TEACHING HIGH SCHOOL COMPOSITION

TEACHING HIGH SCHOOL
COMPOSITION

GARY TATE
University of Tulsa

EDWARD P. J. CORBETT
Ohio State University

NEW YORK
OXFORD UNIVERSITY PRESS
LONDON   1970   TORONTO

PREFACE

It is an ironic and disturbing fact that English teachers are seldom trained to teach composition effectively. The education of the typical English teacher is predominantly a literary education, and few colleges require the future teacher to take a single composition or rhetoric course beyond the freshman level. Prospective teachers seldom complain during their college years about this situation because most of them have been drawn to English studies in the first place because of their interest in literature. Yet when they become teachers of English, they soon discover that they are judged, to a large extent, not by the literary sophistication their students achieve but by the writing ability their students acquire. That this discrepancy between what their college education prepared them for and what they are expected to accomplish in their own classrooms is eventually disturbing to most English teachers can be verified by merely questioning any group of experienced teachers. The majority of them will say that it is for the teaching of composition that they feel most poorly prepared and, consequently, frustrated.

We have prepared this volume of readings in the belief that the training of composition teachers can be better than it usually has been. Indeed, their training must be better than it has been if teachers are to retain that pride in their profession which comes from the assurance that they have been adequately prepared for their appointed tasks. The thirty-four articles and the two bibliographies reprinted here will introduce English teachers to a sampling of the most thoughtful writing on the teaching of composition produced during the past two decades. Two of the articles were written by the editors especially for this volume. The long list of Additional Readings at the end of the book has been organized so that present and future teachers of composition can pursue in depth those topics that particularly interest them.

We would like to thank Glen Love, of the University of Oregon, for first suggesting that our earlier book, *Teaching Freshman Composition,* might be modified so as to be appropriate for courses in the teaching of high-school English. The "modification" turned into a full-scale revision, with only seven of the articles from the first volume being retained in this collection. We were pleased to find so many excellent articles concerned specifically with the teaching of composition on the secondary level. This collection of theoretical and practical articles should give those teachers who are concerned with helping their students to improve their writing a point of departure for their efforts.

June 1969

G.T.
E.P.J.C.

CONTENTS

BIBLIOGRAPHIES

GENERAL

JAMES R. SQUIRE AND ROGER K. APPLEBEE / *The Teaching of Composition*

Certainly the component of English which is the most elusive and difficult to assess is the teaching of composition, and observers faced many problems in trying to characterize individual programs. Although corrected class sets of papers were usually made available to visitors during their one- or two-day stay, and although these papers were solicited with the understanding that they would be typical efforts of students, there is reason to believe that in a number of instances the papers had been handpicked to show both students and teachers to their best advantage. Observers were also hampered by limitations of time and could not always read all of the papers at hand. Nevertheless, these papers, supplemented by interviews with students and teachers, afforded direct knowledge about the program; indirect data concerning the frequency of writing and the emphasis and point of view in writing instruction came from questionnaires.

The most discouraging conclusion which the project staff reached concerning instruction in writing is that there is simply very little of it. On the basis of classroom observation, teachers at all levels in all schools combined spent only 15.7 percent of their class time emphasizing composition. There was slight variation among grade levels and even less between those groups considered terminal and those labeled college preparatory, but the relatively

From James R. Squire and Roger K. Applebee, *High School English Instruction Today*. New York: Appleton-Century-Crofts, 1968, pp. 121–38. Reprinted by permission of the National Council of Teachers of English and James R. Squire and Roger K. Applebee. This survey, entitled the National Study of High School English Programs, was conducted primarily by members of the English and education departments of the University of Illinois. Cosponsored by NCTE the survey covered 158 high schools in 45 states over a four-year period.

small incidence of teaching directed to writing improvement came as a surprise to observers. Moreover, the bulk of the instruction during the 15.7 percent of total class time devoted to writing was instruction *after* the fact —after papers had been written.

The primary process of writing instruction consists of having students write compositions followed by teacher "correction" and the subsequent return of compositions—in many cases to be read by students and revised. This is a time-honored system that will doubtless continue to carry much of the weight of instruction, but it is a tenuous chain of action and reaction which, like the chain letters of two decades or so ago, can be useful only if all links follow in orderly progression. From the observation of project visitors the chain is seldom continuous; and the result of these efforts is, at best, a fragmentary approach to the writing process.

The Correction and Annotation of Papers

A sampling of thousands of papers that had presumably gone through the complete cycle revealed one third that had not been revised in any way, another third with gross errors of spelling and usage corrected. Only in about 12 percent of the high schools had most students revised their writing completely in response to teacher "correction." There was no way to determine statistically, of course, how effective this process was either with the minority of students who revised or with the vast majority who did not. In spite of the lack of empirical knowledge, however, there can be little doubt that those students who are forced to think back through their first writing and then rework the original into something better must gain in fluency and precision.[1]

For most teachers, correcting papers is synonymous with teaching writing. To a question posed during the interview with entire English departments about the proportion of teaching time or emphasis on composition, the most typical response was that more time and emphasis on composition were impossible with existing class loads. In other words, there was simply not time to correct more papers than were currently being produced. According to individual questionnaires, teachers spend an average of nine to twelve hours weekly reading and correcting papers, a sizable proportion of time considering their other professional obligations. Similarly, students report that they submit an average of one theme a week, with able senior students tending to write more frequently and tenth grade students somewhat less

[1] Richard Braddock, Richard Lloyd-Jones, and Lowell Schoer, *Research in Written Composition* (Champaign, Ill., National Council of Teachers of English, 1963), pp. 35–36.

often. It is difficult to imagine how this enormous paper load might be increased and still have any significance for either student or teacher.

The average English teacher in these schools meets about 130 pupils daily. If he spends as much as 8.6 minutes in annotating each theme—the average number of minutes which Dusel reported required "to teach writing and thinking," [2] then eighteen hours weekly would be required for paper correction alone. When it is realized that the average number of pupils per teacher nationally is about 150,[3] and that some teachers, even in this sampling, are expected to teach writing to as many as 200 pupils in six different classes, it would be irresponsible criticism to assert they are not doing justice to one of the main elements of English instruction. The simple fact is that they cannot.

One method for reducing the paper load of classroom teachers is to employ lay readers, a practice being followed in a significant number of high schools across the country.[4] Among those schools participating in the National Study, 20 percent indicated that readers were used to one degree or another. In larger districts, they are usually assigned to schools after they have satisfied certain requisites, including the successful completion of a qualifying examination. In the case of schools in smaller, more autonomous districts, readers are employed directly on the basis of personal contact and previous experience; more often than not they are former teachers in the respective schools.

It would be impractical to assume that outside readers could upgrade a school's writing program merely by increasing the frequency of writing, and, indeed, no direct relationship between the frequency or quantity of student writing and the use of readers was found. What readers can do is relieve the laborious burden of correction to allow more time for the *teaching* of writing. If classroom teachers must spend ten or more hours a week reading papers, they have substantially less time to prepare thoughtful and purposeful lessons. No doubt this demand has much to do with the sometimes superficial marking that observers noticed on sets of papers.

Lay reader programs differ in a number of respects. In some, readers always remain behind the scenes, in a few instances transacting most of the paper exchange through the mail; in others, readers are required to visit classes when writing assignments are made, or even to hold conferences with students. Rarely do readers grade and correct more than a minority of

[2] William J. Dusel, "Determining an Efficient Teaching Load in English, *Illinois English Bulletin,* 43: 1 (October, 1955).

[3] Committee on National Interest, *The National Interest and the Teaching of English* (Champaign, Ill., National Council of Teachers of English, 1961), pp. 98–99.

[4] A good discussion of such programs appears in Virginia Burke, *The Lay Reader Program: Backgrounds and Procedures* (Milwaukee, Wisc., Wisconsin Council of Teachers of English, 1961).

student papers, and usually teachers review grading by sampling a number of papers from each set marked by a reader. In some programs, notably in the so-called Rutgers Plan,[5] graders are assigned to specific teachers and classes—i.e., those classes following the Rutgers plan in other respects. Less structured programs allow several teachers to call upon a reader as they require.

Interviews with students who have had experience with theme readers revealed mixed reactions. Interestingly, some students are delighted with the notion that an "outsider," someone who doesn't know them, will read their papers and pass judgment from what they believe to be a more objective point of view. Other students prefer the more intimate touch and object to their work being read by anyone other than the teacher. It is fair to say that, in general, student response to the employment of theme readers is negative, but not overwhelmingly so.

Teachers, too, are as a whole ambivalent in their attitudes toward a lay reader program, though, for a sizable portion of the teaching community, feelings run very high. Ten percent feel lay readers are detrimental, 8 percent that they are absolutely essential, and the majority that they are of only minor importance. During department interviews, the subject of lay readers arose with some regularity in response to the question of how departments might spend a sum of money added to their department's budget, but it was ranked after such items as recordings, overhead projectors, supplementary books, and clerical help. It is clear that most teachers do not view the establishment of lay reader programs with any great urgency; indeed, most are quite emphatic in stating that funds would be better spent in reducing the number of students per teacher.

Clearly, lay readers do not provide a panacea for a poor writing program, though they can make a good one better, and reports from project observers make possible a number of generalizations about successful programs. The best enlist the services of very able readers who write well themselves, can recognize problems that others may have, and are able to translate their analyses into terms which high school students can comprehend. Frequently, though not always, such people were themselves English teachers. These readers work on a regular basis with one or two teachers, observing some classes to become more familiar with the capabilities of the students and the teaching methods used. In the best programs the reader is more than a proofreader, encouraging and commenting on good efforts as well as pointing to errors in mechanics and usage. To this end, a series of conferences with students as well as the teacher can greatly enhance the effectiveness of the reader. No matter how well structured the lay reader pro-

[5] Paul Diederich, "The Rutgers Plan for Cutting Class Size in Two," *English Journal,* XLIV (April, 1960), pp. 229–36, 266.

gram may be, however, the teacher must still teach writing. To foist onto others the burden of reading and correcting without accepting the responsibility for continuous instruction would be to renege on the contract implicit in the provision of readers.

The reports of project observers make clear that individual English departments must give more thought to their objectives and practices in the teaching of student writing. Much that was seen suggested little more than mechanical activity: assignments manufactured to suit the time of year, compositions of cryptic symbols relating to the mechanics of writing rather than to its substance. Department chairmen did report, when asked about instruction in writing, that the element of primary importance was organization of ideas followed by clear thinking or logic. These concerns rated well ahead of such matters as diction, style, or originality and somewhat ahead of the more pedestrian "correct" mechanics and usage. Similarly, when asked to give priority to criteria for evaluating student writing, chairmen considered clarity of thought and organization, appropriate development, and sentence structure, in that order, to be of greatest importance. Yet these conditions simply do not obtain even in these schools. In reviewing student assignments made available to them, observers noted that two thirds of the papers were corrected from a negative point of view involving only correcting faults and assigning grades. In only 17 percent of the schools could they say that comments were designed to teach writing and thinking—the avowed purpose of the whole cycle of writing, correcting, and revising. If there is little instruction in these important matters by way of teacher comments on individual papers, and none at all in the classroom, where are students to learn about them?

The Focus of Instruction

One source of instruction, of course, is the occasional or systematic use of textbooks. Figure 1 shows, however, that less than a third of the teachers interviewed indicated that they regularly made use of such texts; even fewer responded favorably to traditional workbooks used to provide drill in grammar and usage. From statistically less solid ground, project observers reported that they seldom saw composition texts in use, although they were often in evidence; most schools lend or rent such books to students or ask students to purchase them. If composition texts are, in fact, as little used on the national scale as they were in the project sample (and there is no reason to assume any great difference), the issue is raised of the considerable public expense versus the slight instructional value of the books. One problem in this regard is that texts frequently must be purchased from lists compiled

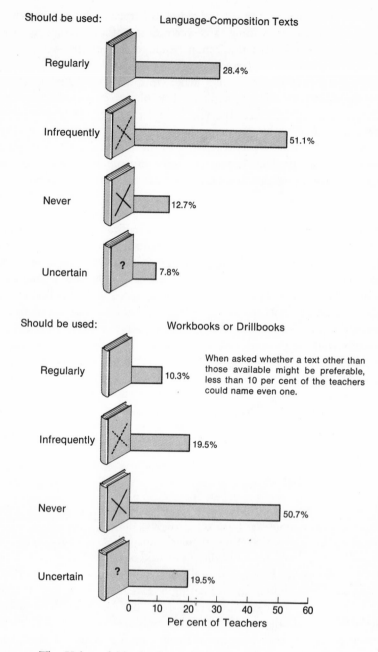

FIGURE 1 The Value of Textbooks and Workbooks in Teaching Composition and Language
(*Interview responses of 370 teachers*)

by local school boards or state authorities, a requirement that can force a teacher to use a book he feels to be inferior to one he might have chosen himself. Significantly, however, less than 10 percent of these teachers who indicated disaffection for the composition-grammar books which were authorized would or could suggest other titles. In large measure this may reflect the failure of commercial publishers to offer materials appreciably different in content or approach from those the teachers already have available.[6]

A content analysis of fourteen sets of composition-gammar textbooks by James Lynch and Bertrand Evans [7] several years ago reveals an interesting parallel between the emphasis found on instruction in composition in the National Study and the proportion of instructional material as evidenced by the number of pages given to composition and rhetoric in the texts. Over twice as many pages dealt with matters of grammar, usage, and mechanics in these books than showed any emphasis on units larger than the sentence. In view of this surprisingly small attention to writing in the composition texts, one almost wonders whether the lack of classroom instruction in writing reported by observers was somehow a reflection of the quantity of treatment in available textbooks. Similarly, the whole mode of teacher correction mirrors the rationale implied in the textbooks: about two thirds to the problems of grammar-mechanics-usage and a much less significant proportion to the rhetoric, the development and organization, of writing. Although department chairmen and well-meaning English teachers feel that the latter are of greater value, these matters are clearly not receiving the priority they deserve.

Lynch and Evans also bewail the lack of any real differentiation in the approaches which these textbooks take at successive stages of composition instruction. A given series will typically list essentially the same topics for each of the four years of high school, topics more often than not concentrating on experiences or ideas assumed to be very close to the students' immediate concerns rather than on literary experiences. While a glance through almost any of these series would corroborate these assertions, one must also note that at least twice as many of the papers reviewed by project observers were based on literature as on all other subjects combined, including personal experiences, the social sciences generally, and imaginative topics involving creative writing. Although no absolute data were tabulated in this regard, teachers themselves generally indicated that a good writing pro-

[6] Within the last few years, however, several companies have offered texts that are different with respect to their viewpoint concerning language and the emphasis given to instruction in writing.

[7] James J. Lynch and Bertrand Evans, *High School English Textbooks: A Critical Examination* (Boston, Mass., Little, Brown and Co., 1963).

gram should allow for diverse writing experiences, including exposition, argumentation, description, and narration, but that literature should "very often" serve to stimulate such writing.

From time to time, high school programs have been criticized for allowing a disproportion of creative writing to more formal and academically respectable assignments in exposition. Indeed, some critics would, in Procrustean fashion, lop off all imaginative writing as extraneous to the legitimate concern of the high school, insisting that appropriate expository assignments based on literature will offer enough to feed the creative impulses of the students. From the point of view of project staff and observers, however, this position is for a number of reasons untenable. Among papers given to observers for review, for example, there were far fewer instances of creative writing than of any other kind. In descending order of frequency, students wrote on: (1) literary topics, (2) subjects close to their own experience, (3) nonliterary subjects requiring special information, and (4) topics classified as "creative writing." Perhaps as a direct result of the rigid assignments and mechanical instruction that characterize so much composition teaching, two thirds of the sixty advanced twelfth grade classes which indicated they would like to see an improved composition program specified more creative writing, an emphasis reflected too in the enthusiasm of students enrolled in such classes. In the opinion of the project staff, the occasional experience of creating a poem or story can carry a number of extrinsic dividends. The opportunity to create something even remotely literary may not turn the student into an artist, but it should help him develop an appreciation of the distinctions between the language and conventions of literature and the language and conventions of his own immediate world. While the project staff does not recommend sudden, wholesale, and capricious efforts, it does feel that the occasional assignment in the area known as creative writing can be of significant value. Whether the note of protest against creative writing and the emphasis on expository themes by committees of the NCTE and the CEEB Commission on English has changed a previously distorted pattern, or whether such writing has never been overly emphasized in the better schools of the country, the National Study reveals no need for a radical shift in the *kinds* of writing being asked of students in most of the cooperating high schools.

Continuity and Sequence

As suggested above, most of the time and attention devoted to composition entails an *analysis* (whether superficial or comprehensive) of the finished product. With a few exceptions, any concerted efforts of English departments have been directed to setting standards for grading or for establishing requirements for student writing in terms of numbers of words or assignments. Although courses of study proclaim worthy enough objectives relating to "improving abilities" or "increasing writing skills," the project staff found little thought or effort given to *how* a student's writing ability can be improved. As a result of this lack of focus on the *process* or *sequence* of writing, the writing experience of students in most programs suffers from either redundancy or fragmentation. Students are therefore inclined to view the program in composition as a disconnected series of activities, and they can scarcely be blamed if, faced with the same topics, they write in the same ways they have found successful before. If growth and improvement are to be expected from the students, they must be built into the program itself.

One method of encouraging continuity and progression in the individual classroom is to use cumulative folders or notebooks to contain all of the consequential pieces that a student writes. Teachers in the cooperating schools were generally in favor of this practice, as it gave them an opportunity to observe student progress throughout the year. Some departments had gone even further, preserving selected writings over a three- or four-year period to add some measure of continuity to the program as a whole. In either case, this procedure, while providing an important perspective on the growth of the individual student, is at best a roundabout method of ensuring sequence and continuity within the writing program of a school.

Perhaps as a result of the currently popular theory of the spiral curriculum, a number of schools have written new courses of study, frequently called "sequential guides" to composition. Inherent in the design of these programs is the principle that the important skills of writing are developed incrementally. This does not imply that the ninth grade students learn all there is to know about constructing sentences; tenth grade students, the paragraph; and juniors, a multiparagraph composition. Instead, a typical guide provides from twenty to fifty writing experiences for each grade level, from which some twelve to twenty will be chosen by the individual teacher on the basis of the needs and capabilities of his class. At all levels students are required to write narration, description, exposition, and argumentation, though in the ninth grade there is likely to be a greater emphasis on narration and description, and in the twelfth, greater concern with more complex and subtle forms of exposition and argumentation. Many of these assignments are clearly related to the literature taught at particular grade levels, and at times students are asked to emulate the style of an author— to write "in the manner of" John Buchan or E. B. White, for example, while developing a personal essay. Sequential composition guides differ in the extent to which they include other apparatus: standards for grading, a style sheet for students, a glossary of technical terms. Some contain explicit instructions to teachers and list questions to direct the class discussion preceding the writing experience; others depend on the teacher and the general context of each course to motivate the sequential assignments. With the shortcomings of composition textbooks as noted above, it is important that high school departments focus in some manner on the essential problems of sequence and continuity in the writing program. Merely to determine how many compositions should be required at each grade level begs the critical questions involved.

The Term Paper

The high school research or term paper is a fairly well-entrenched requirement in many English programs. About 71.7 percent of the teachers in the Study schools support a requirement for at least one such paper in every student's high school career. Although there is no discernible pattern for such papers, ranging as they do among subjects in literature, history, politics, science, and current events and varying in depth and scope, the tradition is somehow maintained that college bound students should be submitted to the process of gathering information, taking notes, and preparing a paper of anywhere from five to fifty pages. For some time the value of this process has been questioned by many high school teachers and college English instructors on the grounds that such writing is frequently a waste of time—time that might more profitably be spent on other aspects of composition or on the study of literature and language. Such writing, it is claimed, is in no sense *research* and more often than not results in both plagiarism of source material and unfortunate superficiality: teachers are prone to emphasize the mechanical aspects of taking notes, preparing footnotes, and compiling bibliographies to the exclusion of processes of thought or logical development; topics are usually unrelated to any other aspect of English, often turning to the trivial or transitory; few high schools have libraries adequate for such research.

These arguments are countered by individuals who feel that it *is* profitable for a student to pursue a subject in depth and to sustain his best writing efforts in an extended paper. In the process, it is assumed, he will learn much about the library and about using source material. Furthermore, the term paper advocates state, other academic departments both expect students to know the proper form and procedure for writing a long source paper and regard the English class as the appropriate place for such instruction. Supporters also claim that former students return from college to tell them how useful this instruction has been in their beginning college course, to some extent refuting the frequent argument that college departments of English do not expect freshman to know how to write term papers and, in fact, would prefer that incoming students be taught other things instead.

The most profitable means of resolving this dilemma is to inquire to what extent the research paper helps students become more able writers in the whole scheme of individual composition programs. Only from this perspective can individual teachers and departments satisfactorily determine whether their efforts at instruction as well as their students' long labors offer an efficient vehicle for writing improvement. Though such a perspective was of its very nature not available to the members of the National Study, their observations do allow a number of inferences about the general practice of requiring long source papers of high school students.

Individually, many observers read some long papers that would suggest the manifest worth of such assignments. Selected samples showed that a number of high school students are capable of writing sustained, coherent, and comprehensive papers. In contrast to these samples, of course, were many others that suffered from all of the ills of bad writing and dishonest thinking imaginable, compounded in these respects by the demand for length. Unless the long paper evolves from other written assignments over a period of years, and unless the subject matter of these efforts has some relationship to English (or else some immediacy to related disciplines), observers feel that the instructional time might better be spent on other writing. The crash programs which they occasionally witnessed, where students were thrown into the school library and asked to produce twenty pages of prose in two weeks, are not worthwhile educational pursuits; nor is mere instruction on the formal aspects of note-taking, footnoting, and manuscript form valuable *per se*. Unless the whole enterprise grows from roots which have already been nourished by other work *in English,* it is the critics rather than the supporters of long source papers who must be heeded. To consider instruction on the long paper as a necessary end in itself, as a service function to other high school departments, or as an assumed college requirement makes the task unrewarding and the practice unsound.

Approaches to Writing

In a small number of participating schools, schoolwide "composition days" have been established, allowing for infrequent but planned occasions when all students write compositions of specified length and type. Teams of readers assess the strengths and limitations of all of these efforts, lending an objective measure to pupil improvement and a positive touchstone to the tenor of the writing program. The most worthwhile by-product of this enterprise is that it focuses attention on this important component of English and, in spite of the mechanical aspects, motivates students to improve their work. Too often, from the observation of visitors to schools, English departments are willing to relinquish the essay in final examinations in favor of the more easily corrected objective question. Whether or not these tests are a valid measure of other aspects of the English program, they neither measure a student's composing ability nor motivate him to improve. Such a device as the schoolwide "composition day" can mitigate some of the shortcomings of the final objective test in English by asserting once again the importance of the act of writing.

Another promising procedure in the teaching of composition is the pupil-teacher conference. In department interviews, teachers conceded that systematic discussion with individual students about their writing would indeed be beneficial. They also pointed, however, to heavy class loads, obligations to police corridors or locker rooms, and "extracurricular" assignments that curtail after-school conferences. At one school this problem was circumvented by naming two additional English teachers as "composition teachers" whose sole function was to teach students singly or in pairs in frequent tutorial sessions. In addition to their regular English classes, the majority of students in two grade levels were assigned to one or the other of these teachers for one conference a week over the entire year. Administrators and teachers at this school were convinced enough of the worth of this program to continue it beyond the experimental phase. In view of the value placed on these face-to-face encounters, teachers might well look more closely at methods to institute conferences on a more frequent basis than obtains at present, even at the expense of other class activities. To be effective, of course, it is incumbent upon teachers to recognize that techniques different from those used in teaching a class are open to them in tutorial sessions. A conference presents an opportunity for the teacher to reach even the most reluctant writer and to come to grips with more salient problems than those implied in "correctness."

Observers watched numerous sets of papers being returned to students during class sessions, but they were struck by the very few times that teachers took advantage of these occasions to teach some facet of writing. Some teachers had prepared lists of "common errors" that were written on the board or reproduced for class correction, but very few took the time to reproduce or analyze an entire paragraph or theme in this fashion. Significantly, even fewer teachers used opaque or overhead projectors to facilitate a common study of the larger aspects of composition, those very elements of organization, logic, and development which claimed high priorities on their questionnaires. In the judgment of observers, such direct instructions can fill an unfortunate void in the whole effort of teaching writing in the schools. Another neglected source of practical instruction is the practice of having students read each other's papers. At the least, such a device can lead to superficial improvements in usage and mechanics; at best it contributes to an overall development of style. Students with a clear notion of audience and a more immediate sense of purpose will write with a clarity and conviction usually lacking when they know that only the teacher will read their work.

A number of programs throughout the country use models to help students achieve a better sense of direction and form in their writing. Particularly those schools with sequential programs have employed literary models (and occasionally student efforts) to suggest patterns that students can emulate. Though there is the built-in hazard that students will ape the original too closely or will consider it too far above their own abilities, the judicious use of models is a positive and valuable device in teaching students to write better. Similarly, it is often valuable for the teacher himself to write an assignment that he has given to a class and then to use his own paper as a model for demonstration. Obviously discretion is necessary, but as an added dividend teachers are made aware of some of the problems and pitfalls that they are prone to overlook when they merely correct the errors of others.

Summary

Needless to say, there are many qualitative differences among the various composition programs. Some committed departments are involved in continuous efforts to improve instruction in writing by a number of methods, whereas others make no concerted effort to create cohesive, schoolwide programs, allowing individual teachers their own frequently haphazard approaches. Optimistically, in observer reports of general strengths, programs in composition were cited fifty times, second only to teaching staff in frequency comment. On the other hand, inadequate programs in composition were cited forty-one times, ranking seventh among general weaknesses of English programs.

When teachers were asked to indicate on questionnaires the aspect of English in which they felt most deficient, composition outranked all others (including literature, language, reading, and speech) by a considerable margin. Approximately 25 percent of the teachers surveyed reported taking a course in advanced composition since they began teaching, and a solid 82 percent revealed that such a college course would be of "some" or "great" importance to them. These figures suggest commitment and a professional need that is not always met, but the newly established NDEA Institutes, many of which offer a composition component or, failing that, oblique instruction in the teaching of writing through their workshops, allow a note of optimism. Furthermore, changing certification requirements are beginning to prompt a noticeable addition of new writing courses to the offerings of colleges and universities.

In spite of the evidence of considerable writing activity in most English classes, observation reveals that there is very little effort directed to *instruction* in writing. For one reason or another, teachers depend heavily on the process of correction and revision to improve student composition. Skillful teachers with enough time to make the process significant and enough patience to complete the cycle through revision are able to promote student achievement, not only in mechanical "correctness" but also in rhetorical power and stylistic flavor. Where the conditions of skill and time are not present, however, instruction through correction is extremely limited.

While teachers are generally conscientious in assigning and grading many sets of papers, there is a clear lack of consistent and progressive instruction in writing. After observing a large number of high school English classes, one can easily get the impression that compositions are often assigned in lieu of any ordered classroom instruction, as though mere practice were all that was needed. The project staff is convinced that the quality of the writing assignments, the care taken by the teacher in correcting the paper, and the continuing dialogue between writer and reader are of greater importance than the frequency of writing. Moreover, unless these qualities are an integral part of the writing program, it is distinctly possible that frequent but routine writing assignments will inspire little more than trivial efforts that promote no growth whatsoever in writing ability.

To add confusion to neglect, teachers are in no clear agreement about methods and priorities in teaching students to write. The responses of students and teachers to a check list of concepts which might be taught at various levels indicate clearly that concepts related to rhetoric and composition are only inconsistently presented; some are overtaught, some not taught at all. Although a good deal of research has been undertaken on the teaching of writing, few of the findings are easily translatable to classroom technique. Indeed, some results appear at least superficially to be in conflict with the claims of other investigations. As indicated in the Braddock report, there remains a manifest need for more controlled research in a number of basic areas related to the teaching of composition.[8]

Confusion about conflicting ideas and ignorance of research, however, provide no rationalization for an inadequate composition program. Teachers cannot wait in expectation of the seminal study on the teaching of writing;

[8] Richard Braddock *et al., op. cit.* See especially Chapter 3, "The State of Knowledge about Composition," pp. 29–53.

they can combine knowledge, experience, and intuition to develop meaningful programs of writing in the high school. To take the position (as some individual teachers have) that writing "cannot be taught," or that the process is too mysterious for words, or that it has no more sequence and content than a bag of tricks, is strangely inconsistent with the general pattern of educational philosophy in our time.

JANET EMIG / *On Teaching Composition: Some Hypotheses as Definitions*

"We teach composition." Whatever can we mean? Our rhetorics and practices down the centuries form a fantastic pop-op mobile—appalling, if we are free enough to be judgmental.

Around the mobile whirls:

> A bar sinister of red pencils crosses a shield of paperback covers;
> Exhortations rise up on a collage of grammar workbook sheets, topical and contradictory as Chinese wall posters;
> "Write more," "Write less"; "Revise," "Throw away";
> At the base turns a combination retroactive multi-rocket tape recorder-opaque projector-computer
> half-engorging a ventilated, crenellated program card;
> At the top, like a Marisol, smiles out a photo of an actual animate—
> A lay reader
> (With that designation, shouldn't she be off gilding manuscripts?
> Or Deweyizing some order's library?)

What have we been thinking? What are we doing?

"Not much," some voices, quiet but acerb tell us—Sledd, Roberts. As Hemingway once wrote Marlene Dietrich, about another matter, "Movement is not action."

What could we possibly mean when we say we teach composition? Surely it is not premature to attempt some kind of systematic response.

From *Research in the Teaching of English,* I (Fall, 1967), 127–35. Reprinted by permission of the National Council of Teachers of English and Janet Emig.

Teaching as Intervention

An essential prelude is to define what is meant, generically, by teaching. Teaching is the intervention, usually by an older person, into a process, usually of a younger person, to improve that process or the product of that process. Teaching can also be mutual intervention, an exchange of insights and competencies between older and younger (rare), or the exclusive unilateral intervention of a younger person into the process of an older person (unheard of).

Sermonettes will occur intermittently throughout this text. Sermonette I: For far too long, for far too many of us, the teaching of composition has been solely product-centered. We have been concerned exclusively with the piece of writing, more particularly the simonized draft submitted for the devastation and the grade. The sciences have long known and taught that getting there, like riding a Greyhound, is at least half the fun. Science and math instructors are quite as interested in the routes students take to a solution as in their identifications of the solutions themselves. Moreover, they know their significant teaching occurs before or during the time the student works in the laboratory, and they regard as very limited evidence of his intellectual evolution the slight, or full, reports the student hands to a lab assistant at the end of the session.

If teaching is intervention, the primal question in teaching composition is, of course, "In what kinds of intervention should we engage?" In teaching composition, as in most other forms of teaching, there are really only two significant modes of intervention: the proffering of freedoms and the establishing of constraints. The teaching of composition consists of determining and enacting strategies for intervention in one or both modes in whatever order best serves the writing process of the individual student and the piece he produces. Teaching can be the spontaneous, unpremeditated response to the moment, the student, or the piece. And it can consist of deciding *not* to intervene, as in dealing with the mature student who has already internalized and now enacts his own appropriate sets of freedoms and constraints. If intervention occurs, however, the double question becomes the highly complex and immensely fragile one of how and when.

Sermonette II: For far too many of us, the definition of teaching composition, like our definition of teaching in general, is solely the specifying of constraints. By the definition given here, this means that we are fulfilling only half, or less, of our function; indeed, that our view of teaching is dangerously truncated, irresponsible, and anti-humanistic.

It is probably helpful to characterize the kinds of interventions, both freedoms and constraints, which we as teachers of composition can extend. The freedoms are all, basically, varieties of cognitive and affective support: (1) the provision of stimuli; (2) the extension of options, including the presentation of skills needed by a student for a given piece; and (3) the acceptance of divergent writing behavior. Species of the third are (a) allowing the student to choose his own subject and style of approach; (b) permitting him, tacitly or explicitly, to break off in process and not complete a given piece of writing; (c) withholding any form of evaluation, perhaps including praise; and (d) giving sanction for the student in some instances not to write at all.

To further define and taxonomize, stimuli are verbal and nonverbal ploys for setting the writing process into motion or for keeping it going. Verbal stimuli can be (a) the right kinds of assignments, oral or written; (b) teacher and student dialogue about the process of writing, professional and peer, and about specific products, most notably, of course, great pieces of literature; and (c) models offered by the writings of professionals and peers. Some might classify modeled writing as a constraint in that syntax is fixed; but many students find models stimuli for getting under way, and they are free to fill sentence patterns with any lexicon they choose. Actually, all of these examples could be regarded as species of both modes. The most skillful intervention may well combine the proffering of a freedom with the issuance of a constraint.

Nonverbal stimuli can be (a) incitements by other modes—music, painting, sculpture, mime, mass communication; (b) rituals; and, especially, (c) confrontations with the natural world. By rituals are meant those habits or compulsions that determine how a piece of writing is begun or continued—choosing certain kinds of writing instruments or paper and pursuing such required indulgences as eating, drinking, or smoking.

The third freedom is the acceptance of divergent writing behavior, such as permitting a student to select his own subject or not to complete a piece of writing. Sermonette III: People outside schools usually have the option in some segment of their lives not to complete what they have begun. The lives of the highly creative abound in the unfinished—manuscripts, quartets, canvases, equations, theories. Why the ruthless puritanism of the schools? Why must the student finish everything he begins, especially when at some early moment both he and the teacher identify a piece as a loser? And when our own writing lives are filled with shards?

The withholding of evaluation is also an examplar of freedom. The student is permitted at times to write without teacher as unsolicited evaluator, or even unsolicited reader.

Expectedly, teacher constraints are counterforms of these freedoms: (1)

the rationing or removal of stimuli, (2) the establishing of parameters, such as helping the student to identify the audience to whom his piece will be directed and to heed conventions in whatever form he has selected, and (3) the interpretation of teacher support as certain kinds of insistences, such as the insistence at carefully selected times upon closure, that work be completed or completed and evaluated. The teacher's goal in this mode may ultimately be to help students appreciate the wisdom of Duke Ellington. When asked why he always composed for one orchestra whose weaknesses he knew as well as its strengths: he replied, "Limitations are a wonderful thing. Everyone should have them."

Writing as Process

What is the nature of the writing process into which we as teachers intervene? In literary, rhetorical and, textbook canon there is a strong tradition that all writers engage in a monolithic process, with that process made up of three discrete components—planning, writing, and revising. Although these canons seldom supply tight or full descriptions for these components, teachers and textbook writers usually agree on the following operational definitions:

> *Planning* is the sum of those activities, mental and written, the writer engages in prior to producing a first draft.
> *Writing* is his effort to formulate—usually observing the grammatical requirements, semantic conventions, and graphic amenities of a language—an effective expressive or expressive-communicative sequence of words.
> *Revising* is that activity, or series of activities, by which the writer adjusts, at a time usually separated from the writing of a draft, part or all of that draft to more closely approximate certain substantive and stylistic aims.

The writing process is treated as a fixed and full ordering of these three components occurring in a lockstep, non-recursive, left-to-right sequence. In other words, one always plans, then writes, then revises with no backsliding or returning to a previous "stage." The straight line is the metaphor implied or stated throughout these descriptions as an apt metaphor for the writing process, both *in parte* and *in toto*. One starts at the beginning of the process and moves without confusion or diversion to the end, like the Israelis marching to the Suez.

I would like to suggest that this description of the writing process is a series of hypotheses calling for, if seldom receiving, systematic scrutiny, especially since it has been belied by many kinds of internal and external data—introspection; examination of our own drafts and those of others, both peer and professional; and our experience as teachers of composition.

One could equally, or more powerfully, hypothesize that the process of writing is not monolithic, or tri-partite, or non-recursive. That is, instead of a single process of writing there may be process*es* of writing, at least a process that can be changed—shortened, lengthened, transmogrified—by a number of variables. Instead of a process or processes inexorably made up of three "stages," there may be more or fewer components. Writing may be recursive, a loop rather than a linear affair—one can write, then plan; or one can revise, then write.

For the rest of this piece I will assume the second multiple hypothesis is valid. Five variables affect the length and nature of processes of writing. Four pertain to the student; one, to the intervener, the teacher. To this last I will devote my culminating discussion. The four that pertain to the student are (1) the sophistication of his skills, (2) his temperament, (3) his ego-strength, and (4) the nature of the mode in which he writes.

(1) The sophistication of a student writer's skills may affect the nature and length of the writing process. In some of my own inquiries, for example, I have found that very able eleventh and twelfth grade writers often do not make any written conspectus for pieces of discursive prose under 500 words. Yet if one questions these students about the plan they followed, they orally give highly elaborated outlines, complete with sub-subtopics and other accoutrements of that art form. And when forced by a teacher to produce a written outline, they invariably oblige by providing a construct *a posteriori*.

(2) Temperament also affects the process of writing. There are student writers, like mature writers, for whom revision is anathema. This does not mean that they are unwilling or unable to reconsider a writing problem. Rather, they prefer a total rewriting to a partial revision.

(3) The ego-strength of the writer is a highly significant variable in the writing process, and one almost wholly ignored. Its presence or absence affects many phases of the process, and particularly the evaluation that follows the process. If teacher evaluation is negative, for example, does the student become daunted and refuse to write, or does criticism spur him to persist?

It is sometimes difficult to tell by behavior alone whether its sources are the same, since behaviors may have different origins. For example, the writer with faint ego-strength and the writer with strong temperament may both refuse to revise. There are, however, quite different motivations for their refusal: for writers with certain temperaments, the task is too boring; for writers with faint ego-strength the task is too threatening or painful.

them, we should ask students to keep writing diaries in which they recount how they set about and persist in writing. To determine dimensions to include, classes can read together and discuss professional writers' accounts of their styles and processes of writing. Anthologies we can use include the two volumes of the *Paris Review Interviews: Writers at Work* (1958 and 1963); *Counterpoint* (1964), edited by Roy Newquist; and the senior in the series, *Modern Writers at Work* (1930), edited by Josephine Piercy. Dimensions students will probably elect to discuss are time and place of writing, rituals associated with beginning and persisting, instruments of writing employed, attitudes toward formal planning, point of view toward revising versus revision, and responses to different kinds of teacher evaluation.

We need also to observe, which means that early in the semester or quarter students should write under our direct surveillance. We need to query the students about what they are doing as well as to observe, allowing, of course, for the artificiality and self-consciousness such a situation will probably evoke.

Commiseration I (in lieu of Sermonette V): Yes, I hear the murmurs and the mutters; and yes, I agree. Such a definition of teaching composition calls for a ferocious amount of work. I would suggest another less complex and taxing way, if I knew one that was honest and valid.

Such a definition of teaching composition calls for more than work. It calls for a certain kind of teacher. Indeed, the key variable that determines the direction and success of that complexity the teaching of composition is, ultimately, the teacher. How and when we intervene in the writing process of our students depends at last upon our knowledge of the writing process and of our students and upon our tact, taste, and sensibility. Most frightening and challenging of all, to establish constraints may well mean that we ourselves are disciplined and controlled persons as well as writers; to proffer freedoms may well require that we ourselves are free.

RICHARD L. LARSON / *In-service Training for the English Composition Teacher*

For many English teachers, "teaching composition" includes assigning themes and grading them—and not much more. Some teachers complement the assigning and grading of themes by holding personal conferences with students, but not many give much real instruction in composition during their classes. Even fewer give their students, in addition to letter grades, discerning commentaries on their themes.

Roger Applebee of the National Council of Teachers of English, reporting in the March 1966 *English Journal* on the results of the National Study of High School English Programs, found that in the schools visited during the study (all of them chosen because of the high quality of their programs in English), only some 16 percent of class time in English was devoted to the study of composition. And James Squire, enumerating in the same publication some characteristics of ideal programs in English, implied that many teachers of composition fail to give "rigorous, incisive attention to the processes of thinking and expression." Thoughtful, constructive analysis of students' papers, Mr. Squire observed, is a "sometime thing" even in the better departments of English visited by the National Study.

If teachers of English give less time than they might to the actual teaching of composition and to the thoughtful scrutiny of students' papers, the reason may be—as is often charged—that teachers are overloaded with students and overburdened with extracurricular and clerical duties. No doubt these burdens do impair teachers' efforts to instruct students in com-

From *The Bulletin of the National Association of Secondary School Principals,* LII (February, 1968), 29–47. Reprinted by permission of the National Association of Secondary School Principals and Richard L. Larson.

position—a more difficult subject to teach than the analysis of literature or (for a teacher who has studied the characteristics of languages and modern grammar) the structure of the English language. But surely as important a reason for the shortcomings in the teaching of composition today is the failure of teacher-training institutions to give their students adequate instruction in composing, not to speak of instruction in the teaching of composition.

Poll on Composition Training

In a recent informal poll of 56 major public and private colleges and universities that prepare large numbers of teachers, I found that nearly 40 percent of the schools polled neither required nor recommended of prospective secondary teachers an advanced course in writing (of discursive prose, or fiction, or poetry). About half of the schools polled required no more than three hours of work in advanced composition of these future secondary teachers. Of the 60 percent that do require or recommend advanced courses in writing to prospective teachers, only about a third offer courses in writing specially designed for these teachers; the other two-thirds allow teachers to meet the requirement or recommendation by taking the same writing course that students in other departments may take.

While this is not the place to argue the merits of special courses in composition for prospective teachers, one can be pardoned for guessing that although the teaching of writing is generally held to be a major responsibility of the teacher of English, he is far less well prepared during his undergraduate and graduate programs to teach composition than he is to teach the analysis and interpretation of literature.

Principals to whom I talked during studies of the impact of NDEA institutes in English suggested that they recognize, though sometimes dimly, the inadequacies of their English teachers' preparation for the teaching of composition. But these principals often expressed this recognition by saying that they wished their teachers had been better prepared in college for the teaching of "grammar," as if the knowledge of grammar somehow brought with it competence in the teaching of writing. These principals appeared willing to encourage teachers to attend courses and workshops in modern grammar, linguistics, or the teaching of standard English as a second dialect, confident that such courses would somehow work enormous changes in the effectiveness of teachers' work in composition.

Yet the results of studies reported by Braddock, Lloyd-Jones, and Schoer in *Research in Written Composition* (Champaign, Illinois, 1963) led those authors to the conclusion that "the teaching of formal grammar has a negligible or, because it usually displaces some instruction and practice in actual composition, even a harmful effect on the improvement of writing" (pp. 37–38). Braddock and his colleagues wrote, of course, before the start of experiments to determine whether direct study of transformational-generative grammar would help students improve their writing.

The "New Grammar"

Two recent studies offer some hope that study of this grammar may help in teaching writing. Donald Bateman and Frank Zidonis, in *The Effect of a Study of Transformational Grammar on the Writing of Ninth and Tenth Graders* (Champaign, Illinois, 1966), found that the ability of ninth- and tenth-graders to write well-formed sentences was increased by the study of transformational-generative grammar. John Mellon, in an unpublished study entitled *Transformational Sentence-Combining* (the Final Report of Cooperative Research Project No. 5-8418) found that a study of transformational sentence-combining in their language course helped seventh-graders to increase their syntactic fluency in composition more than is normally achieved in that grade.

Even though these studies may point toward possible applications of the "new grammars" in composition classes, the new grammars cannot at the moment help with units of composition longer than the sentence. There remains the task of teaching students to build complete essays—a task for which the study of grammar and of methods of teaching standard English to speakers of dialects have not yet demonstrated any power.

Nor can teachers gain the competence in teaching composition that they need simply by taking a course in writing in the evenings or in summer session. Such courses, unless designed specifically for teachers of English, often try to do little more than improve participants' performance in writing. They help participants to acquire an intuitive "know-how," and that is all. But, as Martin Steinmann, Jr., comments in the January 1966 issue of *College English* (p. 278):

> There are two senses of "knowing": knowing *how* and knowing *that*. In the first sense, a person is said to know something (a language, say) if he possesses a certain ability, if he can perform in certain ways (speak the language). He has knowledge because he knows *how* to do something. In the second sense, he is said to know something (a language, say) if he possesses a theory (of grammar and semantics) explaining exercise of a certain ability (speaking the language) or information about some historically given events (certain utterances). He has knowledge because he knows *that* something is the case. Neither sort of knowledge entails the other.

How, That, and Why

The teacher of composition lives not primarily by performing (by knowing how, and doing); he lives by helping others to perform. For that work, he does not need only to know *how* (i.e., he does not need only to be able to write himself); he needs to know *that* (he needs to possess a conscious understanding of the writer's tasks, as well as of the means available for completing these tasks). And, if I may add to Steinmann's two kinds of knowledge still a third, he needs to know—or be able to discover—*why* (why one method of accomplishing the task may produce better results than another, and why, precisely, one piece of writing can be said to be better than another).

This teacher needs, not just practice in writing, but a philosophy about writing, information about what strategies work better in what circumstances, and concepts for use in his teaching. He needs, in short, a viable theory about the rhetoric of written discourse and some of its applications. He needs in-service training that will leave him with a fresh, up-to-date view of the complex art of composing and with a determination to help his students as fully as he can, through classes and analyses of students' papers, to understand that art.

What are some of the concepts or attitudes about composition that the teacher of English, whether he is well- or ill-trained in the performance of writing, should put into practice? I shall enumerate seven of what I take to be the more important concepts and implied attitudes, and then suggest what might be the emphases in an in-service program designed to develop them.

I shall be bold enough to hope that such a program may not simply implant new ideas about composition but may also help the teacher improve his "know-how," his performance as a writer. For this reason some of my examples are drawn from possible writing experiences faced by teachers themselves as well as those faced by students.

Purpose

First, most discursive prose—letters, editorials, articles, reviews, books of historical and political analysis, essays in interpretation of literature, and so on—is written for a reader or a group of readers, in order to accomplish a purpose. One can ask, in examining a piece of discursive prose, for what purpose its author has decided to come before his reader(s), and one can evaluate the piece by determining how successfully it promises to achieve its stated or implied purpose. If these questions can apply to the work of professional writers, they can apply equally well to the writing of students— and, for that matter, to the writing of their teachers.

To be sure, the audience to be addressed by a student in a composition course always includes the teacher, and possibly his classmates, but it is a valuable exercise for the student also to imagine, on many assignments, an audience outside the classroom—parents, school administration, citizens in the community, and so on. Teachers do not need to "imagine" their audience; they know to whom their writing is addressed (much of it to their students), and they can evaluate what they write, as can the professional writer, by judging how well it will achieve its purpose with the group to which it is addressed.

Strategy

Second, the writing of a piece of discursive prose is in part a process of making decisions, of solving problems. The writer's most general problem is to discover what plan or strategy to adopt in presenting material so as to accomplish his purpose most effectively. A student trying to convince his classmates that one of Dickens' two endings for *Great Expectations* is "better" than the other has, for example, the problem of deciding on criteria for evaluating the endings of novels and perhaps on criteria for evaluating novels in general, and then of making his criteria as well as the application of them seem defensible to his classmates. The teacher, reporting to his superiors or to parents about a disruptive student, has the problem of demonstrating that the student is indeed disruptive and not the victim of the teacher's prejudices or of honest errors in the teacher's judgment about how he should be taught.

This problem of discovering a plan or strategy sometimes includes another, more knotty problem: to find a balance between the exact way the writer perceives his subject, including his feelings about that subject, and the way he must present his subject to his reader(s) in order to accomplish his purpose. There may, of course, be little difference between what the writer sees or feels, on the one hand, and what he says to his reader, on the other; or there may be considerable difference between the two. In writing about the ending of *Great Expectations,* the student may have feelings so intangible that to write his paper mainly about them would convince no one that the ending he prefers is "better." And the teacher may need to do considerably more than record his experiences and perceptions of the student he considers disruptive.

"Invention"

Third, an important step in the determination of a strategy for a piece of discursive prose is the systematic examination of the subject, the gathering of data, and the reasoning about those data—in short, the search for matter that might be included in the piece. This is the process that theorists of rhetoric call "invention"—the *finding* of substantive material that the writer did not previously have and the *discovery* of ways of looking at or presenting the subject.

The importance of this process is often overlooked by teachers in the teaching of composition as well as by students in the writing of essays. A young writer will find it profitable to practice identifying the areas that must be investigated to assure adequate treatment of his subject, recognizing the assumptions that underlie various statements that might be made about the subject, determining the kinds and sources of evidence needed to support his conclusions, and applying questions that may offer fresh views of the subject—for instance, questions about how an issue came to become an issue, about the causes and consequences of an event, about the precise similarities and differences between one event and others apparently like it, etc.

If such investigation is profitable for the writer, the teacher will find it useful to encourage students to carry it out thoroughly before they start to write. If their subject is the preferred ending of *Great Expectations,* to continue with the previous example, he might stimulate discussion of how one finds criteria for choosing between alternative endings for a story. If these criteria include "consistency" in the behavior of characters between the body of the story and its conclusion, he might ask whether the criterion can take into account logical or reasonable development of character. If it can, then what makes a character's development "reasonable"? How does one identify in a story signs that a character is "developing"? How does one go about comparing what a character is like at one point in a story with what he is like at another point? What sorts of data disclose character? If another criterion that can be used in judging endings is "appropriateness of tone," what makes tone "appropriate"? How do we identify the "tone" of a passage in a story? And so on.

Similarly, the teacher will find it useful to conduct the same sort of mental investigation of subjects on which he must write. Writing about a disruptive student, the teacher will need to record specific details of the student's behavior, the consequences of that behavior, possible reasons for it that might excuse it or at any rate mitigate a reader's judgment upon it, its possible significance in disclosing problems or difficulties in the entire class, and so on.

To be sure, almost no writer uses in his work all of the materials he has "invented" in his investigation of a subject. One of his problems is to decide which of the materials he has gathered will best serve his purposes in addressing his audience. He must make this decision consciously, deliberately; making it is a major step in composing. But without the effort at "invention" already described, it is likely to be an uninformed decision, a less wise decision than it might have been.

Organization

Fourth, a writer's plan for the presentation of his material ought to be the result of deliberate choice, governed by the demands of the material he has chosen to include and, where possible, by his purpose and the needs or interests of the audience addressed. It may not be possible to say with assurance in advance of writing that one plan of organization is more likely to accomplish the writer's purpose than another. (Some students of communication today try to test experimentally the differences in impact on the same audience of two or more articles that present the same information according to different plans.) But at the very least the writer can select a plan which will assure that he presents at the beginning of his piece what the reader is going to need to understand in order to follow the later parts of his discussion, or which assures that he will present necessary explanations of important ideas where the need for them arises.

Selection of a plan of organization is more of a problem than most texts on composition make it out to be. Where the texts imply that there are four or five basic patterns of organization that the student should practice and adopt (narration, illustration, comparison-contrast, and cause-and-effect are frequently listed), essays by practicing writers exhibit widely varying organizational plans.

Some plans, to be sure, are more common than others. (One that appears frequently but is rarely mentioned in texts on composition is to give the details of an event or condition—adoption of a plan to "rebuild" a city, for instance—and then to point out what it reveals about society or a social group, or what it has caused.) Teacher and student should both recognize that the measure of an effective organizational plan is its clarity, its internal logic, and its probable effectiveness in transmitting the writer's ideas and feelings to his reader(s) with due emphasis. The test is whether the plan is clear and works, not whether it conforms to a textbook stereotype.

Comparison of Plans

Class discussion of how a student might arrange his materials in an essay on the ending of *Great Expectations,* for instance, might focus on the comparative advantages of such plans as (1) simply listing the reasons for preferring one ending to the other, (2) comparing principal features of the two endings and picking the one that seems most reasonable, (3) enumerating and defending the criteria for an effective ending for a novel and testing each ending against those criteria, or (4) tracing the progress of Pip and Estella through the second half of the novel, noting what happens to each, and concluding that in one ending their behavior is more "in character" than in the other; and so on. The student would be left to choose the plan he preferred; he would decide which plan enabled him to present most clearly and emphatically the ideas he had elected to set forth and was likely to make the logic of his argument most cogent for his readers.

Similarly, the teacher who is thinking how best to present his views on the disruptive student might consider such plans as (1) narrating the history of the student's behavior and concluding with a summary evaluation, (2) enumerating those kinds of behavior that he classed as disruptive, or (3) defining a disruptive student and showing how his student fits the definition. One of these plans might suit a report to the principal better than it would a report to parents, and vice versa. Just as the student before writing his essay should evaluate his options, so the teacher before preparing his statement might evaluate his own options, recognizing that there is no "right" or "wrong" plan of organization, but that one might accomplish better than others the job he has set out to do.

Commitments

Fifth, regardless of the organizational plan a writer adopts, by his opening sentences and paragraphs he makes a commitment to his reader concerning the subject he will discuss and the approach he will take to it. He generates in his reader's mind some expectations about what his essay will do. And he has the responsibility to keep his promise, to satisfy those expectations— or to give his reader a satisfactory explanation of why he has decided not to do so. (This is the principle of "commitment and response," best enunciated by Robert Gorrell in his article, "Not by Nature: Approaches to Rhetoric," in the April 1966 *English Journal.*)

If the student promises at the start of his essay on *Great Expectations,* for example, to show that one ending is preferable because in it the characters' behavior is more consistent with their actions earlier in the novel, he cannot spend all the rest of his essay talking about whether the tone of either ending is consistent with the rest of the book. He must deal with the behavior of the characters and, if possible, give a reason for believing that consistency in their behavior is a valid reason for preferring one of the endings.

This principle furnishes us an important basis for evaluating the design and the content of any piece of discourse. By asking the student to recognize to what he is committing himself by his opening, the principle also encourages him to make a close examination of his organizational plan, to determine whether it will enable him to discharge that commitment.

Effectiveness

Sixth, there is no way to assess absolutely the rightness or wrongness of the means of expression in any essay. All one can measure is the suitability and effectiveness of the words and sentences to one's subject matter, purpose, and audience. To be sure, one can judge whether or not a writer's sentences observe the conventions of English grammar, and whether the individual words are used in a manner likely to be consistent with a reader's understanding of them—whether they will get across to the reader the ideas the writer wishes to advance. But these judgments are the least important and the least interesting of those that need to be made about words and sentences. Much more important are judgments about the clarity, emphasis, economy, and appropriateness of a writer's diction and syntax.

Student and teacher alike should try to avoid ambiguous statements, vague statements, and excessively general statements. These are flaws of style to which a teacher may want to call specific attention. So are sentences whose structure puts apparently important ideas where they seem less important, sentences that use more words than necessary to make their point, and diction, idiom, and figures of speech that establish a tone or imply an attitude inconsistent with the rest of the discourse and not supported by it. Both student and teacher must learn to recognize the effects of their words and sentences on their readers and to consider alternative means of expression that will avoid possible weaknesses.

Granted that this advice focuses on qualities of expression to avoid, it still suggests virtues to be sought, although it may not highlight sufficiently the major goal that students and teachers alike need to seek: words, figures, and sentences that express vividly and vigorously the writer's central ideas. Finding this sort of vivid and vigorous expression often is the result of trial and error—a process of conceiving, evaluating, and choosing among ways of making a point. (One book that analyzes the usefulness of different kinds of diction and sentence structure is Halverson and Cooley's *Principles of Writing,* published by Macmillan.) Thus a teacher's goal in discussing written expression is not only to help students avoid locutions that will perplex and disturb the reader, it is also to help them discover means of expression that will reach the reader forcefully and please him.

Discovery

Seventh, and to be grasped only through the experience of writing: to compose is to discover. However carefully a writer may identify the problems he thinks he will meet in addressing his audience and however carefully he has investigated his subject and determined his strategy, he usually finds that the process of setting forth ideas and of choosing among means of expression brings with it new understanding of the subject—an understanding that the writer must incorporate as he goes along, and that may even lead him to change altogether his strategy. Even though it can hardly plan for the effects of such discovery, no theory of composition can fail to take into account its occurrence. No teacher, therefore, can reasonably demand adherence to a rigid organizational framework or a predetermined outline.

All writing, imaginative or discursive, is the result of a creative process that works in mysterious ways. It cannot be regulated and rigidified; the attempt to regulate it stultifies a young writer and dampens his energies. A teacher can help the student recognize and solve the problems presented by a writing task, but he can no more dictate to the student a single solution to these problems than he can refuse to recognize that in his own writing he must constantly choose between alternatives that he discovers.

Application of Concepts

I have described these concepts in a detail perhaps more appropriate to an essay for chairmen of English departments than for principals, but principals who have been feeling uneasy about the performance of their English staff in the teaching of composition may find in these concepts an explanation of the weaknesses they sense in that performance. In any event, what has been said points toward action that the principal must initiate. For listing these seven concepts or propositions is only a first step; the important questions remain: how to familiarize active teachers with these concepts, and how to illustrate implications or applications of these concepts in the classroom?

One obvious answer is to encourage teachers to take a regular writing course in a university in the late afternoon or evening during the school year, or during the summer. The simplicity of taking a regular writing course is appealing, particularly to a school administrator who needs to take no action beyond recommending such a course to his teachers. (If his school has money, he may be able to offer teachers released time for such courses.) But unless the courses his teachers take are designed specifically to help them learn "that" and "why" about composition as well as "how," their gains from such courses may be less than the principal and the teacher hope for.

This is not to say that study in the academic year or the summer, particularly in institutes designed expressly for teachers, cannot be helpful; it merely reasserts that most regular courses in composition are not designed to give participants the kind of conceptual understanding about composition, along with the opportunities to discuss ways of using the concepts, that I have been describing.

Values of Special Courses

At a time when principals often want the in-service work pursued by their teachers to be regular university courses, it may seem an anomaly to dwell on the values of a short in-service course, possibly conducted at the school, or of a university course designed especially to serve a particular group of teachers. But teachers of English composition, unlike teachers of most other academic subjects, are not trying to impart knowledge, encourage effective habits of thinking, and lead their students to respect humane values; they are trying to develop students' capacity for effective *performance* in writing.

If concepts and procedures that may help students toward effective performance can be identified, as I have tried to do, special in-service courses or special university courses (if a principal can request that such courses be designed) may be both the most effective and the most efficient means of helping teachers understand these concepts. Such courses may at once help teachers improve their performance as teachers and as writers.

I shall not attempt to propose a specific length for an in-service program or a special university course designed to help teachers understand the seven concepts I discussed. The courses can be longer or shorter, depending on the time available to the teachers and the school. Instead I shall mention five components that I take to be essential in an in-service course for teachers of composition, and indicate briefly why each of these components seems essential.

TEACHERS SHOULD READ, AND MAKE RHETORICAL ANALYSES OF, SOME EX-
AMPLES OF PROFESSIONAL WRITING.

Such analyses should begin by identifying the evident audience and purpose for which each piece was written, should consider any obstacles that
stood in the way of the author's accomplishing his purposes, and should
examine the strategy he used to overcome these obstacles. Teachers may
want to discuss possible alternate strategies that he might have used, in
order to determine the advantages and disadvantages of the one he chose.
They should then evaluate the probable success of each piece in achieving
its purpose with the audience addressed—a practice which will help teachers
evaluate what they themselves write. They might also ask of each essay:
What does the author promise or claim that he will do in his piece? Does
he keep his promise and make good his claim?

THEY SHOULD WRITE OUT THE INSTRUCTIONS FOR SAMPLE ASSIGNMENTS THAT
THEY MIGHT GIVE THEIR STUDENTS.

Then they should discuss how clearly the instructions each teacher has
written will communicate to the student what is expected of him, what tasks
he must perform, what problems he must solve. Not every set of instructions for a theme, of course, needs to identify for the student the problems
he must solve in writing it. But in these practice assignments teachers
might specify what they think are the problems presented by their assignments, so that other participants may help each other to determine how well
each of them sees what is demanded by his assignments.

In addition to assuring that their draft assignments are as clear and precise as need be, participants should practice specifying an audience and a
purpose for their assignments, so that they and later their students can get
into the habit of judging their work by how well it promises to achieve its
purpose. Participants in the special course might also practice designing assignments to meet special demands, such as the assignment that "take[s]
the form of, or [is] construable into, a proposition." (See *Freedom and
Discipline in English,* the 1965 report of the Commission on English, p. 94.)

THEY SHOULD PRACTICE "INVENTING" MATERIALS FOR THE SUBJECTS THEY
ASSIGN—OR FOR SUBJECTS ASSIGNED BY THE INSTRUCTOR—BY TRYING OUT DIF-
FERENT KINDS OF QUESTIONS THAT MIGHT HELP THEM TO SEE THE SUBJECT MORE
CLEARLY AND BY SPECIFYING WHERE THEY MIGHT GO FOR INFORMATION ABOUT
THE SUBJECT.

In so doing, they would be practicing one of the activities preliminary to writing that help a writer in determining his strategy. Such discussions will give participants a "feel" for the sort of class discussion they might lead in conjunction with theme assignments, besides giving them practice in a procedure that may help their own writing.

FOR SEVERAL ASSIGNMENTS THAT THEY DRAFT, THEY SHOULD DISCUSS DIFFERENT PLANS THAT MIGHT BE USED FOR ARRANGING MATERIAL IN AN ESSAY.

Such discussion would highlight the fact that the arrangement of data, like the selection of things to say, is a decision the writer makes on the problem of how to achieve his purpose most effectively, and that his decision will usually be better if he is aware of the several alternatives open to him. Such discussion will also give the teachers a sense of what might take place in their classrooms, and practice in the kind of decision-making required, though they may not have realized it, in their own writing.

THEY SHOULD WRITE ESSAYS THEMSELVES, INCLUDING ONE ON THE SAMPLE ASSIGNMENT THEY DRAFTED.

This is not just a restatement of the maxim that "one learns to write by writing," although it is always desirable for a teacher of writing to practice what he teaches. There may be no better way of alerting the teacher to the problems his students face in their assignments and to the ways in which his instructions may compound these problems than asking him to write one (or indeed most) of the themes he assigns. Participants may also discover unseen difficulties in their assignments, and possibly even some hidden assumptions they are making in all of their assignments about students and writing problems. Further, they will learn that however carefully a writer may plan his essay in advance, he discovers as he composes, and that it is therefore folly to insist that an essay stay within the straitjacket of a preplanned outline.

THEY SHOULD ANALYZE THEMES WRITTEN BY THEIR STUDENTS (POSSIBLY EVEN THEMES WRITTEN IN THEIR GROUP IN RESPONSE TO THEIR OWN ASSIGNMENTS) TO DETERMINE HOW EFFECTIVELY THESE THEMES ACHIEVE THIER PURPOSE. AND THEY SHOULD PRACTICE ANNOTATING THESE THEMES AS PRECISELY AS POSSIBLE TO DEMONSTRATE WHERE AND HOW THE THEMES SUCCEED OR FAIL.

This process, though it can be harrowing for a teacher unused to writing and unused to hearing judgments from his peers, can instruct each participant about weaknesses in his writing and—much more important—can let him see how difficult it is to communicate judgments about writing so that the author will understand and accept them.

The process is also a further exercise in writing to an audience and for a purpose. But it does no good if participants focus their comments on small matters of detail rather than looking at the substance and design of the whole piece, as is required if one is to determine how well the piece achieves its purpose. A thorough analysis of the whole theme is needed—an analysis such as might result from applying the "Considerations" listed in the Appendix to this article.

Objectives of the Training

The program or course proposed here should serve three objectives simultaneously: to help participants develop a philosophy and understand some important concepts about composition; to give them some experience that might show how these concepts can be translated into teaching practice; and to give them additional experience in writing. It gives participants the opportunity to move from the perspective of the teacher to that of the writer, and back again. It touches the "knowing how" of composing, but gives principal attention to the "knowing that" and the "knowing why."

No one of the objectives can be separated from the other two. All three operate simultaneously; the conceptual knowledge about composition, as well as the practice in invention and choice of strategies, should reinforce the benefits teachers will gain from again (possibly for the first time since freshman English) writing under supervision.

Writing, essentially, is not a routine process or even a skill; it is an art, and it requires the constant exercise of judgment by the writer. We may not all wish to label the teaching of writing an art, though some would surely judge it so. But it, too, is more than a routine process of making assignments, red-pencilling papers, and logging in dutifully completed revisions of themes.

The teaching of writing, like writing itself, requires a constant exercise of judgment; that is what makes teaching a profession instead of a trade. Where composition is carelessly taught or where hard-working teachers are found assigning compositions rather than teaching composition, the reason may be that these teachers have not been led to respect what they are doing as a professional responsibility. They have not been trained to think of their work as a profession.

Probably no special in-service course or even a specially designed university course can lead previously untrained teachers of composition to re-gard their work as a serious professional responsibility. But it can at least remind them—possibly inform them for the first time—that the writer has a purpose in going before his audience and that the achieving of that pur-pose requires many complex choices among available data, alternative strategies, and possible methods of expressing each idea. The teacher can-not make these decisions for his students, and he cannot supply them with a formula for making them.

What the teacher can do is help students recognize the problems they face in writing, help them identify the options available to them, and help them assess the results of choosing each option. That is what we need to train our teachers of composition to do. That is what the program described in this article seeks to do.

Appendix

CONSIDERATIONS IN THE READING OF THEMES

Subject Matter

Interest and significance (Is the subject worth reading about?)
Aptness for prospective audience
Aptness to assigned purpose or purpose assumed by the writer
Limitation of subject (appropriate to length of occasion and purpose as-signed)
Relevance of subject to assignment if the subject was not specified
Relevance of all details to subject of essay
Adequacy of matter "invented" to the purpose of the essay (Does the essay achieve what the author claims he will do?)

Reasoning

Reporting of data: accurate? (If the theme is based on an essay or work of literature, is the substance of the essay accurately reported or the literary work described reasonably? If the theme is based on experience or obser-vation, is the experience or observation accurately described?)
Generalizations: reasonable? soundly derived from data?
Assumptions: recognized and defended, if significant? If not explicitly de-fended, are the assumptions reasonable?
Cause-and-effect inferences: fair in light of data?

Distinctions between facts, opinions, statements of evaluation, statements of preference: regularly and wisely made?

Deductive or inductive procedures, if any: soundly used?

Data used to support general conclusions drawn by writer: adequate and convincing?

Statements of prediction, if any: reasonable in light of data cited?

The Rhetoric of the Whole Theme

Appropriateness of division of subject into parts

Clarity and aptness (for subject? for audience?) of the plan of organization

Coherence of parts

Suitability of expository procedures used (to purpose and subject? to audience being addressed?)

> Definitions (Are they provided where needed?)
>
> Illustrations
>
> Explanations of processes or sequences of events
>
> Interpretations of data
>
> Uses of comparison or contrast

Introduction (adequately comprehensive? not over-inclusive?)

Body of the paper: does it carry out what the introduction promised or explain why it departs from the plan originally announced?

Lucidity and gracefulness of movement from section to section

Conclusion (apt in view of the matters discussed in the paper? informative? significant, i.e., more than a repetition of points clearly made before?)

Paragraphs

Adequacy of introductory sentence(s) as expressions of the writer's "commitment"

Clarity and aptness of way of arranging material within each paragraph (Is the desired emphasis established?)

Unity (Does each paragraph advance a single major proposition? If not, can the absence of unity be defended?)

Coherence (preservation of consistent point of view, use of apt transitional words, etc.)

Individual sentences (clarity of purpose, achievement of purpose)

Conclusion (relevant to body of paragraph, useful and not superfluous)

Are related sentences in the whole essay kept together by the paragraph punctuations?

Voice and Tone

Freshness and distinctiveness

Suitability to subject, audience, writer's responsibility, writer's assumed "role"

Reasonable consistency (Are changes in tone accidental and uncontrolled, or purposeful and effective?)

Sentences

Clarity of predication (Are major assertions contained in the sentence communicated clearly?)

Clarity of structure (i.e., freedom from ambiguity in arrangement of clauses and phrases)

Aptness of syntactic structures to ideas being communicated and emphasis intended

"Reasonableness" of length (in respect to intended audience, in respect to the student's power of *controlling* sentence)

Economy of structure (Are the structures used the ones that will make the point most concisely?)

Appropriateness of punctuation to the relationship of ideas being communicated

Diction

Precision (absence of ambiguity and unnecessary vagueness)

Are denotations and connotations of words clearly understood by the writer?

Vividness

Freshness (including avoidance of jargon and cliches)

Respect for standard usage and idiom (if required by purposes of theme and imagined "occasion" for the writing of it)

Economy

Aptness of figurative language (if used)

Balance of abstractness/concreteness, generality/particularity, non-sensory/sensory, as appropriate to subject

Fundamental Literacy

Observance of standard conventions of grammar, mechanics, spelling

JAMES MOFFETT / *Learning To Write by Writing*

Most of what I have had to say so far has concerned curriculum. In this chapter my concern is method, in particular the sort of method most appropriate for the notion of curriculum that has been expounded.

What is the main way in which human beings learn to do things with their minds and bodies? Let's not think first about learning to write—we'll get to that soon enough. Let's think about learning to walk, ride a bicycle, play a piano, throw a ball. Practice? Coaching by other people? Yes, but why does practice work? How do we become more adept merely by trying again and again? And what does a good coach do that helps our trials get nearer and nearer the mark? The answer, I believe, is feedback and response.

Feedback

Feedback is any information a learner receives as a result of his trial. This information usually comes from his own perception of what he has done: the bicycle falls over, the notes are rushed, the ball goes over the head of the receiver, and so on. The learner heeds this information and adjusts his

This essay was delivered as a lecture on April 7, 1967, at the Yale Conference on English and then printed in the *Papers of the Yale Conference on English,* copyright © 1967 by the Office of Teacher Training, Yale University. Later it appeared, with slight alterations, as Chapter Six of James Moffett's *Teaching the Universe of Discourse* (Boston: Houghton Mifflin Co., 1968), pp. 188–210. It is reprinted by permission of Edward Gordon, Director of the Yale Conference, and of James Moffett.

next trial accordingly, and often unconsciously. But suppose the learner cannot perceive what he is doing—does not, for example, hear that the notes are rushed—or perceives that he has fallen short of his goal but does not know what adjustment to make in his action. This is where the coach comes in. He is someone who observes the learner's actions and the results, and points out what the learner cannot see for himself. He is a human source of feedback who supplements the feedback from inanimate things.

But, you may say, learning to write is different from learning to ride a bicycle or even learning to play the piano, which are, after all, physical activities. Writers manipulate symbols, not objects. And they are acting on the minds of other people, not on matter. Yes, indeed. But these differences do not make learning to write an exception to the general process of learning through feedback. Rather, they indicate that in learning to use language the only kind of feedback available to us is human response.

Let's take first the case of learning to talk, which is a social activity and the base for writing. The effects of what we do cannot be known to us unless our listener responds. He may do so in a number of ways—by carrying out our directions, answering our questions, laughing, looking bored or horrified, asking for more details, arguing, and so on. Every listener becomes a kind of coach. But of course a conversation, once launched, becomes a two-way interaction in which each party is both learner and source of feedback.

Through their research in the early stages of language acquisition, Roger Brown and Ursula Bellugi have been able to identify two clear interactions that take place between mother and child.[1] One is the child's efforts to reproduce in his own condensed form the sentence he hears his mother utter. The other is the mother's efforts to expand and correct the child's telegraphic and therefore ambiguous sentences. Each time the mother fills out his sentence, the child learns a little more about syntax and inflections, and when the child responds to her expansion of his utterance, she learns whether her interpretation of his words was correct or not. Linguists never cease to marvel at how children learn, before they enter school, and without any explanations or teaching of rules, how to generate novel and well-formed sentences according to a paradigm or model they have unconsciously inferred for themselves. In fact, many of the mistakes children make —like *bringed* for *brought*—are errors of overgeneralization. This ability to infer a generality from many particular instances of a thing, which also accounts for some children's learning to read and spell even without phonics training, is of course itself a critical part of human learning. The learner's

[1] Reported in "Three Processes in the Child's Acquisition of Syntax," *Language and Learning*, Janet Emig, James Fleming, and Helen Popps, eds. (New York: Harcourt, Brace, and World, 1966).

abstractive apparatus reduces a corpus of information, such as other people's sentences, to a usable rule. It is a data-processing gift that enables us to learn *something,* but not how to *do* something.

To learn to talk, the child must put his data into action and find out what happens. Thus he learns his *ir*regular verbs when he says, "I bringed my cup," and some adult replies, "Well, I'm glad you brought it." Throughout school, imitation of others' speech, as heard and read, remains a major way of learning language forms, but conversational response is the chief means the child has for making progress in speech production itself. Later, after the syntax and inflections have become pretty well fixed, the responses the learner gets to what he says are not expansions but expatiations. That is, his listener reacts to his ideas and his tone, picks up his remarks and does something further with them, so that together they create some continuity of subject.

Learning to use language, then, requires the particular feedback of human response, because it is to other people that we direct speech. The fact that one writes by oneself does not at all diminish the need for response, since one writes for others. Even when one purports to be writing for oneself—for pure self-expression, if there is such a thing—one cannot escape the ultimately social implications inherent in any use of language. As George Herbert Mead argued so well, even in our unuttered thoughts, we speak as though to another because we have long since incorporated the otherness of the social world to which language is irrevocably tied. Furthermore, we have all had the experience of looking back on something we have written earlier and of responding much as another person might do. Thus, once beyond the moment of writing, the writer himself becomes "other," and can feed back helpfully to himself.

But no feedback of whatever sort can help the learner if his will is not behind his actions, for will is the motor that drives the whole process. Without it, we ignore the results of what we have done and make no effort to adjust our actions so as to home in on the target. The desire to get certain effects on an audience is what motivates the use of speech. This is what rhetoric is all about. So the first reason why one might fail to learn is not caring, lack of motivation to scan the results and transfer that experience to the next trial. The other principal cause of failure is, on the other hand, a lack of response in the audience. One cares, one makes an effort, and no one reacts. For me, the character Jerry, in Albee's *The Zoo Story* epitomizes the desperation of one who cannot get a response. To get some effect on the unresponsive Peter, he runs through the whole rhetorical gamut—chitchat, anecdotes, questions, shocking revelations, quarreling, until finally he resorts to tickling, pushing, and fighting. It is Jerry who says, "We *must* know the consequences of our actions." And sarcastically: "Don't react, Peter, just listen."

Speaking from his experience with autistic children who had withdrawn and given up, Bruno Bettelheim has touched on the importance of both initiation and response. From the very first, he says, an infant should be given the chance to communicate his needs, not have them anticipated, and be responded to when he is communicating the need, not fed according to some other timing.

> It is for this reason that time-clock feedings are so potentially destructive, not merely because they mechanize the feeding, but because they rob the infant of the conviction that it was his own wail that resulted in filling his stomach when his own hunger timed it. By the same token, if his earliest signals, his cry or his smile, bring no results, that discourages him from trying to refine his efforts at communicating his needs. In time he loses the impulse to develop those mental and emotional structures through which we deal with the environment. He is discouraged from forming a personality.

But those are infants, not adolescents, and we teach our students to write, we don't feed them. Bettelheim continues:

> Even among adults the joke that fails to amuse, the loving gesture that goes unanswered, is a most painful experience. And if we consistently, and from an early age, fail to get the appropriate response to our expression of emotions, we stop communicating and eventually lose interest in the world.

"But," we say, "I praise my students, I give them an encouraging response."

> But this is not all. If the child's hungry cry met with only deep sympathy and not also with food, the results would be as bad as if there had been no emotional response. . . . should his smile, inviting to play, be met with a tender smile from the parent but lead to no playing, then, too, he loses interest in both his environment and the wish to communicate feeling.[2]

Smiling, gushing, or patting the back are not to the point. A response must be real and pertinent to the action, not a standard, "professional" reaction. Any unvarying response, positive or not, teaches us nothing about the effects of what we have done.

If, as I believe, writing is learned in the same basic way other activities are learned—by doing and by heeding what happens—then it is possible to

[2] These quotations are from "Where Self Begins," *The New York Times Magazine,* February 17, 1966. The article itself was drawn from *The Empty Fortress,* by Bruno Bettelheim (New York: Free Press of Glencoe, Inc., 1967).

describe ideal teaching practices in this way and compare them with some current practices. Ideally, a student would write because he was intent on saying something for real reasons of his own and because he wanted to get certain effects on a definite audience. He would write only authentic kinds of discourse such as exist outside the school. A maximum amount of feedback would be provided him in the form of audience response. That is, his writing would be read and discussed by this audience, who would also be the coaches. This response would be candid and specific. Adjustments in language, form, and content would come as the writer's response to his audience's response. Thus instruction would always be individual, relevant, and timely. These are precisely the virtues of feedback learning that account for its great success.

Clearly, the *quality* of feedback is the key. Who is this audience to be, and how can it provide a response informed enough to coach in all the necessary ways? How is it possible for every member of a class of thirty to get an adequate amount of response? Classmates are a natural audience. Young people are most interested in writing for their peers. Many teachers besides myself have discovered that students write much better when they write for each other. Although adolescents are quite capable of writing on occasion for a larger and more remote audience and should be allowed to do so, it is difficult except in unusual situations to arrange for this response to be relayed back to the writers. For the teacher to act as audience is a very intricate matter fraught with hazards that need special attention.

First, although younger children often want to write to a "significant adult," on whom they are willing to be frankly dependent, adolescents almost always find the teacher entirely *too* significant. He is at once parental substitute, civic authority, and the wielder of marks. Any one of these roles would be potent enough to distort the writer-audience relationship; all together, they cause the student to misuse the feedback in ways that severely limit his learning to write. He may, for example, write what he thinks the teacher wants, or what he thinks the teacher doesn't want. Or he writes briefly and grudgingly, withholding the better part of himself. He throws the teacher a bone to pacify him, knowing full well that his theme does not at all represent what he can do. This is of course not universally true, and students may react in irrelevant and symbolic ways to each other as well as to the teacher. But in general, classmates are a more effective audience.

The issue I want to make clear, in any case, is that the significance of the responder influences the writer enormously. This is in the nature of rhetoric itself. But if the real intent of the writing is extraneous to the writing—on a completely different plane, as when a student turns in a bland bit of trivia to show his indifference to adult demands—then the effect is actually to dissociate writing from real intent and to pervert the rhetorical process into a weird irony. Much depends of course on the manner of the teacher, and, curiously enough, if the teacher shifts authority to the peer group, which is where it lies anyway for adolescents, and takes on an indirect role, then his feedback carries a greater weight.

But, it may be argued, students are not informed and experienced enough about writing to coach each other. Won't their feedback often be misleading? How does the teacher give them the benefit of his knowledge and judgment? Let's look a moment at just what students can and cannot do for each other. Part of what they can do is a matter of numbers; multiple responses to a piece of writing make feedback more impersonal and easier to heed. Group reactions establish a consensus about some objective aspects of the writing and identify, through disagreement, those aspects that involve individual value judgments. It is much easier for peers than for the teacher to be candid and thus to give an authentic response, because the teacher, usually aware of his special significance, is afraid of wounding his students. A student responds and comments to a peer more in his own terms, whereas the teacher is more likely to focus too soon on technique. A student, moreover, may write off the comments of a teacher by saying to himself, "Adults just can't understand," or "English teachers are nit-pickers anyway," but when his fellow human beings misread him, he has to accommodate the feedback. By habitually responding and coaching, students get insights about their own writing. They become much more involved both in writing and in reading what others have written.

Many of the comments that teachers write on the themes can be made by practically any other person than the author and don't require a specialist. The failure to allow for the needs of the audience, for example, is responsible for many difficulties indicated by marginal comments like, "misleading punctuation," "unclear," "doesn't follow," "so what's your point?", "why didn't you say this before?", and so on. Irrelevance, unnecessary repetition, confusing organization, omitted leads and transitions, anticlimactic endings, are among the many things that anyone might point out. Again, numbers make it very likely that such things will not only be mentioned if they are problems, but that the idiosyncrasy of readers will be cancelled out. Probably the majority of communication problems are caused by egocentricity, the writer's assumption that the reader thinks and feels as he does, has had the same experience, and hears in his head, when he is reading, the same voice the writer does when he is writing. It is not so much knowledge as awareness that he needs.

What help can a teacher give that peers cannot? Quite a lot, but the only time he makes a unique contribution to the problem of egocentricity is when the students all share a point of view, value judgment, or line of thought that they take for granted, in which case one may question whether the teacher can or should try to shake their position, which is probably a factor of their stage of growth. Imposing taste, standards, and attitudes that are foreign to them is futile and only teaches them how to become sycophants. But there is value in the teacher's expressing his point of view so they at least know that theirs is not universal.

Where the teacher can be most help, however, is in clarifying problems after students have encountered or raised them. Adolescents—or, as I have discovered from experimenting, even fourth-graders—can spot writing problems very well, but often they do not have enough understanding of the cause of a problem to know how to solve it. This insufficient understanding more than anything else causes them to pick at each other's papers in a faultfinding spirit or to make shallow suggestions for change. A student reader may complain, for example, that a certain paper is monotonous in places and suggest that some repeated words be eliminated. But the real reason for the monotony, and for the repeating of the words, is that there are too many simple sentences, some of which should be joined. The teacher projects the paper with the comment about monotony and leads a problem-solving discussion. This is where the teacher's knowledge, say, of a generative grammar comes in—not as technical information for the students but as an aid to the teacher. Embedding some of the sentences in others involves, as well as transformations, the issue of subordination and emphasis, so that the problem of monotony can now be seen as also a lack of focus.

The teacher, in other words, helps students to interpret their initially vague responses and to translate them into the technical features of the paper that gave rise to them. Notice the direction of the process—the emotional reaction first, then the translation into technique. This amounts to sharpening response while keeping it paramount, and will help reading as well as writing. While helping to solve specific writing problems, the teacher is at the same time dispelling the negativism of comments and creating a climate of informed collaboration in which feedback is welcomed.

The role of the teacher, then, is to teach the students to teach each other. This also makes possible a lot more writing and a lot more response to the writing than a teacher could otherwise sponsor. He creates cross-teaching by setting up two kinds of group processes—one that he leads with the whole class, and a smaller one that runs itself. It is in the first kind, which I just illustrated, that the judgment and knowledge of the teacher are put into play. Periodically, the teacher projects papers for class discussion, without presenting them as good or bad examples and without trying to grind some academic ax. No detailed preparation is needed. He picks papers embodying issues he thinks concern students and need clarifying, getting his cues by circulating among the small groups, where he learns which problems are not getting informed feedback. He asks for responses to the projected paper and plays these responses by alert questioning designed to help students relate their reactions to specific features of the paper before them. If they indicate problems, he asks them to suggest changes the author might make. In these class discussions the teacher establishes tone and a method of giving and using feedback that is carried off into the small groups.

The procedure I recommend is to break the class into groups of four or five and to direct the students to exchange papers within their group, read them, write comments on them, and discuss them. This would be a customary procedure, run autonomously but constantly reinforced by the model of class discussion the teacher continues to lead. It can be of help *during* the writing process, before the final draft. The small size of the group, the reciprocity, tend to make the comments responsible and helpful. The teacher makes it clear that all reactions of any sort are of value—from strong emotions to proof-reading. A writer should know when he has succeeded in something; honest praise is very important. Descriptive remarks are very helpful—of what the paper seems to be or do, and of the effects it had on the reader. All these responses can be compared by talking over together the comments on each paper. Later in this discussion, the author says what he meant to do, and suggestions for bringing the paper more in line with his intentions are made if needed. The teacher sits in on the groups in rotation, acting as consultant and joining the discussion without necessarily having read the papers.

After the sessions, the papers may be revised. The more use to which they are put, the better. In fact, the small groups would most of the time act as editorial boards to prepare papers for some purpose. Themes should be printed up, exchanged with other groups just for reading, performed, and many other things. Eventually they go into folders kept for each student and when the teacher has to evaluate student work for the benefit of administration, he makes a general assessment of the writing to date. No grades are given on individual papers.

The teacher of course may respond individually to any paper at any time during a discussion or during a conference. Whether he writes comments on the paper himself depends on several things. Do his students still need an adult to validate and give importance to their work? Is his commentary helping or hindering? Is it necessary? If a student does not want a certain paper read by anyone but the teacher (which happens less often in small groups, where trust is stronger), the teachers honors the request and serves as reader and commentator himself. For some assignments the teacher may feel that his comments are especially relevant, for others not. In any case, if student cross-commentary occurs during the writing process and is at all effective, the amount of commentary the teacher needs to make should be small, as indeed it should be anyway. Mainly, the teacher has to know the effects of *his* action, how students are taking his feedback. First-person comments are best and will set an example for student cross-commentary. A teacher should react as an audience, supplementing the peer audience. Above all, a piece of writing should not go to a dead-letter office. Both the non-response or the irrelevant response persuade the learner that nothing is to be gained from *that* line of endeavor, and the impulse to write withers.

Trial and Error

I would like now to go back to aspects of the action-response model of learning other than the quality of the feedback. These have only been implied so far. Plunging into the act, then heeding the results, is a process of trial and error. That is the first implication. Now, trial and error sounds to many people like a haphazard, time-consuming business, a random behavior of children, animals, and others who don't know any better. (Of course, by "random" we usually mean that we the observers are ignorant of the reasons for the behavior.) Trial and error is by definition never aimless, but without help the individual alone may not think of all the kinds of trials that are possible, or may not always see how to learn the most from his errors. And if it is a social activity he is learning, like writing, then human interaction is in any case indispensable. So we have teachers to propose meaningful trials (assignments) in a meaningful order, and to arrange for a feedback that insures the maximum exploitation of error.

The second implication is that the teacher does not try to prevent the learner from making errors. He does not preteach the problems and solutions (and of course by "errors" I mean failures of vision, judgment, and technique, not mere mechanics). The learner simply plunges into the assignment, uses all his resources, makes errors where he must, and heeds the feedback. In this action—response learning, errors are valuable; they are the essential learning instrument. They are not despised or penalized. Inevitably, the child who is afraid to make mistakes is a retarded learner, no matter what the activity in question.

In contrast to the exploitation of error is the avoidance of error. The latter works like this: the good and bad ways of carrying out the assignment are arrayed in advance, are pretaught, then the learner does the assignment, attempting to keep the good and bad ways in mind as he works. Next, the teacher evaluates the work according to the criteria that were laid out before the assignment was done. Even if a system of rewards and punishments is not invoked, the learner feels that errors are enemies, not friends. I think any learning psychologist would agree that avoiding error is an inferior learning strategy to capitalizing on error. The difference is between looking over your shoulder and looking where you are going. Nobody who intends to learn to do something wants to make mistakes. In that sense, avoidance of error is assumed in the motivation itself. But if he is allowed to make mistakes with no other penalty than the failure to achieve his goal, then he knows why they are to be avoided and wants to find out how to correct them. Errors take on a different meaning, they define what is good. Otherwise the learner engages with the authority and not with the intrinsic issues. It is consequences, not injunctions, that teach. We all know that, don't we?

But doesn't this process lead to more failures? A learner needs very much to feel successful, to score. If he learns everything the hard way, doesn't he get discouraged by his mistakes? For one thing, trial-and-error makes for more success in the long run because it is accurate, specific, individual, and timely. For another, if the teacher in some way sequences the trials so that learning is transferred from one to the next, the student writer accumulates a more effective guiding experience than if one tried to guide him by preteaching. And feedback of the sort I am advocating—because it is plentiful and informed—does not just leave a feeling of failure, of having "learned the hard way," in the sense of coming out a loser. When response is real and personal, it does not leave us empty, even if our efforts missed their mark.

The procedure, moreover, of getting feedback *during* the writing instead of only *afterwards* allows the learner to incorporate it into his final product (as, incidentally, adults do when we are writing professional articles). I recommend also a lot of chain-reaction assignments, such that one paper is adapted into another. This amounts to a lot of rewriting, not mere tidying up but taking a whole new tack under the influence of suggestions from other students. It is with the isolated, sink-or-swim assignment that the student goes for broke. Finally, the error-avoiding approach has hardly given students a feeling of confidence and success; since it is the predominant method of teaching writing, it seems fair to attribute to it a lot of wariness and sense of failure so widespread among student writers today.

The Case Against Textbooks

The third implication of action—response learning follows from the last one about futility of preteaching writing problems. If we learn to write best by doing it and by heeding the feedback, then of what use is the presentation of materials to the learner? Don't presentations violate the trial-and-error process? Don't they inevitably entail preteaching and error-avoidance? My answer is yes. If I reject all prepared materials for writing, it is not that I am failing to discriminate among them. I know that they come in all sizes, shapes, and philosophies. It is not the quality but the fact of these materials that I am speaking to.

The assumption I infer from textbooks is that the output of writing must be preceded and accompanied by pedagogical input. Now, there are indeed some kinds of input that are prerequisites to writing—namely, conversation and reading—but these are very different from the presentations of textbooks. Let's look at the sorts of materials that are used to teach writing.

This material may be classified into six overlapping sorts, all of which might appear in any one unit or chapter. The first sort consists of advice, exhortation, and injunction. It is the how-to-do-it part, the cookbook material. Here are some fabricated but typical samples. "Make sure you allow for your audience." "Catch the reader's interest in the first sentence." "Make sure your punctuation guides the reader, instead of misleading him." "Connect your ideas with linking words that make transitions." "Write a brief outline of the points you want to make, then write a paragraph about each point." "For the sake of a varied style, it is advisable to begin some sentences with a main clause and others with subordinate clauses or phrases." "A vivid metaphor will often convey an idea more forcefully than a lengthy, abstract explanation." "Build up your descriptions from details that make your readers see." "A good narrative has a focus or point to it that is not obscured by irrelevant details (remember what we learned about focus in the last unit?)."

What is wrong with practical pointers and helpful hints? As I have suggested, preteaching the problems of writing causes students to adopt the strategy of error-avoidance, the teacher's intention clearly being to keep them from making mistakes. The learner is put in the situation of trying to understand and keep in mind all this advice when he should be thinking about the needs of the subject. The textbook writer is in the position of having to predict the mistakes that some mythical average student might make. The result is that, in true bureaucratic fashion, the text generates a secondary set of problems beyond those that an individual learner might truly have to deal with in the assignment itself. That is, he has to figure out first of all what the advice means at a time when it can't mean very much. Often he makes mistakes because he misconstrues the advice. In trying to stick to what he was told, he is in fact working on two tasks at once—the fulfillment of the advice and the fulfillment of the assignment.

Since not all learners are prone to the same mistakes, some of the pointers are a waste of time for the individual personally; he would not have erred in those particular ways. The exhortations and injunctions often inhibit thought. But most critically of all, they prevent both the learner and his responders from knowing what he would have done without this preteaching. It is essential to find this out. The learner has to know his own mind, what it natively produces, so that he can see what he personally needs to correct for. Students who fulfill the advice well have passed the test in following directions but have missed the chance to learn the most important thing of all—what their blind spots are.

After all, allowing for the audience, catching interest in the first sentence or paragraph, guiding the reader with punctuation, making transitions, varying the style, using metaphors, giving narrative a point—these are common-sense things. What interests me is why a student fails to do these things in the first place. The fact is, I believe, that writing mistakes are not made in ignorance of common-sense requirements; they are made for other reasons that advice cannot prevent. Usually, the student *thinks* he has made a logical transition or a narrative point, which means, again, he is deceived by his egocentricity. What he needs is not rules but awareness. Or if he omits stylistic variation, metaphor, and detail, he does so for a variety of reasons the teacher has to understand before he can be of use. Scanty reading background, or undeveloped eye or ear, a lingering immaturity about not elaborating are learning problems that exhortation cannot solve. Particular instances of failing to do what one thinks one is doing, and of failing to use the full resources of language, should be brought to light, the consequences revealed, the reasons explored, the need for remedies felt, and the possibilities of solution discovered. Unsolicited advice is unheeded advice, and, like time-clock feeding, imposes the breast before there is hunger.

A second class of material found in textbooks is expository. Here we have the definitions and explanations of rhetoric, grammar, logic, and semantics. In other words, information about language and how it is used. Part of the game played here is, to borrow the title of a Henry Read poem, the naming of parts. The assumption seems to be the primitive one that naming things is mastering them. It goes with the attempt to convert internal processes into an external subject. By pedagogical slight of hand, an output activity is transformed into something to be read about. The various ways of constructing sentences, paragraphs, and compositions are logically classified and arrayed. The student can then be put to work on writing as if it were any other substantive content: he can memorize the nomenclature and classifications, answer questions on them, take tests, and on some fitting occasion, "apply" this knowledge.

The explanations tell him what it is he is doing when he strings utterances—not he, of course, but some capitalized He, for this is the realm of general description and theory. The material may be up to date—the new linguistics and the new rhetoric—but the method couldn't be older: "There are three kinds of sentences: simple, complex, and compound." "Articles, demonstratives, and genitives make up the regular determiners." "An inductive paragraph goes from particulars to the main statement, and a deductive paragraph begins with the main statement and descends to particulars." "Ideas may be presented in any of several patterns: they may be repeated, contrasted, piled up in a series, balanced symmetrically, and so on." "The elements of fiction are plot, character, setting, and theme." "People use the same words, but don't mean the same things by them."

Such generalities, like advice, induce in the students a strategy of avoiding errors, of trying to do what the book says instead of doing justice to the subject. Whereas advice tells you what you *should* do with language, exposition tells you what people *do* do; it codifies the regularities of practice. The message is essentially the same: apply these rules and you will be all right. Good teaching, rather, helps the individual see what he in particular is doing with language and, by means of this awareness, see what he in particular might be doing. There is no evidence that preteaching general facts and theories about how people use language will help a student learn to write. (The teaching of grammar as an aid to composition is such a special and notorious case in point that I dealt with it separately in the last chapter.)

Since the most natural assumption should be that one learns to write by writing, the burden of proof is on those who advocate an indirect method, by which I mean presenting codifications about rhetoric and composition in the hope that students will apply them. Today there are many good theories of rhetoric and composition. Teachers should study these, for, like grammatical formulations, they may help the teachers understand what their students are doing or not doing in their writing. But to teach such formulations, through either exposition or exercises, would hinder more than help.

A third class of materials comprising textbooks is exercises. Sometimes the student is asked to read some dummy sentences and paragraphs and to do something with them. For example: "Underline the one of the following words that best describes the tone of the sentence below." "Rewrite the sentence that appears below so that one of the ideas is subordinated to the other." "Change the order of the sentences in the following paragraph so that the main point and the secondary points are better presented." "Read this paragraph and underline the one of the sentences following it that would serve as the best topic sentence." "Make a single sentence out of the following." Or the student may be asked to make up sentences or paragraphs of his own: "Write a sentence describing some object or action, using modifier clusters as in the examples." "Write a descriptive paragraph following a space order (or a time order)."

Exercises are obviously part and parcel of the preteaching approach characterized by advice and exposition. A point raised and explained in the text is simply cast into the form of directions so that the student will apply the point directly. The philosophy here is a curious blend of hard-headed logical analysis and folklorish softheadedness. That is, the teaching of "basics" is construed in this way. Basics are components, particles—words, sentences, and paragraphs. The learner should manipulate each of these writing units separately in a situation controlling for one problem at a time. He works his way from little particle to big particle until he arrives at whole compositions resembling those done in the outside world. The single-unit, single-problem focus derives from linguistic and rhetorical analysis done in universities, not from perceptions about learning.

The folklorish part is represented in the old saw about having to crawl before you can walk. But crawling is an authentic form of locomotion in its own right, not merely a component or subskill of walking. For the learner, basics are not the small-focus technical things but broad things like meaning and motivation, purpose and point, which are precisely what are missing from exercises. An exercise, by my definition, is any piece of writing practiced only in schools—that is, an assignment that stipulates arbitrary limits that leave the writer with no real relationships between him and a subject and an audience. I would not ask a student to write anything other than an authentic discourse, because the learning process proceeds from intent and content down to the contemplation of technical points, not the other way.

First of all, when it is the stipulation of the text or the teacher and not the natural limit of an utterance, a sentence or a paragraph is too small a focus for learning. How can you teach style, rhetoric, logic, and organiza-tion in a unit stripped of those authentic relationships to subject and au-dience that *govern* the decisions about word choice, sentence structure, paragraph structure, and total continuity? Judgment and decision-making are the heart of composition. With exercises the learner has no basis for choosing one word or sentence structure over another, and rhetoric becomes an irony once again. It is a crime to make students think that words, sen-tences, paragraphs, are "building blocks" like bricks that have independent existence and can be learned and manipulated separately pending the oc-casion when something is to be constructed out of them.

And when students make up a sentence or paragraph demonstrating such and such kind of structure, they are not learning what the teacher thinks they are: they are learning that there is such a thing as writing sentences and paragraphs for their own sake, that discourse need not be motivated or directed at anyone, that it is good to write even if you have nothing to say and no one to say it to just so long as what you put down illustrates a linguistic codification. The psychological phenomenon involved here—called "learning sets" by H. E. Harlow, and "deutero-learning" by Gregory Bateson [3]—is that when someone learns a certain content, he also *learns that way of learning*. This second kind of learning tends to be hidden because it is not under focus, and yet for that very reason may be the more lasting. The student learns how to do exercises, and this learning is of a higher order, ironically, than the learning of the different sentence or paragraph structures contained in the exercises. Thus in an a-rhetorical learning situation, he learns to discourse a-rhetorically!

When decomposition precedes composition, many such unintended and harmful side-effects occur that seem to go on unnoticed because we are fastened on the logic of the subject instead of the psychologic of the learner. Scientists have long been aware that when you isolate out a component for focused observation, you are changing it. Live tissue under a microscope is not live tissue in the body. A sentence or paragraph stripped of its organic context, raised several powers, and presented in the special context of analysis and advice represents serious tampering with the compositional process, the consequences of which are not well recognized.

Second, a student doing a paragraph exercise, say, knows the problem concerns paragraph structure, whereas in authentic discourse the real problem always is this, that *we don't know what it is we don't know*. A student may do all of the exercises correctly and still write very badly because he is used to having problems plucked out of the subjective morass and served to him externally on a platter, and has subsequently developed little in the way of awareness and judgment. For example, he *can't* decide how to break into paragraphs because he must write only one paragraph.

Third, students adopt a strategy for beating the game of exercises: they take a simplistic approach, avoid thinking subtly or complexly, and say only what can lend itself readily to the purpose of the exercise. To make the paragraph come out right, they write things they know are stupid and boring.

Fourth, the poetic justice in this strategy is that the exercises themselves ignore the motivational and learning needs of the student. The result is just the opposite intended: the learner dissociates the technical issues in the exercise from honest discourse. The learner becomes alienated, not only by this but by the hidden message of exercises, which says, "We are not interested in what you have to say; we just want a certain form." His defense is to do the exercise by the book in an ironically obedient fashion

[3] See pp. 215 and 216 of *Communication: The Social Matrix of Psychiatry,* by Jurgen Ruesch and Gregory Bateson (New York: W. W. Norton & Company, Inc., 1951).

to show them for just what they are. You bore me and I'll bore you. This dissociation in the minds of students between school stuff and writing for real is one of the deep and widespread symptoms that has made English teaching ripe for reform.

The last three kinds of materials are not bad in themselves but suffer from being embedded in the paraphernalia I have been polemicizing about. For this reason I will deal with them briefly. The first is the presentation of samples of good writing to serve as models. As I have said, learning to write entails a lot of reading, but when passages from the old pros are surrounded by rhetorical analysis and pesky questions about how Saroyan got his effects, a disservice is done to both reading and writing. How would you as an adolescent react to a message such as this: "See how Steinbeck uses details; now you go do that too." And there is no evidence that analyzing how some famous writer admirably dispatched a problem will help a student recognize and solve his writing problems. From my own experience and that of teachers I have researched with, I would say, rather, that models don't help writing and merely intimidate some students by implying a kind of competition in which they are bound to lose. The assumption is still that advance diagnosis and prescription facilitate learning. The same reading selections can be helpful, however, if merely interwoven with the writing assignments as part of the regular reading program but without trying to score points from them. Learners, like the professional writers themselves, incorporate anyway the structures of what they read; what they need is more time to read and write authentically. The service publishers could do is to put out more straight anthologies of whole reading selections grouped according to the various kinds of writing but unsurrounded by questions and analysis. The student should write in the forms he reads while he is reading them. There can be a lot of discussion of these selections, but the points of departure for discussion should be student response to the reading.

Another kind of textbook material—writing stimulants—is closely related to models because sometimes these prompters are also reading selections. Or they may merely be the text writer's own prose as he tried to set up ideas or talk up topics, two intentions that are better realized in class conversation. Sometimes the stimulants are photographs—possibly a good idea, but the pictures are always too small in the textbook. Whatever the kind of stimulant, the wiser course is to let it arise out of the daily drama of the student's life in and out of school, including his regular reading. In this way the stimulants are automatically geared to what the students know and care about. To present stimulants in a book is to run an unnecessary risk of irrelevance and canned writing.

At last we come to the assignment directions themselves. They, of course, are justified, but for them who needs a book? Even the windiest text writer could not get a textbook out of assignment directions alone. It is better anyway for the teacher to give the assignment because he can adapt it to his particular class—cast it in a way that they will understand, relate it to their other work, and so on.

Let me summarize now my concerns about presenting materials to students as a way to teach writing. They install in the classroom a mistaken and unwarranted method of learning. They take time, money, and energy that should be spent on authentic writing, reading, and speaking. They get between the teacher and his students, making it difficult for the teacher to understand what they need, and to play a role that would give them the full benefit of group process. They add secondary problems of their own making. They sometimes promote actual mislearning. They kill spontaneity and the sense of adventure for both teacher and students. They make writing appear strange and technical so that students dissociate it from familiar language behavior that should support it. Their dullness and arbitrariness alienate students from writing. Because they predict and prepackage, they are bound to be inappropriate for some school populations, partly irrelevant to individual students, and ill-timed for all.

I believe the teacher should be given a lot of help for the very difficult job of teaching writing. A lot of what is in textbooks should be in books for teachers, and is in fact partly there to educate them, not the students. The real problem, as I think many educators would admit, is that too many teachers cannot do without textbooks because they were never taught in schools of education to teach without them. Textbooks constitute a kind of inservice training in teaching method and in linguistic and rhetorical analysis that they never received before. Thus the trial-and-error approach would be considered too difficult for most teachers; they wouldn't have the background, perception, and agility to make it work. The extreme of this belief is that teacher-proof materials are necessary to compensate for teacher inadequacy. If this is so, then let's be frank and solve the problem by renovating teacher training and by publishing more books for teachers on the job, not by putting materials in the hands of students. If it is acknowledged that textbooks do not exist because they embody the best learning process but because teachers are dependent on them, then we would expect them to dwindle away as the education of teachers improves. But I don't see that texts are a mere stop-gap measure. There is every indication that they will become more powerful, not less. The investments of everyone are too great. I don't mean just the publishers, who are merely supplying a demand; I mean that we are all caught in a self-perpetuating cycle that revolves among education schools, classrooms, school administrations, and publishers. The teaching of writing will not improve until the cycle is broken. It is not up to the publishers to break it; they will put out whatever teachers call for. Although a number of teachers do teach writing without texts, it is too much to expect a revolution to start in classrooms without a lot of change in school administration and schools of education, which is where the cycle can be broken.

If I have strayed here into essentially noneducational considerations, it is because I believe the only justification for textbooks in writing is an essentially noneducational one. My main purpose has been to propose that writing be taught naturalistically, by writing, and that the only texts be the student productions themselves. I regret that I have had to speak so long against something, but it is not enough to propose; a way must be cleared. I see tremendous evidence against the preteaching approach, embodied in textbooks, and no evidence for it. The great advances in language theory, on the one hand, and in programming techniques on the other, are unfortunately reinforcing that approach. The prospect that frightens me is that we educators are learning to do better and better some things that should not be done at all. We are rapidly perfecting error. Which is to say that I think we should heed better the feedback we get about the consequences of our own teaching actions.

BRUCE E. MILLER / *On Composition as Art*

Of the three main divisions of the English curriculum—literature, gram-mar, and composition—composition is notoriously the most difficult to teach. As the number of articles on motivating composition attests, few students voluntarily write, and teacher morale staggers under the burden of theme correction. Most students acquire writing skill so slowly and painfully that neither they nor their teachers have much heart for continuous effort. After years of teaching composition at high school, undergraduate, and graduate levels, I still find that writing is the part of English instruction which de-mands the most effort and which yields, on the whole, the least satisfying results. Other teachers have the same experience. My purpose here is to suggest a reason why learning to write poses the difficulty it does for most students and then to explore some of the pedagogical consequences of that reason.

Composition is an art, and it is the only one which high schools demand that students attempt to master at a fairly high level of proficiency as a prerequisite for graduation. To be sure, schools make some other ·art ex-perience available. If a student is lucky, he may get a taste of painting and perhaps clay sculpture, and generally schools offer music to a more ad-vanced level; but these arts are in nearly all cases elective. Schools insist, however, that all students should be able to write, and indeed to write in a fairly specialized and demanding *genre,* the expository essay.

Not nearly enough has been made of the artistic character of student

From *English Journal,* LVIII (October, 1968), 1017–19. Reprinted by permission of the National Council of Teachers of English and Bruce E. Miller.

writing, and some of our disappointments in teaching composition may owe to this fact. Like other arts, composition requires not only a particular collection of ideas but also the ability to put those ideas into effect in the making of a construct. The artist not only *knows* something; he also *makes* something. In this sense, few school subjects involve artistic skill. Social studies, at least as commonly taught, requires little more than the accumulation of ideas, which may be sorted and arranged but rarely reduced to a practical application. Other subjects—mathematics, natural science, language (including English in the study of grammar or usage)— may feature some practical outcome, but usually this result is itself a pattern, not an original creation. In mathematics the correct proof is the standard one, in natural science the experiment must duplicate other experiments with the same elements, and in language study the test of propriety is conformity to a received pattern that constitutes grammar.

Composition, on the other hand, requires a different kind of activity. Its merit is uniqueness, not conformity. A student essay that expresses the same content as other student essays is condemned for banality or investigated for plagiarism. Still more difficult for the student to attain is uniqueness of form, but if he fails in this task he is graded down for using clichés or being verbose or having faulty organization.

When we ask a student to write an essay, therefore, we are asking very much from him, if he is an ordinary sort of person. We are asking him, in the first place, to call up a large fund of information—about lexicography, social convention, rhetoric, grammar, spelling, euphony, logic—and then we are asking him to bring all that to bear in a creative effort. In other words, we are asking him to be an artist for the nonce. We do not fully appreciate his dismay, perhaps, because although we are not artists ourselves by and large, still we are at least artistic; we have some taste and some creative power. That is why we are English teachers. If we want to realize just how uncommon artistic aptitude is, let's look at another field. Arnold Haskell, the ballet critic and Director of the English Royal Ballet School, reports that the great national ballet companies find acceptable only one in ten of the students training in their own schools, even though these are highly motivated persons who have been subject to careful screening and intense training.[1]

That proportion of success—10 per cent—is not surprising in dance or indeed in any other artistic discipline, for although many are called to enjoy art, few are chosen to create it. The grim truth of the matter is that for the marvellous few who dance through life there is an equal number who

[1] *Ballet Retrospect* (London: B. T. Batsford, 1964), p. 131.

stumble and a vast many who merely plod, or, if they insist on what they imagine is excellent, caper and prance. Instruction benefits those who are naturally gifted, of course, but it is ineffectual with those who have no inclination for art, and it aids very little those whose creative endowment is slight. Most people would readily grant all this, would take it as axiomatic in fact, of all the arts *except writing*. But writing is useful; it helps us to get ahead, both in school and later on in business or one of the professions. Thus it is concluded that since business and professional people *need* to write, they *must* be taught composition, whether they are capable of learning it or not. And so it is that boys who want to be engineers and girls who want to be nurses—perfectly able but linguistically untalented—are forced all through high school and the first year of college once a week to make clowns of themselves in themes that delight all the powers of darkness. Although these people scarcely show any perceptible improvement—so little that according to one experiment they would have learned to write as well by just reading [2]—still they have one consolation: if they can survive composition through Freshman English, nine out of ten will probably never write another essay as long as they live.[3]

If it is true that writing is an art and that few can master it, then some of the peculiarities in teaching composition become more understandable. In this connection, the reason why some few students learn to write much more easily than the great majority is that few possess the specialized aptitudes that go into composition. Most students—many of them intelligent— make very little progress because they simply are not apt for writing and never will be. They do not readily command the manifold elements that go into an essay. Even when such students progress in one respect—punctuation say—they fall back in other ways and write formless, tasteless essays unintentionally enlivened from time to time by well-punctuated but ludicrous solecisms. At the end of the school year they have little more to show for their effort than a succession of dreary themes and conscientiously elaborate error charts—those pathetic memorials of vain endeavor.

When we recognize that writing is a high level art, we should be able to see the inappropriateness of our present expectations and thus take a step towards ascertaining the right goals. In the first place, if writing means the intelligible and agreeable expression of ideas together with supporting reasons, then the plain fact—or at least the probability—is that we can

[2] Frank Heys, "The Theme-a-Week Assumption: A Report of an Experiment," *EJ*, 51 (May, 1962) 320–22.
[3] Does anyone really believe that term papers are required by social science instructors? A colleague of mine who teaches courses in guidance recently told me that many of his graduate students say that they have never written an essay since they took Freshman English.

never teach the greater number of our students to write. And a paper a week (or a day) will not help much. Of all vocations art is peculiarly the one in which the rich get richer and the poor poorer. My own experience is that the average high school student, by the time he has reached the eleventh grade, has been educated all the way up to his capacity in writing and will learn no more except, rarely, at a very disproportionate expense. On the other hand, there are some—perhaps 20 per cent—who have an inclination for writing and can still learn more about it.

Therefore, I should like to see English teachers revise a curriculum which now requires everyone to work away at an acquirement which only a few can master. For the students who cannot learn to write we nevertheless have much to offer: we can strengthen their appreciation of literature, we can help their readiness and ease in speech, we can teach them such border-line composition skills as the writing of courtesy notes and factual business correspondence and the filling out of personnel forms, tax forms, and order blanks. And of course such students can learn much else. Then the smaller number of students, those specifically gifted with the qualities that go into writing, could get the amount of attention which their talents deserve.

Curriculum changes slowly, I realize, but a teacher who wants to can act upon the spirit of this advice in his own way. A teacher who has a mixed batch of papers need not give the same amount of energy to the "C minus minus" student writer that he gives to the more promising one. Moreover, alternative assignments or even some modifications of the old contract method are possible.

But conscience, or compulsiveness, makes cowards of us all. In fact many of us concentrate our efforts on the "C minus minus" writer because we feel that he needs us. Such a student does not really need us, for writing is not the only way through which a person may improve himself; there are others. Furthermore, we help such students very little; we merely harass them into sullenness and complicate the problems of rapport. Those jokes about the antipathy between English teachers and physical education teachers usually are told at the expense of the coaches. But the coaches can teach us something about resignation to facts; at least they rarely insist that scrawny ectomorphs play tackle.

JOHN C. SHERWOOD / *How to Escape Teaching Composition*

In an interesting and valuable article in a recent issue of the *Bulletin*,[1] Professor Bruce Dearing has entered a protest against the present tendency in teachers of English literature to desert their traditional activities for new and unfortunate experiments in which literature either is used as an occasion for teaching something else or is treated in a narrow and specialized fashion. It is possible that some of his alarm is unnecessary, but a good deal of it is perfectly justified. It would be even more justified if he were treating the conduct of teachers of English in their other capacity as teachers of composition; for in this area they show to an even more alarming degree a tendency to desert their main enterprise for all sorts of activities which are distracting and often absolutely irrelevant. We would have to admit, I think, that all the experiments mentioned by Mr. Dearing do represent possible ways of teaching literature and ways which might conceivably be successful, although in some, and especially in the sociological approach, there is grave danger that all literary values may be lost. In the case of some of the activities carried on under the name of composition, not even this much could be claimed, and the danger that they will damage or destroy the whole discipline is even greater. For this reason, it is time to take a look at some of the common distractions which appear in composition courses and substitute themselves for the teaching of composition itself.

[1] "The Sirens on the Shore," *AAUP Bulletin*, XXXVIII (Winter, 1952–53), 589–98.

From the *AAUP Bulletin*, XL (Summer, 1954), 282–90. Reprinted by permission of the American Association of University Professors and John C. Sherwood.

These distractions are so numerous, and are so often resorted to, that one would almost think that a composition teacher would rather do anything than teach his own subject.

II

The substitute which has been doing damage for the longest time is undoubtedly the teaching of grammar. It may seem surprising to speak of grammar as a substitute for composition, since for so long the teaching of grammar *was* the teaching of composition, or the greater part of it. But it needs only a little reflection to see that the two cannot be identified. If we assume, as we should, that the attainment of the kind of correctness in writing demanded by the older grammar is desirable, yet we still have to recognize that a student who has attained it has attained nothing except the ability to write individual sentences which make sense. There is no guarantee that he can put sentences together into a sensible piece of writing; and, in fact, he has only begun to learn composition. The teaching of some grammar is certainly a necessary prerequisite for successful work in writing, whatever progressive superintendents of schools may think; but if all composition work is reduced to grammar, and the diagramming of sentences and filling in of exercises replaces actual experience in writing, then grammar ceases to be a tool of composition and becomes a substitute for it, and such excess is to be deplored and avoided. It may be better to teach grammar alone than to pay no attention at all to language, and if heavy class loads force a teacher to make the choice, he would do well to stick to the grammar; but otherwise there is not much to be said for it.

It might be replied that the teaching of grammar is no longer much of a menace, except in very benighted circles, because the old prescriptive grammar of rules (alleged to be unscientific, undemocratic, perhaps un-American) has been overthrown and usage elevated as a standard in its stead. Our present objection, however, is not that the old grammar was rigid and unrealistic, but that it was taught as an end rather than a means, and taught in preference to more important things; and exactly the same thing can happen with the teaching of the grammar of usage. Actually, "usage" can be far more complicated than "grammar," since the single standard of correctness is replaced by a separate standard for each "level" of language, and since every rule acquires a multitude of qualifications and exceptions. If any reader doubts that the study of usage could become a mechanical activity and take up the time needed for the larger elements of composition, he should look at the proposals for "A Course in Language and Communication," set forth in the volume *Toward General Education* published a few years back.[2]

There is a minor vice which we might mention here because it resembles the teaching of grammar in its mechanical character and has much the same status as a minor study which sometimes tends to crowd the major one. This is vocabulary building. As in the case of grammar, it has its place; but also as in the case of grammar, it can become mere exercise-work, a matter of memorizing lists and analyzing etymologies, and quite ineffective. A good active vocabulary is not built by exercise work, but by reading and listening, and by active use.

Another activity which has menaced composition courses and tempted teachers from the strait path from time immemorial is the teaching of literature. (Under this heading we would not, of course, include the teaching of literary works which are taught as models for writing.) Now, the teaching of composition and literature are related, and, properly carried on, they support each other, since both depend on a mastery of language. Whether they should be taught together in the same course is another question; I am inclined to think that they should be kept apart, though in some college programs this may not be possible. But whether they are together or apart, it needs to be emphasized that they are not equivalent and that the one is not to be substituted for the other. The emphasis is especially needed because the teaching of literature is likely to be easier and more entertaining than the teaching of composition, and most beginning teachers know the literature better; hence, where the course is mixed the literature tends to crowd the composition, and even where the courses are kept separate, we are likely to find the composition staff trying to slip over into literature by means of book reports or some such device. In one sense the displacement of composition by literature is not as bad as the displacement by grammar, since the activity substituted is worth while in itself; but in another way it is worse, since it is a quite distinct activity, not even related to the other as the part to the whole. However the program is set up, the boundary line between composition and literature should be clear, and composition should be protected against the aggression of the more attractive discipline.

III

If grammar and literature are the chief distractions for the older generation of teachers, those who came into the profession during the depression years and later seem to be most attracted by an activity which for lack of an

[2] Earl J. McGrath and others, *Toward General Education,* New York: The Macmillan Company, 1948, pp. 77–78.

official term we will call stimulation, or the sociological approach to composition. As far as stimulation is justified by reference to the central purposes of a composition course at all, it is founded on the assumption that students write best about what really interests them; or, as Goethe puts it,

> . . . What is uttered from the heart alone
> Will win the hearts of others to your own . . .
> Good sense, Sir, and rightmindedness
> Have little need to speak by rule.

This proposition is a dangerous half-truth; it would be nearer the truth to say that a person in a state of excitement will probably write vigorously and sincerely, but not necessarily with order, clarity, or logic. For illustration of this point we need only look at the editorial pages of college newspapers, where students write with incoherent passion of sports, fraternities, and other things that "really interest them." As for the stimulators, they commonly begin by giving the student readings in provocative essays on topics of "timely" and (occasionally) permanent interest and follow up the reading with a bull session on the content of the essay, presumably with the notion that this will give the student ideas and motivation sufficient to generate a theme. Their texts, usually labelled as essays for today, for our time, for "an air age," are organized into divisions which have no reference to the rhetorical features of the pieces included, but only to their social significance. "War and Peace," "Science and Society," "Problems of Education" are typical labels; one book has a section which is simply called "issues," and it is not unusual for a text compiled on other principles to include a provocative section as a concession to the stimulators. Where exercises are provided, they read something like this (a composite, but the individual sentences are authentic):

> Do you consider ——'s indictment of American immaturity too sweeping? Are most Americans, as you know them, blatant, discourteous, vulgar? What to you now constitutes "a satisfying and significant life"? What suggestions would you make for improving faculty-student relations? What is your own attitude toward Frank Sinatra? What are the basic problems of American life? Are new ideas necessarily sounder than old? Did Hardy possess alert senses? Do you know a better place to picnic than Pond Island? What aspects of American life are neglected by the comfortable classes? Or are you the victim of your own cleverness?

And so on. The essays are "think pieces," the exercises are "discussion-stimulative" (to use the publisher's jargon), and the intent seems to be to reduce the composition course to a very debased and diluted social-science survey.

This sort of thing is not, of course, a sound or adequate course in the social sciences, and if it were so labelled it would immediately be denounced by the social scientists as superficial. The essays read are sometimes by men with scholarly reputations in their fields, but they are more likely to be the work of politicians, journalists, and amateur prophets—the sort of people, in other words, who stimulate more than they inform. If the staff is a normal composition staff, it will consist of people trained in literature, so that between the instructor and the text, the student is likely to be robbed of his composition without getting anything much in return. The best he can hope for is that the "think pieces" will be subjected to close analysis as a preliminary to the stimulating discussion; then he will get some training in reading and perhaps some sense of organization in prose.

It is not easy to explain how composition teachers ever got on the stimulation track, but the spirit goes back to the depression years when most young English teachers were, if not pink, at least boiling with social consciousness, and thought that the greatest service they could do humanity was to unsettle the middle-class prejudices of their students; and it has been kept alive, after the fading out of depression liberalism, by the spirit of socialized education as propagated in schools of education. There are thousands who would still defend the necessity of such unsettling experience in college life; but if it is necessary to give such a course, it ought to be treated quite frankly for what it is and appear in the catalogue under its proper colors:

SOCIOLOGY 1 and 2. *Stimulation of Immature Minds.* Eradication of bourgeois prejudices. Casual reading of provocative essays. Lively discussions. Three hours each semester.

To call such a thing composition is a fraud, and if some college faculties were more conscious of what was going on, they would either eliminate the required composition course altogether, or turn it over to the social scientists, who are after all more expert in what has become the main part of the course, and who would handle what is left of the instruction in writing no worse than the composition instructors handle the sociology.

Occasionally the stimulator pauses from his invasion of the realm of the political scientist to take up psychology and counseling, encouraged by the modern trend in education which saddles the teacher with all the responsibilities formerly assumed by the home and the church. At least there is one text whose headings are a direct challenge to the freshman to reform himself:

    I. How strenuously do you propose to live?

    II. Are you satisfied with your personality?

    III. Do your habits help or hinder?

I take it, however, that it is not as common to organize courses around the student's private emotions as it is to organize them around his political opinions, and this particular distraction is not at the moment much of a threat, or some composition teachers might find themselves in trouble for practising psychiatry without a license.

IV

Though the stimulation movement has faded somewhat, it is still the strongest threat to composition, and more important than the innovations which have made headway since the war. Of these, one of the more interesting is the introduction into composition of certain elements of logic and semantics. This tendency is not bad in itself; certainly no one would protest against the demand that writing be logical, or against the use of a little instruction in formal logic, provided we recognize that writing modeled on the logic of the philosophers would be intolerably stiff and rigid, and that the study of logic beyond a certain point would not help writing much and would be beyond the capacities of the average freshman class. The case is much the same with semantics. In moderation semantics can do much to make the student sensitive to the finer points of language; but as pursued by professionals, it becomes involved with all sorts of difficulties and profundities which have absolutely no significance in the study of writing. As a matter of fact, the very difficulty and dullness of semantics in its higher reaches would effectively prevent its ever being used to excess in freshman courses were it not for the existence of an unfortunately popular book in which semantics is at once vulgarized and made obscure by being expounded in a pretentious and difficult jargon. The book is especially dangerous in that it lends itself to simple minds who enjoy playing with the jargon without really understanding it, or perceiving that the ideas which it conceals are extremely simple and obvious; and the amount of time which can be wasted on semantics when considered in this way is very great.[3] Fortunately, more recent texts present the matter in a simpler and more usable form.

[3] "Here though we think it profoundly necessary to discuss varying levels of abstraction and hence varying degrees of exactness in communication, we are not suggesting that the course be turned into one in general semantics. Especially we should think it desirable to avoid the terminology of the general semanticists which too often drives their prose into the very obfuscation they deprecate." (McGrath and others, *op. cit.*, p. 79.)

Some composition courses have lately shifted their emphasis from writing to reading, usually as a result of some further deterioration in pre-college training. This change falls within the scope of our subject, since it does seem to involve the displacement of composition by something else; but in practice it is not much of a threat. The teaching of reading, if properly done, will consist mostly of the careful analysis of passages, which is what most good composition teaching above the level of grammar largely is. Some care will have to be taken to see that the passages read are suitable models for composition, and that the particular problems which come up in writing but not in reading are given a place. With these precautions, the two ought to go along happily together.

A more complex problem is that raised by the appearance of communications courses in which speech and composition are combined, usually with the addition of reading and "listening." While recognizing that there are many practical objections to this type of course, for which it is extremely difficult to find a competent staff, we would have to admit that there is a certain logic in the combination, and that where the practical difficulties can be overcome, there might be some gain in running the two together. At the same time, we need to make very clear that speech and composition are not equivalent, that speech is not an acceptable substitute for composition, and that if both are to be taught, they cannot be taught properly in the brief time normally allowed for composition. Another thing to be guarded against is the real possibility that instructors not trained in speech will take up speech and listening in an amateurish way as a device to fill up time and take away from the instruction in writing without accomplishing anything of any consequence with the other. All they need to do is to revive the old stimulation bull session and rechristen it a "panel discussion"; the thing will be easy to manage and can be advertised as novel and progressive. For the rest, if speech is to be added, then additional time must be allowed, and the staff should be trained enough so that the speech and listening will not be mere babble.

V

This completes our survey of the principal activities which creep and intrude and climb into composition courses and distract staff and students from their real business. In some cases a minor part of the course, such as grammar, has come to take up time beyond its real value and must be put back in its place; in others, a related but not strictly equivalent activity has managed to substitute itself and must be put out altogether. The reasons for such intrusions and substitutions are not hard to find. In some cases the activity serves merely to fill up time, and is resorted to because the instructor lacks the experience or the ingenuity to do what he ought to be doing and has to turn to Beowulf or Bessie the Cow to see him through to the end of the hour. Some substitutes appeal because they are simple and definite; it is easier to explain a comma than to show why a particular essay is put together as it is or why a particular line of reasoning is unsound. Literature appeals because it is more entertaining than composition; and stimulation because it has the appearance of being more useful from a social and political point of view than mere good writing. Still, all these temptations would be resisted better than they are if it were not for the depressing circumstances under which a freshman writing course must operate. The staff is largely composed of beginners, who are often overworked; the students are a completely unselected group, often ill-trained and mostly reluctant. The subject, finally, is hard to teach and hard to learn, and it is extremely difficult to get satisfactory results in the short time the course lasts. Under the circumstances, it is not surprising if things often go wrong.

It does not seem likely that these circumstances will change very soon, and none of the problems of composition will be cured overnight, least of all the one which is the subject of this essay. Nonetheless, there is a good deal of improvement possible. If composition staffs had a little better instruction in their particular jobs, they would know what it is to teach writing, and not go on supposing that it is an endless series of boring exercises or an extended discussion of all the problems of life. In part, all that is needed is a little more pride and confidence in the work, a feeling that good writing is in itself a very worthy attainment and that a teacher who is helping others toward that attainment need not try to justify his existence by trying to do something else along with it. Along with this confidence, however, there needs to go a certain amount of humility; an English teacher ought to realize that he is not necessarily qualified to solve all the woes of the world in his little three-hour course. We do not solve our problems by multiplying them; and why it should be supposed that an instructor who is not doing very well in eradicating sentence fragments will be improved if he has to undertake speech and psychoanalysis in addition is not easy to explain. Such, however, would seem to be the assumption behind many innovations in the teaching of composition, innovations which seem destined to continue and against which we should make constant protest.

CURRICULUM

JAMES M. Mc CRIMMON / *A Cumulative Sequence in Composition*

"How can principles of rhetoric, logic, and grammar be arranged cumulatively according to the pupil's maturity level?" To avoid duplication with Professor Gorrell, who deals with the interrelation of grammar, and composition, and with Professor Hook, who deals with the interrelation of grammar, logic, and rhetoric, I will place my emphasis on what I shall call *rhetorical structure*. Let me explain that term.

The rhetorical structure is the organization of symbols to which we respond in any unit of communication. For example, Keats's sonnet, "On First Looking into Chapman's Homer," has at least three major structures—a grammatical structure, a metaphorical structure, and the generic structure of the Italian sonnet. All these together make up the rhetorical structure of the sonnet. I use the phrase *rhetorical structure* to get away from the divisiveness of the trivium—grammar, logic, and rhetoric. As Professor Hook has pointed out, rhetoric includes grammar and logic; it also includes semantics. Whatever elements in a communication affect our response are parts of the rhetorical structure of that communication.

What I want to do here is to illustrate how rhetorical structures may be arranged in a sequence which is cumulative in the sense that each new structure tends to include those preceding it, so that when a student learns how to handle one kind of structure, he can use that experience to master the next kind. The particular sequence I will illustrate for Grades 7, 8, and 9 has been influenced by the writings of Jerome Bruner, Albert Upton, and

From *English Journal*, LV (April, 1966), 425–34. Reprinted by permission of the National Council of Teachers of English and James M. McCrimmon.

others, but it is chiefly the result of experiments and experience in the class-rooms of the laboratory school of the University of Illinois. For the most part, the illustrations which I will use are lessons taken from the curriculum being developed at that school.

Specification. The first stage in the sequence I am concerned with is speci-fication. If we ignore errors in spelling, punctuation, conventional sentence structure, and grammatical agreements of various kinds as matters of usage rather than of composition, I think we will all agree that the greatest weak-ness of inexperienced writers—and this holds true for college seniors as well as for seventh-graders—is their addiction to undeveloped, unsupported, and unexplained statements. For example, I ask a seventh-grader to write an essay about why he liked a particular short story, and he answers in a single sentence that he liked it because it was "interesting." He does not understand that his answer gives me no additional information, that he has merely substituted the abstraction "interesting" for the abstraction "likeable." I must now ask him what events in the story he found interesting. Only when his words point to specific events in the story does he begin to com-municate to me.

Some of you will have noticed that part of the blame for this failure to communicate was mine. By asking a general question, I invited a general answer. Had I asked a more specific question, I might have guided the stu-dent into a more specific response, and such a response might have helped him to bring himself into a relation with the story and so evaluate its ef-fect on him. As those of you who have read *how the french boy learns to write* must know, some of the bad writing we get from our students is a result of our failure to specify the assignment. Young students have to be guided into good writing. They can best be led into being specific by putting them into situations which require specific responses. This is especially true when they are being asked to revise inefficient work. It is not enough to ask them to be more specific; they must be shown what kind of specificity is wanted, and where. One way to direct such a revision is shown in the following assignment.

The purpose of this exercise is to revise a student essay so as to make it a more specific communication. At successive points in the essay, numbers have been introduced, and for each number a question is asked at the end of the essay. You are to answer these questions on a separate sheet of paper. When you have answered all the questions, you will be asked to revise the essay.

> *The Secret Life of Walter Mitty* tells about a man's daydreams.[1] His
> wife nags him [2] and he begins to dream. In his dreams he is a hero who
> has many adventures, such as a pilot and a doctor.[3] In real life **he is a**

very ordinary person,[4] but he becomes a great man in his dreams.[5] He does a lot of exciting things.[6] His wife is not very nice.[7] She bosses him terribly.[8] The story tells how he escapes from her bossing in his daydreams.

1. Is the purpose of the story simply to tell about his daydreams, or are the dreams chosen for a special reason? State the purpose of the story.

2. Give examples of her nagging.

3. If a reader of this essay does not know the story, will he know what "such as a pilot and a doctor" means? What adventures is the author of this essay thinking of? State the adventures so that a reader will understand them.

4. What kind of ordinary person is he? Describe the "real" Walter briefly but specifically.

5. What kind of "great man"? Give an example.

6. If examples are given in 5, this statement will not be necessary, since the example will show the exciting things he does.

7. In what ways is his wife not nice? If she is something more than bossy, give an example here. If she is only bossy, ignore this sentence.

8. Give examples of her bossiness.

9. Study your answers to these questions and group them under three headings: (1) the purpose of the story, (2) Mrs. Mitty's treatment of Walter and the way he accepts that treatment, and (3) his daydreams.

10. Starting with the purpose, rewrite the essay in the light of your answers.

This exercise was put on a transparency and projected on a screen for class discussion. I find it useful to do a good deal of this kind of work in the classroom. I have little confidence in the kind of help I can give a student by my written comments on his paper. That procedure is more useful for proofreading than for teaching composition. But I find that if selected essays are projected and discussed in detail by the whole class, not only is the revision more efficient, but the whole attitude toward revision is changed. It is no longer a question of a particular student's trying to appease a fault-finding teacher; it is an experience in communal authorship, which can be discussed at every stage of the composition. Teachers often complain—and rightly so—of the burden of grading compositions, but it seems to me that they often confuse evaluation with teaching. It is usually necessary at the end of each term to assign a grade which is a fair estimate of the quality of the student's work, but it is not necessary that every paper written during the term be graded. A graded assignment once a month would meet the evaluation requirements; the rest of the writing can be designd as learning experiences in which the class discovers by writing and criticism some of the differences between good and bad writing.

But I must return from this digression on grading. The best approach to specificity, I think, is through semantics. The minimum prerequisite is at least a rudimentary knowledge of the abstract nature of language and of the difference between words that point to things which we can see, hear, feel, taste, and smell and words which refer to classes of things. And the best pedagogical device for teaching this lesson is the abstraction ladder, which shows a range between very concrete and very abstract terms. The old distinction among proper nouns, common nouns, and abstract nouns is a less efficient method of teaching the same lesson. All nouns are abstract. It is only when they are restricted by modifiers and descriptive details that they point to individual and specific things. The following lesson illustrates this point:

THE MEANING OF CLASS NAMES
(X_1 IS NOT X_2)

Here are pictures of two objects. A rectangle has been placed around them to indicate that they are to be understood as "real" objects, not pictures. You can cut them with a fork and eat them.

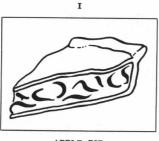
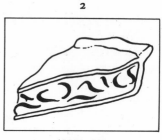

APPLE PIE   APPLE PIE

1. Are these objects the same? Alike? If you were hungry and were offered one, which would you choose, and why?

2. What do the names under the objects tell you about them? If the objects are different, why do they have the same name?

3. The apples in the pie at the left (No. 1) were first quality Jonathans grown in New York State. The flour was milled in Minneapolis from wheat grown in Kansas. The butter came from a Wisconsin dairy famous for its dairy herd. The pie was baked by the chef of the Waldorf Astoria from his own private recipe.

I made the other pie (No. 2). I got the apples off our driveway where they had fallen from the old apple tree that I had been meaning for years to cut down. I cut out all the worms and most of the bruised spots and I rejected any apples that had been run over by the car. I got the flour from an open package at the back of the top shelf of the kitchen cabinet.

I don't know how long it had been there, but it had no weevils in it, at least none that I could see. We were out of butter, so I used the contents of the can into which my wife drains the used cooking grease. I was very careful in preparing the crust, because I had never baked a pie before, but the recipe was so smudged that I had to guess at some of the measurements and ingredients. To make sure it was well cooked, I baked it in a hot oven for two hours. The crust got a little scorched but, except for that, it looked pretty good to me.

4. If you were hungry and were offered one of these objects, which would you choose, and why?

5. What does the name "apple pie" tell you about these objects? What does it not tell you? What do the numbers above the objects tell you about them?

6. What do we mean by the statement, "Apple pie_1 is not apple pie_2"?

7. If apple pie_1 is not apple pie_2, do you think a similar distinction can be made between seventh-$grader_1$ and seventh-$grader_2$? $Teacher_1$ and $teacher_2$? $Democrat_1$ and $Democrat_2$? X_1 and X_2, where X is any noun?

8. Using the example in 3 as a model, write a two-paragraph composition to illustrate *one* of the following statements: Woman $driver_1$ is not woman $driver_2$; $Redhead_1$ is not $redhead_2$; X_1 is not X_2, where X can be any class name you choose.

The lesson that class names, or common nouns, do not point to things but to characteristics that classes of things have in common is basic to specification. All description depends on it. The describer must use words that point through the class to the individual member with which he is concerned. This leads to what Matthew Arnold called writing with one's eye on the object, and one of the things that an emphasis on specification leads to is a concern with what the object actually looks like. It is not an exaggeration to say that at this stage in the teaching of composition we teach students to write by teaching them to see what they are writing about. Some of you, no doubt, remember the accounts of how Agassiz taught his students to understand the anatomical structure of fish by forcing them to look and look and look again at the structure of particular specimens. We composition teachers would be wise to follow his example, and to drill into our students that observation is a prerequisite for thinking, and thinking a prerequisite for writing. The structure of the writing must reflect in all significant details the structure of the subject as the writer perceives it. At least in the best of all possible worlds, rhetoric recapitulates experience.

This emphasis on the structure of the subject can be extended to the structure of a piece of writing. American children are supposed to have a genius for taking things apart to see how they work. They should be invited to take rhetorical structures apart and to see the interrelation of the parts. The following lessons invite them to take paragraphs apart to see how the general idea of the topic sentence is specified through examples.

PARAGRAPH STRUCTURE

Study each of the following paragraphs and answer the questions that follow it.

(1)

(1) The greater the speed, the less control the driver has over the car. (2) For example, a man driving at 30 miles an hour needs only 73 feet to bring the car to a complete stop, but a man driving at 60 miles an hour needs 222 feet.

a. Which sentence expresses the main idea of the paragraph? Call that the *topic sentence.*
b. What is the relation of sentence 2 to sentence 1? Which sentence is lower on the abstraction ladder?
c. In the light of these answers, describe the structure of the paragraph.

(2)

(1) Beauty is a quality what tends to endure. (2) In a house that I know, I have noticed a block of spermaceti lying about closets and mantelpieces for twenty years, simply because the tallowman gave it the form of a rabbit; and I suppose it may continue to be lugged about unchanged for a century. (3) Let an artist scrawl a few lines or figures on the back of a letter, and that scrap of paper is rescued from danger, is put in a portfolio, is framed and glazed, and, in proportion to the beauty of the lines drawn, will be kept for centuries. (4) Burns writes a copy of verses and sends them to a newspaper, and the human race takes charge of them that they shall not perish.

a. What is the topic sentence of the paragraph?
b. What is the relation of sentence 2 to sentence 1? Is sentence 2 higher or lower on the abstraction ladder?
c. What is the relation of sentence 3 to sentence 1? Which sentence is lower on the abstraction ladder?
d. What is the relation of sentence 4 to sentence 1? Which sentence is lower on the abstraction ladder
e. In the light of these answers describe the structure of the paragraph.
f. Now suppose we added a final sentence to the paragraph:

(5) People treasure beautiful things and usually try to preserve them.

What is the relation of this sentence to sentence 1? Describe the structure of the expanded paragraph.

g. To save time and space we can use symbols to represent the parts of the structure of these paragraphs. We can use TS for "topic sentence," E for "example," and R for "restatement of the topic sentence." With these symbols we can describe the structure of the paragraphs as follows:

Paragraph 1: $TS + E$

Paragraph 2 (original): $TS + E_1 + E_2 + E_3$

Paragraph 2 (expanded): $TS + E_1 + E_2 + E_3 + R$

Once students have a good grasp of the structure of this kind of paragraph, they can extend it to multi-paragraph essays by using two or more sustained examples and allowing a paragraph for each example. The structure is generative in the sense that, once a student learns it, he can generate more examples for himself. Think what any normal 12-year-old could do by applying this structure to the theme, "Why don't grown-ups practice what they preach?"

I have spent so much time on specification because I think it is a prerequisite for almost everything else that the student will do in composition. If we divide composition into two major concerns—organization and development—we are here dealing chiefly with the problem of development. The student will always be dealing with that problem. But if, during the seventh and eighth grades, he acquires the habit of spelling out, through specific reference and illustration, the implications of general statements, he will have already reached a level of rhetorical maturity that many college freshmen never achieve. Yet that level is not beyond his capacity. It is not difficult to have him give an example of what he means or to have him point to specific things and events. He does this all the time with his peer group. The difficult thing is to persuade him that the standards of communication inside the classroom are not fundamentally different from those outside of it.

Before I move on to the next stage, I should like to add that this approach to specific communication has useful by-products. As we deal with the relation of topic sentence and paragraph development, of theme and examples, we are already beginning to lay a foundation of purpose and unity in a piece of writing. We are also, through our concern with these relations, creating an awareness of rhetorical structure.

Comparison and Contrast. In specifying we are concerned chiefly with reporting, with using words to point to things, and with explaining general statements by means of examples and illustrative details. In the next stage, comparison and contrast, we are getting into judgment. We are interpreting experience by selecting material and organizing it into some shape imposed by our interest in it, or by our purpose. Students who have already had some work in semantics will recognize this activity as part of the process of classifying. Indeed, observation, comparison, and classification are successive stages in a continuum. Each new stage subsumes the one preceding it, but in simple classifications the stages are so closely related that they seem to occur simultaneously. Since what experiences are selected in a comparison depends on the purpose for making the selection, work on comparison-contrast provides a natural introduction to the concept of purpose.

Exercises in comparison may be made as simple or as complex as the teacher thinks appropriate to the student's ability and previous experience. These exercises may be used for a wide variety of purposes—to compare two characters, actions, or themes in a novel or play; to explain different points of view, customs, or values; to explore alternative solutions to a problem or to weigh the advantages and disadvantages of a proposal. Since comparison-contrast is a common starting point for inference making, exercises in comparison lend themselves conveniently to inductive teaching in many subjects.

In developing a contrast of two subjects, A and B, we have a choice of two basic patterns, which I shall call $A + B$ and $A/B + A/B$. In the $A + B$ pattern we say all that we wish about A before saying anything about B, so that the paragraph or essay is structured as two balanced halves. In the $A/B + A/B$ pattern the contrast is established cumulatively, sentence by sentence, and the balance lies within the sentence. As the Kennedy inaugural address illustrates, the second pattern is chiefly a ceremonial form today. For most purposes, and certainly in junior high school classes, the $A + B$ structure is the more useful.

The following lesson requires students to analyze the structure of a paragraph which develops a contrast by first stating it generally in the first four sentences, then developing A and B in turn by illustrative details, and finally restating the theme in a concluding sentence. If this paragraph were expanded into a multi-paragraph essay, as it might be, its structure would be expanded but not changed. The first paragraph would be an introductory statement announcing the theme of the essay and explaining the contrast at a general and introductory level. The second paragraph would apply the theme to the ant society, the third to the goose society. The fourth paragraph would be a concluding restatement of the theme. In other words, the structure shows the same logical relation among the parts whether the comment is presented in one paragraph or several.

> When a comparison or contrast follows an $A + B$ structure, the essay or paragraph naturally tends to break into two parts. From your earlier work on paragraph structure, do you remember a structure in which the topic sentence was followed by two or more subtopic statements? Study the structure of the following contrast and answer the questions that follow.

(1) The Wart's adventures as an ant and a goose were contrasted lessons in government. (2) Both adventures were designed by Merlin to prepare the Wart for kingship. (3) Each illustrated a society in operation and the values held by that society. (4) The Wart was expected to learn a lesson from the contrast. (5) As an ant he saw the tyranny of a dictatorship which reduced individuals to automatons. (6) The ants had no freedom. (7) They were brainwashed by propaganda both in peace and in war. (8) They could make no personal choices. (9) All that was not forbidden to them by the state was compulsory. (10) Their lives were governed by "Done" and "Not done," and what was done or not was decided by their leader. (11) By contrast, as a goose, the Wart saw how individuals lived in a free society. (12) The geese chose their leaders freely for their skill in guiding the migrations. (13) They followed these leaders willingly but were not subject to them. (14) They accepted the mutual responsibility of taking turns as guards to warn of the approach of danger; but the thought of war with their own kind was so abhorrent to them that Lyo could not accept the Wart's question about war as serious. (15) When she realized that he was serious she was so shocked that she would not speak to him. (16) In the contrasted lessons of the ants and the geese Merlin showed the Wart society at its worst and best.

a. Which is the topic sentence of the paragraph? Mark it TS. Which two sentences serve as subtopic statements to introduce the ant and the goose adventures? Mark them st-1 and st-2 respectively. These divisions mark out the general outline of the paragraph. Is that structure $A/B + A/B$ or $A + B$?
b. What is the function of sentences 2, 3, and 4? Do you remember what we called sentences like these? What is the function of sentences 6, 7, 8, 9, and 10? Of sentences 12, 13, 14, and 15? Of sentence 16?
c. If this paragraph were to be divided into two, where would the division occur?
d. If the paragraph were to be expanded into a four-paragraph essay, what would be the content of each paragraph?

I suggested earlier that comparison-contrast tends to include specification. The comparison establishes the main structural divisions—in this example, the topic sentence and the subtopic statements. But within these divisions the development is by specification. This specification is just as essential here as in our earlier examples. Without the illustrative details provided by sentences 6, 7, 8, 9, 10 and 12, 13, 14, 15, the contrast required by the purpose does not get adequately established. It is not surprising, therefore, that nine of the 16 sentences in this paragraph develop the theme by specification.

From comparisons of the kind we have been considering, it is a short step into analogy and metaphor, the structures of which can usually be described as a proportion: *a* is to *b* as *c* is to *d* in some identifiable sense. Thus Keats's first reading of Chapman's Homer was like an astronomer's first sight of a new planet in the sense of the thrill of discovery. The following assignment provides at least a rudimentary model from which a student may generate his own analogy.

> Using the following short analogy as a model, develop an analogy for the following topic sentence: The relationship between a _____ and a _____ may be illustrated by an analogy with _____. Fill in the blanks with the terms of your choice.
>
> The relationship between a writer and a reader may be illustrated by an analogy with dancing. Anybody who has danced knows that both partners move in accordance with patterns which both understand and take for granted. The man, by his leading, indicates which pattern he wishes to set; the girl follows. If the man leads his partner to expect one kind of movement and then switches to another, the girl will have difficulty following.
>
> The relationship between a writer and a reader is similar. Each assumes that the other is familiar with the basic patterns of sentence structure. The reader, like the girl in the dance, must follow the writer's lead, and as long as the writer keeps to an accepted pattern the reader has no trouble. But if the writer sets one pattern in the first half of a sentence and then shifts to another, the reader is likely to be confused.

Every student can do something with a model like this, and some students will do surprisingly imaginative work. I had an eighth-grade student who filled in the blanks in this model to make the statement that the relationship between a teacher and a student may be illustrated by an analogy with photosynthesis. Then she went on to develop the figure that the teacher, like the sun, provided the light, and the student, like the plant, absorbed it and converted it into nourishment. But, she continued, photosynthesis is a function of the plant, not of the sun, and it occurs only when the plant is actively converting sunlight into food. When it stops converting, no chemical reaction takes place. The sunlight still falls on the plant, but nothing happens.

It is not difficult to give students—even quite young students—a sense of the structure of comparison, but, of course, the quality of what is said in that structure will depend on the talent that the student brings to the comparison. The perception of the similarities and differences between things is an intellectual activity, and the greater a student's mental powers are, the more sensitive, imaginative, and significant his comparisons will be. Nevertheless, I think that experience with the structure of comparison, especially if it is carried on through analogy and metaphor, will help students to think more efficiently. Professor Upton of Whittier College is said to have raised the IQ of a group of college freshmen by ten points by exercises in critical comparisons and analyses. Certainly if the new rhetoric is going to be worth cultivating, it must go beyond clarity and grace of expression and provide a procedure for helping students to improve the substance as well as the style of their comments.

Classification. The next stage after comparison is classification. As I suggested earlier, this is an extension of comparison. To be able to classify things, a student must first observe that they have something in common. But classification goes beyond this recognition and, by organizing and shaping perceptions, it creates new knowledge.

Classification may be approached inductively and deductively. Inductive classification is the heart of the discovery method. It is the means by which we organize and record experience. It is primarily a form of self-communication. Deductive classification is a method of communicating with others. When we have interpreted experience inductively, we explain the results to others deductively. The following assignment will illustrate both processes.

The following words illustrate the chief types of semantic change (changes in meaning) in English. For each word, the first meaning given in parentheses is the old or original meaning; the second meaning is the modern one. Look over the words, then follow the directions given below them.

1. *acorn* (various kinds of nuts—the seed or nut of oak trees)
2. *bonfire* (a fire for burning bones or corpses—any large outdoor fire)
3. *boor* (a farmer—an ill-mannered person)
4. *boycott* (an Irish captain who was ostracized by his neighbors—refusal to associate with any person or group)
5. *cad* (a younger son of an aristocratic family—an ill-mannered fellow)
6. *cattle* (property or wealth—cows, bulls, and steers)
7. *champagne* (wine from a French district—any wine resembling French champagne)
8. *corn* (a hard particle—the seed of a particular cereal crop)
9. *cunning* (knowing or skillful—tricky or meanly clever)
10. *dean* (an officer in charge of ten people—a major college administrator)
11. *deer* (any small animal—a particular animal with antlers)

12. *discard* (reject a card—throw something away)
13. *ferry* (travel—travel by boat)
14. *gossip* (a godparent—a spreader of rumors)
15. *hussy* (a housewife—a woman of low morals)
16. *knave* (a boy—a villainous man)
17. *knight* (a young male servant—a titled person)
18. *lady* (a breadmaker—a woman of quality)
19. *martinet* (a French general who was a stickler for discipline—any rigid disciplinarian)
20. *minister* (a servant—a clergyman or statesman)
21. *pedagogue* (a slave—an educator)
22. *shibboleth* (a password used in the Bible—any word or phrase that identifies a particular group)
23. *shirt* (a loose outer garment worn by either sex—a garment worn by a man)
24. *skirt* (a loose outer garment worn by either sex—a garment worn by a woman)

1. Examine the words to see if you can detect any patterns of change. That is, do you find certain words showing the same kind of change— for instance, *bonfire—boycott—discard* show one kind of change, and *boor—cad* another.

2. Group all the words that illustrate one type of change in a list and over the list write a heading which describes that change. This procedure will give you Class I and the name or description of that class. Repeat the procedure until you have established the four major classes of semantic change.

3. Convert your findings into an outline of the following form:

Title: _____
    I. _____
   II. _____
  III. _____
  IV. _____

4. Fit the following words into the classes which you have already established:

brat—child; *butcher*—a killer of goats; *campus*—a field; *citizen*—a city dweller; *clerk*—a cleric or clergyman; *count*—a companion; *cupboard*—a shelf for holding cups; *daft*—neat; *dismantle*—take off a cape; *eaves*—edges of any kind; *ferry*—to travel in any way; *fowl*—any bird; *frock*—a loose garment worn by a monk; *front*— forehead; *idiot*—a private person as contrasted with a public official; *liquor*—a liquid or fluid of any sort; *nice*—foolish; *a prude*— a modest person; *sergeant*—a servant; *silly*—happy or blessed; *starve*—to die in any manner; *steward*—the keeper of a pig sty.

5. For each of the four Roman numerals in the outline, write a paragraph consisting of a topic sentence developed by all the examples that are pertinent in that paragraph.

6. Now write an introductory paragraph which converts the title into a sentence which states the general conclusion of the study and explains that statement by one or more clarifying statements.

7. Finally write a concluding paragraph that sums up the content of the essay.

There are four things I'd like to point out about this assignment. First, difficult as the task may seem, it is really only a more challenging application of techniques which the student has already learned—the techniques of comparison and specification. Through comparison the student selects and organizes his material; through specification he illustrates the conclusions he has reached. What I am saying now is merely a restatement of what I said earlier. From specification to comparison to classification there is a straight line of sequence, and each segment of the line recapitulates the one before it.

Second, whether the assignment is difficult or easy depends more on the teaching procedure than on the subject matter. If students are required to work independently on this assignment, many of them will have difficulty and some of them will be frustrated. But if they are allowed to work as a group, sharing each other's insights and doubts, they will tend as a group to profit from individual contributions and to correct false leads. Indeed, it is at least theoretically possible that a brilliant student could lead the class to a quick break-through. He might see that *bonfire, boycott,* and *discard* were alike in that their meanings had become extended from narrow to wide. He might see that *boor* and *cad* had changed in the direction of taking on unpleasant meanings. He might then reason that for every class there is likely to be an opposite class, and so he might set up the hypothesis that the four changes were from narrow to wide, from wide to narrow, from good to bad, and from bad to good. If he tested that hypothesis, he would find that it worked, and he would have solved the problem without plodding through every word. I must admit that I have not actually had such a student, but I have had groups of students who, working together, achieved similar results.

Third, the teacher's contributions to the discovery is the structuring of the assignment. Once he has organized the specific steps in the total process, he withdraws from the solution, or at most limits himself to asking questions designed to challenge and invite reconsideration of a wrong turn in the thinking. If he obtrudes into the solution he will deprive the class of the thrill of discovery. He will then be like some critic telling Keats how wonderful Chapman's translation of Homer is. I doubt that any sonnet would ever have been written.

Finally, the method of doing this assignment can be generalized into a strategy for attacking other problems. The student has learned more than the common patterns of semantic change. He has learned an operational procedure which he can use in situations in which it is applicable, and these situations exist in all subject areas. As a result, the student is likely to have increased confidence in his ability to solve other such problems, perhaps even increased confidence in English as a subject.

One more point before I finish. I am not proposing this sequence as a universal composition curriculum for junior high schools. I am too clearly aware of individual differences among students and teachers alike to suggest that one sequence will satisfy everyone. I think it is important that there be a sequence in the composition work in successive grades, and I think that sequence should have some kind of explicit rationale—that is, it should be a true sequence, not just a succession of unrelated units. But I have no conviction that all students should follow the same sequence or that they should follow any sequence at the same rate. I am not, therefore, giving you a ready-made composition curriculum to apply in your own classes, but rather working out the implications of a point of view. There are other points of view, and many of them yield useful sequences. What is important, I think, is for the teacher to commit himself to some sequence, not necessarily to this one.

ALAN D. ENGELSMAN / *A Writing Program That Teaches Writing*

Too frequently, composition programs make writing a mere adjunct to reading and fail to develop specific writing skills in a planned sequential fashion. Consider the following examples:

> Choose one character from *All the King's Men,* and in a well-organized essay show how his view of the nature of good and evil changed during the course of the novel.

> Considering our class discussion on Hemingway's style, read the short story "Soldier's Home." Then write a well-documented essay in which you assert that the style in "Soldier's Home" is either typical or atypical.

These assignments are good in that they reinforce *reading* skills; they ask the student to reveal what he has learned about characterization and style. However, they don't adequately stress specific *writing* skills. It is true that the first assignment calls for a "well-organized" essay and the other a "well-documented" one, but neither provides any guidelines about *how* to organize or what kind of evidence constitutes good documentation.

Teachers should not ignore literature as subject matter, but they must bear in mind that the primary objective of a composition program should be to teach writing and their assignments should reflect this objective. The two assignments above would be much more effective if they provided some guidelines to the writer, and they would be most effective if they were a part of a series of assignments all dealing with a single skill.

From *English Journal,* LVI (March, 1967), 417–21, 442. Reprinted by permission of the National Council of Teachers of English and Alan D. Engelsman.

Perhaps some exercises and assignments which have proven successful in my eleventh-grade classes will illustrate what I mean by a sequential program. Coming after several assignments which have emphasized using concrete evidence, these stress the skill of organizing evidence within a theme. Before introducing them, I spend a period discussing classification. I call for a random naming of objects or things: elephant, garbage can, duck, pencil, rose, shoe, and so on. When we have a fairly long list on the board, I ask the students to classify the items into homogeneous groups: animal, vegetable, mineral; animate, inanimate; large, small. Then, choosing one of these classes, say animals, we extend that list and explore the possible patterns for organizing it: size, biological complexity, habitat, number of feet, and others. This leads to some generalizations about patterns of organization: the most frequently used ones and the relationship of pattern to purpose. Then the students are ready for the next assignment which happens to be the fifth in the year's sequence.

Assignment No. 5 asks students to assume the role of an expert and choose a topic which they think they may know a little more about than most of their friends; then it says

> . . . for the benefit of the layman write a paper in which you give or explain eight examples (types) of . . . ., or eight ways to . . . ., or eight reasons for . . . .

The blank is to be filled in by the student with his topic. After some sample topics are suggested, the assignment concludes:

> This assignment is specifically designed to emphasize the process of organization and the necessary use of transitions. The eight elements of your topic must be placed in some logical order, and this must be made apparent in the transitions from one element to the next. Your paper will probably consist of an opening paragraph; eight paragraphs of development, each introduced by or containing a transitional word, phrase, or thought; and a concluding paragraph.

This final paragraph makes the assignment a *writing* assignment and focuses the student's attention on a single skill. Furthermore, it clearly implies that in this particular case the subject matter is not as important as the way it is presented. The student then is given a plan sheet as an additional guide. He must fill it out and submit it one week before the paper is due.

PLAN SHEET

I. Briefly state your topic.

_____
_____
_____
_____

II. List the key word(s) or sentence(s) showing the eight parts of your topic in the order you will discuss them.

1. _____
   _____
2. _____
   _____
3. _____
   _____
4. _____
   _____
5. _____
   _____
6. _____
7. _____
   _____
8. _____
   _____

III. Briefly explain the reason for this order.

_____
_____
_____
_____

Example:

There are eight methods of cheating that some students practice in high school.

1. checking homework answers with a friend
2. copying someone else's homework
3. changing answers on a quiz which the student corrects himself
4. checking with someone who had a test the period before
5. copying from someone's paper during a test
6. feigning illness on the day of a test
7. taking notes into an exam
8. adding a paragraph after a test is returned and demanding a reevaluation

These are arranged in order of importance from least serious to most.

The plan sheet goes on to explain to the student how he may organize his paper using two guiding principles yet keeping one dominant.

When the instructor returns the plan sheet to the students with precautionary comments, he amends the assignment to call for "Five or six ways to ...." This allows the students to combine some of their items which overlap or to eliminate their weakest points entirely. The resulting essays are usually interesting and orderly. They are also varied enough in subject matter so that the students enjoy discussing several sample essays in class. The discussions focus on the appropriateness of the pattern of organization to the purpose of the paper.

After examining the samples and receiving their own papers back, the students are ready for the next assignment which both limits the subject to literature and emphasizes the need for a relationship between the organizing principle and the purpose.

Writing Assignment No. 6
WHAT RELATIONSHIPS WITH OTHER CHARACTERS REVEAL

In the last assignment you applied what you have learned about organization to a subject that you were familiar with. Had someone else explained that same topic to you in a haphazard manner, you probably would have been able to reorganize mentally what he said as you read or listened to his explanation; lack of order poses few problems when you are dealing with familiar subjects.

However, a writer should assume he is presenting new ideas or unfamiliar material which the reader does not already understand. He must, therefore, organize it clearly. Moreover, when a writer is approaching material which he himself is unfamiliar with, it becomes imperative that he discover a pattern or order before he writes. In other words, finding and using a meaningful order is an important step in clear thinking as well as in clear communication. Organization also serves an additional purpose in building to a conclusion.

This assignment asks you to discover and use an appropriate principle of organization in an essay about a central character in one of the novels or plays we have read this semester. By examining his (or her) relationship with three other characters, come to some significant conclusion about his situation or his problems.

Two hints about procedure:

1. The order in which you discuss the three other characters and their relationship with the central character will depend on your conclusion. For example, if you want to show that Holden Caulfield's failure to communicate with others was primarily the fault of the people he spoke to, you might order your paper in this way:

a. Spencer:	was too righteous	order:
b. Ackley:	was too defensive	seriousness of the
c. Sally Hayes:	was too self-centered	other's failures

If, however, you want to demonstrate that the fault was Holden's because he was too demanding or too critical, you might choose the following order:

a. Sally:	Holden expected too much from her.	order: seriousness of
b. Ackley:	He was too critical of him.	Holden's failure
c. Spencer:	He allowed petty flaws to overshadow this man's genuine interest.	

2. The three subordinate characters you choose should be comparable in some way. The three in the examples above, for instance, though disparate in their backgrounds, are united by the fact that Holden tries to communicate with each. It would also be possible to choose three whose backgrounds are similar but whom the central character regards differently, such as Ackley, Stradlater, and James Castle, all prep school acquaintances of Holden.

Although this assignment is more complex, I do not require the student to submit a plan sheet. However, he is encouraged to make one for his own use.

After the class has completed Assignment No. 6, it seems advisable to interject an in-class exercise, because Assignment No. 7 calls for an even more sophisticated understanding of organization and transitions. The exercise presents a statement about authors using insects as a device for commenting on the foibles of mankind. Then, in part, it continues:

In writing a composition with the above statement as your thesis and the following works as examples:

"A Considerable Speck" by Robert Frost,
"The Ephemera" by Benjamin Franklin,
"The Battle of the Ants" by Henry David Thoreau

suggest two different orders you might present the examples in.

A. 1. _____   The organizing principle
   2. _____   for this arrangement is
   3. _____   _____

B. 1. _____   The organizing principle
   2. _____   for this arrangement is
   3. _____   _____

The exercise concludes by asking the student to choose one of the two orders and write an introductory paragraph and three transitional sentences for each succeeding paragraph. The filling in of the blanks can be completed rather quickly, and students can then discuss the various patterns of organization they chose: chronological, relative seriousness of author, relative seriousness of foible, and others. Later, by exchanging papers they can also comment on the effectiveness of each other's transitions. Then, perhaps, they are ready for the last assignment in the sequence.

Assignment No. 7 asks students to write an essay examining a theme which appears in three different works of literature. I read and discuss a model essay in class (Bruce Catton's "The Feel of the Lash," February 1963 issue of *American Heritage*), and the assignment itself again provides further guidelines for writing this particular kind of essay.

The entire sequence speaks for itself. Each assignment presents a slightly more difficult task for the writer, yet each builds on skills learned in the previous assignment. Most important, the student is made acutely aware that, though he may have a chance to reveal his skill as a reader, the assignment is primarily designed for him to learn and practice a skill relating to *writing*.

I should like to make it clear that with these examples I am illustrating a philosophy and an approach and *not* proposing a specific curriculum or sequence of assignments. Those who see virtue in this approach will be happiest if they construct their own program. This can be done by individual teachers or, even better, by an entire English department. For the teacher who wishes to begin such a program, the following suggestions may be helpful.

First, he must decide what skills need emphasis in his school and at his grade. It is in this area that a pooling of colleagues' opinions is most helpful. Ideally, a year's sequence should focus on no more than three or four basic writing skills, each to be emphasized in three or four themes. By suggesting this, I do not mean to preclude the teaching of corollary skills, but I am suggesting that if a student can learn four skills *well,* he will have made significant progress in writing during the year. Once he has selected the skills he wants to stress, the teacher must further decide which one deserves the greatest emphasis and which ones should be taught first. All this should be done before he begins to compose the individual assignments.

When writing the assignments, the teacher should bear in mind that, though work in composition should be related to work in literature, it should not be subordinated to the literature. In fact, when introducing new skills, sometimes it is better to let the students have a free choice of subject (as in Assignment No. 5 above) and then to limit them to literature in the subsequent assignments which reinforce the same skill. On the other hand, the reading program should not become a slave to the writing program; a composition assignment which is written months in advance as part of a sequence can usually be worded so that, if a teacher desires, he can fit it to a specific work (or works) at the time he makes the assignment.

Next, the assignment should be worded so that the student clearly understands what skill is being stressed. The samples illustrate how this can be done. Moreover, in most instances the teacher should precede and/or follow the assignment with a lesson or an exercise involving that skill. Finally, the assignment should specifically refer to skills introduced in previous assignments so as to encourage the student to continue using devices and techniques that he has practiced earlier in the sequence.

Building a successful program of sequential writing assignments will take time. The teacher starting from scratch may only be able to develop one well-planned sequence of three assignments during the first year. But by revising these and adding new sequences in the following years, he will eventually have a writing program that is substantial, meaningful, and effective.

KEN MACRORIE / *To Be Read*

We ask students never to judge ideas or events out of context, but fail to see our composition classes in any larger world. That is why they are such astonishing failures. For decades we have been smearing bloody marks (*sp, awk, gr*) in the margins of what we call "themes." These papers are not meant to be *read,* but *corrected.*

Now we are living in a great series of revolutions, testing whether the present forms of school, church, state, family, and relationships between blacks and whites will endure. Already high school students are following the lead of college students—publishing underground newspapers, asking for a voice in making the rules of their schools. Tomorrow they will be suggesting or forcing changes in the classroom—in what they are asked to read, to write, and in how their work is to be evaluated.

A textbook named *Correct Writing, Forms A, B, C, and D* is likely to receive only a hoot of derision from students who are communicating with each other and with administrators and teachers in dozens of new ways. As the television generation, they are not any longer going to suffer learning in grade school that the White House is where the President lives, in junior high what the President's name is, and in senior high that the house is located on Pennsylvania Avenue. Many of them have been there, and to the Pentagon as well.

These are perilous moments for American establishments. They will be destroyed or they will reform. We have a small chance to keep our students

From *English Journal,* LVII (May, 1968), 686–92. Reprinted by permission of the National Council of Teachers of English and Ken Macrorie.

from turning our schools into the shambles remaining after revolutions in Watts, Newark, and Detroit. But it is a chance.

Four years ago I stumbled into a way to induce students to write so they excited each other and me. Now that I have worked out a program and seen it elicit lively and valuable writing from all levels of students (from seventh grade through graduate school) and all ranges of students (from "remedial" to "honors"), I know trying to reform writing in the schools and colleges makes sense.

Here is the program:

1. Ask students to place themselves outside of class anywhere they can be alone and quiet. Then write for ten minutes as fast as they can, putting down whatever comes to mind. If they can't think of a word, they should start by reporting what they see in front of them. Let the mind and pencil go until they fill a large-sized notebook page. Twice, so they have two papers to bring to the next class.

2. Ask for honesty. Say you know school doesn't often nurture it, that at times you will be dishonest, as everyone is without realizing—but you will try to speak truth. Pass out an example of phony writing—pretentious, empty:

> But the area which caused Henry and I to become steadfast friends was outdoor sports.

Also pass out an example of honest writing, like this:

> He doesn't have legs. Not ones that feel or move. It's been that way almost four years now. Wheels. I was scared to talk at first, felt like a kid asking what it is that everyone's talking about. But we did. We used to goof around and tell dirty jokes. I always felt a little fake. Dan and I took him to the bathroom every day. Had to be done in a special way. We were there once, Dan asked a question—I don't remember what it was—something involving my ability to work.
>
> "What do you think I am, a cripple?" That's what I said. I didn't look at anyone, just the wall. For about half an hour. I felt very whole, but my stomach was tin foil. They were quiet, both of them. Quiet as being alone. I wished someone would cut off my arms.

3. Ask students to keep all papers in a folder. At the end of the semester you will choose the six to ten best papers and give a course grade on them. If the student needs a grade earlier—to convince his father he should buy him a car or so he can apply for college—you will grade his folder as of the moment. His classmates and you will be constantly commenting on his

papers in this seminar-style class, and some papers will be reproduced as examples of fine writing; so he will know how he is doing.

If students' free writings turn out too personal or confessional, they should try others. Ask them not to submit writing that embarrasses them because of its intimacy. If they write close to their heart, they may ask you to withhold their names when their papers are presented to the class.

4. Ask students to bring two free writings to the second meeting and to exchange papers with another student. They should underline (or indicate in the margin) any phrases or sentences they like for content or expression, or both.

5. Discuss the marked passages with students. Ask students to comment on some before you praise them. Look for truth and liveliness. Take papers home, mark passages or phrases you like. Ditto these excerpts. Write nothing on the papers.

6. At the third meeting continue discussion of good passages. Tell students that for the first month or so they should make only positive comments on each other's writing. If the class numbers no more than twenty, begin the first few meetings with the group seated in a circle, or around a giant table made from a number of tables. If the class is more than twenty, for part of the period separate students into smaller groups. Seven is good because it puts pressure on writers so they cannot dismiss criticism—good or bad—as merely a gesture from friend or enemy. Do not visit the groups. In the first month ask no student to read his paper aloud to others unless you think it a smashing success. Otherwise, you read it to the class or ask students to exchange papers several times so they may be read aloud without the class knowing who wrote them.

7. Ask students to write two fifteen-minute free papers trying to focus on one subject, not letting the mind skip as freely as in the first writing. If they get off the subject and are going marvelously, they should continue on the detour.

8. As you and the students discuss the writing, allow them to react even when they can't say what they like about the writing. Twelve heads nodding up and down in appreciation will charge any writer's batteries. Begin now occasionally to point out why a writing is good: strong metaphor, rhythmic sentences, tension between two ideas or facts, fresh expression instead of clichés, insight, memorable sensuous details. Don't feel obliged to offer all the papers to class criticism, even if you have a two-hour period in which to work.

9. Show students how to tighten writing. Ask them to choose their best free writing and cut all wasted words—outside of class. Urge what pro-

fessional editors suggest (not necessarily what English textbooks emphasize): for example, eliminating unnecessary uses of *which, that,* and *who.* Show students where they have repeated words powerfully.

10. Ask students to write a forty-five minute free paper focusing on one subject.

11. Encourage and encourage, but never falsely. When you get a fine piece of writing with a weak beginning and ending that need chopping, type it on a ditto master in the most powerfully cut version you can arrange without changing any words, and then—if the author approves—post it on the bulletin board in the hall. Correct all spelling errors and mechanical weaknesses before publishing it in any way. Publishers never knowingly embarrass their writers.

Try to place several writings in the student newspaper or magazine early in the semester. Don't expect students to take that initiative. For years they have been indoctrinated to believe they can't write. Their papers have been massacred—all that blood in the margins.

12. Ask students to write an informal case history of a day or hour (or several days, hours, or weeks condensed into one) on a job, or in a process or activity they've gone through many times. Or to tell what happens during a half-hour in the school library at a certain spot. They should put the reader there, not try for clinical detachment unless they need it. If they wish, they can write freely several times about the experience and then try to find a center (some tension, meaning, or lack of meaning) in the activity that helps tell them which details to discard and which they need more of. This paper may run two pages or ten.

13. Read aloud a few of these case histories the day they are due. Ask students to point out anything they like. Take them home, read them, try not to comment unless you have a major suggestion. Do not correct. Do not mark mistakes. Ditto two to four (one or three if your class lasts only fifty minutes) that you think compelling.

Occasionally during the semester you will find a paper that becomes excellent when cut massively. Ditto the cut version, then append the cut paragraphs or sentences. Remind students that this surgery is only one possibility and that the author has the *authority* to restore any of the material cut. After class discussion of case histories, ask all students to take their papers home and do their own revising and adding to. Let them know reworking of papers is expected in all major assignments, except when a paper seems strong all the way through upon first writing. Tell students that the wastebaskets of professional writers are full of discarded pages.

14. Ask student to record short fabulous realities in a notebook or journal. Examples:

> a. Boy and girl talking, he standing in gutter, she on curb, for better eye-to-eye contact.
> b. Sign downtown: "Four Barbers, No Waiting," and then below: "Television While You Wait."

Written skillfully these fabulous realities embody six essentials of most good writing: The writer (1) makes an event happen before the reader, (2) locates it significantly, (3) presents materials that create a tension or point, (4) uses only details that bear upon that tension or point, (5) does not waste words, and (6) saves the punch till the end, where it gains from suspense. The first fabulous reality above could be improved by reordering:

> Boy and girl talking—for better eye-to-eye contact she stands on the curb, he in the gutter.

The surprise is now at the end.

15. Ask students to think of expanding one fabulous reality into a little story. If they have nothing expandable, they needn't try. Conduct this class for writers, not hothouse scholars. When writers have worked hard and nothing goes right, they give up a project and start another. Good writing usually is produced half by civil engineering and half by hidden springs that suddenly start flowing.

16. Ask students to write a longer paper remembering some childhood incident that shook them up. They should put the reader there, not generalize about feelings. Start with "One day—" and recreate that young world.

In this, and in all of their writing, do not allow clichés. If students can't think of another way of saying "It rained cats and dogs"—one that hits precisely the mood and intensity they want—let them say, "It rained hard." In casual conversation clichés are to be expected and endured; in writing—inexcusable. A writer asks his reader to look at his sentences. His first duty is not to bore him.

17. When childhood papers come in, introduce the elementary kinds of organization—Before-After, The Journey (we did this or went here and then did that and went there—whether this is a movement in ideas or action), and The Hook (at the end tying back to the beginning, perhaps with irony). Suggest that students may want to use one of these patterns in reshaping their childhood papers. (Call writing "writing" or "papers," never "themes." Whoever would voluntarily read something called a "theme"?) From now on in seminar sessions point out weaknesses in students' writings as well as strengths, but in front of the class don't be hard upon the paper of a student not yet praised by the group.

18. Ask students to keep a journal for three weeks or more, making entries only when they see or think of something striking. Present excerpts from strong journals, like Thoreau's, to show range and diversity of entries.

Ask students to try several short free writings in their journals, and not to worry if they don't hit a subject that goes beautifully. A journal is a place for many failures and a few successes. Ask that entries be communications to others, not Dear Diary private statements. In five or ten years the student looking at this journal should be able to put himself back in his experience. He can't do that with comments like these: "What a terrible week it has been. Tommy just isn't the sort of guy I thought he was going to be. I'm really miserable." He can with an entry like this:

> We went for a ride in the fog last night, out on Ravine Road. There are no lights and no houses. So in the fog we were isolated. All that existed in the universe was about ten yards of yellow ribbon and my eyes, and that curving conveyor belt which I had to steer my eyes along—very much like my life at times.

19. Ask students to try word play in journals. Read Lewis Carroll's *Through the Looking Glass,* the text for word play. Make words speak to each other, as Shakespeare or a good newspaper headline writer does. Puns, rhymes. Revive dead metaphors. Record good word play heard in TV commercials or seen in advertisements, or around school. Examples:

 a. Love Is a Many Splintered Thing. [student word play]
 b. Watch how Gossard [girdles] makes tummies disappear in ten seconds flat.

20. Ask students to write an article for the school magazine or newspaper. They must think of readers and give them news in fact or expression— something that hits the writer and will hit the reader. At the outset, the article should grab and hold and tell the reader enough to satisfy his need for completeness. What persons say should be exploited, but only the words that strike hard in what they say or how they say it.

21. In assigning the article suggest that students try and discard and try again. Let them know you expect some of the articles to be published. Ask them to study campus publications for length of story, style, and kinds of responsibility shown by the writer. Don't restrict students to a tight, "straight" news article. Allow feature stories or columns of personal opinion if the writing seems to move in that direction.

22. Let students know that at any time in the semester you will allow them to depart from an assignment if they have motive and materials boiling. This freedom must be balanced with discipline. About halfway through

the course, when students are apt to slough off (feeling wearied and harried, like you) by using rewriting possibilities as an excuse for not turning in work, begin the practice of requiring two pieces of writing every week, even if only short free writings. You are developing writers. They are persons who write.

23. When you use professional models, whenever possible point out how students have employed the techniques you are pointing to. You have dittoed student work to refer to. For example, this paper—

> I had always wanted a BB gun, but I never had one until now. We were going out to a friend's farm near Paw Paw and my dad bought me one to take along. At first I took it home to practice. I thought it was a big thing to hit an empty Joy bottle from twenty feet.
>
> After I got to the farm, the owner asked me to shoot some blackbirds for him. For a long time no blackbirds came around. At last one landed in a walnut tree in the yard. I walked under it quietly so I wouldn't scare it. The stupid thing just sat there begging to be shot. I fired my first shot. I saw the little gold BB fly past his head. Dumb bird. It still didn't move. I shot again and the bird's face reacted with pain. It fell over, hanging upside down by one foot from its branch. I shot again. It still hung there. I could see blood on its feathers even from where I stood. With the fourth shot, it fell, its black feathers red.

The last phrase, "its black feathers red," exhibits poetic concentration and carries the weight of the boy's revelation. During the experience he changed his feelings from sadism to sympathy, but he lets the reader infer the change. He does not tell him. He speaks no joy or condescension after "the bird's face reacted with pain." Like a professional writer, he allows some of the smallest details to rise to the surface, and they turn out aptly ironic and symbolic. Practicing to kill, he is shooting a Joy [name of a detergent] bottle. He uses gold BB's for blackbirds. He probably did not intend these extra meanings, but they are present, they work, and he did not excise them.

Because this paper on shooting blackbirds is a small piece of literature, it embraces many of the qualities of good explanatory or persuasive writing, while carrying a different intention and purpose. Show students how "personal" writing usually makes up part of all good critical essays and descriptions and explanations, like those written by Emerson, Bernard Shaw, or E. B. White. The sharply chosen details of the story about the blackbird constitute evidence for its large and unexpressed assertions. "Too subjective," says one teacher. Nonsense. The writer here looked hard at himself over a period of time that gave him distance, recreated the thoughtless killer he once was, took the reader inside his sadistic attitude, and then revealed the change through action rather than explanation. Subjectivity and objectivity are both present and never confused. A trainer of literary critics could ask for no more. (The stories about the boy in the wheelchair and the shooting of blackbirds were written in classes of John Bennett, teacher at Central High School in Kalamazoo, who has used this approach to teaching writing.)

24. After three weeks of journal keeping, ask students to turn in journals. Excerpt from them some of the best writing and ditto it for students. You need not look at journals again if you do not want to. You may suggest to students that journals make useful banks for ideas and beginning pieces of writing.

25. Ask students to write a paper about something they have read. They should tell how and why some part of the work delighted, enraged, or stamped itself onto their memories. At the beginning and end of the paper they may present experience from their lives that illuminates the work. They may discuss book, magazine, short story, poem, sign, instruction sheet, letter, whatever. For this assignment one boy wrote of how successful Truman Capote had been in making the murderers in *In Cold Blood* seem human. The boy showed that in many ways they lived and thought like his own acquaintances and friends, who were not violent, sadistic, or murderous. Students should make their experience touch the experience in what they read, but not distort the author's world. Sometimes only part of this paper will go well. That part may be so good it can be lifted out to stand by itself.

26. Call attention to sound effects in both professional and student writing. Ask for several free writings (in journals or elsewhere) that experiment with sounds.

27. Ask students to write an indirect paper, in which they say the opposite of what they mean, create a fantasy that parallels some life situation, or speak in a pompous or otherwise false voice in order to satirize. Remind them frequently that they use these techniques in conversation with other students when they mimic, speak praise when they mean blame, or talk roughly to convey admiration or love. Don't use the word "satire." In this writing they must maintain one approach and tone. They cannot write "straight" part of the time and ironically the rest of the time.

Explain that some contemporary writers and artists using what has been called the "Put-On" mix tone and approach so the audience is never sure where the communicator stands. This ploy is sometimes appropriate and effective but more often irresponsible. In every activity of this course, except the assignments on word play and indirect writing, a few sophisticated students may feel they are being pushed into an old-fashioned, traditional mold. If you sense this reaction, say that most artists master the traditional techniques and forms of their art before significantly breaking them.

28. Throughout the course take up matters of usage and dialect when occasions present themselves. Language styles change. Today what we teachers once considered unpublishable vulgarity and obscenity is being printed, frequently by good writers and editors. Make students justify any use of material that shocks you. Does the material, the occasion, the audience, seem to the students to call for the language employed? You don't have to like it yourself, but don't inhibit the student's language to the point that he loses the rhythms inherent in his voices. Remember he has many voices. Frequently he should be able to find one that speaks clearly and excitingly to his classmates, to you, and to him.

By reading aloud passages from students' writing, constantly remind them of the differences between rhythmic sentences and stiff, flat, awkward sentences—the authentic and the badly borrowed. This emphasis on genuine voice does not mean you need to encourage only one style—informal, conversational, of the alley. Most good writers of ideas and experience—Shakespeare, Emerson, James Baldwin—employ a style which alternates between homely, kitchen language and elevated words. This alternation provides variety and tension and insures precision without artificiality.

29. Tell students that if they attend this seminar-style class regularly and write and criticize others' writing, they will write several, perhaps half a dozen, pieces that deserve to be published to the whole school community. That is a promise.

Expect student seminar criticism to improve slowly. Students need to test your assertion that you want truth. They need to discover ways of helping writers rather than injuring them. They need your more sophisticated and experienced judgment. Several times a week for periods of fifteen to twenty minutes, talk about writing clearly and authoritatively. If you do not know a great deal more about craft than most students, you should learn or quit teaching. In valuable seminars the teacher lets the students do most of the talking but comes forward strongly when he feels he can inform or lead. He is never the authoritarian but often authoritative.

In general, do away with individual conferences with students about their papers. Most teachers dominate those sessions. Few such conferences provide the long-term support a writer needs to improve on his own. The teacher-student dialogue in the office has bad connotations for the student. In this course you are doing something different for him: providing praise from both his fellow students (whom he must trust more than you at the outset) and the most convincing approval—publication of one kind or another.

When you find a student who is not improving, take him aside and ask for four or five free writings again. Look for what is good in them. If nothing, try again. Bring him out of his doldrums or fear by honest praise for what he has done well, if only a sentence or paragraph.

30. Finally, the students' writing will be as good as the amount of discovery and wonder it contains. Old ideas, if held dearly, are valuable when expressed in new ways. Otherwise, the materials students present to others and to you should be news. The surest way for a writer to find newness is to try almost unbearably for truth. Last year in *The Reporter* magazine, Gene Baro said of Edward R. Murrow: "He told the truth in order to see it."

RHETORIC AND COMPOSITION

ROBERT GORRELL / *Not by Nature: Approaches to Rhetoric*

Dogberry in *Much Ado* displays his learning by informing the Watch that

> To be a well-favored man is the gift of fortune; but to write and read comes by nature.

Dogberry, of course, with the usual perversity of his mind, was neatly mixing matters, reversing the attitude of his day. We often seem to play Dogberry the unfair trick of taking him literally. Because we do not really know how "to write and read comes," we behave comfortably as if we believe that writing and reading come by nature. That is, we manage to teach everything we can think of except writing—literary biography, telephone manners, how to choose a vocation, for examples—and hope that somehow or other writing will flourish. We behave in this way partly because we realize that teaching writing is difficult, and we are not quite sure how to do it. The faith healing often works; I suppose that to write and read does come partly by nature.

But often it does not. I think that when it does not, we need not despair. There is a subject matter that can be called *composition* and can be both respectable and profitable. A subject called *rhetoric* exists and has been a recognized academic discipline for 2,500 years. It is a central business for those of us who teach English. I am aware that rhetoric is *in* this year, that the word *rhetoric* carries some of the magic inspired by hope or desperation. I do not want to look on rhetoric as trickery or as a panacea for the illit-

From *English Journal,* LV (April, 1966), 409–16, 449. Reprinted by permission of the National Council of Teachers of English and Robert Gorrell.

eracies that plague students. I want to look on it rather as a difficult and demanding subject, one that we know too little about, but one that by its very inclusiveness is important.

There is, of course, a great tradition of rhetorical discussion available, both theoretical and practical, much of it highly useful. But I do not propose to rehearse the tradition here. I want rather to submit three principles, partly because they seem to me to describe accurately what happens in writing but more significantly because they seem to me to provide some practical approaches to writing and the teaching of writing. These are simply three different ways of looking at the same phenomena, often the same constructions. They do not exhaust the subject, nor do they provide anything like a comprehensive rhetorical theory. Furthermore, they overlap; they do not provide a logical analysis of the problems of rhetoric. I am proposing them as approaches, as ways of thinking about writing which seem to me fruitful. I am calling them the principles of addition, continuity, and selection.

Writing can be considered as a process of addition, of adding comments to topics. The approach is so fundamental that it seems obvious; and in a way it is, based on the observation that writing is saying something about something. It is, for instance, a rather over-simplified way of describing notionally what happens in a sentence. But the implications of the approach are perhaps not obvious, or at least not obviously observed. For one thing, the process of addition may produce a two-word sentence or an extended composition, depending on how much comment we wish to add. The topic *birds* may have as its comment a single word *sing,* or it may have a volume on ornithology. Consider the following paragraph, which may illustrate rather too neatly:

> (1) Some English words have a negative, but no positive. (2) Anything which is *indelible* cannot be erased, but there is no *delible.* (3) An *uncouth, unkempt* person is crude and untidy, but even if he should reform his ways, he would not be *couth* and *kempt.* (4) We can speak with *impunity,* but not with *punity,* be *immune* to disease, but not *mune.* (5) All these words, and others, were originally formed from a negative prefix and a positive word. (6) In some cases the positive word was never taken into our language, but only the combined form with a negative meaning; in other cases the positive word eventually dropped out and only the negative combination remained. (7) *Unkempt,* for instance, is from English *un-,* not, and *kempt,* a dialect form of *combed.* (8) We no longer use *kempt,* but have kept *unkempt,* which from the original meaning of "uncombed" came to mean "generally untidy." (9) *Indelible* is from Latin *in-,* not, and *delibilis,* perishable. (10) We adopted

the Latin word *indelibilis*—but not delibilis—and changed it to *indelible*. Helene and Charlton Laird, *The Tree of Language* (World, 1957).

The paragraph contains about 175 words arranged in ten varied sentences to convey a good deal of information. It has the complexity of any piece of prose, and thorough examination of every aspect of this group of words might involve a volume of linguistic analysis. But the paragraph can also be considered as very simple, as an extended comment on a single topic, *words*. The basic comment is contained in a few key words, *have negative but no positive*. All the remaining words in the paragraph continue and elaborate the comment about *words*. They attach to the basic framework in various ways. To begin with, *Some English* restricts the group of words being considered. And then nine sentences augment and clarify the opening statement, as in the following diagram:

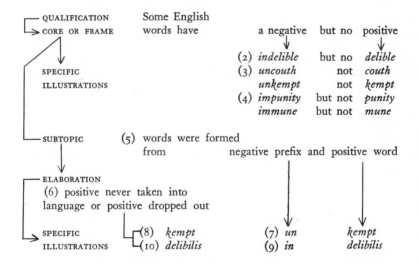

As the diagram shows, sentences 2, 3 and 4 add specific examples of the key assertion. Then sentence 5 varies the comment of the opening sentence explaining why the words have a negative but no positive by telling how the *words were formed;* and sentence 6 adds elaboration to 5. Then, just as 2, 3, and 4 illustrate 1, sentences 7, 8, 9, and 10 illustrate 5 and 6.

The principle of addition, of course, does not explain the psychological generation of a sentence. A writer does not produce a simple sentence like *The ash tray fell on the floor* by choosing a topic like *ash tray* and then casting about for a comment to make on it. Obviously, it is the comment which motivates the utterance; the writer observes what happens to the ash tray, and therefore the comment suggests the topic. And it is the comment that gives any unit of writing its individuality.

The paragraph above, for example, in the book from which it is taken, serves as only part of a series of comments on the topic *words*. The opening framework, *words have negative but no positive,* is one of several comments on the general topic of this section of the book. This comment, however, becomes a topic on which the next three sentences comment. And 5 and 6 are part of the comment on 1 as well as the presentation of a new topic for additional comment in the final four sentences. Patterns interlock, carrying the reader step by step through a composition by specifying and clarifying the relationships between topic and comment.

Complex as thoughts may get, these basic relationships between topic and comment can be considered as only four. Two of them, predication and linkage, are basic in the development of the English sentence. Two others, coordination and subordination, are important within the sentence but also in the structure of larger units.

Predication. Although basic in the grammatical structure of the English sentence, the relationship of subject to verb and sometimes to objects—which I am calling predication—is difficult to describe. Grammatically the relationship is expressed in the kernel sentences of English and their main transforms. It can sometimes be described as the relation of actor to action to goal. Or it can be described as the relationship among ideas in which something does or affects something else. It is, of course, the relationship revealed in the key words of the opening sentence above, *words have negative but no positive.* It is perhaps the most common way of making a comment on a topic. Word order usually reveals the relationship.

Linkage. Although the patterns expressing the relationship I am calling linkage look like predication patterns, they express a quite different relationship. Like predication, linkage produces kernel sentences, but in linkage patterns the topic is regularly coupled with something else. A subject is joined by *be* or a linking verb to a noun or a modifier. The relationship might be described as identification, or sometimes almost of equation. That is, something is or is like something else. Sentence 3 in the paragraph above is an example; *person* is linked by *is* to the modifiers *crude* and *untidy.*

Coordination. Coordination may relate individual words or other units within a sentence, sentences within a paragraph, or paragraphs or other longer units in a longer composition. Coordination describes the relationship between items similar in status; coordinate elements have the same function in their contexts. The relationship is sometimes expressed by putting the coordinate items in parallel form, sometimes by placing them in parallel positions in their contexts, and sometimes by joining them with words like *and* or *or*. In the opening sentence of the paragraph above, *a negative* and *no positive* are related as coordinates within the sentence. Moreover, sentences 2, 3, and 4 are coordinate sentences in the paragraph, all of them bearing the same status in relation to the opening sentence.

Subordination. Subordination is one of the most common processes of addition, and one of the most difficult to describe. By subordination, secondary characteristics of a word or a full statement or a developed idea can be added. Most commonly, subordination is modification of some sort. That is, subordinate additions qualify or clarify or illustrate. In the first sentence of the paragraph above, *some English* is an addition subordinated to *words,* modifying *words* within the sentence. Less obviously, sentences 2, 3, and 4—which are coordinate with each other—are subordinate to the opening, providing concrete examples.

These devices of addition—predication, linkage, coordination, and subordination—are obviously basic to all writing. The writer needs to learn what the devices do so that he can use them wisely. And the devices will not work on the basis of rules or dogma attempting to define what must appear in structures. For instance, predication cannot be managed simply by some such formula as "Always make the most important idea the subject." The choice of subject depends on what the writer wants the sentence to do. Neither will a rule like "Put ideas of equal importance in parallel form" hold. The design or purpose of the whole guides the writer in framing ideas to show the relationships he wishes to emphasize. Coordination or subordination is not necessarily inherent in the ideas themselves—in their importance or any other characteristic. The writer coordinates ideas, because he wants to present them in this relationship. Similarly, the common injunction to subordinate less important ideas is misleading, the result of taking too literally a grammatical term which developed by analogy. In the paragraph about words, the first sentence is not in itself "more important" than the next three. It is more general, which may be important, as I shall suggest later.

My first principle, then, the principle of addition, is simple enough in outline. It is that by predication, linkage, coordination, and subordination we can add the comments to topics to produce composition. Filling in the details of the outline would add complexities and puzzles, but the principle provides one way of imposing some order on the complexities.

A second principle is that writing can be considered as continuity, as a series of commitments and responses. That is, the patterns which reveal the relationships of addition described above can also be looked at as a flow or a sequence. Within the sentence, for instance, every predication or link-age pattern takes form partly because every word the writer chooses com-mits him in some way to what is to follow—limits him, sometimes quite narrowly, to the words—the responses—which may follow. When, for instance, the writer chooses a sentence subject, he commits himself in sev-eral ways to certain types of responses. If he chooses to begin with an abstraction like *his insistence* or *the reason,* he limits possibilities for follow-ing verbs. He eliminates action verbs like *jump* or *grumble;* he increases considerably the likelihood that his verb will be *is* or *was.* If he does select *is* or *was,* he is again committed, grammatically at least, to a modi-fier or subject complement as a response.

The principle is more significant, however, as an approach to longer units than sentences—as a way of looking at the development or generation of prose as a sequence of ideas. Consider the beginning of the paragraph above about words. The opening sentence

Some English words have a negative, but no positive.

makes a commitment; that is, it limits the possibilities that can follow. As a relatively general assertion, it creates an expectation in the reader; the reader expects in the following sentence to get further enlightenment about what the opening sentence means. The sentence commits the writer to saying more explicitly what he means—to illustrating, explaining, justifying, elab-orating his opening assertion. Sentence 2 responds with a concrete, specific illustration, which clarifies the assertion of sentence 1. But sentence 2 also makes a commitment, and sentence 3 responds by citing another example. Sentence 4 responds to 3—and, of course, both 3 and 4 also respond to 1—with two more illustrations. One could go on through any segment of prose, analyzing various elements—words, sentences, parts of sentences, parts of paragraphs—as sequences of commitments and responses.

But I am interested in the concept less as a device for the analysis of existing prose than as a guide for the generation of prose—as a way of thinking about composition. The application of the principle to writing is obvious: every unit of composition must be conceived and tested both as a commitment to what follows and a response to what precedes. The im-plications of the principle are perhaps less obvious and are certainly far-reaching; they encompass much of practical rhetoric. They direct the writer—and of course the teacher of writing—to two basic considerations:

1. *Commitment.* Any unit of continuing prose makes a commitment, but it is convenient here to consider sentences. The writer must be aware of the kind of commitment each sentence makes. The opening sentence of

the above paragraph might have been cast in many different ways, but any change would change the commitment. For example, the writers of the paragraph might have begun:

> Some English words offer variations which seem illogical and inconsistent.

The commitment here is much less restricting than in the original. The paragraph might go on to talk about spelling variations, about unusual semantic changes—or about negatives without positives. The sentence offers less help than the original. If the sentence were still broader,

> Some English words present very interesting problems.

it would be almost useless as an opening for the paragraph, because it commits the writer so extensively that he can respond only in a book. On the other hand, a generalization as broad as this—though hopefully less vague and more meaningful—might serve usefully as an opening, making a commitment to several paragraphs or chapters. Because commitments vary in scope, a sentence may make a commitment to only the sentence following it, to three or four sentences—as does the opening sentence of the original— or to a whole book. If the writers had omitted the opening sentence, begun the paragraph with sentence 2, a different sort of problem would have existed: the opening sentence would have limited the possibilities of what could follow but would not have extended its influence so widely over the entire paragraph.

Such speculation about alternatives suggests obvious broad precepts, mostly variations on don't bite off more than you can chew, but bite off something. That is, at each stage in his composition the writer is making commitments—in form and in content. The commitment must not be so great that no sensible response is possible; a generalization must not include everything, but it must say something.

2. *Response*. Although obviously an unlimited number of specific sentences may follow any other, the types of likely responses to any commitment seem to me surprisingly few. In general, the writer seems to me committed to one of the following: a. Specification, b. Repetition, c. Diversion.

a. *Specification*. Probably the most common response to a commitment is an illustration, an example, an explanation. In the paragraph above, sentence 2 obviously responds to sentence 1 in this way. Or, in the following three sentences, William James moves to one level of increased specificity and then goes to examples:

> But, with all this beating and tacking on my part,
> I fear you take me to be reaching a confused result.
> I seem to be just taking things up and dropping them again.
> First I took up Chautauqua, and dropped that; then Tolstoi and the heroism of common toil, and dropped them; finally, I took up ideals, and seem now almost dropping those.
> —*The Will to Believe and Other Essays* (Reynolds, 1897).

The second sentence turns the paragraph to discussion of the first part of the first sentence, sharpening the focus. The third responds to the second with examples. In the following, the second sentence specifies somewhat differently.

> Because it is small, the small firm has one potential advantage over the big one. It can't afford big research teams to administrate or interlocking committees to work up programs, and it doesn't have a crystallized company "family" to adjust to.
> —William H. Whyte, Jr.,
>   *The Organization Man* (Simon and Schuster, 1956).

The first sentence asserts that the small firm has an advantage which is its very smallness. Then the second lists two or three specific aspects of this advantage of smallness.

Often the specification moves farther, selecting only part of a preceding sentence as its commitment and providing a specific emphasis for what is to follow. The second sentence of the paragraph above on words, for example, might have gone something like this:

> These words seldom cause difficulty, but they could provide temptations for anyone who likes to play games with words.

This kind of sentence would turn the generalization of the opening in a new direction, establishing a new kind of commitment. A third sentence, then would have to be something like:

> They might stimulate someone to praise the convenience of *delible* ink, to come to an *evitable* conclusion, and to speak with *punity*.

The paragraph could go on, although it would be moving in a different way. The following illustrates the same sort of variation:

If the essence of history is the memory of things said and done, then it is obvious that every normal person, Mr. Everyman, knows some history. Of course we do what we can to conceal this invidious truth.

—Carl Becker,
"Everyman His Own Historian,"
American Historical Review (January 1932).

The second sentence responds to only part of the assertion of the first, turning the direction enough that it might be considered a deviation as well as specification. As might be expected, the third sentence offers specification for sentence 2, for how we "conceal this invidious truth":

Assuming a professional manner, we say that so and so knows no history, when we mean no more than that he failed to pass the examinations set for a higher degree; and simple-minded persons, undergraduates, and others, taken in by academic classifications of knowledge, think they know no history because they have never taken a course in history in college, or have never read Gibbon's *Decline and Fall of the Roman Empire.*

Interestingly, however, the paragraph after another sentence or two moves back to respond more directly to the opening sentence, providing specific support for the statement that Mr. Everyman knows some history.

b. *Repetition.* It is also common to follow a sentence with another of the same sort, in effect paralleling or repeating a response to an earlier commitment. In the paragraph about words, sentence 3 responds to 2 by repeating on the same level of specificity adding a parallel example, and sentence 4 follows 3 in the same way. Or notice the sentence that follows those quoted above from William H. Whyte, Jr.:

Because it hasn't caught up yet with modern management, to put it another way, it provides an absence of the controls that make the scientist restive.

The sentence may move slightly toward greater specificity than the one preceding it, but essentially it is a parallel, putting it another way.

c. *Deviation.* Often a writer achieves movement of his ideas by using one sentence as the basis for a shift in a direction in a following one. That is, a possible response to a commitment may be a deviation, which turns the course of discourse, even reverses it. A possible second sentence for the paragraph on words might have shifted direction:

Most English negatives, however, have a corresponding positive.

Such a sentence would seem to commit the third to respond with examples of pairs: *intangible* and *tangible, invisible* and *visible,* and so on. Or, the second sentence might have gone even farther afield:

> This suggests that English speakers generally have taken a pessimistic view toward life.

Obviously, such a turn does not provide a very promising way to continue. A response which provides a deviation occurs most frequently along in the middle of a paragraph as a way of providing a kind of subtopic, as in the following:

> By temperament I lean to the side that considers composing in our community as a natural force—something to be taken for granted— rather than the freakish occupation of a very small minority of our citizens. And yet, judging the situation dispassionately, I can see that we ought not to take it for granted.
>
> —Aaron Copland,
> *Music and Imagination* (Harvard University Press, 1952).

The paragraph continues with specification to develop the second sentence.

I have used examples of sentences in pairs to emphasize the continuity from sentence to sentence, but variations should be pointed out. Sometimes a response is made to an earlier commitment, as discourse breaks into units longer than a single sentence. In the paragraph above, for instance, sentence 5 is actually a response to the commitment of sentence 1, starting a new sequence in which 6 specifies 5, and the remaining sentences are parallel specifications of 6. On the other hand, a single sentence may present not only the commitment and response involved in the basic predication but also illustrative specification:

> Scholars have introduced learned spellings in many words,
>   e.g., *debt, doubt,* on account of Latin *debita, dubito,* formerly written
>   as in French *dette, doute;*
>   *victuals,* formerly *vittles.*
>   —Otto Jespersen,
>   *Essentials of English Grammar* (Allen and Unwin, 1933).

And, of course, responses do not necessarily fit neatly into the categories I have listed but frequently combine; a diversion often specifies, for example.

My third observation is that writing can be looked at as selection, as a series of choices among alternatives. In one sense, I am using selection to describe the practical problems of addition and continuity, to include, I suppose, most of rhetoric. That is, for the writer or the teacher of writing, notions like the principles of addition or continuity are useful mainly as they direct choices of words or structures. A topic is chosen because the writer wants to comment on it; the topic directs the choice of comments. A phrasing for a commitment is selected because of what it requires in a response, and the response is limited by its obligations to the commitment. But there are many other influences on selection, of which I shall mention only two or three.

Grammar. Anyone writing obviously uses the grammatical patterns of his language, and his selections are partly determined by them. That is, the writer does not say "The dog me bited" or "Rapidity artichoked filigree," because they are not grammatical. He also, however, has the problem of making choices among the grammatical patterns that are available, and this can be more difficult and often more important. For example, he may need to decide whether to use a basic kernel pattern or a transform of it, whether to say "The children broke the record" or "The record was broken by the children." Or, to look from another direction, he may need to know how to choose the grammatical structure which will reinforce the relationship of a response to a commitment.

Semantic Compatibility. Questions of grammaticalness are not always simple, are often bound up closely with questions of meaning. I can black my shoes but not brown them. It is possible to tar and feather a person but not to egg him. Although many combinations are possible if a meaning is discernible, selection depends frequently on customs which place certain words in certain contexts. We are likely to *deliver* a lecture or *make* a speech but not to *make* a lecture. The writer selects words which work in meaning with the words around them.

Usage. All of the many questions of usage influence selection. Whether to use *contact* as a verb or *type* as a modifier is one kind of selection problem, with the writer's decision depending on his assessment of the consequences of using alternatives.

Tone and Purpose. In a broader sense, selection is constantly influenced by the writer's commitment to his audience and his attitude to his subject. These are obviously subjects too complicated for treatment here, but they are fundamental to most questions of selection.

*   *   *

I am not sure that the principles I have mentioned are of much significance for a theory of rhetoric, but I am interested in them as practical approaches to writing. Practically, I think they are useful, because they provide ways of getting at important writing problems, of thinking about writing as a composing process, of thinking of choices made for reasons more meaningful than an arbitrary rule. For the teacher, such approaches offer almost unlimited opportunities for both criticism of student writing and productive practice in writing problems. Various kinds of exercises are possible with sentences or longer sequences, and I shall simply mention a few at random.

> 1. Students might be asked to think of a comment on a topic, a comment that seems to them worth making. They then might list additional comments, as many as possible. Then they might be guided in putting the additions into a sentence or sentences.
>
> 2. Or working from the other direction students might be given a subject, topic, or an actual sentence and then a list of all the additions. Their task would be to construct a sentence, and their results could be compared with the original sentence.
>
> 3. Students might be given a sentence, possibly the topic sentence of a paragraph, asked to analyze the commitment it makes and then asked to frame possible responses. Such an exercise could be handled effectively with an overhead projector with the teacher offering alternative responses as well as the one actually in the paragraph.

Obviously various kinds of exercises, for analysis of existing writing or for development of new writing, could be devised.

These principles will not solve all writing problems nor create a new generation of highly literate students. But I think that Dogberry was probably wrong—at least for most students—and I think that there are things about writing that can be taught and that should be taught.

RICHARD L. LARSON / *Teaching Rhetoric in the High School:*
Some Proposals

The phrase, "Some Proposals," is included in my title [1] to make clear that
this discussion is not to be a survey of courses in rhetoric currently being
taught in high schools. If I were to attempt such a survey, I fear that it
would turn up a few such courses. Possibly the major methods now being
used to introduce rhetorical principles into high school curricula are the
units on rhetoric and composition produced by curriculum study centers
such as those at the Universities of Oregon and Nebraska; these units are
being tested in the schools in areas surrounding the centers. But these units
are new, and they were exposed to teachers outside the immediate vicinity
of the study centers for the first time in NDEA institutes held during the
summer of 1965; their impact, I think, has yet to be measured.

Instead of presenting a survey of writing courses, then, this paper makes
some suggestions about the structure and emphases of high school courses
in composition. (My suggestions apply principally to courses that require
expository writing. I leave aside for the present courses in speech or "oral
English.") Let me reassure you at once that these suggestions do not include the introduction into the high school curriculum of another course
(or even another unit)—this one in the history of rhetoric or in rhetoric as
a body of theories about language and communication. Nor do my suggestions include the substitution of Aristotle's *Rhetoric* or Cicero's *De
Oratore* or Quintilian's *Institutes* for the texts on composition now in use,

[1] Based on paper read at the NCTE meetings in Boston, November 1965.

From *English Journal*, LV (November, 1966), 1058–65. Reprinted by permission of
the National Council of Teachers of English and Richard L. Larson.

although some of the current texts, as we all know, deserve to be replaced. What I am suggesting is that teachers of expository writing in high school look at expository writing from the perspective employed by most classical and many modern writers on rhetoric, and encourage their students to adopt the same perspective. I am urging teachers of composition to view writing not as a process of observing the rules of grammar, or of engaging in "creativity" as an end in itself, or of negotiating the expository "methods" that are regularly described in standard texts on composition, but rather as an art by which the writer tries to assure that his readers understand what he has to say, respect his opinions, and, if they reasonably can, come to agree with them.

Before developing further the values of the "rhetorical perspective" that I am proposing, I must explain how I am using the term "rhetoric." I have in mind a broader definition of the term than that of Aristotle, who, as you recall, defined rhetoric as "the faculty of discovering in the particular case what are the available means of persuasion."[2] My definition is also broader, I think, than that of Professor Corbett, who more or less adopts Aristotle's definiton when he descrbes classical rhetoric as "the art of persuasive speech," and adds that the end of rhetoric "was to convince or persuade an audience to think in a certain way and act in a certain way."[3] Two of Kenneth Burke's definitions[4] of the term, as "the use of words by human agents to form attitudes or induce actions in other human agents" and as "the use of language as a symbolic means of inducing co-operation in beings that by nature respond to symbols," seem more pertinent for teachers of composition today, if Burke would agree that when a reader desires seriously to entertain and explore the ideas of the writer (the user of words), he has formed an "attitude" and is engaged in a species of "cooperation." I also find Richards' early re-definition of rhetoric as "the study of verbal understanding and misunderstanding" helpful as a guide to teachers of writing, since it focusses on the whole question of how a writer's words are received and understood by his readers.[5]

For my purposes in this paper, however, the most helpful definitions of rhetoric are those offered by Donald Bryant.[6] After noting the superficial

[2] *Rhetoric*, 1. 2, trans., Lane Cooper (New York: Appleton-Century-Crofts, 1962), p. 7.
[3] Edward P. J. Corbett, *Classical Rhetoric for the Modern Student* (New York: Oxford University Press, 1965), p. 21.
[4] Kenneth Burke, *A Rhetoric of Motives* (New York: Prentice-Hall, 1950), pp. 41, 43.
[5] I. A. Richards, *The Philosophy of Rhetoric* (New York: Oxford University Press, 1936), p. 23.
[6] Donald Bryant, "Rhetoric: Its Function and Scope," *The Quarterly Journal of Speech*, XXXIX (December, 1953). Reprinted in Joseph Schwartz and John Rycenga, editors, *The Province of Rhetoric* (New York: Ronald Press, 1965). Page references are to this reprint.

meanings ("bombast," "propaganda," and the like) frequently associated with "rhetoric," Bryant reminds us that rhetoric is often concerned with questions of what *probably happened* in a given set of circumstances or what *will probably happen* if proposed action is taken. Observing, then, that rhetoric is often concerned with establishing probabilities, he calls rhetoric the strategy "for deciding best the undecidable questions, for arriving at solutions of the unsolvable problems, for instituting method in those phases of human activity where no method is inherent in the total subject-matter of decision" (p. 11). But Bryant does not limit rhetoric to the art of determining what irrevocable action should be taken in the presence of inadequate information. He finds that what he calls "rhetorical situations" have in common the use of language by human beings "to effect a change in the knowledge, the understanding, the ideas, the attitudes, or the behavior of other human beings" (p. 17). And he describes the rhetorical function as that of "adjusting ideas to people and people to ideas" (p. 19). Rhetoric directs the creative activity by which language is used "for the promulgation of information, ideas, attitudes. . . . Its characteristic is publication, the publicizing, the humanizing, the animating of [ideas and information] for a realized and usually specific audience" (p. 19).

Two features of Bryant's definitions will help teachers to understand the details of my suggestion that they adopt a "rhetorical perspective" in teaching composition. The first, of course, is his focus on the relationship of the writer (or speaker) and his listener. The second is his implicit assumption that rhetoric need not be preoccupied or even principally occupied with persuading or propagandizing, and that the transmitting of any information, the promulgation of any ideas, depends for its success on the adjustment of what is presented to the backgrounds, capacities, and needs of a particular group of receivers (the audience) on a particular occasion. When I speak of "rhetoric," then, I speak of how a writer can most effectively transmit a group of ideas to particular hearers or readers. And I do not insist that the effectiveness of the transmission is measured by the willingness of the audience to believe or act upon what is said. The transmission is effective if the audience understands and respects what has been said, i.e., if the audience is willing to give serious attention to the writer's ideas.

To some who are familiar with Aristotle's painstaking analysis of the interests and dispositions of various kinds of human beings, my insistence that the writer take the needs and interests of his reader into account may seem an unnecessary restatement of the obvious, but recent textbooks that include the term "rhetoric" in their titles suggest that it is not. I am now teaching a course in advanced exposition—with several prospective secondary school teachers of English enrolled—with the aid of a text (I did not help to choose it) whose title proclaims rhetoric as one of its twin subjects. But nowhere in the book do I or my students find significant attention paid to the relationship of writer and reader; nowhere does the author show that he understands the writer's cardinal responsibility to think, before writing, about how best to assure that his message will be received and "respected" by its audience.

Professor Bryant's definitions, then, help us in establishing a rhetorical perspective for teaching exposition in high schools. But even his definition, I think, does not make clear in sufficient detail the responsibilities of a writer whose work is guided by a concern for how his thoughts will be received. We can make the writer's task clearer by recalling the first three of the traditional five parts of the subject of rhetoric: invention (finding ideas), disposition (arranging these ideas in the discourse, and allocating appropriate space to each), and elocution (expressing the ideas in words and sentences). We can say that rhetoric is the art of adapting the ideas, structure, and style of a piece of writing to the audience, occasion, and purpose for which the discourse is written.

If this definition is accepted, it reminds us of this important fact: that any writing requires the systematic and purposeful making of choices. The principal areas of choice are three: what to say, how to arrange and allocate space to what is to be said, and how to express in words what is to be said. And the major controls on the choices—the forces in consideration of which the writer makes his decisions—are also three: the audience (those who will receive the communication), the occasion (the external circumstances, together with the emotional and intellectual pressures, under which the discourse is composed), and the writer's purpose (what he hopes to accomplish by writing—what he hopes to have his audience know, think, feel, or do as a result of his writing). In identifying these "controls," of course, we recognize that the subject itself and the writer's abilities or personality may also control the ideas, structure, and style. The responsible writer can hardly make statements that his subject or his information will not permit, nor will he, in all probability, adopt a style or voice in which he feels uncomfortable or at a severe disadvantage.

Rhetoric, then, requires the continued making of decisions as one plans and writes. Viewed from the perspective of rhetoric, writing ceases to be the carrying out of mechanical procedures and becomes, instead, an activity that requires great sensitivity and discretion. Writing is a continuous exercise in the meeting of responsibilities to one's readers.

Now suppose that the teaching of expository writing in a high school were to be designed so that students were required to produce themes directed toward a designated audience, to serve a specific purpose, in response to the demands of a particular occasion. What would result? An example may suggest an answer. The theme of comparison is about as traditional and conventional an assignment in high school courses in writing as any, with the possible exception of assignments in description and narration. But the student is usually asked to write a theme of comparison as if the process of comparing were an end in itself—as if the value lay simply in the completion of the process. Teachers teach comparison because their syllabus tells them to, or they assign comparison papers because such assignments are easy ways of forcing students to talk about two or more literary works or characters that the class has just studied. They trot out the standard methods of organizing a comparison (the last report I heard was that there are seven such methods), remind the student that the comparison must be balanced (corresponding features of both items under examination must be discussed), set the student a subject, and tell him to proceed. If he uses one of the methods of organization consistently (it doesn't usually matter which one), observes the requirement of balance, exhausts the subject (or at least covers the points the teacher has in mind), and preserves the conventions of grammar and usage, he receives an *A* and passes on to the next assignment. But he may have learned nothing of the uses to which he can put comparison as a technique of arriving at or transmitting knowledge.

The teacher with a rhetorical perspective, on the other hand, will ask students to regard comparison as a way of organizing information to achieve a purpose. In fact, students will find that comparison may serve many purposes. By comparing assigned subjects, first of all, students may *discover* important features—ones they had not already seen—of the subjects compared. Comparison, students will find, can also *provide emphasis*. By putting apparently like (or unlike) things together, a writer may discover and give the reader a livelier appreciation of the differences (or similarities) between these things. When the subjects appear side by side, what had earlier been scarcely noted may all of a sudden be sharply observed. Comparison can also *clarify*. The writer may help his reader to understand more fully the properties of an unfamiliar object by reminding the reader of the features of a similar, but more familiar, object. Next, comparison—putting items side by side—can assist a writer in judging each and *ranking* the two. (Comparison thus used is an essential tool in the making of decisions, the resolving of issues, the selecting of courses of action from among alternatives.) Finally, comparison may *argue*. The writer may make his proposition plausible by comparing his subject to another subject about which a similar proposition has already been established. The teacher with a rhetorical perspective, then, helps the student learn how to employ comparison as a method of examining or arranging data when the student's purposes in writing will be best served by that method. Comparison becomes a tool rather than a self-serving exercise. Other traditional expository procedures (definition, enumeration, classification, and the like), when viewed from a rhetorical perspective, will also become tools for a purpose rather than pointless activities in which the students simply get purposeless drill.

One more consequence of adopting this rhetorical perspective will be a reevaluation of the grouping of writing into four "forms": description, narration, exposition, and argument. The groupings, of course, are supposed to designate different ways of ordering statements within paragraphs and paragraphs within the whole piece. But instead of emphasizing the distinctions among these patterns, the teacher with a rhetorical perspective will show students how they often interpenetrate. On occasion, to be sure, the writer's purpose may be only to "describe," i.e., to realize an object, scene, or person vividly for his reader by pointing out in succession various details of the appearance or constitution of his subject. On occasion, too, the writer's purpose may be served entirely by "narrating," i.e., by relating a sequence of events. But to "describe" an object frequently entails narrating a sequence of events in which the object is involved. To engage in "exposition," i.e., to set forth a group of ideas for the reader according to an orderly plan, frequently requires the describing of persons, places, or objects and the narrating of events. Even to argue a proposition may require the describing of objects, the narrating of events, and the explaining of causes and effects, not to mention the enumerating of grounds of belief and the prediction of the results of action (all of these last three activities would without doubt be regarded as "expository"). A teacher with a rhetorical perspective will encourage students to consider their purposes and the needs of their audiences in deciding what details to give and what kind of order to impose on these details.

Now to say that teachers of exposition in high school should adopt a rhetorical perspective may elicit agreement, but it does little to direct the teacher in employing this perspective in the classroom. Let me make some suggestions about how a teacher can encourage his students consistently to view writing as an effort to put ideas across to an audience so as to win its respect, even if it withholds agreement.

First, in many if not most of his writing assignments, the teacher can stipulate the audience to whom the students should address their papers. He can also suggest the purpose that sudents should try to achieve in their writing, and he can specify an imagined or an actual occasion for writing. If the designated audience is live and present (school administrators, officers of student government, members of the class just behind or just ahead of those writing), so much the better. If the papers cannot reasonably be addressed to an audience outside the classroom, other members of the class can furnish a live audience for any single student to envisage. A useful variation of the procedure might be to ask students to stipulate their own audience, purpose, and occasion. Still another variation might be to ask students to write on the same subject for different audiences (or for different purposes or on different occasions), and to discuss in class the differences among the papers that result. Students could profitably discuss, even write papers explaining, why they chose one arrangement and style for one audience, another arrangement and style for the second audience.

Second, whatever the audience or purpose for a theme, the teacher can encourage students to approach it with these questions in mind: what procedures ought I to follow in selecting and arranging my material so as to assure that I communicate completely with my reader? Given what I know of my audience and given my purpose, what strategies are available to me and which one will probably work best? Answers to these questions may suggest the amount and kinds of information the student will need to include in his theme, and the pattern of organization best suited to bringing this information together. The answers may even help students to decide how to develop individual paragraphs. To rely on the traditional types of paragraphs (illustration, cause to effect, effect to cause, and so on), students will discover, is grossly to over-simplify the task of arranging material. Quite often several different patterns of movement will have to combine in a single paragraph if that paragraph is to play its proper role in the developing action of the paper.

Third, the teacher can invite students to make rhetorical analyses of contemporary writings and speeches. Students can decide for themselves what selected editorial writers, essayists, political orators, and advertising copy writers are trying to accomplish in their pieces, and can discuss why particular combinations of data, plans of organization, patterns of sentences, levels of language, and figures of speech appear in the pieces under study. Teachers who feel uncertain about carrying on such analyses should find Corbett's *Classical Rhetoric for the Modern Student* especially helpful. Along with samples of spoken and written discourse from Greece and Rome, England, and modern America, Corbett prints extensive rhetorical analyses of many pieces. Particularly instructive for the teacher trying to employ a rhetorical perspective in teaching exposition is Corbett's discussion of President Kennedy's inaugural address. Another book that features extensive rhetorical analyses—this time mostly of essays designed for publication rather than oral delivery—is Israel Kapstein's *Expository Prose: An Analytic Approach* (Harcourt, 1955). Kapstein explores his examples in much greater depth than students or even most teachers will want to follow, but the analyses are nonetheless instructive. For teachers wishing a brief introduction to rhetorical analysis, I suggest the kinescope or the kinescript, entitled "Organization: Rhetorical and Artistic," by George Williams of Duke University, available from the Commission on English of the College Entrance Examination Board.

In asking his students to engage in rhetorical analysis, the teacher should not accept easy generalizations or fuzzy, subjective descriptions of style or argument. To understand the choices made by a speaker or writer, the student needs to identify specifically the role played by each paragraph and sentence.[7] Indeed he should be encouraged to consider why the writer used particular words and phrases—instead of alternatives that come readily to mind—at strategic points in his discourse. The student may need, for example, to decide for himself whether a particular metaphor does indeed accomplish the work of a given sentence more neatly than a plain statement. If the student disagrees with the speaker's choices, he can learn much from defending the organizational plan or figure of speech he prefers in the context. If teacher wishes his students to attempt rhetorical analysis experimentally or on a small scale, following the example set by Williams in the analysis of opening paragraphs will give them good practice—besides telling them something of value about opening paragraphs. One can, to be sure, bear down to heavily on rhetorical analysis (such analysis can produce in students the kind of self-consciousness that paralyzes thought and invention), but when used judiciously, as an instrument to help students learn about writing, rather than as an end in itself, detailed analysis of the workings of sentences and paragraphs can teach as much about exposition as any method I know.

The teacher can draw another useful assignment from the rhetorical analysis of prose: he can encourage students to imitate, perhaps better still to parody, the techniques of authors under study. Imitation used to be a commonplace method of teaching writing or learning to write, but it is now out of fashion. Wisely used, however, imitation can help the student learn how it feels to write in other than his normal idiom; the exercise may help free him from inflexible, perhaps tedious, habits of expression, and may help him learn what it means to adapt style to the occasion and purpose of

[7] On the rhetorical value of different kinds of sentence structure, teachers may wish to consult Richard Weaver, *The Ethics of Rhetoric* (Chicago: Henry Regnery Company, 1953), Chapter 5.

writing. Parody, because it is fun, may be an even more effective learning procedure than direct imitation. To parody a writer's style requires a pretty thorough understanding of that style; the pleasure in recognizing both the likeness and the exaggeration in parody will reward the student for showing that he has understood the distinctive features of that style.

Finally, why not introduce high school students to a few of the "topics," as they are interpreted by modern scholars? Four teachers at the University of Chicago show how definition and classification (argument from *genus*), comparison, analysis of cause and effect, and the use of authority can be taught as methods of *argument* to freshmen in college.[8] Mark Ashin has also shown how these "topics" work in Madison's *Federalist* No. 10.[9] There seems little reason why college preparatory classes in today's high schools cannot profit from similar instruction when they confront assignments in argument. Such assignments appear frequently in high school courses in composition, although often they appear in other guises, as assignments on controversial subjects in the interpretation of literary works, for example. Explicit discussion of a few "topics," as the teachers from Chicago demonstrate, will give students valuable practice in locating and using arguments to support their propositions—including their propositions about literary texts. Attention to the uses of testimony, in addition, will help students develop a discriminating attitude toward ostensibly authoritative statements; they will learn to evaluate the sources of testimony about events and about literary characters. From these studies they will also learn to argue more effectively about propositions that can be no more than "probably" true. Recall that Professor Bryant spoke of rhetoric's concern with deciding "undecidable" questions, with issues of what is more and less "probable."

The procedures suggested here are varied, but they come together in demanding that the student look at writing not as a sterile exercise to be performed at home or in class and shared with the teacher alone, but as a way of getting a message to someone for a purpose. Hopefully they come together, also, in encouraging the student to view writing not merely as a task in achieving correctness or outguessing the teacher, but as a discipline that requires the making of reasonable decisions—plans for verbal action, one might call them—in the face of the many different problems in written communication.

[8] Manuel Bilsky and others, "Looking for an Argument," *College English*, 14 (January, 1953), 210–18.
[9] Mark Ashin, "The Argument of Madison's Federalist No. 10," *College English*, 15 (October, 1953), 37–45.

In adopting this view, I echo the comments made by Walker Gibson: that every writer consciously or unconsciously assumes a role and adopts a "voice" when he begins to write, and that he is better off if he chooses deliberately, or at least recognizes, the role he is adopting, than if he is unconscious of how he appears to his reader.[10] I also concur in the observations by Robert Gorrell that were quoted by Gibson.[11] But I think that the choices required of a writer, when his task is viewed from the perspective that modern students of rhetoric have given us, are more numerous than those Gibson described. It is not merely a role and a voice that the writer must choose; he also has the responsibility for selecting the substance, arrangement, and proportioning of his work. (Professor Gibson would probably concur. His discussion was limited to the writer's assumption of role and voice through stylistic choices.) Bringing to bear on the high school composition course the perspectives of rhetoric can help students learn to choose wisely in deciding every feature of their papers, and to bear in mind always the purposes for which they write. One cannot claim that they will always write "better" as a result of adopting this perspective (how hard it is to define "better writing"!), but they may at least write more thoughtfully, responsibly, and convincingly.

[10] Walker Gibson, "An Exercise in Style," a paper delivered at the 1965 convention of the National Council of Teachers of English in Boston, Massachusetts. [Reproduced in the section on style in this volume.]
[11] Robert Gorrell, *"Very Like a Whale—A Report on Rhetoric,"* CCC, 16 (October, 1965), 142.

WAYNE C. BOOTH / *The Rhetorical Stance*

Last fall I had an advanced graduate student, bright, energetic, well-informed, whose papers were almost unreadable. He managed to be pretentious, dull, and disorganized in his paper on *Emma,* and pretentious, dull, and disorganized on *Madame Bovary*. On *The Golden Bowl* he was all these and obscure as well. Then one day, toward the end of term, he cornered me after class and said, "You know, I think you were all wrong about Robbe-Grillet's *Jealousy* today." We didn't have time to discuss it, so I suggested that he write me a note about it. Five hours later I found in my faculty box a four-page polemic, unpretentious, stimulating, organized, convincing. Here was a man who had taught freshman composition for several years and who was incapable of committing any of the more obvious errors that we think of as characteristic of bad writing. Yet he could not write a decent sentence, paragraph, or paper until his rhetorical problem was solved—until, that is, he had found a definition of his audience, his argument, and his own proper tone of voice.

The word "rhetoric" is one of those catch-all terms that can easily raise trouble when our backs are turned. As it regains a popularity that it once seemed permanently to have lost, its meanings seem to range all the way from something like "the whole art of writing on any subject," as in Kenneth Burke's *The Rhetoric of Religion,* through "the special arts of persuasion," on down to fairly narrow notions about rhetorical figures and devices. And

From *College Composition and Communication,* XIV (October, 1963), 139–45. Reprinted by permission of the National Council of Teachers of English and Wayne C. Booth.

of course we still have with us the meaning of "empty bombast," as in the phrase "merely rhetorical."

I suppose that the question of the role of rhetoric in the English course is meaningless if we think of rhetoric in either its broadest or its narrowest meanings. No English course could avoid dealing with rhetoric in Burke's sense, under whatever name, and on the other hand nobody would ever advocate anything so questionable as teaching "mere rhetoric." But if we settle on the following, traditional, definition, some real questions are raised: "Rhetoric is the art of finding and employing the most effective means of persuasion on any subject, considered independently of intellectual mastery of that subject." As the students say, "Prof. X knows his stuff but he doesn't know how to put it across." If rhetoric is thought of as the art of "putting it across," considered as quite distinct from mastering an "it" in the first place, we are immediately landed in a bramble bush of controversy. Is there such an art? If so, what does it consist of? Does it have a content of its own? Can it be taught? Should it be taught? If it should, how do we go about it, head on or obliquely?

Obviously it would be foolish to try to deal with many of these issues in twenty minutes. But I wish that there were more signs of our taking all of them seriously. I wish that along with our new passion for structural linguistics, for example, we could point to the development of a rhetorical theory that would show just how knowledge of structural linguistics can be useful to anyone interested in the art of persuasion. I wish there were more freshman texts that related every principle and every rule to functional principles of rhetoric, or, where this proves impossible, I wish one found more systematic discussion of why it is impossible. But for today, I must content myself with a brief look at the charge that there is nothing distinctive and teachable about the art of rhetoric.

The case against the isolability and teachability of rhetoric may look at first like a good one. Nobody writes rhetoric, just as nobody ever writes writing. What we write and speak is always *this* discussion of the decline of railroading and *that* discussion of Pope's couplets and the other argument for abolishing the poll-tax or for getting rhetoric back into English studies.

We can also admit that like all the arts, the art of rhetoric is at best very chancy, only partly amenable to systematic teaching; as we are all painfully aware when our 1:00 section goes miserably and our 2:00 section of the same course is a delight, our own rhetoric is not entirely under control. Successful rhetoricians are to some extent like poets, born, not made. They are also dependent on years of practice and experience. And we can finally admit that even the firmest of principles about writing cannot be taught in the same sense that elementary logic or arithmetic or French can be taught. In my first year of teaching, I had a student who started his first two essays with a swear word. When I suggested that perhaps the third paper ought to start with something else, he protested that his high school teacher had taught him always to catch the reader's attention. Now the teacher was right, but the application of even such a firm principle requires reserves of tact that were somewhat beyond my freshman.

But with all of the reservations made, surely the charge that the art of persuasion cannot in any sense be taught is baseless. I cannot think that anyone who has ever read Aristotle's *Rhetoric* or, say, Whately's *Elements of Rhetoric* could seriously make the charge. There is more than enough in these and the other traditional rhetorics to provide structure and content for a year-long course. I believe that such a course, when planned and carried through with intelligence and flexibility, can be one of the most important of all educational experiences. But it seems obvious that the arts of persuasion cannot be learned in one year, that a good teacher will continue to teach them regardless of his subject matter, and that we as English teachers have a special responsibility at all levels to get certain basic rhetorical principles into all of our writing assignments. When I think back over the experiences which have had any actual effect on my writing, I find the great good fortune of a splendid freshman course, taught by a man who believed in what he was doing, but I also find a collection of other experiences quite unconnected with a specific writing course. I remember the instructor in psychology who pencilled one word after a peculiarly pretentious paper of mine: *bull*. I remember the day when P. A. Christensen talked with me about my Chaucer paper, and made me understand that my failure to use effective transitions was not simply a technical fault but a fundamental block in my effort to get him to see my meaning. His off-the-cuff pronouncement that I should never let myself write a sentence that was not in some way explicitly attached to preceding and following sentences meant far more to me at that moment, when I had something I wanted to say, than it could have meant as part of a pattern of such rules offered in a writing course. Similarly, I can remember the devastating lessons about my bad writing that Ronald Crane could teach with a simple question mark on a graduate seminar paper, or a pencilled "Evidence for this?" or "Why this section here?" or "Everybody says so. Is it true?"

Such experiences are not, I like to think, simply the result of my being a late bloomer. At least I find my colleagues saying such things as "I didn't learn to write until I became a newspaper reporter," or "The most important training in writing I had was doing a dissertation under old *Blank*." Sometimes they go on to say that the freshman course was useless; sometimes they say that it was an indispensable preparation for the later experience. The diversity of such replies is so great as to suggest that before we try to reorganize the freshman course, with or without explicit confrontations with rhetorical categories, we ought to look for whatever there is in common among our experiences, both of good writing and of good writing instruction. Whatever we discover in such an enterprise ought to be useful to us at any level of our teaching. It will not, presumably, decide once and for all what should be the content of the freshman course, if there should be such a course. But it might serve as a guideline for the development of widely different programs in the widely differing institutional circumstances in which we must work.

The common ingredient that I find in all of the writing I admire—excluding for now novels, plays and poems—is something that I shall reluctantly call the rhetorical stance, a stance which depends on discovering and maintaining in any writing situation a proper balance among the three elements that are at work in any communicative effort: the available arguments about the subject itself, the interests and peculiarities of the audience, and the voice, the implied character, of the speaker. I should like to suggest that it is this balance, this rhetorical stance, difficult as it is to describe, that is our main goal as teachers of rhetoric. Our ideal graduate will strike this balance automatically in any writing that he considers finished. Though he may never come to the point of finding the balance easily, he will know that it is what makes the difference between effective communication and mere wasted effort.

What I mean by the true rhetorician's stance can perhaps best be seen by contrasting it with two or three corruptions, unbalanced stances often assumed by people who think they are practicing the arts of persuasion.

The first I'll call the pedant's stance; it consists of ignoring or underplaying the personal relationship of speaker and audience and depending entirely on statements about a subject—that is, the notion of a job to be done for a particular audience is left out. It is a virtue, of course, to respect the bare truth of one's subject, and there may even be some subjects which in their very nature define an audience and a rhetorical purpose so that adequacy to the subject can be the whole art of presentation. For example, an article on "The relation of the ontological and teleological proofs," in a recent *Journal of Religion,* requires a minimum of adaptation of argument to audience. But most subjects do not in themselves imply in any necessary way a purpose and an audience and hence a speaker's tone. The writer who assumes that it is enough merely to write an exposition of what he happens to know on the subject will produce the kind of essay that soils our scholarly journals, written not for readers but for bibliographies.

In my first year of teaching I taught a whole unit on "exposition" without ever suggesting, so far as I can remember, that the students ask themselves what their expositions were *for.* So they wrote expositions like this one—I've saved it, to teach me toleration, of my colleagues: the title is "Family relations in More's *Utopia*." "In this theme I would like to discuss some of the relationships with the family which Thomas More elaborates and sets forth in his book, *Utopia*. The first thing that I would like to discuss about family relations is that overpopulation, according to More, is a just cause of war." And so on. Can you hear that student sneering at me, in this opening? What he is saying is something like "you ask for a meaningless paper, I give you a meaningless paper." He knows that he has no audience except me. He knows that I don't want to read his summary of family relations in *Utopia*, and he knows that I know that he therefore has no rhetorical purpose. Because he has not been led to see a question which he considers worth answering, or an audience that could possibly care one way or the other, the paper is worse than no paper at all, even though it has no grammatical or spelling errors and is organized right down the line, one, two, three.

An extreme case, you may say. Most of us would never allow ourselves that kind of empty fencing? Perhaps. But if some carefree foundation is willing to finance a statistical study, I'm willing to wager a month's salary that we'd find at least half of the suggested topics in our freshman texts as pointless as mine was. And we'd find a good deal more than half of the discussions of grammar, punctuation, spelling, and style totally divorced from any notion that rhetorical purpose to some degree controls all such matters. We can offer objective descriptions of levels of usage from now until graduation, but unless the student discovers a desire to say something to somebody and learns to control his diction for a purpose, we've gained very little. I once gave an assignment asking students to describe the same classroom in three different statements, one for each level of usage. They were obedient, but the only ones who got anything from the assignment were those who intuitively imported the rhetorical instructions I had overlooked—such purposes as "Make fun of your scholarly surroundings by describing this classroom in extremely elevated style," or "Imagine a kid from the slums accidentally trapped in these surroundings and forced to write a description of this room." A little thought might have shown me how to give the whole assignment some human point, and therefore some educative value.

Just how confused we can allow ourselves to be about such matters is shown in a recent publication of the Educational Testing Service, called "Factors in Judgments of Writing Ability." In order to isolate those factors which affect differences in grading standards, ETS set six groups of readers —business men, writers and editors, lawyers, and teachers of English, social science and natural science—to reading the same batch of papers. Then ETS did a hundred-page "factor analysis" of the amount of agreement and disagreement, and of the elements which different kinds of graders emphasized. The authors of the report express a certain amount of shock at the discovery that the median correlation was only .31 and that 94 per cent of the papers received either 7, 8, or 9 of the 9 possible grades.

But what *could* they have expected? In the first place, the students were given no purpose and no audience when the essays were assigned. And then all these editors and business men and academics were asked to judge the papers in a complete vacuum, using only whatever intuitive standards they cared to use. I'm surprised that there was any correlation at all. Lacking instructions, some of the students undoubtedly wrote polemical essays, suitable for the popular press; others no doubt imagined an audience, say, of *Reader's Digest* readers, and others wrote with the English teachers as implied audience; an occasional student with real philosophical bent would no doubt do a careful analysis of the pros and cons of the case. This would be graded low, of course, by the magazine editors, even though they would have graded it high if asked to judge it as a speculative contribution to the analysis of the problem. Similarly, a creative student who has been getting A's for his personal essays will write an amusing colorful piece, failed by all the social scientists present, though they would have graded it high if asked to judge it for what it was. I find it shocking that tens of thousands of dollars and endless hours should have been spent by students, graders, and professional testers analyzing essays and grading results totally abstracted from any notion of purposeful human communication. Did nobody protest? One might as well assemble a group of citizens to judge students' capacity to throw balls, say, without telling the students or the graders whether altitude, speed, accuracy or form was to be judged. The judges would be drawn from football coaches, jai-alai experts, lawyers, and English teachers, and asked to apply whatever standards they intuitively apply to ball throwing. Then we could express astonishment that the judgments did not correlate very well, and we could do a factor analysis to discover, lo and behold, that some readers concentrated on altitude, some on speed, some on accuracy, some on form—and the English teachers were simply confused.

One effective way to combat the pedantic stance is to arrange for weekly confrontations of groups of students over their own papers. We have done far too little experimenting with arrangements for providing a genuine audience in this way. Short of such developments, it remains true that a good teacher can convince his students that he is a true audience, if his comments on the papers show that some sort of dialogue is taking place. As Jacques Barzun says in *Teacher in America,* students should be made to feel that unless they have said something to someone, they have failed; to bore the teacher is a worse form of failure than to anger him. From this point of view we can see that the charts of grading symbols that mar even the best freshman texts are not the innocent time savers that we pretend. Plausible as it may seem to arrange for more corrections with less time, they inevitably reduce the student's sense of purpose in writing. When he sees innumerable W13's and P19's in the margin, he cannot possibly feel that the art of persuasion is as important to his instructor as when he reads personal comments, however few.

This first perversion, then, springs from ignoring the audience or overreliance on the pure subject. The second, which might be called the advertiser's stance, comes from *under*valuing the subject and overvaluing pure effect: how to win friends and influence people.

Some of our best freshman texts—Sheridan Baker's *The Practical Stylist*, for example—allow themselves on occasion to suggest that to be controversial or argumentative, to stir up an audience is an end in itself. Sharpen the controversial edge, one of them says, and the clear implication is that one should do so even if the truth of the subject is honed off in the process. This perversion is probably in the long run a more serious threat in our society than the danger of ignoring the audience. In the time of audience-reaction meters and pre-tested plays and novels, it is not easy to convince students of the old Platonic truth that good persuasion is honest persuasion, or even of the old Aristotelian truth that the good rhetorician must be master of his subject, no matter how dishonest he may decide ultimately to be. Having told them that good writers always to some degree accommodate their arguments to the audience, it is hard to explain the difference between justified accommodation—say changing *point one* to the final position—and the kind of accommodation that fills our popular magazines, in which the very substance of what is said is accommodated to some preconception of what will sell. "The publication of *Eros* [magazine] represents a major breakthrough in the battle for the liberation of the human spirit."

At a dinner about a month ago I sat between the wife of a famous civil rights lawyer and an advertising consultant. "I saw the article on your book yesterday in the Daily News," she said, "but I didn't even finish it. The title of your book scared me off. Why did you ever choose such a terrible title? Nobody would buy a book with a title like that." The man on my right, whom I'll call Mr. Kinches, overhearing my feeble reply, plunged into a conversation with her, over my torn and bleeding corpse. "Now with my *last* book," he said, "I listed 20 possible titles and then tested them out on 400 businessmen. The one I chose was voted for by 90 per cent of the businessmen." "That's what I was just saying to Mr. Booth," she said. "A book title ought to grab you, and *rhetoric* is not going to grab anybody." "Right," he said. "My *last* book sold 50,000 copies already; I don't know how this one will do, but I polled 200 businessmen on the table of contents, and . . ."

At one point I did manage to ask him whether the title he chose really fit the book. "Not quite as well as one or two of the others," he admitted, "but that doesn't matter, you know. If the book is designed right, so that the first chapter pulls them in, and you *keep* 'em in, who's going to gripe about a little inaccuracy in the title?"

Well, rhetoric is the art of persuading, not the art seeming to persuade by giving everything away at the start. It presupposes that one has a purpose concerning a subject which itself cannot be fundamentally modified by the desire to persuade. If Edmund Burke had decided that he could win more votes in Parliament by choosing the other side—as he most certainly could have done—we would hardly hail this party-switch as a master stroke of rhetoric. If Churchill had offered the British "peace in our time," with some laughs thrown in, because opinion polls had shown that more Britishers were "grabbed" by these than by blood, sweat, and tears, we could hardly call his decision a sign of rhetorical skill.

One could easily discover other perversions of the rhetorician's balance— most obviously what might be called the entertainer's stance—the willingness to sacrifice substance to personality and charm. I admire Walker Gibson's efforts to startle us out of dry pedantry, but I know from experience that his exhortations to find and develop the speaker's voice can lead to empty color- fulness. A student once said to me, complaining about a colleague, "I soon learned that all I had to do to get an A was imitate Thurber."

But perhaps this is more than enough about the perversions of the rhetori- cal stance. Balance itself is always harder to describe than the clumsy poses that result when it is destroyed. But we all experience the balance whenever we find an author who succeeds in changing our minds. He can do so only if he knows more about the subject than we do, and if he then engages us in the process of thinking—and feeling—it through. What makes the rhetoric of Milton and Burke and Churchill great is that each presents us with the spectacle of a man passionately involved in thinking an important question through, in the company of an audience. Though each of them did every- thing in his power to make his point persuasive, including a pervasive use of the many emotional appeals that have been falsely scorned by many a freshman composition text, none would have allowed himself the advertiser's stance; none would have polled the audience in advance to discover which position would get the votes. Nor is the highly individual personality that springs out at us from their speeches and essays present for the sake of selling itself. The rhetorical balance among speakers, audience, and argu- ment is with all three men habitual, as we see if we look at their non- political writings. Burke's work on the Sublime and Beautiful is a relatively unimpassioned philosophical treatise, but one finds there again a delicate balance: though the implied author of this work is a far different person, far less obtrusive, far more objective, than the man who later cried *sursum corda* to the British Parliament, he permeates with his philosophical per- sonality his philosophical work. And though the signs of his awareness of his audience are far more subdued, they are still here: every effort is made to involve the *proper* audience, the audience of philosophical minds, in a fundamentally interesting inquiry, and to lead them through to the end. In short, because he was a man engaged with men in the effort to solve a human problem, one could never call what he wrote dull, however difficult or abstruse.

Now obviously the habit of seeking this balance is not the only thing we have to teach under the heading of rhetoric. But I think that everything worth teaching under that heading finds its justification finally in that balance. Much of what is now considered irrelevant or dull can, in fact, be brought to life when teachers and students know what they are seeking. Churchill reports that the most valuable training he ever received in rhetoric was in the diagraming of sentences. Think of it! Yet the diagraming of a sentence, regardless of the grammatical system, can be a live subject as soon as one asks not simply "How is this sentence put together," but rather "Why is it put together in this way?" or "Could the rhetorical balance and hence the desired persuasion be better achieved by writing it differently?"

As a nation we are reputed to write very badly. As a nation, I would say, we are more inclined to the perversions of rhetoric than to the rhetorical balance. Regardless of what we do about this or that course in the curriculum, our mandate would seem to be, then, to lead more of our students than we now do to care about and practice the true arts of persuasion.

FRANCIS CHRISTENSEN / *A Generative Rhetoric of the Sentence*

We do not have time in our classes to teach everything about the rhetoric of the sentence. I believe in "island hopping," concentrating on topics where we can produce results and leaving the rest, including the "comma splice" and the "run-on sentence," to die on the vine. The balanced sentence deserves some attention in discursive writing, and the enormous range of coordinate structures deserves a bit more. The rhythm of good modern prose comes about equally from the multiple-tracking of coordinate constructions and the downshifting and backtracking of free modifiers. But the first comes naturally; the other needs coaxing along.

This coaxing is the clue to the meaning of *generative* in my title. (It is not derived from generative grammar; I used it before I ever heard of Chomsky.) The teacher can use the idea of levels of structure to urge the student to add further levels to what he has already produced, so that the structure itself becomes an aid to discovery.

This system of analysis by levels is essentially an application of immediate constituent analysis. IC analysis reveals what goes with what. In such analysis the free modifiers are cut off first. The order in which initial, medial, and final elements are cut off is immaterial, but one might as well start at the beginning. Thus, in sentence 2, the first cut would take off the whole set of initial modifiers. Then the members of a coordinate set are separated and, if the dissection is to be carried out to the ultimate constituents, analyzed one by one in order. In sentence 1, the first cut would come at the end of the base clause, taking off levels 2, 3, and 4 together

From *Notes Toward a New Rhetoric*. New York: Harper & Row, 1967, pp. 1–22. Reprinted by permission of Harper & Row, Publishers and Francis Christensen.

since they are dependent on one another. Another cut would come at the end of level 2, taking off levels 3 and 4 together since 4 is a modifier of 3. Medial modifiers have to be cut *out* rather than *off*.

If the new grammar is to be brought to bear on composition, it must be brought to bear on the rhetoric of the sentence. We have a workable and teachable, if not a definitive, modern grammar; but we do not have, despite several titles, a modern rhetoric.

In composition courses we do not really teach our captive charges to write better—we merely *expect* them to. And we do not teach them how to write better because we do not know how to teach them to write better. And so we merely go through the motions. Our courses with their tear-out work books and four-pound anthologies are elaborate evasions of the real problem. They permit us to put in our time and do almost anything else we'd rather be doing instead of buckling down to the hard work of making a difference in the student's understanding and manipulation of language.

With hundreds of handbooks and rhetorics to draw from, I have never been able to work out a program for teaching the sentence as I find it in the work of contemporary writers. The chapters on the sentence all adduce the traditional rhetorical classification of sentences as loose, balanced, and periodic. But the term *loose* seems to be taken as a pejorative (it sounds immoral); our students, no Bacons or Johnsons, have little occasion for balanced sentences; and some of our worst perversions of style come from the attempt to teach them to write periodic sentences. The traditional grammatical classification of sentences is equally barren. Its use in teaching composition rests on a semantic confusion, equating complexity of structure with complexity of thought and vice versa. But very simple thoughts may call for very complex grammatical constructions. Any moron can say "I don't know who done it." And some of us might be puzzled to work out the grammar of "All I want is all there is," although any chit can think it and say it and act on it.

The chapters on the sentence all appear to assume that we think naturally in primer sentences, progress naturally to compound sentences, and must be taught to combine the primer sentences into complex sentences—and that complex sentences are the mark of maturity. We need a rhetoric of the sentence that will do more than combine the ideas of primer sentences. We need one that will *generate* ideas.

For the foundation of such a generative or productive rhetoric I take the statement from John Erskine, the originator of the Great Books courses, himself a novelist. In an essay "The Craft of Writing" (*Twentieth Century English,* Philosophical Library, 1946) he discusses a principle of the writer's craft which, though known he says to all practitioners, he has never seen discussed in print. The principle is this: "When you write, you make a point, not by subtracting as though you sharpened a pencil, but by adding." We have all been told that the formula for good writing is the concrete noun and the active verb. Yet Erskine says, "What you say is found not in the noun but in what you add to qualify the noun . . . The noun, the verb, and the main clause serve merely as the base on which meaning will rise . . . The modifier is the essential part of any sentence." The foundation, then, for a generative or productive rhetoric of the sentence is that composition is essentially a process of *addition*.

But speech is linear, moving in time, and writing moves in linear space, which is analogous to time. When you add a modifier, whether to the noun, the verb, or the main clause, you must add it either before the head or after it. If you add it before the head, the direction of modification can be indicated by an arrow pointing forward; if you add it after, by an arrow pointing backward. Thus we have the second principle of a generative rhetoric—the principle of *direction of modification* or *direction of movement*.

Within the clause there is not much scope for operating with this principle. The positions of the various sorts of close, or restrictive, modifiers are generally fixed and the modifiers are often obligatory—"The man who came to dinner remained till midnight." Often the only choice is whether to add modifiers. What I have seen of attempts to bring structural grammar to bear on composition usually boils down to the injunction to "load the patterns." Thus "pattern practice" sets students to accreting sentences like this: "The small boy on the red bicycle who lives with his happy parents on our shady street often coasts down the steep street until he comes to the city park." This will never do. It has no rhythm and hence no life; it is tone-deaf. It is the seed that will burgeon into gobbledegook. One of the hardest things in writing is to keep the noun clusters and verb clusters short.

It is with modifiers added to the clause—that is, with sentence modifiers—that the principle comes into full play. The typical sentence of modern English, the kind we can best spend our efforts trying to teach, is what we may call the *cumulative sentence*. The main clause, which may or may not have a sentence modifier before it, advances the discussion; but the additions move backward, as in this clause, to modify the statement of the main clause or more often to explicate or exemplify it, so that the sentence has a flowing and ebbing movement, advancing to a new position and then pausing to consolidate it, leaping and lingering as the popular ballad does. The first part of the preceding compound sentence has one addition, placed within it; the second part has 4 words in the main clause and 49 in the five additions placed after it.

The cumulative sentence is the opposite of the periodic sentence. It does not represent the idea as conceived, pondered over, reshaped, packaged, and delivered cold. It is dynamic rather than static, representing the mind thinking. The main clause ("the additions move backward" above) exhausts the mere fact of the idea; logically, there is nothing more to say. The additions stay with the same idea, probing its bearings and implications, exemplifying it or seeking an analogy or metaphor for it, or reducing it to details. Thus the mere form of the sentence generates ideas. It serves the needs of both the writer and the reader, the writer by compelling him to examine his thought, the reader by letting him into the writer's thought.

Addition and direction of movement are structural principles. They involve the grammatical character of the sentence. Before going on to other principles, I must say a word about the best grammar as the foundation for rhetoric. I cannot conceive any useful transactions between teacher and students unless they have in common a language for talking about sentences. The best grammar for the present purpose is the grammar that best displays the layers of structure of the English sentence. The best I have found in a textbook is the combination of immediate constituent and transformation grammar in Paul Roberts's *English Sentences.* Traditional grammar, whether over-simple as in the school tradition or over-complex as in the scholarly tradition, does not reveal the language as it operates; it leaves everything, to borrow a phrase from Wordsworth, "in disconnection dead and spiritless." *English Sentences* is oversimplified and it has gaps, but it displays admirably the structures that rhetoric must work with—primarily sentence modifiers, including nonrestrictive relative and subordinate clauses, but, far more important, the array of noun, verb, and adjective clusters. It is paradoxical that Professor Roberts, who has done so much to make the teaching of composition possible, should himself be one of those who think that it cannot be taught. Unlike Ulysses, he does not see any work for Telemachus to work.

Layers of structure, as I have said, is a grammatical concept. To bring in the dimension of meaning, we need a third principle—that of *levels of generality* or *levels of abstraction.* The main or base clause is likely to be stated in general or abstract or plural terms. With the main clause stated, the forward movement of the sentence stops, the writer shifts down to a lower level of generality or abstraction or to singular terms, and goes back over the same ground at this lower level.[1] There is no theoretical limit to the

---

[1] Cf. Leo Rockas "Abstract and Concrete Sentences," *CCC,* May, 1963. Rockas describes sentences as abstract or concrete, the abstract implying the concrete and vice versa. Readers and writers, he says, must have the knack of apprehending the concrete in the abstract and the abstract in the concrete. This is true and valuable. I am saying that within a single sentence the writer may present more than one level of generality, translating the abstract into the more concrete in added levels.

number of structural layers or levels, each [2] at a lower level of generality, any or all of them compounded, that a speaker or writer may use. For a speaker, listen to Lowell Thomas; for a writer, study William Faulkner. To a single independent clause he may append a page of additions, but usually all clear, all grammatical, once we have learned how to read him. Or, if you prefer, study Hemingway, the master of the simple sentence: "George was coming down in the telemark position, kneeling, one leg forward and bent, the other trailing, his sticks hanging like some insect's thin legs, kicking up puffs of snow, and finally the whole kneeling, trailing figure coming around in a beautiful right curve, crouching, the legs shot forward and back, the body leaning out against the swing, the sticks accenting the curve like points of light, all in a wild cloud of snow." Only from the standpoint of school grammar is this a simple sentence.

This brings me to the fourth, and last, principle, that of texture. *Texture* provides a descriptive or evaluative term. If a writer adds to few of his nouns or verbs or main clauses and adds little, the texture may be said to be thin. The style will be plain or bare. The writing of most of our students is thin—even threadbare. But if he adds frequently or much or both, then the texture may be said to be dense or rich. One of the marks of an effective style, especially in narrative, is variety in the texture, the texture varying with the change in pace, the variation in texture producing the change in pace. It is not true, as I have seen it asserted, that fast action calls for short sentences; the action is fast in the sentence by Hemingway above. In our classes, we have to work for greater density and variety in texture and greater concreteness and particularity in what is added.

I have been operating at a fairly high level of generality. Now I must downshift and go over the same points with examples. The most graphic way to exhibit the layers of structure is to indent the word groups of a sentence and to number the levels. The first three sentences illustrate the various positions of the added sentence modifiers—initial, medial, and final. The symbols mark the grammatical character of the additions: SC, subordinate clause; RC, relative clause; NC, noun cluster; VC, verb cluster; AC, adjective cluster; A + A, adjective series; Abs, absolute (i.e., a VC with a subject of its own); PP, prepositional phrase. The elements set off as on a lower level are marked as sentence modifiers by junctures or punctuation. The examples have been chosen to illustrate the range of constructions used in the lower levels; after the first few they are arranged by the number of levels. The examples could have been drawn from poetry as well as from prose. Those not attributed are by students.

[2] This statement is not quite tenable. Each helps to make the idea of the base clause more concrete or specific, but each is not more concrete or specific than the one immediately above it.

1

1 He dipped his hands in the bichloride solution and shook them,
  2 a quick shake, (NC)
    3 fingers down, (Abs)
      4 like the fingers of a pianist above the keys. (PP)

Sinclair Lewis

2

  2 Calico-coated, (AC)
  2 small-bodied, (AC)
    3 with delicate legs and pink faces in which their mismatched eyes
      rolled wild and subdued, (PP)
1 they huddled,
  2 gaudy motionless and alert, (A + A)
  2 wild as deer, (AC)
  2 deadly as rattlesnakes, (AC)
  2 quiet as doves. (AC)

William Faulkner

3

1 The bird's eye,/remained fixed upon him;
  2 bright and silly as a sequin (AC)
1 its little bones,/seemed swooning in his hand.
  2 wrapped . . . in a warm padding of feathers (VC)

Stella Benson

4

1 The jockeys sat bowed and relaxed,
  2 moving a little at the waist with the movement of their
  horses. (VC)

Katherine Anne Porter

5

1 The flame sidled up the match,
  2 driving a film of moisture and a thin strip of darker grey before
  it. (VC)

6

1 She came among them behind the man,
  2 gaunt in the gray shapeless garment and the sunbonnet, (AC)
  2 wearing stained canvas gymnasium shoes. (VC)

Faulkner

7

1 The Texan turned to the nearest gatepost and climbed to the top
  of it,
  2 his alternate thighs thick and bulging in the tight trousers, (Abs)
  2 the butt of the pistol catching and losing the sun in pearly
  gleams. (Abs)

Faulkner

8

1 He could sail for hours,
  2 searching the blanched grasses below him with his telescopic eyes, (VC)
  2 gaining height against the wind, (VC)
  2 descending in mile-long, gently declining swoops when he curved and rode back, (VC)
  2 never beating a wing. (VC)

Walter Van Tilburg Clark

9

1 They regarded me silently,
  2 Brother Jack with a smile that went no deeper than his lips, (Abs)
    3 his head cocked to one side, (Abs)
    3 studying me with his penetrating eyes; (VC)
  2 the other blank-faced, (Abs)
    3 looking out of eyes that were meant to reveal nothing and to stir profound uncertainty. (VC)

Ralph Ellison

10

1 He stood at the top of the stairs and watched me,
  2 I waiting for him to call me up, (Abs)
  2 he hesitating to come down, (Abs)
    3 his lips nervous with the suggestion of a smile, (Abs)
    3 mine asking whether the smile meant come, or go away. (Abs)

11

1 Joad's lips stretched tight over his long teeth for a moment, and
1 he licked his lips,
  2 like a dog, (PP)
    3 two licks, (NC)
      4 one in each direction from the middle. (NC)

Steinbeck

12

1 We all live in two realities:
  2 one of seeming fixity, (NC)
    3 with institutions, dogmas, rules of punctuation, and routines, (PP)
      4 the calendared and clockwise world of all but futile round on round; (NC) and
  2 one of whirling and flying electrons, dreams, and possibilities, (NC)
  3 behind the clock. (PP)

Sidney Cox

13

1 It was as though someone, somewhere, had touched a lever and shifted gears, and

1 the hospital was set for night running,
  2 smooth and silent, $(A + A)$
  2 its normal clatter and hum muffled, (Abs)
  2 the only sounds heard in the whitewalled room distant and un-
    real: (Abs)
     3 a low hum of voices from the nurses' desk, (NC)
      4 quickly stifled, (VC)
     3 the soft squish of rubber-soled shoes on the tiled corridor, (NC)
     3 starched white cloth rustling against itself, (NC) and, outside,
     3 the lonesome whine of wind in the country night (NC) and
     3 the Kansas dust beating against the windows. (NC)

14

1 The beach sounds are jazzy,
  2 percussion fixing the mode—(Abs)
     3 the surf cracking and booming in the distance, (Abs)
     3 a little nearer dropped bar-bells clanking, (Abs)
     3 steel gym rings,/ringing,/(Abs)
      4 flung together, (VC)
     3 palm fronds rustling above me, (Abs)
      4 like steel brushes washing over a snare drum, (PP)
     3 troupes of sandals splatting and shuffling on the sandy cement,
     (Abs)
      4 their beat varying, (Abs)
       5 syncopation emerging and disappearing with changing paces.
      (Abs)

15

1 A small Negro girl develops from the sheet of glare-frosted walk,
  2 walking barefooted, (VC)
     3 her bare legs striking and coiling from the hot cement, (Abs)
      4 her feet curling in, (Abs)
       5 only the outer edges touching. (Abs)

16

1 The swells moved rhythmically toward us,
  2 irregularly faceted, (VC)
  2 sparkling, (VC)
  2 growing taller and more powerful until the shining crest bursts,
  (VC)
     3 a transparent sheet of pale green water spilling over the
     top, (Abs)
      4 breaking into blue-white foam as it cascades down the front
      of the wave, (VC)
      4 piling up in a frothy mound that the diminishing wave pushes
      up against the pilings, (VC)
       5 with a swishsmash, (PP)

4 the foam drifting back, (Abs)
5 like a lace fan opened over the shimmering water as the
spent wave returns whispering to the sea. (PP)

The best starting point for a composition unit based on these four principles is with two-level narrative sentences, first with one second-level addition (sentences 4, 5), then with two or more parallel ones (6, 7, 8). Anyone sitting in his room with his eyes closed could write the main clause
of most of the examples; the discipline comes with the additions, provided
they are based at first on immediate observation, requiring the student to
phrase an exact observation in exact language. This can hardly fail to be
exciting to a class: it is life, with the variety and complexity of life; the
workbook exercise is death. The situation is ideal also for teaching diction—
abstract-concrete, general-specific, literal-metaphorical, denotative-connota-
tive. When the sentences begin to come out right, it is time to examine the
additions for their grammatical character. From then on the grammar
comes to the aid of the writing and the writing reinforces the grammar.
One can soon go on to multi-level narrative sentences (1, 9–11, 15, 16) and
then to brief narratives of three to six or seven sentences on actions with
a beginning, a middle, and an end that can be observed over and over
again—beating eggs, making a cut with a power saw, or following a record
changer's cycle or a wave's flow and ebb. (Bring the record changer to
class.) Description, by contrast, is static, picturing appearance rather than
behavior. The constructions to master are the noun and adjective clusters
and the absolute (13, 14). Then the descriptive noun cluster must be taught
to ride piggy-back on the narrative sentence, so that description and narration are interleaved: "In the morning we went out into a new world, a
glistening crystal and white world, each skeleton tree, each leafless bush,
even the heavy, drooping power lines sheathed in icy crystal." The next
step is to develop the sense for variety in texture and change in pace that
all good narrative demands.

In the next unit, the same four principles can be applied to the expository
paragraph. But this is a subject for another paper.

I want to anticipate two possible objections. One is that the sentences
are long. By freshman English standards they are long, but I could have
produced far longer ones from works freshmen are expected to read. Of
the sentences by students, most were written as finger exercises in the first
few weeks of the course. I try in narrative sentences to push to level after
level, not just two or three, but four, five, or six, even more, as far as the
students' powers of observation will take them. I want them to become
sentence acrobats, to dazzle by their syntactic dexterity. I'd rather have to

deal with hyperemia than anemia. I want to add my voice to that of James Coleman (*CCC*, December, 1962) deploring our concentration on the plain style.

The other objection is that my examples are mainly descriptive and narrative—and today in freshman English we teach only exposition. I deplore this limitation as much as I deplore our limitation to the plain style. Both are a sign that we have sold our proper heritage for a pot of message. In permitting them, the English department undercuts its own discipline. Even if our goal is only utilitarian prose, we can teach diction and sentence structure far more effectively through a few controlled exercises in description and narration than we can by starting right off with exposition (Theme One, 500 words, precipitates *all* the problems of writing). There is no problem of invention; the student has something to communicate—his immediate sense impressions, which can stand a bit of exercising. The material is not already verbalized—he has to match language to sense impressions. His acuteness in observation and in choice of words can be judged by fairly objective standards—is the sound of a bottle of milk being set down on a concrete step suggested better by *clink* or *clank* or *clunk?* In the examples, study the diction for its accuracy, rising at times to the truly imaginative. Study the use of metaphor, of comparison. This verbal virtuosity and syntactical ingenuity can be made to carry over into expository writing.

But this is still utilitarian. What I am proposing carries over of itself into the study of literature. It makes the student a better reader of literature. It helps him thread the syntactical mazes of much mature writing, and it gives him insight into that elusive thing we call style. Last year a student told of rereading a book by her favorite author, Willa Cather, and of realizing for the first time *why* she liked reading her: she could understand and appreciate the style. For some students, moreover, such writing makes life more interesting as well as giving them a way to share their interest with others. When they learn how to put concrete details into a sentence, they begin to look at life with more alertness. If it is liberal education we are concerned with, it is just possible that these things are more important than anything we can achieve when we set our sights on the plain style in expository prose.

I want to conclude with a historical note. My thesis in this paragraph is that modern prose like modern poetry has more in common with the seventeenth than with the eighteenth century and that we fail largely because we are operating from an eighteenth century base. The shift from the complex to the cumulative sentence is more profound than it seems. It goes deep in grammar, requiring a shift from the subordinate clause (the staple of our trade) to the cluster and the absolute (so little understood as to go almost unnoticed in our textbooks). And I have only lately come to see that this shift has historical implications. The cumulative sentence is the modern form of the loose sentence that characterized the anti-Ciceronian movement in the seventeenth century. This movement, according to Morris W. Croll,[3] began with Montaigne and Bacon and continued with such men as Donne, Browne, Taylor, Pascal. To Montaigne, its art was the art of being natural; to Pascal, its eloquence was the eloquence that mocks formal eloquence; to Bacon, it presented knowledge so that it could be examined, not so that it must be accepted.

But the Senecan amble was banished from England when "the direct sensuous apprehension of thought" (T. S. Eliot's words) gave way to Cartesian reason or intellect. The consequences of this shift in sensibility are well summarized by Croll:

> To this mode of thought we are to trace almost all the features of modern literary education and criticism, or at least of what we should have called modern a generation ago: the study of the precise meaning of words; the reference to dictionaries as literary authorities; the study of the sentence as a logical unit alone; the careful circumscription of its limits and gradual reduction of its length; . . .[4] the attempt to reduce grammar to an exact science; the idea that forms of speech are always either correct or incorrect; the complete subjection of the laws of motion and expression in style to the laws of logic and standardization—in short, the triumph, during two centuries, of grammatical over rhetorical ideas.

Here is a seven-point scale any teacher of composition can use to take stock. He can find whether he is based in the eighteenth century or in the twentieth and whether he is consistent—completely either an ancient or a modern—or is just a crazy mixed-up kid.

Postscript

I have asserted that "syntactical ingenuity" can best be developed in narrative-descriptive writing and that it can be made to carry over into dis-

[3] "The Baroque Style in Prose," *Studies in English Philology: A Miscellany in Honor of Frederick Klaeber* (1929), reprinted in *Style, Rhetoric, and Rhythm: Essays by Morris W. Croll* (1966) and A. M. Witherspoon and F. J. Warnke, *Seventeenth-Century Prose and Poetry,* 2nd ed. (1963). I have borrowed from Croll in my description of the cumulative sentence.

[4] The omitted item concerns punctuation and is not relevant here. In using this scale, note the phrase "what we should have called modern a generation ago" and remember that Croll was writing in 1929.

cursive writing. The count made for the article on sentence openers included all sentence modifiers—or free modifiers, as I prefer to call them. In the total number of free modifiers, the 2000 word samples were almost identical—1545 in the fiction and 1519 in the nonfiction, roughly one in three sentences out of four. But they differ in position:

Nonfiction   initial 575   medial 492   final 452
Fiction   initial 404   medial 329   final 812

And they differ in some of the grammatical kinds used in the final position:

Nonfiction   NC 123   VC 63   Abs 9
Fiction   NC 131   VC 218   Abs 108

Thus the differences are not in the structures used, only in the position and in the frequency of the various kinds of structures. It will be well to look at a few more sentences of discursive prose.

17

1 His [Hemingway's] characters,/wander through the ruins of Babel,/
   2 expatriates for the most part, (NC)
   2 smattering many tongues (VC) and
   2 speaking a demotic version of their own. (VC)

Harry Levin

18

1 From literal to figurative is one range that a word may take:
   2 from *foot* of a person to *foot* of a mountain, (PP)
      3 a substituted or metaphoric use. (NC)

1 From concrete to abstract is another range:
   2 from *foot* to *extremity*, (PP)
      3 stressing one of the abstract characteristics of foot, (VC)
         4 a contrast for which the terms *image* and *symbol* as distinguished from *concept* are also used. (NC)

Josephine Miles

19

   2 Going back to his [Hemingway's] work in 1944, (VC)
1 you perceive his kinship with a wholly different group of novelists,
   2 let us say with Poe and Hawthorne and Melville: (PP)
      3 the haunted and nocturnal writers, (NC)
      3 the men who dealt in images that were symbols of an inner world. (NC)

Malcolm Cowley

20

1 Even her style in it is transitional and momentous,

  2 a matter of echoing and reminiscing effects, and of little clarion notes of surprise and prophecy here and there; (NC)

   3 befitting that time of life which has been called the old age of youth and the youth of old age, (AC or VC)

   4 a time fraught with heartache and youthful tension. (NC)

Glenway Wescott, of Collette's *Break of Day*

21

  2 Aglow with splendor and consequence, (AC)

1 he [Sterne] rejoined his wife and daughter,

  2 whom he presently transferred to his new personage at Coxwold, (RC)

   3 an old and rambling house, (NC)

    4 full of irrregular, comfortable rooms, (AC)

    4 situated on the edge of the moors, (VC)

     5 in a neighborhood much healthier than the marshy lands of Sutton. (PP)

Peter Quennell

22

1 It is with the coming of man that a vast hole seems to open in nature,

  2 a vast black whirlpool spinning faster and faster, (NC)

   3 consuming flesh, stones, soil, minerals, (VC)

   3 sucking down the lightning, (VC)

   3 wrenching power from the atom, (VC)

    4 until the ancient sounds of nature are drowned out in the cacophony of something which is no longer nature, (SC)

     5 something instead which is loose and knocking at the world's heart, (NC)

     5 something demonic and no longer planned—(NC)

      6 escaped, it may be—(VC)

      6 spewed out of nature, (VC)

      6 contending in a final giant's game against its master. (VC)

Loren Eiseley

The structures used in prose are necessarily the structures used in poetry, necessarily because prose and poetry use the same language. Poets may take more liberties with the grammar than prose writers are likely to do; but their departures from the norm must all be understood by reference to the norm. Since poets, like the writers of narrative, work more by association than by logical connection, their sentences are likely to have similar structures. They seem to know the values of the cumulative sentence.

The first example here consists of the first two stanzas of "The Meadow Mouse"; the slashes mark the line ends. The other example constitutes the last four of the five stanzas of "The Motive for Metaphor." It shows well how structural analysis of the sentence reveals the tactics of a difficult poem.

23

1 In a shoebox stuffed in an old nylon stocking/Sleeps the baby mouse I found in the meadow,/
  2 Where he trembled and shook beneath a stick/Till I caught him up by the tail and brought him in,/ (RC)
    3 Cradled in my hand,/ (VC)
    3 a little quaker, (NC)
      4 the whole body of him trembling,/ (Abs)
    3 His absurd whiskers sticking out like a cartoon mouse,/ (Abs)
    3 His feet like small leaves,/ (Abs)
      4 Little lizard-feet,/ (NC)
      4 Whitish and spread wide when he tried to struggle away,/ (AC)
        5 Wriggling like a minuscule puppy. (VC)

1 Now he's eaten his three kinds of cheese and drunk from his bottle-cap watering trough—/
  2 So much he just lies in one corner,/ (AC)
    3 His tail curled under him, (Abs)
    3 his belly big/As his head, (Abs)
    3 His bat-like ears/Twitching, (Abs)
      4 tilting toward the least sound. (VC)

Theodore Roethke *

24

  2 In the same way, (PP)
1 you were happy in spring,
  2 with the half colors of quarter-things, (PP)
    3 the slightly brighter sky, (NC)
    3 the melting clouds, (NC)
    3 the single bird, (NC)
    3 the obscure moon—(NC)
      4 The obscure moon lighting an obscure world of things that would never be quite expressed, (NC)
        5 where you yourself were never quite yourself and did not want nor have to be, (RC)
          6 desiring the exhilarations of changes: (VC)

7 the motive for metaphor, (NC)
6 shrinking from the weight of primary noon, (VC)
7 the ABC of being, (NC)
7 the ruddy temper, (NC)
7 the hammer of red and blue, (NC)
7 the hard sound—(NC)
    8 steel against intimation—(NC)
7 the sharp flash, (NC)
7 the vital, arrogant, fatal, dominant X. (NC)

Wallace Stevens *

* "The Motive for Metaphor," copyright 1947 by Wallace Stevens. Reprinted from *The Collected Poems of Wallace Stevens* by permission of Alfred A. Knopf, Inc.

LINGUISTICS AND COMPOSITION

For well over a decade now, English teachers have been told by linguists, or by other English teachers interested in linguistics, that an objective study of the structure of the English language will help students improve their writing.[1] Some structuralists in the 1950's made extravagant claims for the efficacy of their variety of analysis. A study of the phonemic structure of English was held up as a useful aid in the teaching of spelling. Punctuation problems were to be solved by the study of suprasegmental phonemes—the degrees of stress, the levels of pitch, and the varieties of juncture. But the most far-reaching claims were made for the careful analysis and imitation of sentence patterns. Teachers began drilling their students to distinguish between a simple S V pattern and an S V O. Many young writers learned to produce an S LV PN or an S LV PA pattern on command.

Most authors of textbooks and journal articles for English teachers seemed to assume, however, that the so-called linguistic approach to writing would somehow work a kind of automatic magic on the compositional abilities of students. The teacher had only to teach the distinction between allophones and phonemes, or the niceties of immediate-constituent analysis (Does one start "cutting" from the left or the right of the head word?) to work an

---

[1] The brief description of the relationship between linguists and composition teachers that follows is necessarily personal. How the teacher views this complicated episode in our professional history will depend largely upon where he was during these years, what journals and books he was reading, and which meetings he was attending. Other versions of the story are certainly possible, but I trust that the broad outlines that I have sketched are generally accurate.

This article was written especially for this volume.

immediate improvement in the composition class. When it became increasingly obvious in the early 1960's that this improvement was not occurring, and that students who had memorized phonemic alphabets and drawn Chinese box diagrams were not writing better than they had before, many of the defenders of linguistics very quickly developed a new reason for keeping the structural study of language in the curriculum: language was, they argued, the carrier of our culture, one of the distinguishing traits of our humanity, and, as such, was worthy of study for its own sake. Indeed, the idea that linguistic analysis should be used only as a "tool" in the composition class was now discounted as trivial. Linguistics should take its place alongside such subjects as history, biology, and mathematics as a necessary component in a truly liberal education.[2]

To complicate the situation, just as what might be called "the failure of structural grammar in the composition class" was becoming evident and linguists were constructing new lines of defense, transformational grammar appeared with a rapidity and force that made the earlier coming of structuralism appear hesitant and timid by comparison. While many English teachers were still experimenting with what they considered the "new" grammar, along came the kernel sentence, the branching-tree diagram, and the rewrite rules to sweep away all but the most stubborn resistance.[3] It was at this point in time, faced with yet another, even stranger kind of grammar, that many composition teachers threw up their hands in despair and turned their thoughts elsewhere. Some, of course, had never "bought" linguistics in the first place. They had remained, and continue to remain, steadfast traditionalists with an unshakable faith in schoolroom grammar and its essential powers. Many others, however, who had struggled on their own or in night classes and summer workshops to learn structural grammar, simply had neither the energy nor the faith required to learn yet another variety of English grammar. They found laughable the contention made in all seriousness from the ivory towers of the nearby universities that they should achieve a command of *all* available systems of grammar. They found disheartening the fact that even transformational grammar did not signal an end to change. Just over the horizon loomed tagmemics,[4] and

---

[2] It should be pointed out that many linguists had always maintained this view. With a few obvious exceptions, the most extravagant claims and the quickest shifts of position were made, not by well-trained linguists, many of whom did not concern themselves with the teaching of English, but by the "converts" from the ranks of English teachers.

[3] Although the casual observer may think that transformational grammar has won the day, the reader should consult two recent, anti-Chomskyan books: Robert A. Hall, Jr., *An Essay on Language,* Philadelphia: Chilton Books, 1968; and Charles F. Hockett, *The State of the Art,* The Hague: Mouton, 1968.

[4] As this is being written, there is in press what I believe to be the first textbook on tagmemics advertised among English teachers: Walter A. Cook, S.J., *Introduction to Tagmemic Analysis,* New York: Holt, Rinehart and Winston, Inc. (forthcoming).

something called "stratificational grammar" was referred to in one popular textbook as the best of them all. And even the brave teacher who ignored all these hints of future developments and who concentrated his attention on studying transformational grammar found little comfort. Transformational grammar itself was changing rapidly. If, for instance, he began his study in the early 'sixties, he learned a great deal about kernel sentences. Within a few years, however, this term was to disappear and he was to be told that deep structure and surface structure were the really significant concepts. Furthermore, he was beginning to discover that those traditionalist colleagues, whom he had learned to revile in the 'fifties, were actually not so misguided after all. To those English teachers who had painfully discarded their traditional ideas under the tutelage of the structuralist, this transformationalist reinstatement of several traditional ideas (mentalism, the traditional parts of speech categories, etc.) was difficult to accept. It is little wonder that there are many teachers today who are discouraged, if not disgusted, by the whole affair.[5]

Most transformationalists, probably remembering the extravagant claims of structuralists in the 'fifties, are hesitant now to claim a close relationship between the study of their grammar and the improvement of writing. The claims that are being made, moreover, are treated with skepticism by the many teachers who feel they were misled once before. Their interests are shifting rapidly to other approaches to the teaching of composition, especially to rhetoric. It could be argued with some persuasiveness, I think, that the shift of interest among composition teachers to rhetoric, both classical and "new," is in part a direct result of their disillusionment with linguistics and their need to find another, less rapidly changing approach to the everyday problems of teaching writing.

The entire situation today can probably best be summarized by taking a glance at the make-up of a typical secondary school English department. In this department one will find a good many traditionalists who still see linguistics as a mere fad or as one more attempt to dehumanize their field of study. In addition, there will usually be a few hardy structuralists, who have rejected traditional grammar but who have not moved on to transformationalism. A few of the members will probably have been caught up in the recent excitement over rhetoric and will thus display little interest in any variety of grammar. Joining this disparate group will be new teachers, recent college graduates, some of whom will undoubtedly be enthusiastic, because of college course work, about transformational grammar. It requires only some such superficial survey to reveal why it is rare to find a

[5] The reader is reminded that I am speaking of the situation strictly from the point of view of the composition teacher. To the linguist, these are exciting times and he cannot be blamed because his work is causing confusion among English teachers.

secondary school English department whose members can sit down together and construct a sensible curriculum sequence for the teaching of writing.

Although there are no easy paths out of this wilderness of conflicting claims, divided loyalties, and, quite often, intellectual arrogance, I believe that some more satisfactory sense of the relationship between linguistics and teaching composition can be achieved. The first step is the recognition of certain simple but important errors that we have all made in discussing the problem. The major mistake, from the point of view of the composition teacher, is the equating of linguistics and grammar. Grammar is a *part* of linguistics, but to think of them as synonomous leads to serious misconceptions. Almost without exception, however, when the composition teacher says that he is using a "linguistic approach" in his classes, he means that he has been leading his students through one of the new grammars. And in spite of assertions to the contrary, many teachers have discovered that doing immediate-constituent analysis or constructing branching-tree diagrams will help a student's writing no more than the traditional exercises that asked the student to label the eight parts of speech and underline the subject once and the predicate twice. In other words, if "linguistic approach" means the substitution of one kind of mechanical exercise for another, the teacher is foolish to expect gratifying results when his students begin to write. Students may find the newer grammars exciting and revealing, as indeed they are, but this enthusiasm should not fool the teacher into thinking that writing improvement is taking place. The fact remains, no matter what the transformationalists say, that grammatical study is esentially a process of analysis, whereas writing is essentially a process of synthesis; and the ability to tear language apart, even in the most sophisticated manner, does not lead to the ability to put it together in the form of decent English prose.

If, therefore, the teaching of composition through a systematic study of grammar, be it old or new, is doomed to failure by the very nature of the two activities, must we then disregard entirely the idea that linguistics has some uses in the composition class? I think not. What we must do is to realize that linguistics is more than grammar, that it encompasses general theories and specific facts, not only about grammar but also about dialects both regional and social, about the history of the language, about the relationship between language and mind, and about a number of other areas that are in some ways far more relevant to the work of the composition teacher than is pure grammar. In addition, I would argue that we, as teachers of writing, need not teach all of these subjects systematically and thoroughly. Ideally, of course, such systematic and thorough study should be a part of the English curriculum of every secondary school, but this should be a separate segment of the curriculum, organized and taught for its own sake. In the past, unfortunately, whatever knowledge about language a student has gained has usually been a chaotic by-product of the composition class in which grammar, usage, a little rhetoric, and a number of other elements have been mixed together in a random and haphazard way. What we need to do, as composition teachers, is to draw forth from all the various areas of linguistics those theories, facts, and principles which are relevant to the composition process. It is these selected items which we should teach, not worrying about whether we are "covering" the subject or not. The composition class is not the place to teach systematic linguistics. If there are no provisions in the curriculum for such study, then they should be made, but to attempt to teach both composition and linguistics in a single class will lead only to superficiality in both.

The important question, then, is which linguistic theories, facts, and principles are important to the student writer. I would think that the most important of these would be the ones that free the student's mind from the misconceptions, prejudices, and fears about the language which have led to what someone has referred to as our national inferiority complex about language. All teachers are familiar with this phenomenon—indeed, they have contributed to it—but there has been little consideration among composition teachers about what can be done about it, possibly because few have realized what a significant effect this attitude has on the student's writing. We have always known the importance of the student's attitude toward the topic about which he is writing. Thus we try to choose or lead the student to choose topics that are interesting, "relevant," or of personal concern. We talk about such topics in class in order to stimulate the interest of the student and to generate ideas. What we have been ignoring, however, is the student's attitude toward the *language* he must use when he writes. I would argue that a great many students often write poorly, not because of the topic they are discussing, but because of their feelings of insecurity about language. We are all familiar with the so-called mental block which students profess to encounter when asked to write. This mental block may sometimes be caused by a lack of ideas—the usual explanation—but it is also, I am certain, sometimes caused by linguistic fear, a fear that can be overcome if the student learns something about the English language.

We have now constructed a specific reason for introducing linguistics into the composition class: to rid students of their fears and misconceptions about language and to liberate their thinking so that they can come to their writing assignments with a greater feeling of freedom and with a willingness to experiment. To "open" the student's mind about language is not difficult. Anyone who has taught a course in linguistics knows that one of the inevitable results of the course, if it is a good one, is that students begin thinking more freely and openly about language. But, as I have stressed before, there is no need for a complete course. The examination of a few principles and facts will do the job just as well. For example, the teacher can easily demonstrate the fact that language changes and that the English language is changing today. To do this he need not go into the details of Grimm's Law or the Great Vowel Shift. Simpler, less technical examples are possible. Rather than illustrating linguistic change by showing students an Old English version of "The Lord's Prayer," one of the usual textbook practices, but one which can be disconcerting to students because of the strangeness of the older form of the language, the teacher might more effectively begin by comparing passages of Early Modern English with passages of contemporary English. Because students are able to read and understand most sixteenth- and seventeenth-century writing, the differences between the language of these centuries and the language of the present century are all the more striking, especially after students have been taught to look for these differences. And certainly almost the entire range of linguistic change can be illustrated by using just these two varieties of our language: change in vocabulary, grammatical change, phonological change, and change in spelling. Some of the most interesting observations can be made about the rather large number of English words that have shifted their meaning but not their form. Even quite young students can understand and be fascinated by the fact that a common word such as *freedom* once meant something like our modern *generosity,* and that *enthusiasm* was at one time frequently used as a term of contempt. Any good book on the history of the English language will provide a large number of additional examples of this type of change.

The question should then be asked: "What do these facts of change mean to you as a writer?" They mean, of course, that the student is dealing with a flexible instrument rather than with a system forever fixed by rule. They mean that his tendency to have problems with "who" and "whom" is not the result of his ignorance, but an indication that these forms are in a state of transition. They mean that his failure to use a genitive form before a gerund is not a sign that he is incapable of writing well, but only that he is reacting to a shift in language patterning. The point here is not that he should ignore the distinctions mentioned, but that he should be made to realize that his difficulties are the results of the ever-present phenomenon of linguistic change and not the result of his personal deficiencies.

Another boost to the morale of students can be given by a discussion of the transformationalist concept of the distinction between *competence* and *performance.* If the composition teacher can convince students that they actually "know" their language in ways they are unaware of, this knowledge provides a helpful antidote to the usual critical and negative admonitions of English teachers. Such considerations cannot help but give a psychological and emotional lift to the discouraged young writer. (It would also be wise to discontinue talking about "teaching students how to write." They already *know* how to write; we merely attempt to improve their performance.)

A study, no matter how brief, of language variation, both social and regional, can do much toward opening the minds of students. Such considerations soon break through the barrier raised by the idea that there is one and only one "correct" form of the language, a form, according to most students, that only the teacher has mastered. A further liberating force in this area of linguistics is the concept that each person speaks and writes his own unique form of the language, a form referred to by linguists as the person's idiolect. Once the student realizes that he should not attempt to develop a style of writing that is exactly like that of other writers—once he realizes that this is an impossibility—then he will be less likely to scorn his own linguistic efforts merely because they do not conform in all ways to some ideal model which he or his teacher has set before him. I am afraid that for too long we have discouraged composition students by preaching individuality but teaching composition as if each student's writing should fit neatly into a single, proper mold.

Finally, the teacher can often effect a significant change in the student's feeling about language merely by introducing him to the simple fact that there is today no single grammatical description of English that claims the allegiance of all English teachers. It comes, indeed, as quite a shock to almost all young students that one can discuss, argue about, and disagree about grammar in the same way that one can discuss, argue about, and disagree about politics, religion, or education. Every attempt should be made to enable students to see grammar as a study susceptible of rational control and formulation rather than as a divinely ordained and permanently fixed system of absolute truths. A great amount of linguistic fear has been instilled in students by their being convinced that critical questions about grammar are not admissible in the English class. Once the atmosphere is cleared, however, and the student and teacher feel free to engage in the kinds of serious discussions of grammatical issues which professional students of language concern themselves with every day, then the student will begin thinking and feeling about his language in a less restricted way, a way that will enable the composition teacher to work more successfully with him as they engage in their mutual attempt to improve his writing.

This list of principles and facts which tend to free the student's thinking about his language could easily be extended, but each teacher must decide, on the basis of his own goals and the needs of his students, which linguistic ideas will best serve to rid his students of their misconceptions. I do not discount entirely, of course, the possibility that some students can learn to solve certain writing problems by studying linguistics in a more systematic and thorough way, but I think it is seldom necessary. There *is* a relationship, for instance, between punctuation and the phenomena of stress, pitch, and juncture, but I am not certain that many students profit from a detailed and systematic study of suprasegmental phonemes. There is a difference, also, between speech and writing—a fact that structuralists dwell upon at great length—but a good composition teacher should be able to demonstrate in a very few minutes why it is important for the writer to keep this fact in mind. He can easily and convincingly show that the writer must use means different from those used by the speaker in order to achieve the same effects. To do this, the teacher need not offer an entire unit on phonology and writing systems. Or, to turn to transformational grammar for a moment, a consideration of "embedding" might well lead some students to an awareness of one element of a mature prose style, but, once again, this feature of English structure can be introduced without a full consideration of the awesome panoply of transformational rules.

My point, then, is that although phonology and grammar (what many teachers consider linguistics) do provide insights which can be of practical value to the young writer and which can be introduced informally into the composition class, the help the student receives from studying phonological and grammatical details is trivial compared with the psychologically liberating effects of a study of selected general linguistic principles and facts concerning such subjects as language change, dialect differences, and the competence of native speakers. We should, I think, stop talking about a linguistic "approach" to writing and begin talking about a linguistic "prelude" to writing, for it is not in the actual teaching of composition that linguistics is primarily useful but in the preparation of the student's mind *before* he begins to write, a preparation that should open and free his mind about his language and the way it can be used. Preparation is not enough, of course. The student must soon turn to rhetoric, to literature, or to whatever kind of study his teacher feels will best serve the student's purposes and aid him in his quest for the ability to write more effectively. But this quest will be immeasurably easier, and probably more successful, if he comes to it with a mind not closed and timid, but venturesome and open.

RICHARD M. WEAVER / *Some Rhetorical Aspects of Grammatical Categories*

In an earlier part of this work we defined rhetoric as something which creates an informed appetition for the good. Such definition must recognize the rhetorical force of things existing outside the realm of speech; but since our concern is primarily with spoken rhetoric, which cannot be disengaged from certain patterns or regularities of language, we now turn our attention to the pressure of these formal patterns.

All students of language concede to it a certain public character. Insofar as it serves in communication, it is a publicly-agreed-upon thing; and when one passes the outer limits of the agreement, one abandons comprehensibility. Now rhetoric affects us primarily by setting forth images which inform and attract. Yet because this setting forth is accomplished through a public instrumentality, it is not free; it is tied more or less closely to the formalizations of usage. The more general and rigid of these formalizations we recognize as grammar, and we shall here speak of grammar as a system of forms of public speech. In the larger aspect, discourse is at once bound and free, and we are here interested to discover how the bound character affects our ability to teach and to persuade.

We soon realize that different ways of saying a thing denote different interests in saying it, or to take this in reverse as we do when we become conscious users of language, different interests in a matter will dictate different patterns of expression. Rhetoric in its practice is a matter of selection and arrangement, but conventional grammar imposes restraints upon both

From Richard M. Weaver, *The Ethics of Rhetoric*. Chicago: Henry Regnery Company, 1953, pp. 115–27. Reprinted by permission of the Henry Regnery Company.

of these. All this amounts to saying what every sensitive user of language has sometimes felt; namely, that language is not a purely passive instrument, but that, owing to this public acceptance, while you are doing something with it, it is doing something with you, or with your intention.[1] It does not exactly fight back; rather it has a set of postures and balances which somehow modify your thrusts and holds. The sentence form is certainly one of these. You pour into it your meaning, and it deflects, and molds into certain shapes. The user of language must know how this counterpressure can be turned to the advantage of his general purpose. The failure of those who are careless, or insensitive, to the rhetoric of grammar is that they allow the counter force to impede their design, whereas a perspicacious use of it will forward the design. One cannot, for example, employ just any modifier to stand for a substantive or just any substantive to express a quality, or change a stabilized pattern of arrangement without a change in net effect, although some of these changes register but faintly. But style shows through an accumulation of small particulars, and the artist in language may ponder a long while, as Conrad is said to have done, over whether to describe a character as "penniless" or "without a penny."

In this approach, then, we are regarding language as a standard objective reality, analyzable into categories which have inherent potentialities. A knowledge of these objective potentialities can prevent a loss of force through friction. The friction we refer to occurs whenever a given unit of the system of grammar is tending to say one thing while the semantic meaning and the general organization are tending to say another. A language has certain abilities or even inclinations which the wise user can draw into the service of his own rhetorical effort. Using a language may be compared to riding a horse; much of one's success depends upon an understanding of what it *can* and *will* do. Or to employ a different figure in illustration, there is a kind of use of language which goes against the grain as that grain is constituted by the categories, and there is a kind which facilitates the speaker's projection by going with it. Our task is an exploration of the congruence between well understood rhetorical objectives and the inherent character of major elements in modern English.

The problem of which category to begin with raises some questions. It is arguable that the rhetoric of any piece is dependent upon its total intention, and that consequently no single sentence can be appraised apart from the tendency of the whole discourse. Our position does not deny that, since we are assuming merely that within the greater effect there are lesser effects, cooperating well or ill. Having accepted that limitation, it seems

[1] To mention a simple example, the sarcasm uttered as a pleasantry sometimes leaves a wound because its formal signification is not entirely removed by the intonation of the user or by the speech situation.

permissible for us to begin with the largest unit of grammar, which is the sentence. We shall take up first the sentence as such and then discriminate between formal types of sentences.

Because a sentence form exists in most if not all languages, there is some ground to suppose that it reflects a necessary operation of the mind, and this means not simply of the mind as psychologically constituted but also as logically constrained.

It is evident that when the mind frames a sentence, it performs the basic intellectual operation of analysis and re-synthesis. In this complete operation the mind is taking two or more classes and uniting them at least to the extent at which they share in a formal unity. The unity itself, built up through many such associations, comes to have an existence all its own, as we shall see. It is the repeated congruence in experience or in the imagination of such classes as "sun-heat," "snow-cold," which establishes the pattern, but our point is that the pattern once established can become disciplinary in itself and compel us to look for meaning within the formal unity it imposes. So it is natural for us to perceive through a primitive analysis the compresence of sun and hot weather, and to combine these into the unity "the sun is hot"; but the articulation represented by this joining now becomes a thing in itself, which can be grasped before the meaning of its component parts is evident. Accordingly, although sentences are supposed to grow out of meanings, we can have sentences before meanings are apparent, and this is indeed the central point of our rhetoric of grammar. When we thus grasp the scope of the pattern before we interpret the meaning of the components, we are being affected by grammatical system.

I should like to put this principle to a supreme sort of test by using a few lines of highly modern verse. In Allen Tate's poem "The Subway" we find the following:

> I am become geometries, and glut
> Expansions like a blind astronomer
> Dazed, while the wordless heavens bulge and reel
> In the cold reverie of an idiot.

I do not propose to interpret this further than to say that the features present of word classification and word position cause us to look for meaning along certain lines. It seems highly probable that we shall have to exercise much imagination to fit our classes together with meaning as they are fitted by formal classification and sentence order ("I am become geometries"); yet it remains true that we take in the first line as a formal predication; and I do not think that this formal character could ever be separated entirely from the substance in an interpretation. Once we gain admission of that point with regard to a sentence, some rhetorical status for grammar has been definitely secured.

In total rhetorical effect the sentence seems to be peculiarly "the thing said," whereas all other elements are "the things named." And accordingly the right to utter a sentence is one of the very greatest liberties; and we are entitled to little wonder that freedom of utterance should be, in every society, one of the most contentious and ill-defined rights. The liberty to impose this formal unity is a liberty to handle the world, to remake it, if only a little, and to hand it to others in a shape which may influence their actions. It is interesting to speculate whether the Greeks did not, for this very reason, describe the man clever at speech as δεινός, an epithet meaning, in addition to "clever," "fearful" and "terrible." The sentence through its office of assertion is a force adding itself to the forces of the world, and therefore the man clever with his sentences—which is to say with his combinations—was regarded with that uneasiness which we feel in the presence of power. The changes wrought by sentences are changes in the world rather than in the physical earth, but it is to be remembered that changes in the world bring about changes in the earth. Thus this practice of yoking together classes of the world, of saying "Charles is King" or "My country is God's country" is a unique rhetorical fact which we have to take into account, although it stands somewhat prior to our main discussion.

As we turn now to the different formal types of sentences, we shall follow the traditional grammatical classification and discuss the rhetorical inclination of each in turn.

Through its form, the simple sentence tends to emphasize the discreteness of phenomena within the structural unity. To be more specific, its pattern of subject-verb-object or complement, without major competing elements, leaves our attention fixed upon the classes involved: "Charles is King." The effect remains when the simple sentence compounds its subject and predicate: "Peaches and cantaloupes grew in abundance"; "Men and boys hunted and fished." The single subject-predicate frame has the broad sense of listing or itemizing, and the list becomes what the sentence is about semantically.

Sentences of this kind are often the unconscious style of one who sees the world as a conglomerate of things, like the child; sometimes they are the conscious style of one who seeks to present certain things as eminent against a background of matter uniform or flat. One can imagine, for example, the simple sentence "He never worked" coming after a long and tedious recital which it is supposed to highlight. Or one can imagine the sentence "The world is round" leaping out of a context with which it contrasts in meaning, in brevity, or in sententiousness.

There is some descriptive value in saying that the simple sentence is the most "logical" type of sentence because, like the simple categorical proposition, it has this function of relating two classes. This fact, combined with its usual brevity and its structural simplicity, makes it a useful sentence for beginnings and endings (of important meaning-groups, not so much of formal introductions and conclusions). It is a sentence of unclouded perspective, so to speak. Nothing could be more beautifully anticipatory than Burke's "The proposition is peace."

At the very minimum, we can affirm that the simple sentence tends to throw subject and predicate classes into relief by the structure it presents them in; that the two-part categorical form of its copulation indicates a positive mood on the part of the user, and that its brevity often induces a generality of approach, which is an aid to perspicuous style. These opportunities are found out by the speaker or writer who senses the need for some synoptic or dramatic spot in his discourse. Thus when he selects the simple sentence, he is going "with the grain"; he is putting the objective form to work for him.

The complex sentence has a different potentiality. Whereas the simple sentence emphasizes through its form the co-existence of classes (and it must be already apparent that we regard "things existing or occurring" as a class where the predicate consists only of a verb), the complex sentence emphasizes a more complex relationship; that is to say, it reflects another kind of discriminating activity, which does not stop with seeing discrete classes as co-existing, but distinguishes them according to rank or value, or places them in an order of cause and effect. "Rome fell because valor declined" is the utterance of a reflective mind because the conjunction of parts depends on something ascertainable by the intellect but not by simple perception. This is evidence that the complex sentence does not appear until experience has undergone some refinement by the mind. Then, because it goes beyond simple observation and begins to perceive things like causal principle, or begins to grade things according to a standard of interest, it brings in the notion of dependence to supplement that of simple togetherness. And consequently the complex sentence will be found nearly always to express some sort of hierarchy, whether spatial, moral, or causal, with its subordinate members describing the lower orders. In simple-sentence style we would write: "Tragedy began in Greece. It is the highest form of literary art." There is no disputing that these sentences, in this sequence, could have a place in mature expression. But they do not have the same effect as "Tragedy, which is the highest form of literary art, began in Greece" or "Tragedy, which began in Greece, is the highest form of literary art." What has occurred is the critical process of subordination. The two ideas have been transferred from a conglomerate to an articulated unity, and the very fact of subordination makes inevitable the emergence of a focus of interest.

Is our passage about the highest form of literary art or about the cultural history of Greece? The form of the complex sentence makes it unnecessary to waste any words in explicit assertion of that. Here it is plain that grammatical form is capital upon which we can draw, provided that other necessities have been taken care of.

To see how a writer of consummate sensibility toward expression-forms proceeded, let us take a fairly typical sentence from Henry James:

> Merton Densher, who passed the best hours of each night at the office of his newspaper, had at times, during the day, a sense, or at least an appearance, of leisure, in accordance with which he was not infrequently to be met, in different parts of the town, at moments when men of business were hidden from the public eye.[2]

Leaving aside the phrases, which are employed by James in extension and refinement of the same effect, we see here three dependent clauses used to explain the contingencies of "Merton Densher had an appearance of leisure." These clauses have the function of surrounding the central statement in such a fashion that we have an intricate design of thought characterized by involution, or the emergence of one detail out of another. James' famous practice of using the dependent clause not only for qualification, but for the qualification of qualification, and in some cases for the qualification of qualification of qualification, indicates a persistent sorting out of experience expressive of the highly civilized mind. Perhaps the leading quality of the civilized mind is that it is sophisticated as to causes and effects (also as to other contiguities); and the complex sentence, required to give these a scrupulous ordering, is its natural vehicle.

At the same time the spatial form of ordering to which the complex sentence lends itself makes it a useful tool in scientific analysis, and one can find brilliant examples of it in the work of scientists who have been skillful in communication. When T. H. Huxley, for instance, explains a piece of anatomy, the complex sentence is the frame of explanation. In almost every sentence it will be observed that he is focussing interest upon one part while keeping its relationship—spatial or causal—clear with reference to surrounding parts. In Huxley's expository prose, therefore, one finds the dominant sentence type to consist of a main clause at the beginning followed by a series of dependent clauses which fill in these facts of relationship. We may follow the pattern of the sentences in his account of the protoplasm of the common nettle:

> Each stinging-needle tapers from a broad base to a slender summit, which, though rounded at the end, is of such microscopic fineness that

[2] *The Wings of the Dove* (Modern Library ed., New York, 1937), p. 53.

it readily penetrates, and breaks off in, the skin. The whole hair consists of a very delicate outer case of wood, closely applied to the inner surface of which is a layer of semi-fluid matter full of innumerable granules of extreme minuteness. This semi-fluid lining is protoplasm, which thus constitutes a kind of bag, full of limpid liquid, and roughly corresponding in form with the interior of the hair which it fills.[3]

This is, of course, the "loose" sentence of traditional rhetorical analysis, and it has no dramatic force; yet it is for this very reason adapted to the scientist's purpose.[4] The rhetorical adaptation shows in the accommodation of a little hierarchy of details.

This appears to be the sentence of a developed mentality also, because it is created through a patient, disciplined observation, and not through impression, as the simple sentence can be. To the infant's mind, as William James observed in a now famous passage, the world is a "buzzing, blooming confusion," and to the immature mind much older it often appears something done in broad, uniform strokes. But to the mind of a trained scientist it has to appear a cosmos—else, no science. So in Huxley the objective world is presented as a series of details, each of which has its own cluster of satellites in the form of minor clauses. This is the way the world has to be reported when our objective is maximum perception and minimum desire to obtrude or influence.

Henry James was explaining with a somewhat comparable interest a different kind of world, in which all sorts of human and non-material forces are at work, and he tried with extreme conscientiousness to measure them. In that process of quantification and qualification the complex sentence was often brought by him to an extraordinary height of ramification.

In summation, then, the complex sentence is the branching sentence, or the sentence with parts growing off other parts. Those who have used it most properly have performed a second act of analysis, in which the objects of perception, after being seen discretely, are put into a ranked structure. This type of sentence imposes the greatest demand upon the reader because it carries him farthest into the reality existing outside self. This point will take on importance as we turn to the compound sentence.

The structure of the compound sentence often reflects a simple artlessness —the uncritical pouring together of simple sentences, as in the speech of Huckleberry Finn. The child who is relating an adventure is likely to make it a flat recital of conjoined simple predications, because to him the important fact is that the things were, not that they can be read to signify this

[3] "On the Physical Basis of Life," *Lay Sermons, Addresses and Reviews* (New York, 1883), pp. 123–24.
[4] On this point it is pertinent to cite Huxley's remark in another lay sermon, "On the Study of Zoology" (*ibid.*, p. 110): "I have a strong impression that the better a discourse is, as an oration, the worse it is as a lecture."

or that. His even juxtapositions are therefore sometimes amusing, for now and then he will produce a coordination that unintentionally illuminates. This would, of course, be a result of lack of control over the rhetoric of grammar.

On the other hand, the compound sentence can be a very "mature" sentence when its structure conforms with a settled view of the world. The latter possibility will be seen as we think of the balance it presents. When a sentence consists of two main clauses we have two predications of similar structure bidding for our attention. Our first supposal is that this produces a sentence of unusual tension, with two equal parts (and of course sometimes more than two equal parts) in a sort of competition. Yet it appears on fuller acquaintance that this tension is a tension of stasis, and that the compound sentence has, in practice, been markedly favored by periods of repose like that of the eighteenth century. There is congeniality between its internal balance and a concept of the world as an equilibrium of forces. As a general rule, it appears that whereas the complex sentence favors the presentation of the world as a system of facts or as a dynamism, the compound sentence favors the presentation of it in a more or less philosophical picture. This world as a philosophical cosmos will have to be a sort of compensatory system. We know from other evidences that the eighteenth century loved to see things in balance; in fact, it required the idea of balance as a foundation for its institutions. Quite naturally then, since motives of this kind reach into expression-forms, this was the age of masters of the balanced sentence—Dryden, Johnson, Gibbon, and others, the *genre* of whose style derives largely from this practice of compounding. Often the balance which they achieved was more intricate than simple conjunction of main clauses because they balanced lesser elements too, but the informing impulse was the same. That impulse was the desire for counterpoise, which was one of the powerful motives of their culture.

In this pattern of balance, various elements are used in the offsettings. Thus when one attends closely to the meanings of the balanced parts, one finds these compounds recurring: an abstract statement is balanced (in a second independent clause) by a more concrete expression of the same thing; a fact is balanced by its causal explanation; a statement of positive mode is balanced by one of negative mode; a clause of praise is balanced by a clause of qualified censure; a description of one part is balanced by a description of a contrasting part, and so on through a good many conventional pairings. Now in these collocations cause and effect and other relationships are presented, yet the attempt seems not so much to explore reality as to clothe it in decent form. Culture is a delicate reconciliation of opposites, and consequently a man who sees the world through the eyes of a culture makes effort in this direction. We know that the world of eighteenth century culture was a rationalist world, and in a rationalist world everything must be "accounted for." The virtue of the compound sentence is that its second part gives "the other half," so to speak. As the pattern works out, every fact has its cause; every virtue is compensated for by a vice; every excursion into generality must be made up for by attention to concrete circumstances and vice versa. The perfection of this art form is found in Johnson and Gibbon, where such pairings occur with a frequency which has given rise to the phrase "the balanced style." When Gibbon, for example, writes of religion in the Age of the Antonines: "The superstition of the people was not embittered by any mixture of theological rancour; nor was it confined by the chains of any speculative system," [5] we have almost the feeling that the case of religion has been settled by this neat artifice of expression. This is a "just" view of affairs, which sees both sides and leaves a kind of balanced account. It looks somewhat subjective, or at least humanized; it gives us the gross world a little tidied up by thought. Often, moreover, this balance of structure together with the act of saying a thing equivocally—in the narrower etymological sense of that word—suggests the finality of art. This will be found true of many of the poetical passages of the King James Bible, although these come from an earlier date. "The heavens declare the glory of God; and the firmament sheweth his handiwork"; "Man cometh forth as a flower and is cut down; he fleeth also as a shadow and continueth not." By thus stating the matter in two ways, through balanced clauses, the sentence achieves a degree of formal completeness missing in sentences where the interest is in mere assertion. Generally speaking the balanced compound sentence, by the very contrivedness of its structure, suggests something formed above the welter of experience, and this form, as we have by now substantially said, transfers something of itself to the meaning. In declaring that the compound sentence may seem subjective, we are not saying that it is arbitrary, its correspondence being with the philosophical interpretation rather than with the factual reality. Thus if the complex sentence is about the world, the compound sentence is about our idea about the world, into which some notion of compensation forces itself. One notices that even Huxley, when he draws away from his simple expositions of fact and seeks play for his great powers of persuasion, begins to compound his sentences. On the whole, the compound sentence conveys that completeness and symmetry which the world *ought* to have, and which we manage to get, in some measure, into our most satisfactory explanations of it. It is most agreeable to those ages and those individuals who feel that they have come to terms with the world, and are masters in a domain. But understandably enough, in a world which has come to be centrifugal and infinite, as ours has become since the great revolutions, it tends to seem artificial and mechanical in its containment.

[5] *Decline and Fall of the Roman Empire* (Bury's ed., London, 1900), I, 28.

ROBERT R. POTTER / *Sentence Structure and Prose Quality:*
An Exploratory Study [1]

> *How should writing be taught?* . . . Should the writing exercises
> be closely linked to formal study of grammar . . . ?
> *What kind of knowledge should the student have about the structure*
> *of the English language, and how can such knowledge, at various levels,*
> *be used to improve his ability to write well?* . . . How much, if any,
> of such linguistic knowledge is appropriate for each grade level? [2]

No one concerned with English education needs to be reminded that these
questions, set forth by the "Basic Issues" conference nearly ten years ago,
are still very much with us today. While the nature of "linguistic grammar"
has changed in the intervening period, the relationship between grammatical knowledge and skill in composition has remained largely a matter
of conjecture. The purpose of this article is to survey some of the issues involved in the problem and to summarize the findings of a new study that
may indicate promising paths for future researchers. The study itself is
presented as an exploratory examination of the hypothesis that a significant
relationship exists between the general merit of tenth grade writing, as determined by English teachers, and certain aspects of sentence structure. The
present writer believes that the study may make a start in indicating which
aspects of sentence structure appear to warrant inclusion in the curriculum
on the basis of their possible effect on composition.

---

[1] A summary of a doctoral project report completed in 1966 under Professor Robert
L. Allen, Chairman of the Department of Languages and Literature, Teachers Col-
lege, Columbia University. The full text is available from University Microfilms, Ann
Arbor, Michigan, under the title *An Exploratory Study of the Relationship Between
Certain Aspects of Sentence Structure and the Overall Quality of Tenth Grade Writing.*
[2] "The Basic Issues in the Teaching of English," *Publications of the Modern Language
Association,* LXXIV (Sept., 1959), 1–12.

From *Research in Teaching English,* I (Spring, 1967), 17–28. Reprinted by permission
of the National Council of Teachers of English and Robert R. Potter.

The Present Situation

Today, the teacher who turns to professional literature for assistance on the grammar-composition problem quickly becomes aware that the field is a controversial one. Theories and panaceas abound, yet there is little agreement among the experts. From one school of educators, we hear that linguistic knowledge can be a great help to the fledgling writer.[3] From another, we hear that a resuscitated traditional grammar is the answer.[4] From still another, we hear that the best grammar, as far as writing is concerned, is the least grammar—the way to teach writing is to teach writing.[5]

The teacher who limits his reading to research studies finds himself equally confused. Investigations in the area are both limited and contradictory. Beyond the well-established fact that traditional grammar taught in isolation has little significant effect on composition,[6] we really know very little. For several reasons, studies purporting to show a positive relationship between knowledge of the new linguistic grammar and composition improvement must be examined with extreme caution:

1. Other studies devoted to the same end show no such positive relationship.[7]

2. With regard to control group conditions, the studies often seem to neglect the difference between *approaches to language study* and *the particular grammar used to describe the language*. Significant differences supposedly caused by the latter might easily be caused by the former. A competent study would take care to see that enthusiasm in teaching, new books,

[3] See, e.g., Verna L. Newsome, *Structural Grammar in the Classroom* (Oshkosh: Wisconsin Council of Teachers of English, 1962); or "Expansions and Transformations to Improve Sentences," *English Journal*, LV (1966), 327–35.

[4] See, e.g., D. M. Wolfe, "Grammar and Linguistics: a Contrast in Realities," *English Journal*, LIII (1964), 73–78, 110.

[5] See, e.g., P. G. Perrin, "Freshman Composition and the Tradition of Rhetoric," *Perspectives on English: essays to honor W. Wilbur Hatfield*, edited by R. C. Pooley (New York: Appleton-Century-Crofts, 1960), pp. 121–32.

[6] Among the most recent investigations of this sort are the Harris study, summarized in R. Braddock, R. Lloyd-Jones, and L. Schoer, *Research in Written Composition* (Champaign, Ill.: NCTE, 1963), pp. 70–83; and Ruth C. Baird, "A Survey of Errors in English Compositions," *Journal of Educational Research*, LVI (1963), 228–35. In their article on "Language, Grammar, and Composition," in *Encyclopedia of Educational Research*, edited by C. W. Harris (New York: Macmillan, 1960), J. R. Searles and G. R. Carlsen conclude that "there is no shred of evidence to substantiate the continued emphasis on grammar prevalent in most American classrooms" (p. 462).

[7] See, e.g., E. H. Schuster, "How Good Is the New Grammar?" *English Journal*, L (1961), 392–97; and the results of a three-year controlled experiment at the University of Illinois in Chicago as reported in A. Schiller, "The Coming Revolution in the Teaching of English," *Harper's Magazine*, CCXXIX (October, 1964), 92.

special materials, and inductive, exploratory, and exciting methods are common to both groups.

3. Several of the studies have extremely narrow definitions of "good writing." For instance, the Bateman-Zidonis study at Ohio State seems upon casual inspection to indicate that generative grammar can be a help in composition. But the careful reader notes that only the grammaticality and the complexity of the writing were taken into account. It remains to be shown that the experimental groups in this study actually produced more "good writing," all things considered.[8]

4. If composition improvement is used to justify instruction in grammar, the question goes beyond the relative effectiveness of grammars A, B, C, and D. Each of the grammars must also be tested against a proven "non-grammatical" method of composition instruction. In this connection, Ellen Frogner's important 1939 study deserves more attention than it has recently received. Frogner tested a good functional grammar approach to composition instruction against an approach that ignored grammatical terminology and concentrated on the grace and effectiveness of the communication of the writer's thoughts. She found that although the "grammar approach" produced some improvement, the "thought approach" taught students more skills in less time. Writing skills gained through the "thought approach" stayed with the students longer than did those gained through the "grammar approach."[9] Other studies such as that of Kraus[10] substantiate this general viewpoint.

Some Basic Assumptions

Many, perhaps most, of the persons who have been trying in recent years to make linguistic grammar a part of the secondary school curriculum have considered language to be a worthy subject of study in its own right— an issue outside the scope of this article. For obvious reasons, these persons have looked with hope upon the possibility that the ability to analyze—or to generate!—a sentence might have something to do with the ability to write a composition. But this belief in grammar as a means to something else has remained secondary to the belief in grammar as an end in itself. As a result, the grammar-composition issue has often been approached from the

---

[8] D. R. Bateman and F. J. Zidonis, *The Effect of a Study of Transformational Grammar on the Writing of Ninth and Tenth Graders* (Champaign, Ill.: NCTE, 1966).
[9] Ellen Frogner, "Grammar Approach versus Thought Approach in Teaching Sentence Structure," *English Journal*, XLVIII (1959), 518–26.
[10] Silvy A. Kraus, "A Comparison of Three Methods of Teaching Sentence Structure," *English Journal*, XLVI (1957), 275–81.

grammar side. Most of the studies have attempted to show that a knowledge of some form of grammar will have a generalized transfer to writing competence.

Looking at the grammar-composition issue from the *composition* side, we are forced, in many ways, to rethink the problems involved. And as we do, we discover a number of assumptions and principles that often remain unconsidered if the focus is placed on something other than composition improvement:

1. Instruction in grammar, the basic patterns and transformations of language, will have little effect on usage, the degree of propriety in different situations of a number of variant lexical forms.[11] Most linguists take precise pains with this distinction. Yet just how much of what composition teachers try to achieve can really be subsumed under *grammar?*

2. For good reason, linguistic science devotes most of its attention to the spoken tongue. Yet our *writing* is not merely a graphic record of "English as she is spoke"; it is also a particular kind of English with rules and conventions of its own. Writing is, in truth, a separate *dialect* of English, a dialect that the student must learn, consciously or not, if he aspires to write acceptable prose. Although linguists from Harold Whitehall to Robert B. Lees have used the word *dialect* in referring to Standard Written English,[12] the implications of this view for education have gone relatively unexplored.

3. If it is a new *dialect* that the student must acquire, we must know the precise differences between this dialect and the spoken dialect he brings to the classroom. Following the lead of John B. Carroll of Harvard, Ruby M. Kelley, the author of one important exploratory study in the area,[13] has used the term *normalization* to refer to the process of converting one's natural and instantaneous flow of words into the patterns of formal written English.

4. More particularly, we need to know exactly what processes of normalization seem to separate good writers from bad. What does the good writer do with the language that the poor writer fails to do? If we could quantify these differences in grammatical terms, we would have made a start in identifying the areas of grammar that might warrant inclusion in the cur-

---

[11] A classic study in this area is P. M. Symonds, "Practice versus Grammar in the Learning of Correct English Usage." *Journal of Experimental Psychology,* XXII (1931), 81–95.
[12] H. Whitehall, *Structural Essentials of English* (New York: Harcourt, Brace and World, 1951), pp. 1–2; R. B. Lees, "Some Neglected Aspects of Parsing," *Readings in Applied English Linguistics,* edited by H. B. Allen (2nd ed.; New York: Appleton-Century-Crofts, 1964), p. 147.
[13] Ruby M. Kelley, *A Study To Identify the Content of Linguistically Based Grammar Instruction of a Junior High School* (U.S. Office of Education, Cooperative Research Project No. 1826. Westport, Conn.: Westport Public Schools, 1962–1963).

riculum on the basis of their possible effect on composition. What grammar shall we teach then? That which demonstrably might do the student some good.

Description of the Study

The present writer recently carried out a study designed to explore some of the grammatical differences between good writing and bad. First, a hundred compositions of five hundred words each on the subject "The Qualities of a Good Teacher" were secured from average tenth grade classes. These classes were not designated "honors" or "slow," nor did they contain a preponderance of students having atypical ethnic backgrounds. The student writers came from five schools in a wide geographical area. High school sophomores were chosen because available research indicates that it is between the ninth and eleventh grades that writing really ceases to be "speech wrote down" and moves rapidly in the direction of the written dialect.[14] One can expect, therefore, that the prose of "good" and "poor" writers in an average sophomore class will disclose more features of successful normalization than will the prose of any other school group. The expository title, admittedly an odd one, offered all students the chance to write on a common subject. Moreover, it did not afford some students the fortuitous advantages given by many narrative titles.

Second, since the object of the study was grammar, not usage, all gross mechanical errors were corrected and the papers were uniformly typed. This was done because there is some indication that raters have trouble resisting the "halo effect" caused by good handwriting, mechanics and spelling.[15]

Third, the papers were submitted to four raters, experienced English teachers of different philosophies and backgrounds. The raters were asked to mark each paper "good," "average," or "poor." They were given no special instructions that might have led them to overemphasize sentence structure in making their decisions. The twenty best papers and the twenty worst papers were then submitted to two additional raters, who confirmed the original judgments with very few exceptions.

Finally, the investigator typed the individual sentences in the two groups of papers onto McBee Keysort cards, which were then coded and punched to indicate the presence or absence of certain grammatical features.

[14] Lou LaBrant, "A Study of Certain Language Developments of Children in Grades Four to Twelve, Inclusive," *Genetic Psychology Monographs*, 1933, *14*, 471; Ellen Frogner, "Problems of Sentence Structure in Pupils' Themes," *English Journal*, XXII (1933), 747–48.
[15] Braddock, Lloyd-Jones, and Schoer, pp. 14–15.

Findings and Conclusions [16]

The two groups of papers were examined first with regard to several established criteria that had been found by other studies to differentiate between "mature" and "immature" writing. These included Lou LaBrant's subordination index (the frequency of subordinate clauses expressed as a percentage of all clauses),[17] Kellogg W. Hunt's "minimal terminable unit" —or "T-unit"—length (the length of grammatically terminable sections of prose discourse, whether or not punctuated as sentences),[18] and sentence length.

The present study indicates that these criteria, developed through contrastive analysis of the writing of students at different ages, do not always retain their usefulness in cases where the *quality* of writing is made the differentiating feature. As one might have expected, the sentences in the good papers were generally longer than those in the poor papers, the former averaging 17.8 words, the latter 15.9. But it was not expected that the T-unit ratio between the two groups (figured on the basis of 16.0 and 14.2 words, respectively) would be exactly the same as the ratio for sentence length. In the Hunt study of the writing of average eighth and twelfth graders, sentence length differed significantly less than did T-unit length. Also, the present study found little usefulness in the time-honored subordination index, which was the same for both groups.

Looking further, we find that the poor writers used 645 T-units, the good writers 568. This indicates, of course, that the poor student writer tends to use more of his words in simple, basic sentence patterns, and correspondingly fewer in internal structures of modification. Moreover, the poor writers in this study more than doubled the good writers' use of T-units under six words in length, while the reverse situation obtained for T-units over thirty words. These findings support neither the familiar injunction to "write short, simple sentences" nor the view that many very short sentences should be mixed with longer ones.

The good writers in the study were much more proficient than the poor

[16] The results of the study, here summarized in the terminology of traditional grammar, were originally set forth in the vocabulary and conceptual framework of "sector analysis," a grammar of written English developed by R. L. Allen of Teachers College, Columbia University. A few important findings, the understanding of which demands a knowledge of sector analysis, are perforce omitted here. The interested reader is referred to the complete project report.

[17] The subordination index proved to be a very significant measurement of maturity in writing in LaBrant's classic study of a generation ago, cited above.

[18] The T-unit is a measurement developed in K. W. Hunt's study, *Grammatical Structures Written at Three Grade Levels* (Champaign, Ill.: NCTE, 1965).

TABLE I   Quantitative Data on "Good" and "Poor" Writing Examined

Item	"Good" Papers	"Poor" Papers
Mean sentence length in words	17.8	15.9
Mean T-unit length in words	16.0	14.2
Total number of T-units	568	645
T-units under six words in length	17	42
T-units over thirty words in length	30	18
Subordination index	.43	.43
Sentence patterns (in raw totals)		
Subject + Verb + Optional Adverbial	65	100
Subject + Verb + Object	216	330
(Passives)	42	21
Subject + Verb + Object + Complement	45	39
Subject + Linking Verb + Complement	208	193
Sentence openers		
Clauses		
Conditional	24	53
Temporal	14	18
Others	9	8
"Thought linking" transitional expressions	64	47
Percentage of T-units having openers	31	31
Prepositional phrases	799	684
Different prepositions used	46	40
Objects of prepositions		
Modified by phrase	100	59
Modified by clause	43	27
Modified by verbal	15	6
Clause as object	15	12
Verbal as object	33	21
Nominal clauses	124	149
Using Ø for "that"	25	54
Using "that"	52	41
Elliptical nominal clauses	10	3
Adverbial clauses	152	181
Introductory "if" clauses	30	60
Adjectival clauses	144	148
Using Ø for "which"	16	37
Using "which"	32	19
Relative in subject position	86	67
Relative in object position	38	44
Verbals		
Used as sentence openers	17	7
Used as subjects	13	2
Used as adjective modifiers	33	6
Used as post-noun modifiers	42	27

writers in the use of coordinating words and devices used to add T-units to grammatically complete sentences. The conjunctions *and* and *but* (about equally divided) accounted for 91% of the poor writers' multiple T-unit sentences, as compared to 67% for the good writers, who preferred *and* to *but* by a 3:2 ratio. The good writers made much more use of the conjunction *for* and the semicolon.

With regard to sentence patterns, the greatest difference between the two groups was found in the relative use made of the common subject-verb-object sentence. The fact that this type of sentence made up 47% of the total for the poor writers, but only 36% for the good, makes one wonder about the worth of the advice contained in many language texts to "write more S-V-O sentences." The data also cast doubt on the standard warning against the passive voice, since exactly twice as many passives appeared in the good papers as in the poor. Apparently, what many poor writers need is instruction in the judicious use of the passive voice, not warnings against a structure they seldom employ in any fashion. Also, the good writers were found to be more adept than the poor writers in the use of minor sentence patterns such as those containing object complements.

With regard to sentence openers, or words and constructions used before nominal structures functioning as sentence subjects, the *total* number was about the same for the two groups. The poor writers, however, used twice as many conditional clauses as the good writers used. On the other hand, the poor writers employed many fewer transitional expressions. Only in the use of *but, and, so,* and *for example* did the poor writers even approach the good writers, who excelled in the use of thirty-odd items, from *after all* to *thus.*

It was noted above that the good writer, with fewer T-units than the poor writer, uses more of his words in structures of modification. Prepositional phrases seem to account for a significant proportion of this difference in the percentage of words used as modifiers. The good papers contained 799 prepositional phrases, the poor papers 684. There was little difference, however, in either the use of the phrases or the prepositions employed. The only important difference concerned an area virtually ignored in the textbooks, the complexity of the objects. The good writers proved superior in modifying their objects with prepositional phrases, clauses, and verbal structures, as well as in using clauses and verbal structures themselves as objects.

Also mentioned above was the fact that the gross subordination index for the two groups of papers was about the same. It is to the particular uses of different kinds of clauses that we must look if we are to find meaningful differences.

Looking first at nominal clauses, we find that the poor writers used more than the good writers used (149 to 124). But this excess can be entirely explained by the poor writer's tendency to start his sentences with the terms *I guess, I think, I feel,* etc., throwing the remainder—and substance—of the sentence into clausal position. The good writers among the subjects of the study tended to use the optional *that* to introduce nominal clauses, while the poor writers tended to ignore this somewhat literary device. Also, the good writers used many more nominal clauses as postponed equivalents of "filler" subjects (e.g., "It's good *that you bought milk yesterday*").

The poor writers also used more adverbial clauses than the good writers used (181 to 152). But again, the difference can be explained by the use of one particular structure—this time, the introductory *if* clause. Leaving *if* clauses out of consideration, the totals were about the same. The good writers did, however, appear to have a greater command of the many clause-introducing conjunctions. *If, when,* and *because*—the "big three"—accounted for 57% of their clauses, as against 68% for the poor writers.

The number of adjectival clauses in the two groups of papers was about the same. Here again, the difference is to be noted in the clause-introducing words. What might be called the basic relative pronouns, *who, whom, which, when,* and *where,* accounted for 57% of the clauses in the good writing, but for only 37% in the poor writing. The poor writers tended to use the substitute word *that* or to leave the position vacant. Also, the poor writers were inept in the use of preposition-relative combinations such as *in which.*

The good papers contained more verbal structures of every type than did the poor papers. The really important differences, however, were found in the *use* of these structures. The good writers used twice as many verbal structures in pre-subject positions as the poor writers used. The good writers also greatly exceeded the poor writers in the use of verbals as subjects and as modifiers of adjectives.

Implications for the Future

Nothing in this study should be interpreted as proving that grammar can be a help in writing. No definite connection between grammar and writing has been established. Because the corpus had to be examined for so many syntactic relationships, it had to be held to a manageable size which was too small to permit a meaningful statistical analysis to be made. Moreover, even if the tentative results of this study were proven by a more thorough investigation to be statistically significant for the general student population, it still remains a possibility that sentence structure might best be taught through a classroom approach that employs the "thought approach" or habit training and ignores any kind of grammatical terminology or analysis.

Still, the data should be of interest to persons concerned with the improvement of composition, especially to those now designing research studies of greater depth. The above evidence indicates that measurable differences in sentence structure can be found between the "good" and "poor" writing of our average students. Because of the similarity in the two groups of papers of many gross measurements (the subordination index, for instance, as well as the sentence length/T-unit length ratio, was found to be exactly the same), it seems likely that future investigators will find more meaning in the way particular structures are used than they will find in gross totals. The data also indicate that some of the "grammar" the typical student now studies can have little effect on his writing, and that other grammatical areas which might make a difference in his composition go virtually unstudied. In some cases, the data contradict time-honored maxims of the language-composition texts. Certain favorite structures of the textbook writers, such as the absolute-phrase sentence modifier and the nominal clause subject, are rare even in the "good" writing of high school sophomores. Teaching the average student structures which have not been mastered by his more able peers seems rather premature, especially when there is so much else of more obvious value he needs to know.

Finally, the data indicate that the assumptions upon which this study is based—that written English is, in effect, a dialect of English, and that learning to write consists in part of acquiring this new dialect—may prove useful in future investigations of the relationship between grammar and writing. Until we know the difference between the grammar of writing and grammar of speech (or poor writing), our knowledge of what good writing is will remain incomplete. Until we know how these differences can be best learned by the student, our knowledge of teaching writing will remain incomplete. The research possibilities involved in this approach are varied indeed.

LITERATURE AND COMPOSITION

JOHN A. HART, ROBERT C. SLACK, AND NEAL WOODRUFF, JR. /

Literature in the Composition Course

The Freshman English course seems these days to have fallen victim to its past. Teachers of the course, when not sunk in baffled uncertainty, disagree vastly on what the entering freshman should be taught and how. Superficially, the uncertainty and disagreement are puzzling, for few teachers will dissent from the judgment that the freshman above all needs desperately to learn to write. He lacks grammatical sense; he has barely a nodding acquaintance with the fundamental decencies of writing; most appalling, he lacks ability to compose—to find workable subjects, to give them substance and form, to communicate them effectively to a reader. Plainly the aim of the freshman course should be to fill these abysmal gaps. But the bafflement arises over *how* to do it, and especially over how to confer some vitality on the process. For the course has been presided over from of old by that nemesis of Alexander Pope, the spectre of Dullness. The tradition has become almost immemorial that senior teachers avoid Freshman English like the plague and that the student does his best to sleep his way successfully through it.

It is easy to see how this state of affairs came to be. In the traditional course, the student purchased a reputable handbook to assist him with problems in grammar and furnish advice on how to organize and polish his compositions. He purchased also a thick anthology of readings, the staple of which was expository essays; these essays supposedly provided him

From *College Composition and Communication,* IX (December, 1958), 236–41. Reprinted by permission of the National Council of Teachers of English and John A. Hart, Robert C. Slack, and Neal Woodruff, Jr.

with models of good prose style and with ideas to write themes about. In the second semester, he reached the high-water mark of the course by reading a nineteenth-century novel of sterling reputation. But because the readings were chiefly expository essays, the course had two strikes against it from the start. For the college freshman was not prepared to deal with the capsulized, abstract statement of expository prose. When he had to write something related to the finished thought of a professional expository piece, he could go no further than acceptance or denial of the thought at the level of generalization. Nine times out of ten he could not support his generalizations in concrete terms because he simply did not know enough. For the student, most theme assignments meant the pursuit of a phantom which was to be brought back to the instructor in full dress. No wonder the instructor yawned as the student's effort grew ever more half-hearted.

Since World War II, experiments have been made in reorganizing Freshman English on a variety of principles, all by teachers bent on giving life to a dying course through new materials and new emphasis. The expository anthology has become a collection of pieces on issues presumably vital in the freshman's restricted world, pieces, it has been hoped, which would make a lively claim upon his personal experience. Or, the anthology has been replaced by a book of "cases" from history or current events, research materials concocted for student analysis and commentary. Emphasis has shifted to semantics and communications; or to logic, to "thinking before you write." Most recently, the teacher has been advised to reeducate his students in English grammar by using the findings of structural linguistics. Each of these expedients has its use and value, but none of them, used to organize the full course, gets it out of the doldrums. The teacher's initial excitement over a method may luckily prove infectious among his students for a time, but soon Dullness prevails again. He may grope for a final solution amongst this proliferation of gimmicks, but his reward is always a handful of dust.

One new development alone shows promise of giving sustained vitality to the course. Entering students, it has been rediscovered, are capable of being thrilled by literature—by *The Brothers Karamazov,* by *Oedipus Tyrannus,* even by *The Education of Henry Adams.* They are excited by such books; they discuss them with eager interest; they respond readily to writing assignments based upon them. And teachers seem equally delighted; their accounts of freshman courses in which such books are read glow with pleasure over the students' response. In consequence, many colleges have adopted a new plan by which major works of literature are read, discussed, and written about in the freshman year. Only one thing seems wrong: the freshman course has become a course in literature. One looks through descriptions of its different versions in vain for a statement of how and when composition is taught, and one concludes that it takes a secondary and slighted place. Thus in licking Dullness, teachers have substituted for one sort of course an entirely different sort. A new route has been found, but it seems to lead to a new destination.

We believe that this rich vein may be profitably worked, that the student's interest may be aroused and maintained, that the instructor may deal with material of which he feels confident—in short, that literature may be used—without deflecting the freshman course from its primary aim, the teaching of composition. In this belief, we have been experimenting over the past few years in our courses at Carnegie Institute of Technology.

In order to use literature effectively in the composition course, we have found, the teacher must observe three conditions. The first may be defined with deceptive ease, but it is perhaps the most difficult of the three for the teacher to follow: he must firmly resist the temptation to *teach* literature. He must avoid considering literary form, presenting biographical data, analyzing structure, and giving interpretation of meaning. He must set aside the natural impulse of the teacher of literature to elucidate, to fill in the background, and to make literary judgments. Further, he should not feel that he needs to teach literature in the interest of composition. It is easy for him to rationalize that he ought to discuss a work in some detail to prepare his students to write well about it in their papers; but even this seems an unwise and unnecessary diversion from the main business of a composition course. After carefully choosing the works of literature to be read by the class, the instructor should let these works make their own way and concentrate his teaching effort upon composition.

The second condition, following directly from the first, is that the literature chosen be the kind that the student can comprehend without elaborate help from his instructor or from class discussion. This means that works must have settings which are relatively close to the student in time, and that they must have a more or less realistic surface which enables him, despite unsophisticated reading habits, to enter immediately into the story. We have found too that comprehension is most likely to occur if each piece of reading is long enough for the student to become thoroughly familiar with a given fictional world. Consequently we have experimented with modern novels (or with novel-like presentations of factual experience, such as Hersey's *Hiroshima*) which are relatively clear and simple in style and in which major thematic concerns stand out plainly. Such books in both substance and idiom speak directly to the student and are most likely to build upon his previous reading experience.

The student is expected—and we find he is able—to comprehend the plain content of the literature. Each book is looked upon as a segment of real life which the student is privileged to see with special clarity, rather than as a structural art-product fashioned by the shaping mind of an author. The student is encouraged to deal with the imaginative world of a novel as a presentation of fact; the characters are assumed to be real people and their decisions thus become actual problems in human conduct. This simplifying emphasis on the mimetic aspect of literature no doubt does some violence to its true nature, but we find that it spares students a great deal of perplexity and that in the end it increases their capacity to read good literature with understanding.

One advantage that this deliberate policy has for the teaching of composition is that every student's writing is based on a definite and verifiable ground of reference—a fictional world which is open to examination. The student's perceptions of that world, as expressed in his writing, can be substantiated by the concrete "facts" of that world, "facts" available to every member of the class and to the teacher. Misreadings of that world can be quickly detected.

We should like to emphasize the importance of choosing works of some length. For our purposes a novel is more satisfactory than a short-story, or even a drama. The novel builds up its imaginary world with a richness of concrete detail, and it develops the problems and motivations of the characters at length. The student is thus supplied with a wealth of raw material. In staying with the world of the novel for a span of time, he becomes intimately familiar with it and the people in it. He *knows* what he is writing about. Furthermore, the nature of the novel is such that without literary instruction the student can and does become emotionally engaged with the characters and events of the story. Thus he not only knows what he is writing about; he *cares* about what he is saying. The subject matter of his composition thus contains a powerful motivating influence which is a bonanza for the teacher of writing.

No doubt there are many books which would produce the results we seek. Among those which we have used with success are *The Rise of Silas Lapham, The Late George Apley, The Moon and Sixpence, Hiroshima, Huckleberry Finn, The Catcher in the Rye, The Ox-Bow Incident, The Age of Innocence, The Great Gatsby,* and *All the King's Men.*

The two conditions which we have outlined—that the instructor remind himself constantly not to teach a literature course, and that the students be asked to read and write about works which immediately make sense to them—are effective only if a third condition is fulfilled. This is that the instructor plan writing assignments and class discussions with two closely related aims in mind: that every writing assignment call upon the student to examine a significant aspect of the novel being read; and that every writing assignment be directed toward a particular kind of compositional problem. These two aims are distinguishable, but they work hand in hand to sustain the student's interest in the subject matter of his writing and to provide material for pointed discussion of individual aspects of composition. Every assignment should shoot at both aims.

Because this third condition is more complex than either of the other two, we will spell it out with some specific examples based on our experience. We divide a novel into relatively short reading assignments. In addition to reading, the student is required for each class to write on a specified subject in the novel. For two days of the week, he writes only a paragraph or two, and for every third assignment—once a week—he writes a fully developed theme concerned with a larger portion of the reading. Every writing assignment calls for material which provides illustrations of whatever compositional problem the instructor wishes the class to focus upon.

If the work to be read is *Huckleberry Finn,* for example, and the instructor wishes the class to discuss different kinds of paragraphing, he will give questions about the reading which require different treatment, such as: "What is Huck's attitude toward conventional religion?" and "In the early chapters of the book, does the behavior of Huck or of Tom Sawyer seem more realistic?" The first question requires straightforward development of an idea; the second necessitates development by means of comparison.

Or if the compositional problem is to be the gathering of evidence, the instructor may ask: "What lies does Huck tell out of loyalty to Jim?" This requires students simply to search out the evidence necessary to establish an answer to the question. If the instructor then wishes to discuss the selection of significant evidence, he may ask: "What lies told by Huck are most important for protecting Jim?" If he wishes to emphasize the interpretation of significant evidence, he may ask the students to write a justification of Huck's lying. The answer to this question would undoubtedly be a full-length theme in which the student would have to consider what lying Huck does, what purpose it serves, and what would happen if Huck told the truth.

It ought to be said that this method may be used equally well in courses where emphasis is given to communication problems rather than problems in composition. For instance, the student may be required to write two answers to the same question—one for a person who has read the novel and the other for a person who has not. Later class discussion takes up the question of what material (and how much of it) will make each answer understandable to the person who reads it. Or, the student may be asked to write a statement for an opinionated reader: "For someone who dismisses *Huckleberry Finn* as a 'kid's book,' write a justification of Huck's lying." This subject opens up a moral issue which is anything but childish, and through it the student can convincingly demonstrate to his reader that this is a novel which deserves careful study. Sometimes the student can be asked to analyze a specific instance of communication which appears in the text of the novel, for instance: "Discuss the respective word skills of the Duke and the King"; or, "Consider Colonel Sherburn's communication to the mob and explain what makes it effective."

Thus, for a given novel, questions may be given to the student which will make him work out almost any problem in composition or communication that the instructor wishes to discuss.

The classroom hour itself focuses on discussion of students' current writing, a procedure which has a number of advantages. The class is dealing always with its own work and with its immediate writing problems. This work is based upon material in possession of each member of the class and verifiable at any time. Discussion can be fruitful and lively because the material itself is concrete and specific, and inherently interesting.

The classroom discussion is given direction by the writing assignment. Since each assignment makes a specific demand on the student, the class session usually turns out to be a collective effort to determine what demand the assignment is making and how best to satisfy it. The instructor guides this effort by asking the right questions, by resolving impasses, and by drawing together loose ends; his aim is always to aid the class in arriving at ideas about composition which it finds meaningful, useful, immediately applicable.

This daily routine may seem likely to diminish, if not destroy, the student's interest in the work of literature read and so defeat the original purpose of using literature. But this will not happen if the second aim of the instructor's planning is kept in mind: that he ask the student continually to examine significant aspects of the novels read. He can do this by building a kind of continuity in the questions given that will lead the students step by step toward the comprehension of some of the central issues or "meanings" in each book. The process may be illustrated by a series of questions based on *Huckleberry Finn*. The nine questions call for daily written answers; every third question demands a full-length theme.

1. What is Huck's attitude toward conventional religion?
2. In what ways does Huck exhibit ingenuity in escaping from his father?
3. Analyze with illustrations the quality and limitations of Huck's intelligence. (based on Chapters 1–12)

These questions attempt to make the student focus on some of Huck's character traits as they are developed in the first part of the novel.

4. Why does Huck play the trick on Jim and how does he feel about it afterwards?

5. What lies does Huck tell to save Jim and how does he feel about them afterwards?

6. Discuss the good and evil consequences of lying, using examples from *Huckleberry Finn*. (based on the novel through Chapter 29)

Questions 4–6 concern the moral strength Huck develops through examining the consequences of his own action rather than relying on conventional dicta.

7. Why is Huck in a dilemma over whether to protect Jim or turn him in to the authorities?

8. Does Huck reveal himself to be more or less intelligent than Tom Sawyer?

9. A superficial look at *Huckleberry Finn* might lead to the conclusion that it is about an ignorant boy who is trying to escape and dodge his responsibilities to society in order to be a loafer. Discuss the extent to which the opposite is actually true. (based on entire book)

The final group of questions highlights the thesis that Huck, endowed with native intelligence, grows through his experience to a maturity denied to Tom Sawyer and the other "conventional" characters. The ninth question requires the student to come to terms with Huck's discovery that gaining freedom entails the acceptance of responsibility.

The sequence of books read during a semester is likewise chosen with care so that they will cluster about some major theme-idea and will serve to reinforce or to contrast with one another. For example, one sequence which we have used successfully develops the theme of personal integrity. In this sequence the class reads in order *The Rise of Silas Lapham, The Late George Apley,* and *The Moon and Sixpence.* A few theme assignments, one given at the completion of each book, brings out the significant relationships.

1. In what sense is this the story of the rise of Silas Lapham?

2. In the light of the whole book, what does this statement of Apley's reveal about his character: "Nothing which is worth while is easy, nor in my experience is the actual doing of it particularly pleasant"?

3. What do you believe integrity is? Which comes closest to satisfying your definition—Lapham, Apley, or Strickland?

To recapitulate, our three conditions for success in using literature in the teaching of composition are these: that the instructor teach composition, not literature; that the literary works chosen be manageable by the student without scholarly or critical aid and afford him a lengthy soaking in an experience which holds his interest; and that the writing assignments based on literature challenge the student to find meaning in what he reads and pose a calculated variety of particular compositional problems. We readily confess that even if these conditions are observed, a class in Freshman English remains less exciting than an evening in the theater, less delightful than an afternoon at the beach. It will probably always be so. But we have found that the use of literature in accordance with these conditions puts life into the student's effort and inspirits the teacher's work. And this carries us a long way in the campaign to conquer Dullness.

EDWARD P. J. CORBETT / *A Composition Course Based upon Literature*

A composition course based upon literature is likely to produce a severe case of ambivalence in the teacher. The teacher is torn two ways: his natural interests and formal training dispose him to teach literature *as* literature; and yet the departmental syllabus dictates that he keep the primary emphasis on composition. If he takes his obligation at all seriously, he may find himself at the end of the semester flat on his back on a psychiatrist's couch, babbling of green fields. Other teachers, noting the seemingly irreconcilable conflict between their natural inclinations and the uncertain demands of the course, save themselves from the same fate by professing to teach composition but really embarking with their students on blithe excursions through the "realms of gold."

Maybe the wisest policy would be to divorce literature and composition and consign them to "separate maintenance." The composition course would have its own innings; the semester devoted to literature would become, pure and simple, an introduction-to-literature course. Students in the literature course would be called upon to write papers in response to their reading, and their papers would be annotated and graded by the teacher, but no classroom time would be spent discussing the papers or instructing the students in the principles of composition. This is the practice that prevails in upper-division literature courses in college. How many teachers can recall any of their undergraduate or graduate professors coming into a literature class some Monday morning after reading a set of papers and saying, "The writing in these papers was so abominable that we are

This article was written especially for this volume.

going to interrupt our excursion through the realms of gold and devote a couple of classes to reviewing the fundamentals of unified, coherent, lucid prose"? Why should the Freshman English instructor or the high-school English teacher be expected to do what his college mentor never did?

But where the syllabus specifies that the emphasis be kept on composition, the teacher who wants to deal with literature in the course has to face up to the problem of how to reconcile the conflicting demands. This paper will attempt to suggest ways in which literature and composition can be rendered compatible in the same course.

The key to resolving the difficulty is to conceive of the course as providing students with instruction and exercise in writing the same kind of expository and argumentative prose that is produced in regular composition courses. In the regular composition course, students rely for their matter on what they have learned from personal experience and formal education and for their models on the prose essays reprinted in anthologies of readings. In the literature-based composition class, students would still be writing the kind of expository and argumentative prose that they wrote in the regular composition course (i.e. "How the Schools Should Respond to Student Demonstrations"), but they would rely for their matter on what they had learned about life, about the world, about ideas and emotions from their reading of such mimetic modes of discourse as poems, plays, short stories, and novels. In order to write a paper on "Willy Loman's Failures as a Father," students would not have to operate as little literary critics, producing the kind of highly technical critical papers demanded of college-level English majors; they would have to respond to the literary text simply on a layman's level—on the same level that they would respond to an automobile accident that they had witnessed on the way home from school or to an account of the accident in the evening newspaper. Conceived of in this way, the course could be kept on target. And at the same time, students could have their valuable exposure to literature, and teachers could savor the delights of dealing with the kind of texts they feel most qualified to teach.

It remains now to spell out more particularly how the teacher could keep such a course on target.

If theme assignments are to be based on literature, considerable classroom time must be spent in analyzing and discussing literary texts. For one thing, we should not presume that our students know how to read literary texts. For another thing, the objectives of the course are not likely to be realized if the teacher simply asks the students to submit book reports on some literary text they have been assigned to read. Besides the doubtful value of book reports—even as evidence that students have read the assigned text—this practice reverts to the kind of writing assignments that are made in college-level literature courses, and the papers submitted are likely to be nothing more than plot summaries or effusions of personal reactions to a reading experience. The value of discussing in class the literary texts that will provide matter for subsequent theme assignments is, first of all, that students will be given some guidance in how to read literary texts and, secondly, that the discussions will generate ideas and suggest possible lines of development for the papers they will be asked to write.

The way in which the literary text is approached in class is also crucial if the course is to be kept on target. I would suggest that very early in the course the students should be led to see the similarities and differences between the expository/argumentative modes of discourse and the mimetic modes. As Marvin Bell points out in his article "Poetry and Freshman Composition" in *College Composition and Communication,* XV (February, 1964),[1]

> If poetry and composition are in some ways dissimilar, they are, in other ways, quite similar. Generally speaking, the student who studies poetry becomes aware that poetry is not, despite certain definitions and credos which imply so, a spontaneous outpouring of language. He learns that most, if not all, of the same techniques which go into the writing of a good poem are available and/or necessary to the writing of a decent composition. Indirectly, he concludes that some measure of art may reside in a composition, providing its author has become a good enough writer. (p. 1)

An obvious way in which expository/argumentative discourse and mimetic discourse are similar is that they both use words as their medium of expression, and for the most part they draw upon a common stock of lexical and syntactical resources. Although the mimetic modes of discourse occasionally make use of a special diction—the so-called "poetic diction"—and of unusual syntactical patterns—departures from regular word-order, especially in poetry and poetic drama—the differences in lexicon and syntax are largely differences of degree rather than of kind. We speak of poetry, for instance, as making *more* use of heightened language, of sensory diction, of images, of figures of speech, than prose discourse normally does. Students should be made aware of how a poet's skillful choice and disposi-

[1] This article and the Robert L. Eschbacher article mentioned later are conveniently reprinted in *Teaching Freshman Composition,* ed. Gary Tate and Edward P. J. Corbett (New York: Oxford University Press, 1967).

tion of words enable him to convey a thought or an emotion more succinctly, more precisely, more memorably than the writer of utilitarian prose does. And that lesson might encourage a student to employ some of the same devices, *when appropriate*, to enliven his own prose.

But the difference between mimetic discourse and non-fictional discourse does not consist solely in the language used. Even students who have not had much experience in reading literary texts sense the profound difference between a prose essay on the one hand and a short story or a novel or a play on the other. None of them, for instance, would put a book or an article about migrant workers into the same category with *The Grapes of Wrath*. Occasionally, the line of demarcation between expository prose and mimetic prose dims, as in the case of John Hersey's *Hiroshima* or Truman Capote's *In Cold Blood,* but even the most unsophisticated student would not mistake these two works for fiction, even though these works make heavy use of fictional techniques. Instinctively he recognizes that these works are not "imitations" but that they are records of historical events.

The difference between *In Cold Blood* and *The Turn of the Screw* lies fundamentally in the fact that the latter is an *imitation,* a fictive representation, of human actions, whereas the former is an artful exposition of historical personages and events. Noting that difference could lead to a consideration of the fascinating question of how *imitations* of human actions differ from *factual accounts* of human actions. This consideration would eventually lead to an investigation of the differences in *manner* and *end* between fictional and non-fictional discourse. A discussion of manner would consider such things as the use of dialogue, point of view, dramatized or narrated presentation, voice, tone, and the various methods of organizing the parts. A consideration of the end could lead to the detection of the essential difference between non-fictional discourse and fictional discourse, and we might arrive at Coleridge's distinction that the end of non-fictional discourse is *truth,* while the end of fictional discourse is primarily *pleasure.*

But wherever such discussions would end up, they would be valuable because they would make students aware of the various uses of language and because a consideration of the various uses of language has special relevance in a composition course based upon the reading of literature. An especially fruitful exercise, after such discussions, would be to take a single theme and show how it is variously treated in a prose article, in a poem, in a short story, and in a play. Following that exercise, it would not be unreasonable to ask the students to write a paper about the differences in effect that result from the treatment of the theme in a prose essay and in one or more of the literary genres. Such an investigation might teach our students more about the art of composition than anything we have done in the regular composition course.

The kind of approach to literature suggested above can keep the course on target because it is primarily concerned with composition—with how a literary text is composed, with the *rhetoric* of literary discourse. The fact that Aristotle wrote both a *Poetics* and a *Rhetoric* indicates that, in his mind at least, there was a real distinction between these two arts.[2] Students in a literature course are likely to be primarily interested in the *poetics* of the literary text; students in a composition course should be interested primarily in the *rhetoric* of the literary text.

Another way for me to help the teacher keep the course on target is to suggest typical and specific theme topics which will elicit from the students the kinds of expository or argumentative papers that, as I have pointed out above, are the desiderata in a course which purports to keep the emphasis on composition rather than on literature as literature. In general, the course will remain on target if the writing assignments result in expository or argumentative themes which rely on the literary texts for data, for evidence, for any kind of substantiation of a generalization or conclusion. But since teachers would undoubtedly welcome something more specific than this, let me suggest some theme assignments which would fulfill the primary objective of the course.

One of the articles that deal with the problem of how to use literature in a composition course and still keep the focus on composition is the article by John A. Hart, Robert C. Slack, and Neal Woodruff, Jr., "Literature in the Composition Course," *College Composition and Communication,* IX (December, 1958), 236–41. Teachers will find helpful the many specific theme-assignments that the authors propose in this article. I should like to repeat just one of the conditions that the authors of the article established for their literature-based composition course: "that the literary works chosen be manageable by the student without scholarly or critical aid." It is very easy for a teacher to forget that most of the students in his classes are not, and do not intend to be, English majors, that they lack the English teacher's expertise in literature, that they do not command the terminology and techniques for talking about the aesthetics of literature in any profound way. The teacher should certainly not expect his students to engage in the kind of historical, textual, genetic, structural, or mythopoetic criticism that he writes for the journals or that he may have written in his college English classes. But his students are capable of understanding and responding to

---

[2] See the Introduction to my *Rhetorical Analyses of Literary Works* (New York: Oxford University Press, 1969), in which I discuss the difference between poetics and rhetoric and between the rhetorical analysis of a literary text and other modes of critical analysis.

literature on an elementary level, and it is on that elementary, non-technical level that the writing assignments should engage the students.

To ask students to show how the image-clusters in *King Lear* help to reinforce the theme of natural vs. unnatural in the play is to engage them on a level of literary analysis for which they may not be prepared, either by temperament or by training. But to ask them to write on whether Lear's mistake in dividing his kingdom among his daughters is consistent with the character of Lear as it is revealed in the play is an assignment that the normally intelligent student who has closely read the play can perform. His assessment of the character of Lear—of any character, for that matter, that he meets with in fiction—is made on the same bases that he makes judgments about character in real life. In real life, he constantly makes judgments about people from what they say and how they say it, from what others say about them, from their actions, from their physical appearance. In fiction, authors characterize, and we make judgments about, the invented people from the same set of phenomena; but in fiction we have the further advantage of being able to assess character from the convention of the exposition of thoughts (in a drama like *King Lear,* this exposition of thoughts occurs in the convention of the soliloquy).

The point I am making is that a student could fulfill an assignment like the second one mentioned above with the skills he had acquired, not from any formal training he had received in a literature course but from his experience of living in the world. The test that the teacher should apply to any theme assignment in a composition course based upon the reading of literature is the simple question—can my students, with their present equipment, fulfill this assignment, can they develop this topic or thesis, without a lot of specialized knowledge about the techniques of creative literature, simply with the data that any normally intelligent person can glean from a careful reading of the text at hand and from his experience of living in the world?

What the student would have to do with the *King Lear* assignment would be, first, to determine, from a study of Lear's speech, actions, thoughts, and the testimony of others in the play, just what kind of person Lear is and, then, make a judgment about whether it is plausible that such a character would partition his kingdom in the way that he does at the beginning of the play. We should expect that some students would judge that action to be implausible and that others would judge it to be perfectly plausible, but that difference in judgment would be the result not of a different degree of expertise in literature but of differences perhaps in skill in reading or of differences in emphasis or personal values. As teachers of composition, we would assess the student's theme by the same general criteria we use in judging a theme he wrote in a regular composition class: how well does he organize, develop, support, and express the arguments he has chosen to substantiate his thesis?

It is difficult to find in literary anthologies used in the schools suggestions for theme topics which do not ask the student to engage in some kind of literary criticism. In the Study Questions and the Suggestions for Writing appended to the literary selections, the editors of such anthologies—even those anthologies that profess to be designed for composition courses— naturally fall back upon the kinds of questions and writing assignments that they were subjected to in their college literature courses. One anthology, however, that frequently suggests the kind of writing assignments I have in mind is the Martin Steinmann and Gerald Willen, *Literature for Writing,* Second Edition (Belmont, California: Wadsworth Publishing Co., 1967).[3] For example, one of the assignments calls for a theme of comparison analyzing the attitudes toward love of four characters who appeared in stories reprinted in the collection—Hawthorne's "Young Goodman Brown," Porter's "Flowering Judas," Lawrence's "Rocking-Horse Winner," and Faulkner's "Barn Burning." The editors suggest that the boy in "Barn Burning" serve as the focal character for the study, and then they point out how crucial to the success of this theme is the formulation of a suitable thesis statement:

> If, for example, your thesis is "The boy in 'Barn Burning' has mixed feelings toward his father," you will be unable to develop a meaningful comparison. If your thesis is "The boy's ambivalence toward love in 'Barn Burning' is an ambivalence shared by at least three other characters in modern short stories," you will be able to develop the necessary comparison, but your theme will still run the risk of being four separate essays; the thesis is more descriptive than it is analytical. A thesis such as "Many works of fiction are concerned, for various reasons, with the failure of love as a guiding force in the modern world" is much more acceptable, for you can then develop meaningful comparisons within a unifying framework. The "various reasons," for example, will have to be explained in detail, with illustrations drawn from the lives of the characters you will be discussing; you will be able to use "Barn Burning" as typical of "Many works of fiction" and the boy as the center of your discussion. And from the boy you should find it easy

---

[3] Although it is difficult to find textbooks that suggest the kind of writings assignments I am advocating, I call attention to Chapter 8 of *Teaching a Literature-Centured English Program* (New York: Random House, 1967), pp. 173–202, in which the authors, James Knapton and Bertrand Evans, suggest dozens of suitable writing assignments based on the reading of novels, plays, poems, short stories, and literary essays.

to get into comparative analyses of the other characters without giving the impression that you have dragged them in merely to fulfill an assignment. (pp. 201-2)

Besides urging the student to formulate for himself a workable thesis statement before even beginning to write—always an advisable practice in the composition process—the editors here suggest ways in which the student might develop his paper and ways in which the texts might be resorted to for supporting and illustrative material. To fulfill the assignment, the student does not have to know a great deal about fictional techniques; he just has to be a good enough reader to be able to abstract from the mimetic presentations what he needs to develop his comparison of the various attitudes toward love. The student who is not yet a good enough reader to be able to do that much is certainly not ready to do what a good many English teachers demand of him—namely, to write an analysis of the poetics of the work. And yet many teachers have no hesitation about asking a student to indulge in highly technical explications of literary works before the student has learned how to read a literary work on the most elementary level.

In a composition course based upon the reading of literary texts, there is no reason why students cannot resort to the same "topics" (in the classical sense) or lines of development that they were taught to use in their expository and argumentative themes in the regular composition course—definition, classification and division, comparison and contrast, cause and effect, example. Robert L. Eschbacher, in his article *"Lord Jim,* Classical Rhetoric, and the Freshman Dilemma," from *College English,* XXV (October, 1963), 22-25, shows how he set up a series of writing assignments on Conrad's novel that exercised his students in all of these methods of development. Here are examples of the kind of assignments he believes can exercise students in the cause-and-effect principle or, as he calls it, process:

> Process, that baggiest of the rhetorical techniques, is often unwittingly embraced by even the baggiest of instructors. The application of this cause-and-effect principle is virtually unlimited in *Lord Jim,* and can rein the most capricious hobby horse. I would seriously consider for essays the processes underlying questions such as these: How does the careful reader come gradually to the discovery that the *Patna* did not go down? How does Marlow manipulate the reader's sympathies in Jim's favor? How does Conrad make anecdotal material relevant to plot and theme? How does Marlow attempt to resolve his own doubts about Jim as he is telling the story? How does Jim err, perhaps, in managing his Patusan career *before* Gentleman Brown arrives? How does Conrad gradually show the perceptive reader that he does not necessarily share Marlow's views? (p. 24)

The study of language is generally acknowledged as belonging to the province of English teachers. Are there some theme assignments on the uses of language in literary texts that teachers could legitimately impose on students who have not yet been exposed to formal courses in the history and structure of their native language? I think that it would not be unreasonable to ask a high-school student to write a paper, for instance, about Holden Caulfield's patois in *The Catcher in the Rye*. The assignment might be posed in this way: Does Holden Caulfield speak like a typical teenager? In preparing to answer that question, the student would have to engage in an inductive study of Holden's diction and speech patterns so that he could present specific examples of Holden's patois. He would not have to be unusually perceptive to discover certain mannerisms in Holden's style of expression—his constant but rather innocuous use of profanity to punctuate his speech, his frequent repetition of pet expressions like "phony" and "I really do," his peculiar mixture of slang and formal language, his inclination to hyperbole. Having collected that kind of data, the student could then start collecting examples of teenage language as he hears it all about him every day. Then having established some norm of "typical teenage speech," he would then have to make some comparisons of Holden's language and the norm and finally make some judgment about the authenticity of Holden's language. One would hope that the student would be shrewd enough to see that changes in particular instances of teenage slang do not necessarily indicate that styles of expression have changed. One generation's "neat" is merely another generation's "cool" or "tough."

After students had been exposed to a variety of English and American poems, it would not be unreasonable to ask them to indulge in some elementary stylistic analyses. Such an assignment might be posed, for instance, in a thesis sentence like this: "The language in contemporary poetry is notably more colloquial, both in diction and syntax, than the language of nineteenth-century poetry." Or if that is too much to bite off, the students might be asked to write a comparative essay on the use of colloquial language in just two poems, one from the nineteenth century, the other from the twentieth century—e.g. Browning's "Soliloquy of the Spanish Cloister" and Housman's "Terence, This is Stupid Stuff." The thesis sentence obviously calls for a definition of the term *colloquial* and invites proof by the citation of examples from the poems studied. Such an assignment, however, requires a preliminary investigation in one or two classroom sessions of colloquial diction and patterns and the establishment of some criteria for deciding the question of degree ("more colloquial"). It might be helpful also to provide the students with pertinent quotations from Wordsworth's *Preface to the Lyrical Ballads* and Coleridge's *Biographia Literaria* about the revolution these two poets hoped to foster by writing poems in "the language really used by men."

What about the appropriateness of explications of literary texts as theme assignments in a composition course? Such writing belongs primarily to the literature course or to the college-level course in practical criticism. But because explications are essentially exercises in expository/argumentative writing, they would qualify, under the terms of my previous recommendation, as suitable theme assignments in a composition course based upon the reading of literature. Since such assignments, however, bear the earmarks of the kind of assignments that are commonly made in a literature or criticism course, I would urge a number of cautions: (1) that teachers not require of their students those highly technical analyses that can be legitimately required of English majors in college; (2) that teachers certainly not demand the kind of exhaustive analysis that is involved in an *explication de texte;* (3) that such assignments be delayed until late in the term; (4) that such assignments not be made until there has been ample demonstration of the technique in the classroom. But if high-school teachers were to press me for what I really think about such assignments, I would discourage them from assigning explications.

My recommendations and suggestions may have created the impression that I am "anti-literature." I certainly am not. I delight as much as the next teacher in the opportunity to teach literature, and in a composition course based upon the reading of literature, I am as much inclined as other English teachers to neglect the teaching of composition and concentrate on the reading of literature for its own sake. But I still have enough of a professional conscience to recognize that if I am commissioned to teach composition, I should teach composition and not something else. The dilemma for us all can be finally resolved by the simple formula—if the primary obligation is to teach composition, then teach composition primarily. We should resist with all the fortitude at our command the temptation to use writing assignments as a mere subterfuge for teaching what we may be most competent and disposed to teach. If we can keep the emphasis where it belongs and can somehow make everything we do in class have some bearing upon the improvement of our students' skill in written composition, we may get from our students in the literature-based composition course the liveliest, the most thoughtful, the most coherent writing that they have ever produced for us. And that is a consummation devoutly to be wished.

ASSIGNMENTS

RICHARD L. LARSON / *Teaching Before We Judge: Planning Assignments in Composition*

Many published discussions of the teaching of composition today still focus on the grading of themes as if it were the central activity in all instruction about writing. The young teacher of composition has at his disposal an abundance of articles, pamphlets, and books that seek to help him in the handling of his students' themes. If he wants to test his grading standards against those of his professional peers, he can find published collections of graded themes written by students in the grade he teaches, in which the basis for the editor's grade on each theme is carefully set forth. If he wishes guidance in writing comments on his students' papers, he can turn to published compilations of themes fully annotated with marginal and general comments. Often the editors of these compilations accompany the comments they would address to the writer of each theme with a paragraph to the teacher, explaining the strategy of their comments. Most of these model comments are exemplary in the friendly constructiveness of their advice to students, and the example these models set for the teacher, if demanding, is often worthy of emulation.

What one misses in many discussions of how to annotate and evaluate themes, however, is attention to the theme assignment itself. Many compilations of themes, despite the thoroughness of the comments on what the students wrote, contain only cursory descriptions of the assignment to which the student was responding, and say little about the instructions and advice to students before they wrote. For all that the young teacher can tell, it

From *The Leaflet*, LXVI, No. 1 (1967), 3–15. Reprinted by permission of the New England Association of Teachers of English and Richard L. Larson.

makes no difference how carefully or how carelessly a theme assignment is made, so long as the theme submitted by the student is dealt with thoroughly. To judge from many of these compilations, moreover, the instruction in writing that preceded an assignment is of no consequence; each assignment, the teacher is free to infer, can be treated as an isolated task.

Now it is, of course, somewhat unfair to censure the compilers of graded themes for failing to describe elaborately the assignments themselves and the preceding instruction. The compilations promise no more than to offer a range of student responses to a representative group of assignments. They deal, as their titles imply, with the *evaluating* of themes, not with the assigning of them.

But even recent books on the teaching of English give relatively little attention to what a teacher ought to consider in planning a specific theme assignment. These books often describe general goals for the program in composition, and make numerous suggestions about the kinds of writing that students in various grades should practice. Occasionally they enumerate subjects that have proven useful or might prove useful for student writing, although the value of these subjects and the problems they would present for students who attempted them are not often discussed in much detail. These texts also offer much advice about annotating and judging themes.

I am convinced that these discussions do not explore in sufficient depth the responsibilities of the teacher in presenting theme assignments to students. For a theme assignment ought not to be given simply to evoke an essay that can be judged. Its purpose should be to teach, to give students an experience in composing (selecting, arranging, and expressing thoughts) from which he can learn as much as he can from the reactions of his teacher to his essay. The very act of writing the assignment should help the student think a little more incisively, reason a little more soundly, and write a little more effectively than he did before encountering it. If it is to give the student this help, a theme assignment cannot be presented haphazardly. Nor can it be made without regard to what the student has been taught about thinking and writing before attempting it, for the student's paper will inevitably be affected by the instructions he has received, even more than by the comments made on earlier papers. Although good comments teach (and teach eloquently), the important work of teaching composition ought to begin at the moment the course is designed and continue with the planning and presenting of each assignment. Evaluation and follow-up of the assignment are the last, and by no means necessarily the most important, steps in the teaching of composition.

This observation about the importance of planning individual theme assignments carefully is really not new; several recent writers have already made the point in general terms. Albert Kitzhaber remarks that "All teachers of composition should recognize that planning an assignment in writing is one of the most important aspects of teaching composition, and it should accordingly receive their closest attention. An offhand assignment or one poorly thought through places every student under a needless handicap and guarantees that a sizable proportion of the papers will be defective." [1] Arthur Carr of the University of Michigan, telling in one of the kinescopes of the Commission on English about a theme assignment dealing with "Fire-Walking in Ceylon," observes "I am persuaded that . . . one important way to do better [as teachers of composition] is to set the writing assignments less blindly . . . and that if we do this we shall be less frustrated as teachers and that our students will make greater headway, headway they themselves can perceive." [2] And the chapter on Composition in *Freedom and Discipline on English,* besides reminding readers that "No part of a teacher's job is more important or more a test of his mettle than the making of sound, well-framed assignments" describes quite specifically the characteristics that the Commission on English thinks a good assignment ought to exhibit.[3] (These suggestions—on pages 92–98 of *Freedom and Discipline*—ought to be required reading for all teachers of composition—in high school or college.) Haphazard assignments, all of these writers imply, are inefficient and often confusing. Only the planned assignment— the assignment that takes final form after the teacher has considered what he wants his students to learn and what problems they must solve in order to learn it—has much promise of success as an instrument of teaching.

Even some of these writers, however, do not deal very much with the specific steps a teacher ought regularly to take in thinking out the problems posed by a possible assignment, the tasks his students must perform in order to handle it, and the best ways of presenting the assignment to the class. (*Freedom and Discipline,* page 97, does offer some valuable suggestions of these points.) Moreover, these writers may encourage teachers to another doubtful assumption: that a theme can be assigned in isolation from those that surround it in the composition course. Yet many teachers now hold that even careful planning of the single assignment is not enough to insure that it will accomplish the maximum of teaching. These teachers argue persuasively that each assignment must fit into, and advance, the entire course, and that, ideally, the composition course in each secondary grade ought to be part of a plan for the curriculum in composition in all six secondary grades.

[1] Albert Kitzhaber, *Themes, Theories, and Therapy: The Teaching of Writing in College,* (New York: McGraw-Hill, 1965), p. 33.
[2] Arthur Carr, "A Student Writing Assignment Based on 'Fire-Walking in Ceylon,'" (a *Kinescript* of the Commission on English, New York, 1965), pp. 6–7.
[3] Commission on English, *Freedom and Discipline in English,* (New York: College Entrance Examination Board, 1965), p. 92.

Much recent work on composition, in response to the arguments of these teachers, has been devoted to the planning of programs covering a full year or several years. Ever since Clarence Hach called in 1960 for a "sequential program in composition."[4] English departments and school districts have been responding with varied programs, some elaborate, some sketchy, but all designed to let the teacher know (or at any rate to force him to decide) what his course is to cover and how it fits into the school's total program in composition. The making of sequential programs of composition assignments has become a common pastime for departments under the leadership of progressive chairmen—and with good results. Leaders of the National Study of High School English programs conclude that in general those schools using or planning sequential programs in composition teach the subject more effectively than those without such a program. Many schools and districts, in fact, are so confident of the value of their programs that they are publishing or distributing them. Many a curriculum guide from one school district inspires imitation from other districts. Published texts on the teaching of English are beginning to contain detailed suggestions for composition curricula. Mary Elizabeth Fowler's *Teaching Language, Literature, and Composition,* for instance, contains an elaborate sequence based on the "spiral" principle—that the same general types of assignments can be given to students in successive grades, if the particular subject matter of work in the higher grades is more complex and demanding than that in the lower grades.[5]

Those who draft sequential programs, however, often neglect to advise teachers how to plan and present the individual assignments in their programs. Their plans, as a result, often are incomplete guides to the teaching of writing. Moreover, in many composition sequences, the principle of "sequence" is often no more than casually observed. In some curriculum guides a sequence of assignments consists simply of a list of subjects or types of writing, arranged in approximate chronological order of suggested use. (Some guides do not even suggest an order in which the types of writing might be assigned.) In many guides, the arrangement of subjects is not explained; often it appears haphazard. To be sure, such programs have the value of letting the teacher know at all times where his course is going (and reminding him of where it has been); they do not, however, encourage him always to think of each specific assignment in relation to those that precede and follow, or to capitalize on what students have learned from one assignment as he moves on to the next. Each assignment, it ap-

[4] Clarence Hach, "Needed: A Sequential Program in Composition," *English Journal,* XLIX (November, 1960), 536–47.
[5] Mary Elizabeth Fowler, *Teaching Language, Literature, and Composition* (New York: McGraw-Hill, 1965), pp. 157–61.

pears, is treated in isolation, although the assignments, when viewed as a group, may assure that the course meets the responsibilities assigned it in the overall curriculum guide for grades 7–12.

But if an assignment is not likely to be an effective instrument of teaching unless carefully presented to students, neither is it likely to do its work fully unless the teacher can connect it to what the student has practiced in previous assignments and will be expected to attempt in later ones. Therefore, while agreeing that the teacher is wise to follow a "sequential" program, I suggest that he should carry out the principle to its conclusion. He should think of a sequential program not merely as a chronological arrangement of assignments but as a structure in which assignments are closely related to each other in service of the goals of the program. Instead of simply deciding what assignments are to be given and then arranging them in any convenient order (as some curriculum guides appear to encourage) he can consider in detail how and why one assignment should follow another and precede a third. He can view the course, to put the matter figuratively, not as a succession of steps to be taken singly, one after another, the later steps scarcely affected by the earlier ones, but as a staircase to be climbed so that at the end the student stands higher, and has a broader prospect beneath him, than when he began. The goal of each assignment in a true sequence should be to enlarge the student's powers of thinking, organizing, and expressing ideas so that he can cope with a more complex, more challenging problem in the next assignment.

A true "sequence" of assignments, then, is an arrangement in which each assignment builds on the one that preceded, and anticipates the assignment that is to follow. For each assignment in a well planned sequence, the teacher can ask students to draw upon and extend habits of thought and writing that they have just practiced or begun to acquire; in each assignment, the teacher may make sure that the student is gaining the preparation necessary for the next assignments in the series.

The planning of assignments requires that the teacher know at what point his students are starting the year, and in what ways each assignment is more demanding or complicated than the last. He must know what new "increments of complexity," if any—what techniques of thinking or organizing or expressing that students have not previously practiced—are demanded in each assignment. And, obviously, he must see that these new techniques of thought or writing are thoroughly understood by his students before they write. If he does not take care to teach new procedures as they are demanded by his assignments, the students will flounder and their papers will fail.

In order to see how each assignment differs from the last, the teacher must examine what mental processes, what operations of mind, the student must go through in order to carry out each assignment successfully. (Observe here my assumption that a teacher ought to know what characteristics the successful papers on any assignment will have, however they may vary in substance and in approach to the assigned topic.) To write an analysis of Lady Macbeth requires different techniques of thinking and composing, for example, than to compare one's school newspaper with that of a neighboring school, and the differences are not fully described by the two verbs "analyze" and "compare." The analysis of a character in a play requires, for example, the ability to draw inferences about the character from his actions, statements, and figures of speech, as well as from the comments of other characters and their reactions to him. It also requires some idea of the goal of "analysis"—to account for the behavior of a character by suggesting a theory? to reveal the importance of the character in the actions of the play? to discover the author's implied evaluation of her, if he implies one? A comparison of two school newspapers also requires a goal (the student must ask: to what discovery will the comparison lead me?), but it also requires powers of direct observation different from those required in the analysis of a play, demands the identification of some bases on which the papers can be compared, and may force the student to develop for himself standards useful in the evaluation of journalism. Again, to compare the newspapers requires different ways of thinking and writing from an assignment asking the student to analyze the significance of the Stamp Act in the years before the American Revolution. The latter assignment requires the student to sift varying kinds of historical evidence and display a lively sense of the potentials and limitations of analyses of cause and effect. The teacher should know the different tasks required by each assignment he gives, make some judgment of which tasks can come before others, and plan his lessons so that the class discusses and practices the necessary techniques before the theme requiring competence in these techniques is to be handed in.

Thus far I have been proposing three separate but closely related theses about the teaching of composition: that the teacher should plan every theme assignment with great care before presenting it to his students; that he should, as a part of this planning, identify the activities and operations of mind in which the student must engage if he is to cope with the assignment; and that he should see each assignment, if possible, as part of a truly sequential course in composition. Let me now try to translate these general suggestions into a series of steps that teachers might try to follow in designing their composition assignments. The proposal is, perhaps, idealistic in its rigor, but it need not be inflexible, and it does, I hope, point to the places where a teacher must make careful decisions about the focus of each assignment and about how he will present the assignment to his students.

First, plan the course at least in broad outline for a term and possibly a year in advance. Decide what you want your students to be able to do when they complete your course. (To be sure, the responsibilities of each course should be decided in general by teachers of several successive grades working together; they must determine what progress a student should make in each grade, and they may want to view the work of each grade as part of a complete sequential program in writing for grades 7–12 or 10–12. But the individual teacher is usually the one to plan a program that will meet the responsibilities assigned to his course.) Decide how many themes you want your students to write, and what tasks in thinking and writing each theme will require of them. You can slow the pace, give more time for some assignments than others, and repeat assignments as necessary, but knowing in advance the purposes of each assignment will give you an invaluable sense of direction as you start the term's work. No assignment need be decided upon in detail while you are planning the course in broad outline, but the major goals to be served and mental activities to be taught by each assignment ought to be at least tentatively determined.

Second, analyze each prospective assignment carefully before you give it. Among the questions to consider before you decide finally on a subject for the assignment are: what can these students reasonably be expected to accomplish at this point in their development? (You may wish on occasion to give an assignment that you know is beyond your students, but you should be aware that the assignment is probably beyond their reach and you should have clearly in mind your purpose in giving it.) What is the student expected to learn from this assignment? What is he to practice when doing it? What, in short, is the purpose of the assignment?

With the purpose of the assignment clearly in mind, you can decide the specific subject (or the kind of subject) you wish the students to discuss. The subject should be of value for itself, and should help students to learn about the act or process of composition. Test the subject to determine whether it will encourage the students to make some discovery, to develop, while planning and writing the theme, a new idea or perception about themselves, their environment, a work of literature, or some other significant object of inquiry. Whether the subject be presented to students in the form of a proposition (as recommended in *Freedom and Discipline in English,* p. 93), or a question, or a problem, or a broad topic which the student must restrict for himself, the assignment ought to help the student to new knowledge or new understanding of his subject.

Moreover, if this new understanding of his subject is to be sound, the student must have adequate data with which to work. The subject must be accessible to him; he must be able to locate the facts and other data needed in the development of his observations. And if he is asked to make a choice between alternatives, between conflicting interpretations of a character or novel, for example, he must have a genuine option; it must be possible for him to defend reasonably, with good evidence, whichever alternative he chooses. Few subjects present a useful problem for discussion if there is only one way to treat them.

Finally, after you have determined that the specific subject to be assigned is likely to be interesting and instructive to the students, check to be sure that, as you have framed it, the subject will serve the purposes of the assignment. If the purpose of the assignment, for example, is to force students to discriminate between facts and opinions on a subject, the assignment must be so presented that the student cannot evade making the discrimination (he might evade it, for instance, by writing a strictly factual narrative).

Third, consider what the student will need to know in order to do well on the assignment. These questions are pertinent: What operations of mind must the student go through in preparing to write the assignment? What powers of observation must he exercise? What acts of induction or deduction must he perform? What problems of rhetoric—selection of materials, organization of materials, and expression of simple or complex ideas—must he solve? Try to determine what a successful piece of writing on the assignment might look like—i.e., what features (of content and structure) it might have. One—admittedly time-consuming—way to determine these characteristics is to write the proposed assignment yourself in a form that you would consider satisfactory, and then determine what mental acts you had to perform in order to write it.

Fourth, decide what you must "teach" now in order to assure students a fair chance to do well on the assignment. This decision will be based on a comparison of what the students now know and can reasonably be expected to do with what the students will need to be able to do in order to carry out the assignment. You will need to consider how well previous assignments have prepared your students to do what you will now ask of them, and what new techniques and procedures—in both thinking and writing—they must master. Decide how you will help them to understand what is expected on this theme. Plan to discuss the special problems of observation, analysis, and organization that they will face. Try to anticipate difficulties the students will face with the assignment, and be prepared before you make the assignment to help the students surmount these difficulties.

Fifth, when the first four steps have been carefully taken, and you are sure that you know what activities and skills you are calling for, draft the written bulletin describing the assignment (or make the notes you will use in giving the assignment orally). Make sure that the instructions are complete and unambiguous. Be sure that the kind of performance—the action—required of the student is stipulated as precisely as possible. (Is he to compare two characters, trace a process, argue in support of a thesis, analyze a scene, and so on? You should even consider carefully what you mean by such verbs as "analyze," which direct the student's performance.) Often it is desirable for students to write as if they are filling a role in which precise communication with another person is required. In such assignments you should stipulate an imagined audience—a reader or a group of readers—to be addressed, an occasion for the writing, and a purpose or purposes to be accomplished. For example, instead of asking for a routine comparison of your school paper with that published in the other high school in town, try instructing the student to propose to his principal (or to the school's newspaper advisor) ways of improving the paper—ways of making it more like the good one in the other school. Instead of asking your aspiring aeronautical engineer to write a "process" paper, ask him to describe how a jet engine works in language that a grandmother taking her first jet flight could understand. Instead of asking routinely for an "analysis" of Lady Macbeth, urge the student to reply to someone who thinks the Lady was a foolish, misguided but loyal wife who was only trying to encourage her husband to better himself. Then check back through your reflections at step 4 to be sure that he has the tools and training (in selecting data, in recognizing and resolving interpretive problems raised by the data) that he will need to meet the problem you have set him.

Sixth, determine what your standards of evaluation on the assignment will be. The standards should, of course, reflect the purposes of the assignment and what you are trying to teach by means of it. Among the bases for evaluation should be the student's success in responding to the audience, occasion, and purpose you specified in making the assignment. The principal question that can be applied to almost any student's paper is: did he keep faith with his reader? did he do the job he set out to do for the audience that he was expected to address? But you will probably regard two or three of the tasks in reasoning, organization and expression presented by the assignment as especially important, and will plan to base your evaluation heavily on the students' success in performing these two or three tasks.

Seventh, explain the assignment to the students fully. Follow the explanation—or, perhaps better still, precede it—by some discussion of exercises or problems that will prepare the student to handle the task. Be sure that he sees the techniques of observation, discovery of ideas, organization, and expression that he needs to use as he writes. Not that writing is reducible always or even often to the application of techniques, but there are ways of drawing good generalizations, forming good hypotheses, drawing good inferences, introducing different kinds of papers effectively, concluding different discussions forcefully, and so on, that the students might know and use consciously as they work. If sources for materials to be used on the assignment are likely to be hard to find, suggest a few such sources. Here, in preliminary explanations of your assignments and perhaps in exercises that let students practice techniques you are teaching, is your chance to make the composition course seem not a guessing game but a program of instruction in a disciplined activity that a student can master.

Also, let the students know on what standards they will be judged. You may even wish to discuss with your students samples of successful work on analogous assignments, if you have such samples. Examples of professional writing that illustrate good solutions of the difficulties in an assignment have long been standard teaching materials for colleges; they can serve well in secondary schools, too. Although professional writing need not always be studied as a model for emulation, there is no harm, especially on difficult assignments, in giving your students a target of excellence at which to shoot.

Eighth, as part of your explanation of the assignment, allow time for students' questions, and be ready to point out pitfalls and difficulties they will encounter as they work on the assignment. You may even want to suggest ways of avoiding these pitfalls, if the assignment is especially demanding. You will not reduce the value of the assignment by alerting students to possible sources of trouble; the students will have difficulty enough in trying to avoid pitfalls they know about, and you may save yourself many unhappy experiences in reading and much red ink if you point out difficulties that students would almost surely not recognize unless forewarned. Some of these suggestions may be given after students have begun to work on first drafts, and possibly after you have looked at a few first drafts to see how the class is doing.

Ninth, in evaluating and commenting on papers, make special note of where the student has and has not succeeded in reaching the objectives of the assignment. Give praise where you can, and remember that the comment ought principally to be a tool for teaching. As such, it ought to point out precisely where a paper fell short of completing the assigned task, and to indicate what difficulties the writer ought specifically to guard against in the next paper, if a similar task is to confront him then. General comments on clarity of organization, accuracy of word choice, and economy of expression are almost always appropriate if warranted, but the teacher should not forget that the student is looking for some estimate of how well he met the specific assignment he faced. Whatever the focus of the comments, they should be full enough to let each student see exactly where he succeeded, where he failed, and why. And they should be constructive enough so that the student can profit from them in writing the next assignment. (Sometimes comments are more carefully heeded if no grade appears on the paper. Grades sometimes deflect students' attention completely from what the comments hope to teach.)

Tenth, discuss the assignments with students when you return them. Distribute, or read aloud, or show on the overhead projector, examples of comparatively successful performances on the assignment, demonstrating where they succeed and, if necessary, where they fall short. Resist the temptation to discuss only papers that show many difficulties; discuss examples of papers that handle the assignment well so that the student can learn by seeing what he should have done. Usually it is wise to involve students in discussion of strong and weak points of an essay; the teacher can intervene to comment if the discussion goes hopelessly astray from important strengths or weaknesses of the paper. But review the pitfalls that seized large numbers of students, and indicate once more (if you have already mentioned them) how these troubles might have been avoided.

Eleventh, ask students to revise or rewrite. For most students, revision ought not to consist simply of correcting errors in mechanics; it ought to be a thorough rewriting of the entire assignment. Some papers may be so good that revision is unnecessary. And on some assignments many students will do so badly that revision is unlikely to be rewarding. In such cases you may want to repeat approximately the same assignment (at the expense of slowing the pace of instruction) on an analogous subject. Whatever the procedure used, however, you should provide some way by which the student can follow up quickly and correct the difficulties he exhibited in handling the assignment.

Of the eleven steps in handling a theme assignment discussed here, eight are completed before the students even approach their final drafts. If the manuals for evaluating themes err in focusing too heavily on how the theme tests what the student has learned, this discussion may seem to focus unduly on what happens before the student has begun seriously to write. Moreover, the suggestions may appear to rigidify the curriculum and make giving even a short assignment into a forbiddingly complex task.

My emphasis on what the teacher must do before the student is allowed to go far with his assignment, though perhaps excessive, is intentional, and I hope the early pages of this essay will justify the emphasis. But this essay does not argue that the curriculum must be rigid. Each assignment should serve the purposes of the course and have a place in its total structure, but specific assignments need not always be decided before the course begins. Assignments often must be made up as the course progresses, to meet the needs of students as these needs appear. I argue only that whatever assignment is made, and whenever it is presented, it should be carefully considered in advance of presentation to the students. Of course, as the year progresses and the assignments become instruments for reviewing and reinforcing what has been taught rather than for the presentation of new techniques and concepts, the amount of explanation given to students before they write may diminish. But the thought given by the teacher to his assignment, I think, ought not to decrease even at the end of the year.

Some readers may object that if the teacher follows these suggestions, the student has less responsibility for learning than the teacher has for spelling out the lesson. Perhaps the charge has some merit. But students learn little from simply trying to outguess the teacher, from striving to write a theme in response to an assignment that seems pointless or confused. And they can hardly be expected to write a good theme if the assignment requires activities of mind that they have not practiced and do not know how to perform. They may, to be sure, learn from failures, but how frustrating it is to be told one has failed when one had no idea of how to seek success. For most students, composition is an uncomfortable subject; few enter with enthusiasm a course devoted primarily to exposition, and the morale even of the eager students is easily shattered by inept instruction. But if students have a goal in writing and are convinced that the teacher is helping them toward that goal, there is at least a better chance that their morale may remain strong.

We can not hope for much success in the teaching of composition unless our students want to learn, and continue wanting to learn throughout our courses. If we try to teach before we test and judge them, perhaps our students will discover that our assignments are helping them learn to write. They may even find that our assignments help them to use their minds more effectively and to organize more successfully their experiences in the world.

ARNOLD LAZARUS / *On the Teaching of Composition*

Ladies and gentlemen, I intend this evening to share with you some ways of involving secondary-school youngsters in imaginative and expository writing, including a certain kind of exposition which, in my own teaching in the Santa Monica, California, schools, I have found workable and educative.

But before I go into these resources and devices I should state the two assumptions undergirding my talk. For if you do not accept these, my lecture will not make much sense to you. The first assumption is that you can teach most pupils at least some of the techniques of writing worth teaching and learning. All of you are by now familiar with Jerome Bruner's celebrated doctrine in his *The Process of Education:* "There is no reason to believe that any subject cannot be taught to any child at virtually any age in some form." (Cambridge: Harvard University Press, 1961, p. 47). Of course Professor Bruner's whole book (as well as the sense of the celebrated Woods Hole Conference which the book reports) stresses the advantages for learners when the teacher wraps his head around his subject so thoroughly as to know every facet of its structure and substructures. My second assumption is that the civilized kinds of writing which most public schools have yet to involve youngsters in should no longer remain the exclusive preserve of the ritzy prep schools. College-bound or not—and most young-

From *Reflections on High School English,* edited by Gary Tate, Tulsa: The University of Tulsa, 1966, pp. 66–75. Reprinted by permission of the University of Tulsa and Arnold Lazarus.

sters today are in fact bound for at least a taste of college—every youngster deserves the discipline and excitement of the kinds of writing that inform his reading.

If you can accept these two assumptions you may be able to accept the following three kinds of writing that I propose to talk about. The first kind let me call *imaginative* rather than creative, for I agree with J. N. Hook and others who insist that all genres of writing can be intrinsically creative. But this first kind can be distinguished at least from the next two which I shall call, respectively, *exposition investigative* and *exposition interpretive*.

For each of these three kinds of writing in general I propose to suggest not only more specific genres but also resources and stimuli for eliciting them from pupils. For all three of these kinds of writing, then, the resources are (A) the pupil's daily-living experiences, (B) his reading of expository literature, and (C) his reading of imaginative literature. But even though any resource, any raw material, any experience may motivate any or all genres of writing whether imaginative or expository, certain kinds of resources seem to me to have elicited one kind of writing more successfully than another. I am thus drawing upon my teaching-experience as well as academic theory in suggesting which resources to exploit for which kinds of writing.

I. Imaginative Writing (Prose and Verse)

I.A. Students' Daily-Living Experiences. At least three celebrated teachers of secondary-school composition—Clarence Hach, Paul Diederich, and Louis Zahner—have stressed the point that most pupils, especially the youngest, should first be involved in writing such short, subjective pieces of prose and verse as are close to their personal experiences. Pupils' daily-living experiences, then, in family, school, church, and club; their sports, hobbies, televiewing, movie-going, and the like comprise the most germinal resources for imaginative writing.

And of all the briefest, most personal kinds of writing, perhaps none is more successful than the *journal-entry*. In fact the journal may itself serve as a kind of reservoir of ideas for longer, more disciplined kinds of imaginative prose or verse. In the journal, preferably during the first ten or fifteen minutes of one or two class-periods a week, the pupil writes informal reactions to his most recent experiences. As illustrated in the following excerpts from pupils' writing, the journal-entry may be a sentence, a paragraph, an epigram or even a limerick:

My tennis is improving. Now I have to work on my temper.

We heard Dr. M—— in convocation today. What misguided energy! How did man *really* evolve? I'll bet there's a lot we'll never find out about this mysterious universe, computers or no computers. Think I'll do my term project on the reconciliation of science and religion.

George Orwell . . . I like the assonance of the O's. I love the *sounds* of words.

How barbaric of the Phoenicians to sacrifice humans (sometimes their own children) to the god, Moloch! Are we guilty of similar sacrifices to Mars?

Idea for short story: Girl who isn't especially good-looking moves to a new town and takes all the boys away from the local girls. One at a time, of course, and ironically without trying.

> Gorgeous Helen and Paris were forces
> Causing Greece to take ominous courses.
> After Troy was subjected
> And Helen collected
> It was home to build more wooden horses.

Whether in the journal or outside of it another creative activity that many pupils enjoy and can manage is the writing of *haiku.* You may remember that this compact three-lined form consists of 5 syllables, 7 syllables, 5 syllables, does not rhyme but is highly suggestive. It re-creates one beautiful or humorous moment. It is almost always tied to a season, explicitly or by implication, and whether or not an extended metaphor or symbol, it contains such beautiful imagery as to suggest all sorts of possibilities of meaning. A tenth-grade girl (whom some teachers regarded as a "slow learner," incidentally) wrote the following haiku:

> Moon's path on lake steals
> slumber from me and all my
> waking dreams of spring . . .

Another kind of imaginative composition is the *personal essay* (also known as "familiar" or "informal" essay). This highly subjective piece of writing need not and probably ought not to be longer than a page or two, certainly no longer than 500 words, with 250 to 300 a happy length. It may be humorous or poetic, and it should throw fresh light on a familiar or even commonplace topic. For specimen essays of this kind, which students have written, see recent issues of *Scholastic* Magazine.

I.B. Students' Reading of Expository Literature. All the imaginative writing mentioned above may also be elicited when the student is stimulated not only by first-hand experiences but also by his reading articles in newspapers and magazines. In fact, some students can be interested in keeping a tickler-file of news-items, which in turn suggest *ballads* and *short stories.* Resourceful teachers have no doubt elicited from their imaginative youngsters, recently, such pieces as "The Ballad of John Kennedy," "The Ballad of Lee Oswald," and "The Ballad of Jack Ruby." Even if the composer of this folk form does not see his ballad published, he or a folk singer can perform the opus, in class, perhaps to the accompaniment of a guitar. The easily composed ballad stanza, the simple story-line, and the note of sadness appeal to student writers. The same raw materials from folklore and the news stimulate some students to write short stories and dramatic skits. Though writing a successful short story is a real challenge for even the most articulate, you have only to look through recent issues of *Literary Cavalcade* to see what some few pupils have been able to create. Perhaps the hardest but most educative technique to be taught and learned in the writing of fiction is how to turn mere reporting into rendering—the selective re-creation of experience by means of sensuous details.

I.C. Students' Reading of Imaginative Literature. All the imaginative kinds of writing already mentioned may also be elicited when the student is stimulated by his reading of one or more of such imaginative genres of literature as poems, stories, plays, and novels. Except for such longer genres as the novel and the three-act play, in fact, any of the shorter genres may themselves serve as models for some students to imitate.

But perhaps one of the most successful writing projects, certainly a viable "culminating activity" related to the study of a literary work, is the pupil-composed *classroom magazine.* This eight or ten-paged mimeographed magazine takes several weeks to put together, and its individual contributions reflect the hard work of revising and refining. But it brings together in one "publication" the diverse talents of practically all the members of a class or of two or more classes co-operatively. Let us say that the master literary work which your class has been studying is Shakespeare's *Macbeth.* The informal essays, short stories, cartoons, limericks, ballads, news articles, editorials, and explications, which the study of this play has elicited, are submitted to the Editorial Board (your most literate students) either appointed or elected. If you haven't already tried this activity, you will be amazed at how effectively the prospect of publication (1) elicits students' writing and

(2) motivates students' industry and growth in smooth communication. You may find yourself giving most of your help to the students who (like some half-educated teachers) over-emphasize the importance of spelling and punctuation at the expense of such comparatively more valuable matters as what has been said that is worth saying and with what logic and directness it has been said or can be said.

Thus the "Dunsinane Newsletter" ("a Broadside for all the people who need people") dated Scotland, December 13, 1057, may contain news items on the events in the play: ("Duncan Slain. Macbeth Rules."); ("Banquo Slain at Banquet. Fleance Flees"); etc., editorials on politics and ethics, explications of the meanings of the blood imagery, "The Ballad of Macbeth," and even classified advertisements. Among the latter—"FOR SALE: For the holidays—Christmas trees straight from Birnham Woods"; and "For antique collectors—black cauldrons, slightly used but in good condition. Contact W. 3-3-3."

II. Expository Writing—Investigative and Factual

II.A. There is no reason why students' daily-living experiences cannot provide the raw material for factual expositions—for papers that objectively explain and describe. But these experiences have almost always turned out to be better inspirations for such non-expository pieces as those already mentioned above, especially for informal personal essays.

II.B. The student's readings in such expository fields as history, geography, anthropology, sociology, economics, government, science, technology, psychology, philosophy, and the like, have traditionally provided him with the "inventio," the matter and the topics for investigative expositions. Many a college freshman composition class devotes most of the semester to this kind of expository reading and writing. Though a certain amount of it is educative, it has been over-emphasized, I believe, in our state colleges and not emphasized enough in our public secondary schools. Nevertheless, that is *not* the kind of exposition we need to give more attention to.

II.C. It will not surprise you that the reading of imaginative literature can provide topics for the writing of investigative expositions. Perhaps all of you have used literary works as springboards for involving pupils in oral reports on the "author's life and works" and on "historical backgrounds of this period." (I hope that nobody here has used a literary work as a springboard for involving himself in lecturing on those topics.) With rare exceptions such expositions are at bottom encyclopedia-copying and hence provide excellent "manageables" for our slowest pupils. While we're at it—at this business of involving average and below-average pupils in writing investigative expositions related to the reading of imaginative literature—let's extend our list of topics beyond "the author's life and works" and "historical background of the period." Let's involve some of our pupils in writing investigative reports on the characteristics of a given genre, on the characteristics of a given mode, perhaps even on the development of a given movement. Another expository manageable, as you well know, is the summary of plot, or setting, or dramatis personae, or the manifest theme and story-line (what Henry James called "the *donnée*"). It is at least far better to have a pupil *write* such factual exposition than to let him inflict it orally.

But all such factual reports along with literary history in general should receive much less time and attention, I hope you agree, than literary interpretation. And it is this latter kind of exposition—explication with an argumentative edge—which deserves more emphasis than it has received in the past few decades in our public secondary schools and in freshmen-composition courses in our state colleges.

III. Exposition Interpretive and Argumentative

III.A. Students' daily-living experiences provide comparatively little resource for this kind of exposition. It all too often degenerates into an aimless autobiographical chronology in desperate search for a point, as the graduate assistants who teach college-freshman composition can testify.

III.B. Students' readings in expository literature provide much keener points for interpretive and argumentative writings. Since most college-composition courses and some secondary-school classes have already been performing well in this field I do not need to add to its discussion. I only wish that some of the secondary-school anthologies would include more expository essays both as models and as stimulators of thought.

III.C. I have saved for the last the kind of expository writing which seems to have been, for the past ninety-five years, a preserve of the ivy-league colleges and of the elite schools that prepare young men and women for such colleges. I refer to expository writing related to interpretive reading of master literary works.

The Why. The chief purpose of this kind of exposition, as has already been suggested, is to explicate, to illuminate, to defend an interpretation. I suspect that some of you are now saying to yourselves, "Here we go again—a long-haired tangle of words, words, words," But your students' interpretations need not and should not reflect the notion that "anything goes," as Laurence Perrine recently wrote. While as teachers we need to be open-minded, we have a right to insist that whatever interpretation a student defends, he supports with details from the primary text rather than with what somebody else may have said about it.

The What. Nor is there any reason why the student's thesis should be restricted to his interpretation of the main theme or of a minor theme. He may find, for his "thesis statement," a germinal topic among one of the following elements of the literary work: a recurring image or symbol; the author's or the speaker's tone-of-voice or his attitude toward his material; the speaker ("persona"); the mode of this piece (in Northrop Frye's lexicon —comedy, tragedy, romance, irony, satire, and the like); a major or a minor character—an analysis, of course, rather than a factual exposition identifying the "dramatis personae" (II.C. above); the language, the vocabulary, and especially the usage or dialect of the author or of a character; the author's mythological world or his use of archetypes; the structure of this work or the structure as it interacts with its content; the author's vision of life as stated or reflected in this work; the comparison of one facet of this work with a counterpart in another work. And one or another literary work will of course suggest a topic peculiarly appropriate to itself. For some other topics as well as some specimen compositions on them see Edgar Roberts, *Writing Themes about Literature.*

The Who. The student-writer will in the end do best to address, as his audience, his own peers rather than you as the teacher. (Experimenting with differential audiences proves to be more fruitful in imaginative than in expository writing of this kind.) He will also do best to assume the role of a defender of his interpretation, a kind of debater; not a polemical critic, mind you, yet an interpreter with a strong conviction. Such a formal voice incidentally calls for formal varieties of usage.

How Long? A viable length for developing a sharply qualified thesis is two or three pages—between 400 and 700 words, with a happy length about 500.

The How. Strategies for ordering one's arguments are in general either inductive or deductive. Inductively the writer may hold back his main generalization to the end, preferring at first to lead the reader to it by presenting the textual evidence. This strategy demands of the writer his most intense discipline. It proves to be beyond the reach of most students. It easily degenerates into a meandering through the miscellaneous unless carefully controlled by writer and teacher. Of course some few students can bring it off even though it makes excessive demands on the teacher's already overcrowded schedule.

The deductive strategies seem to be more manageable for most students. One of the more challenging of the deductive strategies follows the Hegelian dialectic. In this pattern the student states a thesis ("Such and such must be so"), then as a gracious concession an antithesis ("But on the other hand, such and such is also true") then finally a synthesis ("All things considered, however, it remains true that—").

But of all the deductive strategies available (and there are almost as many as there are syllogisms), the pattern that several of my colleagues and I have found the most manageable by most students is as follows:

Thesis statement: _____
Thesis question: _____
    Answer I: _____
       Support A: _____
       Support B: _____
       Support n: _____
    Answer II: _____
       Support A: _____
       Support B: _____
       Support n: _____

More specifically filled in, a model outline for a 500-word exposition related to Shakespeare's *Macbeth* may look something like this:

> *Thesis:* Lady Macbeth functions less as a believable woman than as as Macbeth's own evil other self.
>
> *Thesis question:* How do we know this?
>
> > *Answer I:* She keeps awakening in him mostly his hitherto un-aroused evil desires.
> >
> > > *Support A:* "Your face, my thane, is a book where men/ May read strange matters."
> > >
> > > *Support B:* "Was the hope drunk/Wherein you dress'd your-self?"
> >
> > *Answer II:* She keeps egging on only his evil desires once they are aroused.
> >
> > > *Support A:* "But screw your courage [to do evil] to the sticking-place."
> > > "What [evil] cannot you and I perform upon/ the unguarded Duncan?"
> > >
> > > *Support B:* "Wouldst thou have that/Which thou esteem'st the ornament of life/And live a coward in thine own esteem?"
> >
> > *Answer III:* She says and does little or nothing else which might identify her particularly as a woman.

Now it is easy to sense that a good many of you teachers, especially the women among you, do not accept this particular thesis. But it should be irrelevant whether we agree or disagree with a student in his interpretation, as Harold Martin and others have recently observed, so long as he is interpreting what is there in a given work, with specific supports from the work's details and context rather than what is in some other work.

For this particular kind of exposition we need to insist on an outline before the student writes the paper rather than after. An outline that comes in with a paper all too often turns out to be an after-the-fact attempt to validate the mish-mash of the paper. Nor should this preliminary blueprint be a topic outline; it should be a short-statement outline representing not only close reading but also disciplined reasoning.

This reasoning almost always succeeds or fails in the thesis statement, as Sheridan Baker points out in *The Practical Stylist*. Not only should the thesis be a statement (as distinguished from a topic or a question) but it should go out on a limb of commitment. It should be a specific point of view on which the student-writer takes a stand. If the statement is too close to the obvious or to the given, it is not a thesis. Thus if a student writes "Lady Macbeth keeps egging Macbeth on," for example, he is simply stating a fact (a fact which he may well use further on in his outline); he is not making a statement that needs defending. *Teacher and class may profitably devote an entire period to composing thesis statements and to discussing which are and which are not viable.*

Once the thesis statement has been written and revised to make it as pointed as possible, the next step is easy. One puts to this statement some such question as "Why?" or "How?" or "How do we know this?" or "What are these?" or "By what devices?" One puts a question to a thesis statement, in short, much as one fires a space-probe—to get it off the ground.

Now the answers to this question—and please notice that *all* the answers, the two or three or "n" answers are in reply to one question asked of the one thesis—are a strategic part of the exposition's unfolding. Whether or not these answers are preceded by Roman numerals (and they probably should be), each of these statements should really answer rather than just repeat the thesis statement. Thus if the student-writer of the above outline on Lady Macbeth had written for his first answer to the question "How do we know [that Lady Macbeth is less a believable woman than she is Macbeth's evil other self]?" "Because she seems more an evil spirit than a flesh-and-blood woman," he would not really be answering, would he! He would only be repeating, of course, even if repeating in disguise—the pitfall of circular reasoning that we would have to work on with our students, incidentally, during the writing of the outlines. Again, we may profitably devote an entire period to this phase of the writing. And if anyone is for a moment wondering whether such an exercise, however profitable, may become dull and stale, those of you who have involved your students in this kind of outlining can testify to the contrary. In fact, students who really reach out in this discipline become emotionally as well as intellectually excited. They certainly grow in skill from one exposition to another.

The supports for the answers may be direct quotations, as in the outline above, or paraphrases, or citations of events, and the like. In your reading of compositions of any kind if you have ever felt like using a rubber stamp with the imprint "Give me specific examples!" you can now appreciate the advantages of having the examples ordered beforehand in the outline.

In writing the paper itself, the student need not feel bound to copy the thesis statement as his very first. He may wish to defer it as the last statement in his first paragraph. But follow his outline he should. In a 500-word paper there is of course no room for a formal paragraph of introduction and a formal concluding paragraph. Introductory matter, like concluding observations, need to be limited to one or two sentences apiece. Certainly the student who sweats out the kind of "dispositio" we've been describing is soon disabused of the notion that an outline consisting only of the words "introduction, body, and conclusion" is meaningful.

While one of the chief advantages of this kind of expository writing is that it informs and sharpens one's reading, it provides one of the most educative opportunities I know of for teaching clear and persuasive communication. It motivates all of us to take a machete to the underbrush. It teaches us how much more effective a simple subject-agent joined to a finite verb can be than an unnecessary passive transformation—indeed, than a concatenation of nounifications and -icities. Not "In this classroom-situation composition will be mastered by the student-population" but "The students write."

BERTRAND EVANS / *Writing and Composing*

Though none wrote *enough,* most students who have entered my freshman composition classes in the past dozen years actually wrote a good deal in high school. With them, it is true, have entered a few unfortunates who wrote hardly anything, but instead—when not doing things quite unrelated to "English"—drilled on spelling lists, identified sentence elements, and punctuated other people's sentences in workbooks. These few spent four years "getting ready" to write, and never got ready.

Ironically, these students often prove to be graduates of high schools whose teachers and administrators believe that their programs are designed to prepare for the college examination in English and for the freshman English course. If not all these administrators and teachers are sure that real purpose is served by incessant drilling on various isolated elements, they nevertheless believe that they are doing "what the colleges want." They are not, of course: however indispensable is grammatical knowledge to the solution of certain problems that occur when one writes, the study of grammar apart from and without writing is a waste.

But the freshman who enters my class after writing almost nothing in high school belongs to a small, unfortunate minority, and this essay has less to say of his problem than that of the "typical" freshman, who wrote a good deal before he came. Indeed, he wrote something for his English class nearly every week—not always something finished and elaborate, but something that was called a "theme," "report," "written exercise," or even "composi-

From *English Journal,* XLVIII (January, 1959), 12–20. Reprinted by permission of the National Council of Teachers of English and Bertrand Evans.

tion." If he took English all four years, his total exceeded one hundred such papers. If the high school English teacher has around one hundred fifty students to deal with, this is an impressive total: it means that the teacher, during the "typical" student's four years, graded above fifteen thousand written exercises. Because most of these were read in after-school hours, the grand total seems the more gigantic.

I present these approximations not as news to most readers, but to evince my awareness and appreciation of them; for I am about to make a severe criticism of the English teacher's efforts, and I want to make clear beforehand that I am at least *not* accusing her of loafing on the job. I repeat, therefore: so far as I can discover by fairly systematic prying into the recollections of college freshmen and talking with teachers about their work, the "typical" high school student wrote at least as much as the "typical" teacher could be expected to read with enough care to do any good. Obviously, I could now go on with the argument that is often made in answer to critics of high school graduates' writing ability—namely, that English classes are too large and that if the number for whom teachers are responsible were halved, twice as much writing could be graded. But I am not going to press that argument just now; for although I have no doubt that much would be gained by having students write twice as much as at present, I am less sure that the special lack with which I am immediately concerned would thus be supplied.

If high school students were given more writing assignments, *presumably they would write more of the same kind of things they have been writing in the past and in the same ways in which they have been writing these*. That is to say, they would write more "themes" on topics like sports, hobbies, interesting experiences, and careers; make more "reports" of various kinds; undertake longer "term papers" on larger fields of study; write "My Autobiography" annually instead of biennially. Further, they would presumably have twice as much practice in "narrowing" topics and in devising outlines to "organize" materials.

In thus representing the sorts of writing activities that my freshmen's evidence persuades me to think typical, I do not mean to be only derogatory. Worthy, even indispensable, skills are practiced by such activities. Writing experiences of *any* kind are better than none—as is evinced by the sad condition of the comparatively few students who have had almost none. All exercises in writing give practice in using words and structuring sentences. Whenever one undertakes to represent anything through the device of written language, the mind is inevitably forced into a degree of activity— and any activity of that organ is surely better than none. Moreover, one sort of written exercise may be as useful as another in bringing language troubles into the open, where attention can be drawn to them and remedies applied. If all writing activities are good, then, it follows that more will be better. It is good for students to write every other week; it would be better for them to write every week; it might be best if they could write every day. They would unquestionably thus learn to write better than at present.

But though they learned to "write" better, would they necessarily learn any more about "composing"? It is with this question that I am concerned here.

At this point, possibly, the harassed English teacher, frantic with trying to reach the bottom of a stack of one hundred and fifty papers on her dining-room table before the next set comes in, will toss me aside: "What! I haven't enough to do with misspelled words, non-parallel elements, grotesque sentences, and chaotic organizations? I must take on something else? I give up!" But what I am going to suggest need not increase the teacher's burden; for it implies not more writing to be read, but less—and better. I mean to say that if she gets a student to *compose* a paragraph she has done something more significant than if she gets him to *write* a twenty-page "term paper" with no higher sense of need than that of accumulating many facts.

Let me make clear at once that my "composing" does not necessitate poems, short stories, novels, dramas, or operas. I have in mind composing expository pieces—essays and, perhaps especially, paragraphs. Probably the "typical" English teacher has meant all along that students should compose rather than write. Her intention was implied each time she instructed them to "write a theme" or "write a composition"—for both "theme" and "composition" carry an injunction to compose, and thus differ from "written exercise" and "written report." Perhaps the teacher would have been more precise had she said "develop a theme" and "compose an essay"—or a paragraph; but in any event her intention was evident.

Writing Not Enough

Nevertheless, most of us who are English teachers have either omitted implementation of our intention or gone off the track in it. The methods by which we have *meant* to teach composition are in fact designed only to teach writing. At our worst—which we may have indulged more often than our best—we have even made it improbable that our students would compose—perhaps, indeed, even impossible for them to do so. What, in broad terms, have we done? To begin with, if my freshmen have told me the truth, we have most often confronted students with "topics to write on" and told them to go ahead and write; or we have told them to choose their own topics. We have said, "Write an essay on 'Hobbies,'" and in due time, an hour or a week, back has come a document of two or three pages—titled, of course, "Hobbies." We have said, "Write a report on *The Red Badge of Courage*," and in due time, back it has come—titled, of course, "The Red Badge of Courage." And sometimes, ambitiously, we have said, "Write a term paper on the Missions of California." In due time, in has come a ten-page paper, abounding with facts, dutifully footnoted, and titled "California Missions."

These exemplify our ordinary practices. At our best, or near-best, seeking to be helpful, we have interposed a step or two. "'Don't write on huge topics like 'Hobbies,'" we have said, *"narrow* your topic." Usually we have referred students to the textbook discussion on "How to narrow the topic" and have required them to perform mechanical exercises in "narrowing" or "limiting" in order to prove their ability before dealing with their particular topic. "On page 197 of the text," we have advised, "are listed twenty-five general topics. For tomorrow, narrow each to make a topic suitable for an essay of 500 words." Page 197 lists fields like "Occupations," "Hobbies," "Careers," "Sports," "Education," "Literature," "Movies," etc. Copying models, the students have narrowed these: Occupations—professional occupations—law—learning to be a lawyer; Sports—baseball—the major leagues—famous pitchers of the American League. No doubt it is better to work under the title 'Famous Pitchers of the American League" than under the title "Sports." Possibly the chance that a student will "compose" rather than "write" is improved with the narrower topic; yet the odds against his composing remain so great that the difference is negligible.

Earnestly striving to be still more helpful, we have required that students identify the main and subordinate divisions of the chosen, duly narrowed topic and submit their results of deliberation in outline form. "Plan your organization before you write," we have exhorted them. "Let I, II, III, and IV represent the main division, A, B, C, and D the secondary divisions, and 1, 2, 3, and 4 the details."

And, finally, seeking to be ultimately helpful,—or acting in desperation—we have preached the necessity for unity and coherence and have demanded that essays have Introduction, Body, and Conclusion. Besides exhorting students to stay within the bounds of the topic, to avoid rambling on at random, and to make sure that parts stick together, we have referred them to the textbook's discussion of unity and coherence, and may even have confronted them with examples of nonunified writing. These exemplify our methods at our absolute best; and if my freshmen have told me the truth, we have not usually done our best.

In order to make my point of view unmistakable, let me recapitulate briefly: I believe that it is better for students to write on giant topics like "Hobbies" than not to write at all; that it is better for them to write on narrowed topics like "Beekeeping—my Hobby" than on "Hobbies"; that outlining is an aid to organization and a valuable experience generally, because it requires perception and representation of logical relationships; that it is quite impossible to place too great an emphasis on unity and coherence; and that every true composition has Beginning, Middle, and End. In brief, I believe that all the instruction and practice in writing that my typical college freshman was given in high school was good in that it made a contribution to his ability to write.

Inadequate Approaches

But it taught him *nothing about "composing," and he rarely composes in units larger than the sentence.* Presumably the devices used to teach him to write have even tended to prevent him from composing, for they have planted and fostered in his mind the false notion that if he takes a large topic, narrows it to a smaller one, breaks this into parts, organizes these by outlining, and finally writes everything out in complete sentences of which the substance and order conform to the divisions of the outline, he has done all that is to be done. Thus if the graduate of these methods, starting anew as a college freshman, is given the topic "My Home Town," admonished to apply what he learned in high school about writing, and told to produce an essay of 500 words by next Wednesday, he sets to work boldly. He first questions whether the topic is too broad and decides that it is not—or perhaps he concludes that, since "My Home Town" was the topic assigned, "My Home Town" is exactly what he must write on. He assumes that "topic" is synonomous with "subject," and, indeed, with "title," and therefore he heads his paper "My Home Town." Next he makes an outline:

    I. Introduction
      A. Name
      B. Location
      C. Size
   II. Recreational Facilities
      A. Skiing in Winter
      B. Swimming in Summer
      C. Fishing
      D. Hunting
      E. The YMCA
  III. Educational Facilities
      A. Grade Schools
      B. High School
      C. Libraries

IV. Sources of Income
    A. Farming
    B. Industry
    C. Business
V. Conclusion

Probably he expands the detail, including sub-points under secondary points. In any event, satisfied with his outline (which is, in fact, somewhat better than the typical freshman makes), he starts writing: "My home town is ...., California. It is situated in the great central valley—." He continues, writing sentences and indenting paragraphs in accord with the outline, giving a paragraph to each main point, a sentence or so to each sub-point, the number depending on how much he can think of. Possibly he thinks of more about II, C, 1—"Fishing for trout in the lake"—than about any other point, or even about all the other points together, and his proportion may thus be thrown off, but on the whole he is blindly faithful to the outline. When he has worked through Body, he tackles Conclusion, in which he does one of two things. Usually he "sums up," repeating in abbreviated terms what he has just covered. But sometimes, now feeling free of the strait jacket of outline that has restrained and intimidated him up to this point—or just feeling a certain exhilaration on nearing the end of his task—he swells out in a general pronouncement or two about his home town, even though to do so exceeds the scope of the outline and has nothing particularly to do with what he has been saying in the body of his essay. Thus he may end with a burst of real feeling: "Whatever its shortcomings in some respects, my home town is a wonderfully exciting place to live in, all the year round."

With this sentence, at the very end, he has stumbled upon the point where "writing" might have stopped and "composing" started. But he is presumably quite oblivious to the fact—and in any event his "essay" is finished.

Finally, wishing to shine in his first college composition, he proofreads for technical mishaps of word and sentence, and he asks the larger questions that his training has equipped him to ask: Has the theme Introduction, Body, and Conclusion? Obviously. Is its organization sound? Of course, since it follows the outline. Has it unity? Yes, since it concerns only his own home town and says nothing about other people's home towns. At last satisfied that he has done everything he has been taught to do with themes for English classes—as, indeed he has—he hands in the paper.

It gets, at best, a "C."

It is, of course, better in significant ways than a few papers in the set, which—written by freshmen who did no formal writing in high school except "My Autobiography" once or twice, occasional book reports according to formula, and a term paper on "California Missions"—are marred by stylistic barbarities and lack not only organization but signs of awareness that organization is a thing to attempt. However, though organization is a virtue and the grade of "C" a just reward for such organization and such avoidance of grammatical blunders as the more typical paper achieves, yet organization is not composition, and so the "C" is also a penalty for failure to compose. Moreover, very much as the poorer paper suggests its writer's ignorance that he should try to organize, the typical paper suggests its writer's ignorance of an obligation to compose. Had he attempted to compose, signs of struggle would show even though the effort, as a whole, proved unsuccessful.

The absence of such signs can mean only that the writer has never caught the essential idea of composition. He aims only at organized accumulation, for he has glimpsed nothing beyond it. Though all that he has learned about accumulating and organizing is good, it has stopped short of that which alone can give meaning to the incidentals of matter and organization. My criticism, then, is not that the typical freshman, given a brief trial, fails to compose a perfect essay, but that he shows no sign of knowing that he should try.

Ideas Essential

The heart of the task is somehow to make students understand that though it is easy enough to "write," it is quite impossible to "compose" without an *idea*. Once they have accepted this as a fact, the way is clear; but they do not readily accept it as fact except possibly in a remote and academic way as something that does not really bear on their own practice. The necessity is therefore to find means of translating an abstract and remote something-or-other into a practical reality which students accept as immediately applicable to their work.

Whatever may be the answer to the problem of convincing students that they will not compose unless they have an *idea,* it is certain that it does not consist merely of confronting them with more "topics to write on," giving more instruction and practice in "narrowing" topics mechanically, insisting on more rigorous organizing by means of outlines, allowing more time for larger accumulation of facts, and lecturing on the necessity for Introduction, Body, and Conclusion.

Far from helping to fix in students' minds the realization that they will not compose unless they have and are directed by *idea,* the widespread practice of assigning a "topic to write on" fosters their supposition that they have no need for any such thing.

The first necessity, then, is to break our vicious habit of always using either a general or a narrowed topic as the starting-point for composition. Perhaps we should never confront students with "topics to write on" until they have gained a firm sense of composition. There is proof to spare that if a student does not possess this firm sense at the time he is given a topic and instructed to write on it, he will not pause long enough to get an *idea* before he begins to write, but will begin writing forthwith. The fact is that, given a topic, students jump *directly* at the task of collecting and putting down "matter," "substance," or "detail" that falls within the bounds of the topic. What they should rather do, of course, is to delay writing until "topic" has been transformed to "subject" by the shaping force of *idea*— and only thereafter move on to "matter." They would then be directed to the selection of appropriate detail not by an awareness of general topic but by *idea*.

If we should not give them a topic to start them off, what should we give them? We can give them an *idea*—and by doing so we take one step toward the fixing of a sense of composition in their minds. There is of course nothing new in this suggestion. All teachers of composition, I suspect, and certainly all writers of textbooks on composition, lay stress on what is called—but, I think, improperly—the "topic sentence." Many teachers make a practice of writing a topic sentence, more precisely a "thesis sentence," on the board and asking the class to write a paragraph developing it; it is probably a rare teacher who does not sometimes use this device. The contrast between the typical paragraph written to develop a given *idea* expressed in a thesis sentence like "My home town is a truly exciting place to live" and the typical paragraph, or longer paper, written on the given *topic* "My Home Town" is striking. Given the idea, the student composes, even though he does not know that he is doing so or that he should be doing so. Given the topic, he merely writes, either setting down points at random and requiring only that they concern the topic, or, at best, "organizing" them if there is time.

Since students will almost invariably compose when they are started off with an idea and will almost invariably merely write when they are started off with a topic, whether general or "narrowed," why not simply start them off always with the idea? Give them not "Hamlet," or "Hamlet's Conduct," or even "Hamlet's Conduct in the Scene with His Mother," but "Hamlet's conduct in the scene with his mother shows him to be raving mad." Give them not *"Gulliver's Travels,"* or "Irony in *"Gulliver's Travels,"* or even "Irony in Book IV of *Gulliver's Travels,"* but "The irony of Book IV of *Gulliver's Travels* appears intended to crush rather than to prick." And, for a non-literary piece, give them not "Hobbies," or "My Hobby—Raising Prize Pigs," but "Raising prize pigs is the best way I know to make money, gain glory, and have fun at the same time."

Unfortunately, the solution to this hardest task of the teacher of composition is not so absurdly simple. The device is incomplete and imperfect by itself, first, precisely because it *does* supply the student with an idea. It limits him to the development of other people's ideas very much as punctuation exercises in a workbook keep him punctuating others' sentences instead of his own. It is uncertain that there is any true purpose in learning to compose rather than write if one is only to assemble elements of matter in support of ideas supplied by others. The device can even be a wicked one, since it will sometimes compel students to accumulate details to support ideas that they do not think true and that may, in fact, be quite false. It may be, for example, that a student who has read *Hamlet* with unusual perceptiveness will regard the statement that "Hamlet's conduct in the scene with his mother shows him to be raving mad" as entirely mistaken; it may seem to him more honest to demonstrate that "Hamlet's conduct in the scene with his mother shows him to be extraordinarily sane." There is, however, a practical remedy for this defect of the device, and that is to provide only the frame of an idea, leaving the key words to be supplied by students according to their sense of what *is* true; thus, "Hamlet's conduct in the scene with his mother shows him to be ...." Perhaps this adaptation of the device of the given idea has greatest value as a bridge, leading students from the development of other people's ideas to the development of their own.

Even with this adaptation, however, and though repeated many times, the device of the given idea is not potent enough to accomplish what most needs to be accomplished: it does not fix the sense of composition in students' minds. Proof of this fact is easy: if one presents students at ten successive meetings with idea-statements to develop and at the eleventh meeting confronts them again with a "topic to write on," they will not pause long enough to build up an idea-statement of their own, but will blithely write on the topic in the same old way. The results will be essentially the same as before—organized accumulations which show no sign of struggle to compose, no sign that the writers have caught a sense of composition, and, more discouraging, no sign that they were aware, in the eleventh exercise, of doing something different from what they had just done ten times over. Obviously, the teacher can draw attention to the contrast between the results of the first ten and the eleventh exercises; the series thus makes it possible to show to students *in their own work* what is and is not "composition," and therefore has a special value. Yet, though a step, the series of exercises around and about the device of the given idea will not surely insinuate a sense of composition into the mind of the student, and in any event it will fail to drive home the point with such finality that he will forevermore feel dissatisfaction in merely writing. Perhaps this sense of dissatisfaction is the prime end of the composition teacher's efforts.

Another Approach

But there is another, far more drastic device which can be used to reinforce this one. Instead of confronting students with either the usual *topic* or the less-usual *given idea* as starting point, one can set before them two or even three random, widely separated elements of "matter" in the form of factual statements, thus: (1) "Jupiter is the largest planet in our solar system" and (2) "Among the richest resources of the Pacific Northwest are its forests of Douglas fir." The directions for the exercise are simple: "Write a single paragraph in which you use these two statements, along with appropriate details which you supply, as integral parts. Do not use either as the topic sentence." It is interesting and may be instructive to add: "Make a note of the time that elapses between your reading this assignment and your beginning on the paragraph."

For the student, this a cruel assignment! For the teacher, the spectacle of straining faces and stalled pencils—which would have started flying instantly had a *topic* been presented—may be a salutary experience. Confronted with a given idea, the student has been able to proceed, without any particular struggle, to think of the details that develop it. Confronted with a given topic, he has always written blithely away without pausing for a directing idea. But confronted with disparate elements of matter, he finds himself helpless to write a word until he has found the means of unifying them. In short, he finds for the first time in his life that he is stopped cold until he finds how to compose.

Of course, the teacher who expects a student to produce a masterpiece in this way will be disappointed: the exercise is only an exercise and should be approached as such. But it may make a point that she had despaired of making. Though there will be no masterpieces, every paragraph will exhibit vivid—often violent—signs of the writer's struggle to compose. Probably its potentiality will not be fully exploited unless the exercise is supplemented by calculated discussion: How long did students delay before they started writing? *Why* did they delay? What was going on in their minds? What were they searching for during the minutes before they began to write? From this discussion perhaps the indispensable realization will emerge: that what they found themselves compelled to search for was an *idea,* without which they could not involve the given disparate elements of matter as integral parts of a paragraph; that, once found, this idea served the same purpose that was served in preceding writing assignments by the idea-statement given by the teacher; and that although the need has never seemed so urgent to them, an idea that will serve the identical purpose is also indispensable when they are asked to "write on a topic"—"My Home Town" or "Hamlet."

Given an idea, students compose, consciously or unconsciously. Given disparate elements of matter with which they are helpless until they have backed up far enough to discover a unifying idea, they seek it out, and, having found it, struggle to compose. But after they have taken exercises in composing from these extremely opposed starting places, will they compose when once more they are confronted with a topic? Will they restrain their impulses to start right off as usual, or will they pause until their minds have evolved an idea that can guide their selection of matter? The obvious way to find whether the sense of necessity for idea has carried over is to confront them again with a topic. Some will fail the test at first: they will start writing at the drop of a hat, as before, or they will pause dutifully to "narrow" the topic mechanically and to "organize" it by outlining; in either event, they will then "write on the topic" in the same old way, saying things about it at random, developing nothing that is a whole, oblivious to the fact that they should try to do so. But by repeating, alternating the three possible starting points of composition—*given idea, given elements of matter, given topic*—the teacher may eventually succeed in insinuating into students' minds, and even in establishing permanently there, the sense of necessity for idea, the sense of dissatisfaction with mere writing, the sense of composition.

JACKSON BURGESS / *Sentence by Sentence*

I believe that students learn to write well only by writing a lot, but I think there is a great deal of fuzziness in many teachers' conceptions of (1) what "learning to write" means, and (2) what "writing a lot" means. "Writing a lot" means writing, studying, correcting and carefully revising a lot of discrete units of composition, certainly, but I want to suggest the unit most appropriate and practical for the beginning of a course is not the traditional theme, but the sentence. Before discussing this suggestion, however, I must touch on question 1—"learning to write."

One part of learning to write is learning certain conventions. The use of capitals, for instance, is governed by convention, and the student must simply remember that the first person singular pronoun is capitalized in conventional writing. That particular convention is arbitrary; others rest to some degree upon reason, as does the rule for punctuation of limiting and non-limiting modifiers, which is derived from and represents the difference between the two forms as spoken. Conventions of the second sort are more difficult to manage, since they may not simply be memorized; their application demands judgment and even—as in the case, say, of the use of italics to indicate emphasis—taste. As a further point, convention ceases altogether to guide the writer, as when he chooses between synonyms, or whether to express a particular opposition in two simple sentences, in a single complex sentence. In the last case, he must arbitrate the claims of euphony, tone,

From *College Composition and Communication*, XIV (December, 1963), 257–62. Reprinted by permission of the National Council of Teachers of English and Jackson Burgess.

rhetorical tactics, and so forth—that is, his decision is principled, rather than conventional.

Yet the principles upon which most of a writer's decisions are based are not principles peculiar to composition. The considerations of euphony which influence a certain word-choice are the same as those involved in everyday speech, in singing, or in the naming of a child. In deciding whether a given thought should be set forth in two sentences or one, in a balanced or a loose construction, the writer has recourse to precisely the same principles he would employ in designing a machine-part or in planning an automobile trip. Nor are these principles obscure: a million footpaths testify to the human awareness that a straight line is the shortest distance between two points. Every student is accustomed to applying such principles, whether or not he can formulate them or recognize their applications in unfamiliar contexts.

This seems to me the "what is to be learned" of writing: the application in the literary-linguistic context of principles already accessible to the average student. Conventions will not suffice, and a great deal of mischief is done by teachers who think that they will. The worst example is the teacher who assures his student that every theme must have an Introduction, a Body, and a Conclusion, as if these designations were as conventional and formal as the spelling of "psittacosis," while in fact he is talking about, or around, the principle of organization. What the student must learn is, first, that writing involves a series of decisions—choices of words, word-orders, constructions, and so forth—and, second, that the quality of these decisions determines the quality of the writing. If the decisions are based upon experience and principle, the results will be good. If they are based upon habits, fashions, or formalism, the results will be bad. "Beware the anger of a quiet man," is superior to "A quiet man's anger is especially to be feared," for the same reasons and in the same way that a short, straight shaft is better than a long, crooked one in most machine operations.

What is "a lot of writing"? I have earlier suggested that these words should mean a great number of discrete units of composition, each one of which is carefully composed, studied, corrected and revised. I would now add that these "units" should be such that the student can discern in them the operations of convention, principle, and taste. This means that they must be manageable in size and complexity, and that each must have a *raison d'être*. The first consideration is self-explanatory; by the second I mean only that there must be behind the composition some rationale beyond the fact that it is required by the instructor. Otherwise, it will scarcely involve any recourse to principles except for the eminently reasonable ones of satisfying, flattering, or at least placating, the teacher. This rationale must be simple and simply identifiable, in order that the decisions made by the student in his composition may be tested against it.

For most students even in the freshman year of college, the traditional theme of 500 to 2,000 words is *not* manageable—although I hope to show that it can easily be made so. It is not appropriate for the demonstration of the nature and importance of the decisions which constitute writing, simply because it obliges the student to make a great number of these decisions without forcing him to consider them—indeed, without permitting him the opportunity of observing that he is making decisions. He submits them not to principle, consequently, but to convention, which will not serve, to his habits, which are usually bad, or to imitation, which can teach him nothing. Under this system, the poor student learns nothing at all and the good one little; the mediocre student learns nothing of English composition but he does learn, to his own impoverishment and anguish of the language, "how to write themes."

All of the basic principles of composition operate in the composition of the sentence. A good sentence, like a good essay or a good book (and far more than "a good theme") requires a reasoned organization, a point of view, a consistent and appropriate tone, form, and diction. The principles of composition can be far more easily exposed and analyzed in the sentence than in longer compositions.

The practical advantages of teaching sentences are vast. In a comparatively short time the student can practice numerous genres and forms and can be given many exercises in revision. Revision, furthermore, is more apt to be thoroughgoing when it does not involve a great sacrifice of time. The best demonstration of these advantages, however, and of the practicability of the method, will lie in a detailed description of my own use of sentence-composition exercises.

II

On the first day, the students are instructed to come to every class prepared to write. The second meeting begins with an assignment to write, in the classroom, a sentence of description. Since I have been fortunate in my room assignments, I've been able to draw the blinds, point out the window, and ask them for a one-sentence description of the Berkeley Hills. I tell them that the sentences must be correct in grammar, punctuation, spelling, and capitalization. Next, each should embody some particular way of looking at the hills—a reason for remarking upon them and something to say about them, although this latter need be no more than "Aren't they beautiful?" or "Aren't they ugly?" In addition, each description must be accurate. Finally,

I suggest that the students who feel confident they've achieved the first three aims may try to make their sentences striking, original, elegant, *stylish*. I suggest that they will be wise to try two or three drafts of the sentence, select the best one and revise it.

They are allowed twenty minutes.

Most of the students finish in five minutes; a few take fifteen. I collect their work and the remainder of the hour is given over to a discussion of, say, the notion of correctness in writing.

At the next meeting I distribute a dittographed sheet of sentences selected from their first day's work, and these are discussed by the class. The following are typical of my recent first-day performances:

> 1. The camel-humped hills of Berkeley are styled into various sizes and shapes, but are nestled together in a common area of heighth.
> 2. The Berkeley hills are broad, alternately tree-studded and barren, and sweeping, and overshadowed only by the haven of intellect nestled at their base.
> 3. The smog-shrouded hills, not too clearly visible, appear to be reaching upward for a breath of fresh air.

The sentences are examined in turn, and minutely. I begin by soliciting criticism from the class, but during the first week I do most of the analysis myself. With the first day's work I am not brutal about such trivia as misspellings, errors of agreement, and "its"—"it's" confusion, and the class is not allowed to dwell too long on these matters. Rather, the emphasis is upon *emphasis:* What, in the hills and in his perception of them, does the writer regard as most important, less important, and unimportant? How does the sentence, by word-order, grammatical subordination and diction, reflect this ranking?

I ask, for instance, just what idea about the hills, or his view of them, is important in Sentence 1. We soon agree that a contrast of diversity ("various shapes and sizes") and uniformity ("a common area of heighth") is the central conception of this sentence: its thesis. The comma and the "but" divide the sentence into two parts, and the use of two clauses makes sense in presenting a contrast. We discuss the efficacy of the ". . . , but . . ." construction in conveying the feeling of contrast, and I mention several alternatives which might call more attention to the contrast: ". . . while at the same time . . ." or ". . . nonetheless . . ." or ". . . even though . . ."

Now we examine the two clauses more closely in the light of the thesis of the sentence, the idea of contrast. What about the parallel verbs, "are styled" and "are nestled"? Why the passive? Does the passive construction really have anything to do with the thesis? The vague implications of agent seem irrelevant to the sentence, and in fact obscure the contrast. We ask " 'Styled' by whom?" and throw out the passive verb, leaving: "The camel-humped hills of Berkeley are various sizes and shapes," and ask how well it conveys the idea of diversity, entrusted to the first clause. "Camel-humped" immediately seems a poor choice, for camel humps are certainly not "various sizes and shapes." Vivid as the phrase may be, it is gratuitous. The second clause, rendered in active voice, becomes: ". . . but (they) nestle together in a common area of heighth." Was the rather quaint personification implied by "they nestle" intended, or accidental? It seems to have crept in under the cover of the passive construction. The class chews over the ordinary senses of "nestle" and decides that the writer couldn't have known what he was doing. Probably he has been betrayed by a vague memory of the "nestled in the hills" cliché into somehow nestling the hills into themselves. We now have: "The hills of Berkeley are various sizes and shapes, but in a common area of heighth." The conflict of "area" and "heighth" is as egregious as the spelling of the latter, and shortly the sentence is reduced to: "The hills of Berkeley are various sizes and shapes, but the same height." That is clear enough, but it is hopelessly vague, since things which are the same height are not "various sizes" except in a very special way.

I recapitulate. The student has accurately perceived that the hills are, indeed, all of about the same altitude, yet otherwise "various." He has chosen a form appropriate to his thesis, since the two clauses with the correlative conjunction do balance one of his perceptions against the other. Why, however, did he not keep in mind exactly what he was saying and suit the details as well as the form to his thesis? Why, once he had got his thesis before him, did he not look again at the hills, knowing exactly what to look at? He saw exactly wherein lay the "uniformity" he perceived, but he didn't think about the "diversity." Had he nailed his own idea down, he couldn't have missed the fact that the hills are "various" particularly in their trees or lack of trees, their steepness or gentleness, and in rounding at the top. He was getting at these things in "shape," but he failed to be specific.

Note that I don't attempt to be exhaustive with every sentence, nor do I pursue every hare that pops out of the brush. Each sentence or group of sentences put before the class is selected for the purposes of a particular subject. Thus two sentences may be compared for their uses of metaphor: one develops a single elaborate simile, the other employs three discrete figures. Two others may be compared for tone: one "poetical" and elevated, the other matter-of-fact. A balanced sentence may be followed by a periodic sentence, and the principles of their operation contrasted. In each case, however, the writer's decisions are judged by reference to his thesis. Generally, I give the class ten or twelve specimen sentences on a dittographed page, but only half of these may be discussed in class and only two or three completely dismembered. Once you get started on this kind of analysis there is a danger of exhausting the class, or convincing them that they are dealing with some sort of maniac.

The students give considerably more care to their second sentences, which they write on the fourth day. Almost everybody uses the full twenty minutes. In this day's work I expect to find few slovenly errors. Punctuation and agreement show a mysterious improvement, for any student who can get into a college can, if he has twenty minutes to labor on one sentence, catch most mistakes of this sort. The sentences are subjected to the same treatment as the first. The sentences become more uniform and more "correct," but they also become more cautious, sober, and timid.

By the time they do their third description, most of the students are able, with pains, to write an accurate sentence whose structure reflects and embodies its thesis, and which has a tone and a point of view. They begin to see that every sentence does, whether they know it or not, contain the germ of a plan, and they begin to look for the sentence whose plan suits their intention. They are starting to compose—to write by consciously making principled literary-linguistic decisions. They are experimenting, because nothing much is lost if you try one sentence form and find it doesn't work. They are revising with some notion of why and how to revise, and they are trying to put words at the service of specific perceptions and ideas.

There are two great dangers in this method: that the instructor will *rewrite* for the student, to the destruction of whatever impulse the student had; and that close word-by-word scrutiny of his sentences may make the student self-conscious and timid. It is important to applaud originality, and it is possible to deplore a sentence not in spite of its excellencies but precisely because the writer has failed to make the most of them. The author of sentence 1, for instance, might be praised for having found a sentence form appropriate to his thesis of contrast (despite the fact that he probably didn't think of it that way) and for the attempt at visualization in "camel-humped" (even though the image was at war with the idea, instead of illustrating it).

It is time to shift the ground. The next assignment is for an expository sentence of the "how-to" variety. All students must give directions, in one sentence, for some piece of work involving a sequence of operations. The example I offer is this: "Cakes are mixed by creaming butter and sugar, then beating in flour, baking-powder, eggs, milk, and flavoring, and they are baked slowly in floured pans." I refer them to their earlier experience by pointing out that I am really asking them to describe a process, instead of a thing or a place.

Next they write a narrative-historical sentence: that is, a description of an event. After that comes a description of a class or category of things, with emphasis upon exhaustiveness and exclusiveness. At the same time, the class has begun the study of definition, aided by the appropriate chapter of a handbook. We discuss problems of definition and examine several essays in extended definition. The next sentence is a critical description of an essay from their anthology. Last of all, the class attempts a one-sentence definition of an abstract term. I have used "weather," "courage," and "religion." As they tackle abstraction, the students revert to their worst writing—which is, in itself, a useful lesson to them. I find a minimum of two definitions is required before the class begins to apply to abstractions the same principles they've learned to use in dealing with the concrete.

I begin, as I have said, concentrating upon emphasis and, as a corollary, subordination. From the very beginning, therefore, we talk about organization—not as Introduction, Body and Conclusion, but as the relation of parts to one another. This relation is much more readily discernible in a single sentence than in an essay, or even a paragraph, but the principles are transferable. Failure to formulate one's thesis with sufficient clarity shows up glaringly in the sentence. Banality and cliché lie naked and vulnerable.

The ideal to which the students are referred throughout is the ideal of correspondence between the sentence and the act of intellection or imagination which it seeks to convey. The limits of this correspondence may have to be pointed out if the class shows signs of being swept away by the fallacy of imitative form, but they are usually in need of perceiving its possibilities, rather than its limits.

When the class can write passable definitions, we turn to the paragraph. My method is simply to offer them the opportunity of extending one of their definitions from one sentence to four or five, reminding them that I expect the same principles to be applied to the the sentences of a paragraph as to the words and clauses of a sentence. The paragraphs are then subjected to the same kind of analysis earlier given to sentences: four or five dittographed, one or two minutely criticized.

After two or three paragraphs, the class is ready for themes. I begin with extended definition and short descriptions, proceeding finally to argument. At this point we are into the writing of themes and past the particulars of sentence composition as an access to principles of writing. My experience convinces me, however, that this approach puts the student in command of terms and concepts which can make his subsequent writing and revision not only easier but more fruitful, than if he came to them, as too many college freshmen do, convinced that Introduction, Body, and Conclusion are, like grace, all-important, but invisible and incomprehensible.

DUANE C. NICHOLS / *The Five-Paragraph Essay: An Attempt To Articulate*

Now a favorite word in our professional jargon, *articulation,* crops up at most joint conferences of high school and college English teachers. Judging from speakers' inflections, I think we are to rejoice if we have articulation, but mostly we don't, and speakers urge us to get some. It is a kind of co-ordination between high school and college programs, a sequence of work that avoids duplication and makes the transition from high school to college easier. Some articulation does exist, but the *English Journal* and my students frequently remind me that we need to prepare students in high school for the kind of writing they are expected to do in college. Constantly freshmen demonstrate some proficiency at the personal sketch, at the informal and humorous essay, and at the lumping together of platitudes to please an audience of foggy-minded adults. They also are quite well trained in mechanics (we used to count comma splices and fragments by the linear inch but now we seldom find them) and have all done some writing. Upon being asked, most freshmen can say all the right things about unity, co-herence, force, and other abstractions without being able to demonstrate them in practice. It is not the fault of their high school education that they don't understand the essence of an essay. They recognize no connection be-tween *essay* as Montaigne used it and a trial or test run of one of their own ideas. Apparently we must explain the concept of *essay* sooner and better than we have been doing.

What follows is a simplified breakdown of an essay—almost any essay—

From *English Journal,* LV (October, 1966), 903–8. Reprinted by permission of the National Council of Teachers of English and Duane C. Nichols.

that has helped freshmen gain this insight at Kansas State University. Until this fall this was no more than another teaching gimmick for me. Finding it useful, participants in our NDEA Institute have been writing back for copies to use in high school. I was even more surprised to find a copy on a bulletin board in a scholarship hall, a copy advertised as "The Easy Way With Comp I." It does serve as an abstract of an expository theme, the kind of writing freshmen do most.

Essentially, this is nothing more than a plan for a five-paragraph essay that can be expanded or contracted and applied to almost any kind of exposition or argumentation. The number five is not sacred or magic. In examining some 3,000 freshmen final examinations from three universities, however, I was amazed to find that about 93 percent of the *A* papers had five paragraphs. Surely no cause-effect relationship exists between the number and the grade, but essay topics assigned for class themes, final exams, and English proficiency tests seem naturally to call for such a pattern. One paragraph each for the introduction and conclusion and three paragraphs in the body explaining the thesis.

Not because they have not been told but because they haven't yet caught on, most of my freshmen do not understand the function of an introduction in exposition. This is strange because they do know what an introduction in a speech must do, and the same usually applies in writing. In the following outline of an introduction, the things marked with an asterisk are necessary to the function of a beginning. A reader deserves to know these things about a paper almost as soon as he begins to read it. They should appear either explicitly or implicitly. They need not appear in this order, and often they can be combined into one sentence.

1. Introduction

   * A. The purpose of the paper and a clear statement of the problem it undertakes to solve or the idea it tests.

   B. Background of the problem (an adequate history of the subject to make the paper's situation intelligible to the reader).

   * C. Scope and limitation of the paper (what the essay is and is not intended to cover).

   D. Definitions of terms necessary to an understanding of the paper.

   E. Acknowledgements (the identification of sources or inspiration if one wishes to avoid footnotes).

   * F. Plan of procedure of the essay (method of approach statement).

   * G. Statement of the thesis of the paper.

Most of these things are best done by implication. Even the least sophisticated freshmen think "The purpose of this paper is . . . ," "This essay is limited to . . . ," and "It is the thesis of this paper that . . ." are too me-chanical. They want something more subtle. It is better, however, to have the blatant statement than to have nothing at all.

Each term English teachers find that, after reading introductions to the first papers, they have no clear idea of the purpose of the papers. Sometimes I can't even see that the purpose was to fulfill the assignment. But this stated purpose need be nothing fancy. Simply, by the time a reader finishes the first paragraph he should have some idea of the subject to be covered and what he is supposed to get out of reading it.

The second item has to do with adapting to an audience. Too frequently the beginning writer assumes, if he thinks about it at all, that each member of his audience has the same information the writer has. If, for example, he writes of the striking effect on guests of the scenery at the Eustace P. Bar-bell Dude Ranch, we might find nothing in the paper indicating the nature of that scenery, be it mountain, prairie, or desert. Or, in another paper, we might be reading about how excited high school students in Someplace Else act on Big Red Day. We may, on the basis of our experience, guess what kind of day that is, but if the writer never tells us, we may guess incor-rectly. The place to set the scene and offer background is in the introduction.

The idea of scope and limitation is apparently difficult to teach. Our pupils often are perfectly willing to give a history of the world with 16 ex-amples in 300 words. One way to avoid the problem is to force them to set a physical limitation in the introduction. If, for example, in a brief paper on chauvinism in his home town, the writer tries to explan all instances of chauvinism, he'll not get done. He has to decide to concentrate on one, two, or three cases while letting the reader know somehow that the paper does not attempt a total analysis. The easiest way to do this is to tell the audience, directly or indirectly, that the essay confines itself to the most obvious or most interesting or most important cases. Then the writer cannot be marked down or judged incompetent for not covering everything his title might in-clude.

Scope and limitation can easily be worked into the method of approach statement which is no more than a sentence or part of a sentence indicating the main topics covered in the body and the order in which they appear. This trick has the obvious advantage of preparing the reader for what is coming and of enabling the author to cut down considerably any kind of inter-paragraph transition in the body. It also gives the reader an idea of what the writer thinks is important and offers, early in the paper, a check on the soundness of that writer's ideas.

The plan of procedure, as well as the limitation, may be subordinated with effect in the thesis statement. "Because of A, B, and C, X is true." Im-mediately the reader knows that the writer confines himself only to an investigation of A, B, and C. We know also that the writer is trying to demonstrate X, the truth of which is his thesis. We can legitimately expect him to take up the subject in the order of A, B, and C. And if we, as readers, are paying attention, we can judge the writer's sense of values by the things he has chosen as A, B, and C. If we were not English teachers having to read papers, think of how often we need read no further. Think of the trivia we could avoid in published material were we to have that trivia identified at the end of the introduction.

Why is it that our student writers can grasp so clearly the concept of a topic sentence or topic idea in paragraphing but have so much trouble seeing that an essay also has a topic idea or sentence or thesis? Our staff spends at least half a period early in the first semester of composition explaining that an essay—a poem, a chapter, a book—ordinarily makes one major point. That an essay explains one thing or proves one thing or describes it or tells about it. Even then many students do not understand, and a major problem of most bad papers is either lack of focus on a topic or an excessively broad major point that cannot be explained in 300–500 words. If a student grasps the idea of a thesis in the same way he understands a topic sentence, the rest of his training is practice and embellishment. He knows how to give his prose direction. While a thesis need not always take the form of a proposition, each essay should have a thesis and in most instances it should be at the beginning of the paper.

Let's look at some introductory paragraphs embodying these ideas. They were written by freshmen for an audience of their classmates. In the first one the student was being very explicit, apparently lacking confidence in his readers' ability to get the point:

> (1) Education is important. (2) Each of us should realize why he comes to college in order to get the most out of it. (3) The thesis of this essay is that I really did not come to college to get an education. (4) The method of approach is to consider in order pressure from my parents, my desire to be socially accepted, and my desire to make a good living. (5) These are the real reasons I came to college.

In spite of the drawbacks, at least we know what is going on when we finish reading this opening paragraph. Its purpose is clear enough. We know the major point. We know that, in the body, the first paragraph will talk about influence of parents on this writer, the second will treat his desire to follow the crowd, and the third his desire to be trained for a good job. While we may question his motives we still must admit that we know what they are. On the basis of the fourth sentence alone we can decide whether the essay is going to make much sense. It also seems clear that his audience, having recently made a similar decision, has adequate background to be able to follow the paper. The paragraph's weakness—the overt signalling—gets in the way of the continuity.

Here's the way another freshman wrote about the same thing, implicitly embodying the important things in his opening:

> (1) Again this fall a higher percentage of the spring high school graduating class makes the pilgrimage to college. (2) As one of the flock caught up in the mass migration, I suddenly find myself wondering why I am here. (3) We all have heard all about the importance of higher education and I, falling into the usual cliché, have stated boldly that I came to college to get an education. (4) Honest investigation of my motives, however, leads me to believe that pressure from my parents, a desire to be with my friends, and a need to be trained for a good job brought me to college.

Wordy and metaphorical though he may be, this student begins with a generality broad enough that his audience can understand it and then narrows quickly to a statement including himself within the generality. Finally it centers on why he came to college. As the reader follows from the general to the particular, the essay's purpose becomes obvious. While many things probably influenced this person to come to college, he limits the discussion to three reasons, reasons he should be able to explain fully in a short paper. Its scope is clear as is the writer's area of responsibility. Finally, the fourth sentence mentions in order the topic ideas of the three paragraphs we can expect to find in the body. Hence, that fourth sentence combines topic limitation, plan of procedure, and thesis in a tight package.

When a young writer can see that an introduction has certain jobs to do and that conveniently nearly every topic of exposition or argumentation can be begun in essentially the same manner, he no longer merely tacks on an introduction. In fact, after finishing the introduction he has practically written the essay. All that remains is expansion. Further, a student easily can modify or improvise upon this basic idea as the occasion demands.

The body of a five-paragraph essay is so simple and so standard that its importance is sometimes missed. In outline form, of course, it looks like this:

II. Body
    A. First main point
        1. Sub-point
        2. Sub-point
        3. Sub-point
    B. Second main point
        1.
        2.
        3.

C. Third main point
   1.
   2.
   3.

Since, however, most of our students neither read nor write outlines, they have to be told something about it. Most of them understand basic algebra, and perhaps an analogy is an appropriate start. Consider IIA in the paper introduced in the second example above. The writer's parents put pressure on him to go to college. We know that is the topic idea of the first paragraph of the body, and a student writing such a paragraph has a number of choices in developing it. Perhaps he chooses to explain why his parents wanted him to go to school. The parents must have had three reasons in some kind of order of importance. Perhaps he chooses to present three examples of the pressure. He might give a reason or an example or both. At any rate, IIA is true because of $1 + 2 + 3$ under it. 1 plus 2 plus 3 equals A. The same addition applies in each paragraph of the body. Taken together the sub-points prove, illustrate, explain, describe, or define—as the case may be—the topic idea of the paragraph. Sometimes this algebraic Mickey Mouse works as an explanation of paragraph organization when all else has failed.

To move ahead to the essay's conclusion. Conclusions are horribly hard to write, a fact that accounts for the tendency of beginning writers constantly to tack on a moral. One would think our pupils were either modern Aesops or journeymen preachers. To avoid ending with a moral or to avoid being didactic, our essayists have several options. In outline form a possible conclusion looks like this:

III. Conclusion
  A. Summary of main points
  B. Conclusions
  C. Recommended action, if appropriate
  D. Significance of the conclusions (the "So-Whatness" of it all)

Summation is a bugaboo. Many better students, writing a short essay, think the main points too obvious to reiterate. Many teachers find the summary nothing more than a verbatim lifting of topic sentences from earlier paragraphs. Reasonably one can justify very brief summations in short papers, and I think we need them. The reader is about to put the paper aside, and an author should want his readers to remember what he has read. Some kind of pulling together of supporting points is helpful. Perhaps it need be nothing more than a "because" clause introducing the conclusion statement. "Because of _____, _____, and _____, it follows that _____ must be the case." Logically a summary can be subordinated to the main idea of the paper which, in the conclusion, follows after it.

Students sometimes are surprised to learn that their English teachers equivocate. In one sense we use *conclusion* to mean that section of an essay that ends it. In the other we talk about the *conclusion* reached in testing the idea. They are two quite different things. Essentially IIIB (conclusions) is the thesis of the paper, the controlling generalization repeated at the end in order to leave the main point fresh in the reader's mind as he puts the paper down. We probably want the writer to rephrase or recast the thesis sentence at the end, especially in a short paper, to avoid a mechanical repetition. But IIIB is the same thing as IG. To continue the algebraic analogy, the whole idea of an expository paper may be phrased: $IIA + IIB + IIC = IG$. IG also equals IIIB. Or IG (IIIB) is true because of IIA and IIB and IIC. IG (IIIB) may best be illustrated by IIA, IIB, and IIC.

But isn't this also too mechanical? Those who have read this far may think that this is just another formula and, to a degree, it is. When we have given the reader that rephrased thesis, we really are not done. After all, the introduction in such a scheme is highly analytic and it makes the points of the presentation quite clear. The conclusion should be synthetic. It should answer questions the essay likely raises. If an essay's conclusion is reliable, valid, or true, *so what?* What difference does it make? What can the reader himself conclude from his new knowledge? A good conclusion goes beyond mere summation and reiteration. It gives a synthesis, a pulling together to complement the introduction's analytical division. Without offering a moral platitude or without making an irrelevant value judgment, it can be very effective if it briefly explains the significance of the thesis. It can explain ramifications of the discovery beyond the immediate context. A reader then may find more point to what he has just seen than if the writer leaves him hanging in the air. The tying of loose ends, the anchoring of the thesis to something outside itself, is much more interesting and, indeed, more important than bare summary.

The kinds of essays we assign, in both high school and college, are highly artificial things, the assignments often arbitrary. Perhaps they bear no relation to reality. Obviously any writing or speaking occasion the student encounters outside the classroom will require much more than three or four hundred words. We justify our assignments, however, by arguing that the techniques of well-ordered explanation are the same in or out of the classroom. Only the length changes. I think this is true. Also subject to expansion is this five-paragraph outline. The length of the body is directly proportionate to the limitation of the topic.

Such a formula has drawbacks as a teaching device. A young and not overly alert writer may try to cram any topic for any form of discourse into this frame. Recently, while examining a fictional narrative in class, one of my literal-minded students criticized it for not having a method of approach statement. This is the same as attacking Mary Roberts Rinehart for not naming the bad guy on the first page. The same student may wrongly conclude that any paper following this organization is automatically good. Appropriate primarily in exposition or argumentation, and even there it must be modified to fit the writing occasion, this system does contain within it the essence of generally acceptable essays. Without really thinking about it, E. B. White and John Ciardi include these characteristics in their prose. Our students, not being Whites or Ciardis, have to be taught to think about it.

The better writers readily can improvise upon this theme and should. For them the device has value mainly as a point of departure. In following such a system writers usually discover that the original analysis may not work, that in working out the topic they reach a conclusion different from that of the outline. In doing so they test their ideas as did Montaigne. Perhaps this is one means of showing good and bad writers, as Geraldine Allen so cogently urges (*English Journal,* 53, November, 1964, 607–9), what kind of writing will be expected of them in freshman English. Simultaneously they must be allowed and encouraged to transcend the formula. Another means of articulation but not, of course, the only one.

THOMAS E. TAYLOR / *Let's Get Rid of Research Papers*

Unfortunately, in many high-school English classes the assignment of research papers is becoming more frequent. Students are being required to acquire the habit of collecting other people's thoughts to fill the pages of an assigned paper instead of being given the opportunity to develop confidence in their abilities to express their own thoughts about the ideas contained in the literature they read. English departments have accepted the responsibility for giving instruction in a skill which has no value in the high-school course of study and which may actually stifle the very creative expression of ideas which those departments are supposed to facilitate.

Why should the high-school English teacher waste his and his students' time with lessons on manuscript style, footnoting, bibliography forms, etc., when he knows that his students are not equipped to carry on meaningful literary research? Why should he accept, in lieu of worthwhile literary scholarship, those adolescent excursions into the subject matter of disciplines in which the English teacher is unprepared to offer expert guidance and instruction? If the research paper is an important tool in the high-school social studies class, let its construction be taught there and let that teacher be responsible for the correction and grading of the finished product. (The argument that only English teachers are equipped to handle the correction and grading of research papers, although convenient for some, is an insult to the thousands of teachers of subjects other than English who have successfully used the research papers in their classes.)

From *English Journal*, LIV (February, 1965), 126–27. Reprinted by permission of the National Council of Teachers of English and Thomas E. Taylor.

The research paper is of no value in the high-school English class, because reasonably correct and creative writing—the goal of instruction in composition—cannot be developed by teaching students to regurgitate the thoughts of others (too often without proper credit). The English teacher should not be concerned with the development of young historians who know a good deal about the political, economic, and social aspects of a given period but who are unacquainted with the human values of a literary work set or written in that period. Hours of "background" lectures and activities and piles of plagiarized papers on the Elizabethan theater, Elizabethan England, or Shakespeare's life are no substitute for the student who can express his reactions to the human values found in *Julius Caesar, Macbeth, Hamlet,* or any other of the plays he reads.

Too many of us turn our English classroom into a poor substitute for the social studies classroom. We spend too much time—ours and the students'—on unnecessary literary and political history and too little time on the literary experience which our students are (or should be) having. In an attempt to re-create our own college English classes, we teach literary history and not literature. We forget that the high-school student lacks the background of literary experience that enables the college student to cope with the additional facts from other disciplines which illuminate his mature study of literature.

Often, we have not paid sufficient attention in our high-school classes to the basics of our own subject, a discipline which naturally excites thoughts about the important questions of human experience as it is recorded in our literary heritage. We have neglected to develop in our students' minds the concepts necessary for an understanding of the literary work of art. There are those who spend class hours "teaching" the tenets of existentialism to students who are none too sure of the meanings of theme, conflict, or plot.

In our attempts to re-create the pleasures of our college English classes, we often adopt not only the content (high-school lessons from college notebooks) but also the requirements of the course—especially the research paper. When we deny the student the means of expressing more clearly his reactions to the literary experience by neglecting to teach him the concepts necessary to such expression, we cannot expect to be otherwise than disappointed at his attempts to present those reactions to us in written form. When we go one step further and substitute the stringing together of quotations for the expression of original ideas, we compound our failure to our students and to ourselves.

It is obviously easier and more pleasant to read polished sentences taken from the authors of "sources" than it is to read the awkward prose of an adolescent. It is easier and more pleasant for that adolescent to find his ideas ready-made and ready-written than it is for him to think for himself. Under those circumstances, however, neither of us is doing the job for which we were brought together in the English class in the first place.

We should return to the social studies teacher those parts of his curriculum we have *borrowed* and those of his responsibilities we have accepted. If the activities necessary for the comprehension of the literature that we teach cannot be kept to a minimum of interference with the literary experience, then we should use other literary works in which that experience is more easily available to our students. We should leave the teaching of the techniques of the research paper to the history teacher, if he finds need for it, or, preferably, to the colleges. We must begin to re-emphasize the personal essay as a medium of truly creative expression.

EVALUATION

T. A. KOCLANES / *Can We Evaluate Compositions?*

Why, indeed, should we evaluate compositions at all? One reason is so that we can put grades on them and then use those grades as a basis for reporting to parents and as a basis for deciding whether or not a student has fulfilled the requirements of the course. In other words, we evaluate in order to measure pupil achievement of "standards" as opposed to "goals," to use the terminology of the NCTE Committee on the Evaluation of Pupil Performance.[1] To measure in such a way means first that we must measure each student according to a single standard, and second, by implication, it means a comparative rating of students.

Is this in fact possible? Research tends to answer this question with a qualified "yes," the major qualification being that we rigorously eliminate the consideration of specific points of subject matter [2] and maturity of judgment [3] as criteria for evaluating compositions. Research dealing with quantitative evaluation, that is evaluation which leads to a grade, is usually concerned with the problems of objectivity, reliability, and validity. Objectivity refers to the consistency with which a number of readers will grade the same composition. In the usual essay testing situation the correlations

[1] Luella B. Cook, "The Search for Standards," *The English Journal*, XLIX (May, 1960), pp. 321–35.
[2] P. B. Diederich, "Measurement of Skill in Writing," *School Review*, LIV (1946), pp. 584–92.
[3] John M. Stalnaker, "Tests of Acceptable and Reliable Habits of Writing," *The English Journal* (College Edition), XXIII (1934), pp. 37–47.

From *English Journal*, L (April, 1961), 252–57, 264. Reprinted by permission of the National Council of Teachers of English and T. A. Koclanes.

for objectivity are quite low, .30 to .50.[4] In fact, it has been shown that the same reader will often disagree with himself on two or more readings of the same composition.[5] Reliability, or the dependability of one piece of writing as a basis for judging the general level of a student's performance, is also low, .60 in one study in which tight controls were exercised over the construction of the test as well as the reading and grading. Without such controls, the correlation is usually considerably lower.[6] Thus, as pointed out by Traxler and Anderson, on an assignment to "write a theme of a thousand words on the pleasures of going camping," the reliability would be so low as to require forty such compositions in order to estimate the general level of ability of the writer.[7] Although, according to one writer, "there is no more direct evidence of ability to write,"[8] essay testing is also low in validity if the essays are graded according to content as well as other criteria. Another writer claims that where there is a marked difference between the grade on an essay test and the grade on an objective writing test, the latter is "a more valid estimate" of writing ability.[9] The conclusions of research in the area of essay evaluation would seem to be that the evaluation of writing exercises is an extremely hazardous affair for the ordinary English teacher, who should instead stick to the realm of objective tests of writing and exercises in proofreading, where he is relatively safe from the evils of subjectivity.

Purpose in Evaluating Writing

However, I do not believe that we need to fear these dangers unless our only purpose in evaluating compositions is to assign a grade. If, instead, we are mainly interested in teaching young people to think carefully about significant ideas and to put forth the effort necessary for clear and exact writing, then I think that we can approach the subject of theme evaluation with confidence. After all, it is one thing to help a student to see how he can improve his communication through the use of known and accepted principles, but it is quite another to attempt to take his exact measurements as a writer, and on the basis of this measurement to assign him to a par-

[4] John M. Stalnaker and Ruth C. Stalnaker, "Reliable Reading of Essay Tests," *School Review*, XLII (1934), pp. 599–605.
[5] *Ibid.*, p. 603.
[6] Arthur Traxler and Harold Anderson, "The Reliability of an Essay Test in English," *School Review*, XLIII (1935), pp. 534–39.
[7] *Ibid.*, p. 538.
[8] Diederich, *op. cit.*, p. 584.
[9] John M. Stalnaker, "Essay and Objective Writing Tests," *The English Journal* (College Edition), XXII (1933), pp. 217–22.

ticular rank among his classmates. I do not mean to suggest that we abandon the grading of compositions altogether. But I do agree with William J. Dusel's contention, in "Some Semantic Implications of Theme Correction," that our primary function as teacher-evaluators is to teach, and that any marks which we put on compositions which do not contribute to this end are superfluous and may often have a negative effect on the development of the writer. Or, as he says in a later article, "We should mark papers in such a way as to communicate our respect for the personality of the writer and our interest in his progress." [10] This point of view is, of course, very much in evidence in Volume III of the NCTE Curriculum Series, *The English Language Arts in the Secondary School,* and is representative of the views held by many English teachers.

If by evaluation, then, we mean *criticism with the intention of teaching individuals how to improve their written expression,* and not *the grading of compositions,* I believe that the question in the title of this paper can be answered in the affirmative. If we approach the task of evaluation of compositions in the way in which we would approach any teaching situation, that is with a full knowledge of the emotional as well as the intellectual status of the young people we are teaching, with a patient understanding that motivation must precede all learning, and with the attitude that it may take many failures to produce a success—then there certainly are definite criteria which we can use as a basis for evaluation. Some of these criteria are fairly objective, too, even when we use them to grade papers, although they become rather indefinite, as do any criteria, when we attempt to make judgments on the basis of too many of them at one time. On the level of highest objectivity is the criterion of correctness: grammar, spelling, and mechanics. Next come matters of organization of ideas along with paragraph structure and development. On the least objective level, what the statistical evaluators would call the subjective level, are the criteria of originality, vitality, and significance of ideas, as well as of the mature and reasoned development of ideas.

The Easiest Phase

The most objective level is also the simplest level of evaluation. In the marking of spelling, grammatical, and mechanical errors there is little soul-searching necessary. A sentence fragment is usually a sentence fragment, no matter who marks the paper, and its presence invariably brings out very strong feelings in the teacher. Likewise, errors in agreement, lack of

[10] William J. Dusel, "How Should Student Writing Be Judged?" *The English Journal,* XLVI (1957), pp. 263–68.

clear reference, failure to punctuate a compound sentence or nonrestrictive clause properly bring little feeling of uncertainty or hesitation. The teacher's duty is clear: mark the error and get on with the job. The only danger at this level is that because it is so comfortable to mark these things, we make a big show of it to the exclusion of other more complex matters of evaluation. We do this not only because marking for correctness of expression is easy and requires little thought, but because we feel the need to impress the student with our vast knowledge of grammar, punctuation, etc. How many times have we marked an error, not because we thought it would really teach any specific point of grammar but because we were just a little concerned about doing a thorough job, in the same way that we are concerned about filling in all of the boxes in a crossword puzzle? And there is also the faint anxiety that the student will discover and call to our attention an error which we missed. As Mr. Dusel points out, the little red marks indicating this type of error often completely overshadow the amount of comment devoted to content and to our reaction to the ideas in the theme, and the student very quickly comes to the conclusion that it is the spelling, grammar, and mechanics which really count in good writing.[11]

And what a sad thing it is when, as sometimes happens in my twelfth-grade English classes, a "good" English student, i.e. one whose grammar, spelling, and mechanics are nearly perfect, receives her neatly-written, error-free composition back with no marks on it except the grade of "D" and a comment to the effect that she (for some reason they always seems to be girls) has failed to develop any significant ideas or that her paragraphs are developed through repeating the topic sentence in different words. At this level the important question seems to be not *can* we evaluate compositions, but *should* we evaluate compositions. Although I myself often fall into the crossword puzzle habit of marking themes, I am inclined to agree with Mr. Dusel that error symbols, and grades as well, often give the wrong impression to the student and do not fulfill the primary requirement for evaluation mentioned earlier—that of teaching.[12] It may be that one writer had the right idea when he suggested in *The English Journal* several years ago that we abandon marking symbols altogether, limit ourselves to a brief comment, and teach correctness by duplicating one or two of the average themes and letting the students do the correcting. It was his feeling that students are much more interested in correcting somebody else's work and that they get more out of it because they are not on the defensive.[13]

---

[11] William J. Dusel, "Some Semantic Implications of Theme Correction," *The English Journal*, XLIV (1955), pp. 390–97.

[12] *Ibid.*, p. 391.

[13] P. B. Diederich, "Making and Using Tests," *The English Journal*, XLIV (1955), pp. 135–40.

On a somewhat less objective level is the evaluation of paragraph development and structure. Although judgments may differ as to what constitutes a good paragraph, most textbooks seem to agree on at least three things which, if taught department-wide and accepted generally by the English staff, constitute fairly objective criteria. These things go by different names: my favorite textbook calls them "adequate development," "unity," and "continuity." At a lower grade level they might be known as "supplying details," "sticking to the point," and "guiding the reader." This, it seems to me, is a much more meaningful level of evaluation, and it is much more complex. Though the objectivity here is probably too low for accurate quantitative marking and ranking of papers, the evaluation of paragraph structure and development can be an excellent means of teaching better expression through writing. On this level, the difficulties are not always easily spotted, and, when they are, it is frequently a problem to word the evaluative comment so that it teaches. Of course, one can always just write "unity" or "cont." or "devel." in the margin and let it go at that, but I have found that, until students have really learned the paragraph formula, these marks suggest little in the way of improvement.

Teaching through evaluation, on this level, involves an understanding of the student's purpose in writing and an appreciation for the particular idea he is trying to explain in any one paragraph. That is, it involves more than just filling in the blanks as in the crossword puzzle; it involves two-way communication. What the student fails to say, because he lacks adequate development, must be sensed by the reader if he is to offer helpful evaluative comments. When the writer strays from his main idea, the reader must have enough of an awareness of what that main idea is supposed to be, though it may have been ever so poorly communicated to begin with, to see what the student is *trying* to do with his words and thus to see where and how he began to get off the track. This kind of analysis can be tedious, and it demands the complete and unhurried attention of the reader if the object is to teach through evaluation. Nevertheless, it can be done, and, if the teacher has been careful to teach the concepts of good paragraphing to begin with, students can be taught to write at least more readable paragraphs, and they are likely to find that it can be fun to develop their ideas in this organized way.

The Most Difficult Phase

Good paragraphing, however, does not necessarily mean good writing, though it may provide the framework for good writing. It doesn't take much effort to imagine a composition which is free from errors in grammar, spelling, mechanics, and paragraphing but which fails to do one or more of the following things: (1) communicate anything of significance; (2) show evidence of a central purpose or idea around which the various paragraphs are arranged in some effectual pattern; (3) adhere to standards of logic and straight thinking in the formation and statement of judgments and opinions; (4) supply an adequate number of relevant facts in support of opinions developed in the composition. There is no doubt that here we are at a level of evaluation at which it is neither possible nor desirable to make accurate comparative ratings. Here each composition is a reflection of the complexity of its writer, and we can no more rate the purpose, organization, and significance of ideas than we can rate the writers as human beings. Nevertheless, we can evaluate them for the purpose of helping the writer to do a better job of saying whatever it is he is trying to say. In other words, we may not be able, at this level, to arrange a class set of compositions in order of excellence, but we can help each student to see how he can achieve his purposes more efficiently. What we are evaluating at this level is nothing less than that exact and organized way of thinking referred to by Francis Bacon when he said that writing makes an exact man.

At this level we may often note that a student has not spent enough time in thinking about and writing the composition. If the major value of writing lies in the fact that it forces us to slow down and think carefully, then it is apparent that one of our tasks as teachers is to teach young people to spend more time at the job of writing, even if it is at the expense of the number of separate pieces of writing required. I believe that we can do this if we allow students adequate time for thinking as well as for writing, in our theme assignments, and if we are understanding but firm in our evaluation of their efforts at thinking in an exact and organized way. If evaluating paragraph structure and development demands a sixth sense on the part of the reader in order to understand what the writer is trying to do, this level of evaluation demands even more understanding. If we are really to teach writing through evaluation, we must certainly do more than make such comments as "your ideas are not clear," or "you fail to develop your main idea," or "poor logic," or "organization weak." We must somehow see what the writer is trying to do and help him to see *how* as well as *where* he has fallen down. If we are to inspire him to communicate more effectively, we must react to what he has said. When he has discovered that he can really communicate through writing, he will also discover that he wants to write good paragraphs and maintain standards of correctness in order to support his attempt to communicate.

It would be misleading if I were to end this paper leaving the impression that my remarks reflect accurately my own practices with my 130 students. The kind of evaluation that I have been writing about, evaluation for the purpose of teaching, is a time-consuming process, and it demands the utmost care in execution. Although these represent my objectives in theme evaluation, I find that in practice I simply cannot do the kind of job that I would like to do. One thing that I have done is to assign fewer themes, give a longer period for completion of the assignment, and then expect more careful work. Another thing which has worked well has been to assign shorter pieces of writing in which a specific skill, such as paragraph continuity, is emphasized. Then in the evaluation of these I mark only for that skill. In my opinion time is the biggest single factor in the improvement of writing through evaluation. With four classes of twenty-five students each, I am sure that just about any method of evaluation would show instant results, provided that the teacher were professionally competent in all ways and enthusiastic about teaching writing. But that is another subject, one which has been capably covered by others.

Lay Readers? No

One way of reducing the paper load, which has been suggested from time to time, is the handing over of the evaluation job, or parts of it, to people other than the English teacher. In other words, can *others* evaluate compositions? I believe that there is real merit in the suggestion that we teach students to evaluate their own themes through practice in evaluating the themes of classmates. If each student has his composition read and marked for correctness by four other students and then is asked to revise his own composition on the basis of this marking before submitting it, both the writer and the student-readers stand to gain, not to mention the fact that the teacher has that much less mechanical checking to do. Also, there is no reason why teachers of subjects other than English should not share in the evaluation of compositions written for their subjects, using criteria other than just accuracy and completeness of subject matter.

On the other hand, I find myself out of sympathy with those who propose the use of "lay readers" for the purpose of increasing the amount of writing that can be evaluated, unless the readers' tasks are limited to marking for correctness or to the marking of short writing exercises with specific purposes. I believe that the evaluation of compositions is the most important and demanding single task that an English teacher is called upon to perform, requiring as it does not only skill in spotting quickly the difficulties of the young writer, both rhetorical and grammatical, but also a wide acquaintance with the best literature of our language, and an attitude toward young people based upon professional study and experience. This, to me, is why teaching in the field of English is a profession requiring special talents and special training; it is not a job that can be handed over to a "lay reader" in order to free the teacher for more demanding tasks. In the teaching of English there is no more demanding task than to read sympathetically and yet critically the work of a young person learning to express ideas in writing.

In summary, then, I believe that we must differentiate between the two different kinds of evaluation, evaluation which measures and compares and evaluation which teaches. While I recognize the need to measure and compare in the area of writing, I feel that it can be done in other ways than in the evaluation of compositions and that this area should be reserved, more or less, for the other kind of evaluation. I believe that although the marking of errors in spelling, grammar, and mechanics has a place in teaching through evaluation, it should not be allowed to become more important than other more complex and significant matters such as teaching paragraph development and structure and motivating students to think more carefully about what they write. Finally, I believe that in order to answer the question "Can we evaluate compositions?" with an unqualified "yes," we need, more than anything else, smaller classes; and I do not believe that we can get around this necessity by the cheap expedient of hiring people outside of the profession to do a job that demands a degree of professional skill beyond that of almost anything else that the English teacher is expected to do.

CARLTON F. WELLS / *Ten Points for Composition Teachers*

Have you as an English teacher ever written out your decalogue of do's and don'ts on how best to read, evaluate, and grade your students' papers? Such a ten-point statement of purposes and procedures might well sharpen your approach to composition and upgrade your semester's performance. Not that there is anything sacred in the number ten. Nor can a department-wide consensus on THE ten key points be easily arrived at. But any ten-point program based on experience and critical observation should provide some terse, exact, common-sense suggestions. Any resourceful department chairman or committee could certainly formulate a clarifying group of guideposts useful both to the new teacher and to the veteran.

For whatever it may be worth by way of suggestion, here is my own decalogue on how student papers should be read and evaluated. Its value for other teachers will be served if it stirs them to put together their own different and better list.

1. Give due weight to both the test of form and the test of substance. Don't become a mere crank on mechanics—an occupational hazard of our profession.

2. Make your corrections and comments *instructional*. If, for example, a vague, empty paper gets a *C* minus, specify why—if only by such marginal comments as "Give examples" or "Where are your facts?" Or if spelling is bad, at least refer to the relevant pages in the handbook on how to spell better.

From *English Journal*, LV (November, 1966), 1080–81. Reprinted by permission of the National Council of Teachers of English and Carlton F. Wells.

3. Find room for the commendatory or affirmative word; avoid the merely negative or satiric. A cautionary note, such as "Proofreading pays off," or "You can do better work than this," does not slam the door on future improvement. And with your worst pupils, don't waste your time or overwhelm them by overcrowding the margins with corrections.

4. Be fair to your students. If by chance an assignment produces a disproportionate percentage of disappointing themes, ask yourself: "Is the fault at least partly mine? Did I provide clear, adequate explanation and motivation in assigning the paper?"

5. Marginal and terminal comments, however brief, should always be legible, precise, and well expressed.

6. Read selectively for particular objectives, at least occasionally. Disregarding other shortcomings, stress just one aspect, such as sentence correctness, paragraph organization, "specific details," figurative originality.

7. Emphasize the role of an effective title (the tests of fitness, brevity, originality, interest) and the title's relation to controlling purpose.

8. Always make some use of student papers in class—as by reading selected papers aloud, by duplicating a paper for class evaluation, by blackboard analysis of passages needing revision, by students in small groups judging each others' papers, or by posting superior papers on bulletin boards.

9. Return papers promptly—always ahead of the "due date" for the next assigned paper.

10. Keep a file of your students' papers, corrected, revised. This emphasizes the cumulative record, facilitates both the student conference and the occasional parent conference, and underscores the importance of the end-of-the-semester appraisal.

JAMES L. GREEN / *A Method for Writing Comments on Student Themes*

Teachers of composition have devised fairly effective means for marking mechanical errors on student themes. Symbols, abbreviations, and handbook rule numbers can be used to pinpoint errors in diction, grammar, punctuation, and, to some extent, in sentence structure. However, they are less effective for indicating problems in content, development, and organization. It is generally agreed that these aspects of writing can best be criticized in written comments to the student. As Albert Kitzhaber points out, marginal symbols "should be supplemented with comments referring both to particular passages and to the entire paper." He adds: "Such comments are most helpful when they are specific, pointed, and constructive." [1]

Unfortunately, the terminal comment, the summary appraisal of a student's theme, seldom fulfills Kitzhaber's requirements. If this appraisal is specific, it usually exploits a mechanical problem which has already been criticized with a marginal symbol. The instructor writes: "You need to review the uses of the comma." If the comment is pointed, it is frequently like the toe of a boot—"This is a childish, insignificant paper." And if it is constructive, it is often negative—"The next time you write a comma splice, I will fail your paper." Frequently, the terminal comment is not specific, pointed, or constructive at all. It is a generalized formula, relying heavily on adjectives, which usually appear in pairs: "Your paper is well-organized,

---

[1] Albert R. Kitzhaber, *Themes, Theories, and Therapy; The Teaching of Writing in College* (New York: McGraw-Hill Book Co., 1963), p. 135.

From *English Journal*, LVII (February, 1968), 215–20. Reprinted by permission of the National Council of Teachers of English and James L. Green.

but content is trivial." "Your idea is excellent, but organization is faulty." There are many ways to tell the student that his paper is fairly good but not as good as it should be.

Because of these problems, we need to clarify the functions of the terminal comment; and we need to devise means of making it specific, pointed, and constructive. A terminal comment should do two things. It should identify those major weaknesses of the paper not already criticized in the margins. And it should reveal to the student ways in which he can improve his writing. If a student has acute problems with grammar, usage, or sentence rhetoric, the instructor may need to use the terminal comment to elaborate on errors already identified with marginal symbols. Usually, however, the instructor's summary remarks should tell the student something significant about the content, organization, and development of his theme. In order to make significant comments about these general aspects of composition, we need to identify specific topics concerning content and structure on which to base our comments. Robert Gorrell's concept of commitment and response suggests what these topics might be and thereby generates one method of writing the terminal comment.

According to Gorrell, each statement in an essay dictates, to a greater or lesser extent, both the content and the organization of the following sentence or sentences. Certain sentences, the thesis statement and the topic sentences, are the most important of these, since they serve as the major semantic and structural markers in the theme. The student must respond to these commitment statements by discussing certain things in his paper, usually by arranging his material in a certain order, and sometimes by following a particular pattern of development.[2]

For example, a student paper begins: "Reinforced with faulty logic, misleading evidence, and hidden persuaders, the advertisement for Wilson golf balls in a recent issue of *Time* appeals to the average golfer's desire to be a professional." This statement controls the scope of the theme, limiting the discussion to three aspects of one advertisement. It specifies the aspects to be discussed—logic, evidence, and hidden persuaders. And it indicates that they will be related to a particular appeal—the reader's desire to be a professional. The statement also implies the kind of organization and development that will follow. There will be three main sections arranged in the order the three topics are mentioned in the thesis statement. Section one, on logic, will elucidate and analyze the chain of reasoning implied in the advertisement. Section two, on evidence, will be developed with citation and

[2] Robert Gorrell, "Not by Nature: Approaches to Rhetoric," *English Journal*, LV (April, 1966), 409–17.

analysis of facts presented in the copy. And section three will probably begin with a definition of *hidden persuader,* which will be followed by citation and analysis of examples. In each case the material will be related to the purpose of the advertisement—the appeal to the golfer's desire to be a professional.

As I have tried to show, the thesis statement or thesis commitment of this paper controls and directs content and organization. I believe this is true of all well-written essays. Most weaknesses in content and organization can be directly related to the thesis commitment, or in matters of paragraph development, to the topic sentences. Consequently, one way to write an effective terminal comment is to analyze the problems involved in the semantic and structural commitments of a theme's thesis statement. These commitments provide us with specific topics for comment.

To illustrate the method, I would like to present examples of weak thesis commitments to show how they lead the student to write certain kinds of ineffective themes and to suggest how the instructor can make specific, useful comments by analyzing the commitments of the student's thesis statement. A good thesis statement marks out the scope of a paper; makes a meaningful predication about a topic—a statement which can be supported with evidence; and often directs the organization of the theme. Usually, if it fails to do any one of these, a poor paper results.

The thesis statement should limit the scope of the paper. A theme handed in by one of my students begins: "In 'A Rose for Emily' Faulkner uses the style that is characteristic of his novels." This assertion commits the student to write a book, not an essay. He begins by discussing the style of *The Sound and the Fury.* On page two he realizes that he is attempting too much, and he starts a new paragraph: "The same is true of 'A Rose for Emily.'" But he discovers that the same is not true and spends a page discussing differences. At the top of page three, perhaps realizing that he has not adequately developed his topic, he half-heartedly concludes: "It can be seen, then, that Faulkner's style in 'A Rose for Emily' is similar to his style in *The Sound and the Fury.*"

Several problems result from the thesis statement. It directs the writer to try to prove something which is not true, and it leads him away from his topic—style in "A Rose for Emily." However, these difficulties derive from the more basic problem of scope. The student commits himself to do too much, actually to compare the style of all of Faulkner's novels with the style of the story. Because he partially attempts to follow this commitment, and because he discovers that he has to make qualifications he did not foresee, he writes an undeveloped, disorganized paper which lacks proper focus.

Based on the relationship between the thesis statement and the development and organization of the paper, a comment such as the following might be written:

> Your thesis statement commits you to discuss several Faulkner novels and to relate their style to that of "A Rose for Emily." You cannot do this in a theme-length essay. Also, since there are differences between the style of any Faulkner novel and the style of the story, you are forced to consider these differences. Consequently, you are not able to discuss adequately, your topic, style in "A Rose for Emily." You should do this and nothing else. At one point you write that Faulkner presents details in the story according to the association of ideas rather than chronologically. This would have been a promising, adequately limited thesis statement. One often discovers a topic as he writes. When he does this he needs to start over, beginning with a new topic.

Instead of being too broad, a thesis statement may limit the scope of an essay too severely. The student begins with an assertion that he can develop in a paragraph. He then writes another statement which he can develop in another paragraph, and so on. Occasionally, he discovers a fruitful topic—usually in his last paragraph. With obvious modifications the comment to this student would be similar to the sample just given. In particular, the student should be told that his theme lacks unity and continuity because he does not *have* a controlling generalization.

Although the problem of scope and the problem of significance overlap— a paper which attempts too much or too little will probably lack significance —thesis statements may mark out a workable scope for the paper and still lead the student to write a trivial theme. The thesis statement will dictate an insignificant theme if it fails to raise a question, state a problem, or present a point-of-view; if it leads the paper away from the assigned topic; or if it cannot be supported with evidence.

If a thesis statement fails to raise an issue or problem that calls for discussion or analysis, the resulting paper will almost certainly lack significance. For example, the assertion " 'A Rose for Emily' is about a woman who goes crazy and commits a murder" only directs the students to write a plot summary. The theme is mediocre, because the thesis statement leads the writer to say something which is obvious to anyone who reads the story. This kind of paper is particularly difficult to evaluate in a terminal comment. Instead of writing the usual "trivial," "insignificant" or "You don't *say* anything" at the end of the theme, the instructor should analyze the thesis statement. By pointing out that it commits the student to say the obvious, he can explain why the resulting theme lacks significance. He might also formulate an effective thesis statement, based if possible on the material in the theme, and show how this assertion makes a significant essay possible.

A second kind of inadequate thesis statement directs the paper away from the topic. Another student begins his paper: "'A Rose for Emily' reminds me of my trip to the South." Immediately, the writer begins to describe his trip. He receives an F on the paper, because he does not focus on the story. He gets into further difficulty, since he is aware that he *should* be writing about the story. His thesis statement commits him to relate certain aspects of the story to his trip. The double emphasis causes him to shuttle back and forth between story and trip, referring to Miss Emily's house, then to his grandmother's, and so on. The result is a disorganized paper which lacks focus. An effective comment will do more than tell the student that he did not write on the topic. It will analyze the thesis statement to show the student how the double commitment dictates a disorganized, pointless paper, by forcing him to write two themes at once, one about his trip, one about the setting of the story. Again, a workable idea needs to be suggested. For example, that the student confine himself to write about setting—to show how realistic detail sets the mood, or reinforces the theme, or makes the story credible.

A third kind of controlling generalization commits the student to write an insignificant paper, because it cannot easily or profitably be developed with evidence. This is frequently a statement of opinion—for example, "'A Rose for Emily' is an interesting story." To develop this proposition the student should offer evidence to show that the story is interesting. Although he can refer to particular aspects of the story, ultimately his *evidence* is opinion, which reveals more about himself than about the story. Even if he takes a more sophisticated strategy and evaluates "A Rose for Emily" in terms of qualities that he believes all interesting stories have, he still writes a subjective paper which is not likely to be significant.

The terminal comment on this paper should reveal that the thesis statement forces the student to prove something which he cannot prove, because his only evidence is opinion. It might also point out that even though the student can tell why he thinks the story is interesting, his paper will lack significance because it does not reveal anything about the story itself. Further, the instructor should give the student a sample thesis statement which can be supported with facts. While arguing that Miss Emily is an interesting character, the student who wrote this theme observed that Faulkner reveals what loneliness and isolation can do to the mind of a human being. This is a promising topic upon which the student might have based his entire essay.

So far I have focused on content commitments—those which reveal *what* the student must say in his theme. However, as Gorrell explains, generalizations also direct organization. Even the weak thesis statements discussed above make structural commitments. The assertion that Faulkner's style in his novels is similar to the style of "A Rose for Emily" dictates a comparison-contrast structure. And the statement that the story reminds the student of his trip to the South dictates a zig-zag structure in which a detail in the story leads to a discussion of an aspect of the trip. The structure of the first essay could be effective if the topic were sufficiently limited. The structure of the second would be inadequate regardless of any change in scope, because it dictates a double emphasis which destroys the theme's unity.

As these examples suggest, the instructor can make meaningful comments about structure by analyzing the structural implications of thesis statements. When students write adequate thesis statements, they still frequently have problems with organization because they fail to recognize or to follow the structural commitments implicit in their controlling generalizations. When this happens, the terminal comment can be used to point out what the student has overlooked in order to get him to study the implications of his thesis statements.

The following assertion makes certain semantic and structural commitments: "Although both 'A Rose for Emily' and 'The Black Cat' deal with insanity and murder, Faulkner emphasizes the social causes of insanity, while Poe relates insanity to the perversity of the human soul." Concerning content, the student must analyze the similarities of the stories and the causes of insanity in each. If he fails to do these things, he has not followed his commitment; and his paper will be inadequately developed. The statement also makes an organizational commitment. The student must write a comparison-contrast theme dealing with similarities and differences. Since the generalization indicates that the similarities are relatively unimportant, that they are a base from which the student will build and concentrate on the differences, the student will want to deal with the similarities first and fairly briefly so he can go on to make his major points.

However, the student may get so involved with the similarities that he gets around to the differences only on the last page. Or he may consider the differences first and conclude with the similarities. If he does either, he has not adequately followed his commitments, and a weak paper will result. If he spends most of his space on similarities, his paper will lack proper balance. The differences should receive the fullest development, since they are the main subject. If the student treats the differences first, he has a problem in emphasis. He should not end his paper on his least important points.

The thesis statement makes a further commitment—or rather, raises a problem. The student must decide which story to treat first. In the actual theme, the writer makes the point that "A Rose for Emily" is more significant than "The Black Cat," because Faulkner treats insanity more realistically than Poe. However, the student analyzes Faulkner's story first, thereby creating a problem in emphasis. He should end on his major point— that "A Rose for Emily" is superior to "The Black Cat." Furthermore, in order to make his point, the student must refer to the Poe story, which he has not yet discussed. If he had analyzed "The Black Cat" first, he could have built his case for the superiority of "A Rose for Emily" more easily.

As this example indicates, even when a student writes a good thesis statement, he may not sufficiently consider the commitments which it makes. In particular, he often fails to analyze the organizational implications of his thesis statement. By relating structural problems to the thesis statement in the terminal comment, an instructor can encourage the student to become aware of, and to deal with, fairly sophisticated rhetorical problems.

For purposes of illustration, I have based my presentation of one method for writing a terminal comment on an analysis of the semantic and structural commitments of thesis statements. However, just as the thesis statement directs content and organization of the entire paper, topic sentences direct content and organization of particular paragraphs. In fact, any generalization which calls for development makes semantic-structural commitments. Consequently, individual themes may go wrong at any number of places—whenever a statement fails to follow from an earlier commitment, or whenever it leads the theme in a direction away from the problem at hand. When this happens, the instructor may need to base his terminal comment on topic sentence commitments or on statements within paragraphs to show how the theme suffers, because a statement does not follow from an earlier assertion or because it makes a commitment which destroys the continuity or coherence of the essay.

Nevertheless, since the thesis statement makes the most important semantic and structural commitments, it is usually the topic upon which the terminal comment should be based. The construction of a sufficiently limited, significant thesis statement which can be developed with evidence and arguments is one of the most important aspects of the writing process.

Once the student learns to write effective thesis statements and to analyze and follow their semantic-structural commitments, he will find that the actual writing is relatively easy.

The practice of basing terminal comments on the commitments of the controlling generalizations of a theme fulfills the two requirements for an effective terminal comment. It allows the instructor to specify exactly where and precisely how a theme goes bad; and by focusing the student's attention on his controlling generalizations and the ways in which they direct his paper, it provides the student with a method for improving his writing—by formulating controlling generalizations with care and by following their commitments.

JAMES W. NEY / *On Not Practicing Errors*

Almost universally, English composition is taught by the you-make-the-mistake-and-I'll-red-pencil-it method. This method, it would seem to me, runs counter to all the theories of current educational psychology unless it parodies B. F. Skinner's progressive approximation. The student is progressively trying to approximate an idealized theme in the teacher's mind. But neither the teacher nor he knows exactly what this theme is like. Since the reinforcement, however, is largely negative, the method results in progressive regression with both the teacher and the student becoming more and more frustrated until the peak of frustration is reached with the final grade and the ensuing faculty-student conference.

This is no way to approach the teaching of writing! Both our knowledge of language and our knowledge of educational psychology suggest a better way to teach writing than this. In the first place, linguists have stated time and time again that the spoken form of languages differs from the written form.[1] For a language like English which has centuries of written tradition,

[1] See Leonard Bloomfield, *Language* (New York, 1933), pp. 281–82. See also H. A. Gleason, *An Introduction to Descriptive Linguistics*, rev. ed. (New York, 1961), pp. 435 and 426–27. The following articles not only operate from a similar premise but also carry a trend of thought in line with the one expressed in this article. Donald J. Lloyd, "The Uses of Structure and the Structure of Usage," *The English Record*, 6 (Fall, 1955), 41–46. Also by the same author, "Grammar in Freshman English," *College Composition and Communication*, 5 (December, 1954), 162–66, and "A 'Linguistic' Approach to English Composition," *Language Learning*, 3 (July–December, 1950), 109–16. James Sledd, "Coordination (Faulty) and Subordination (Upside-

From *College Composition and Communication*, XIV (May, 1963), 102–6. Reprinted by permission of the National Council of Teachers of English and James W. Ney.

stylized forms in writing have developed which differ from the spoken forms in both vocabulary and grammatical structures. Now the average student of English composition has mastered at least one spoken form of the language thoroughly. Living in the speech community and using speech for years has given him an extensive knowledge of one type of spoken English in any case. Thus the student, when he approaches writing, has at least one form of the language to work from. But few English composition teachers find this form of the language acceptable in written work because it does not correspond to the historically established patterns of written English.

Now the student has learned the first form of the language by observation and by trial and error. In times past, he has, for instance, pluralized *foot* into *feets*. Then with raised eyebrow and rising voice, mother has corrected him —"No Johnny, not *feets*, but *feet*." Thus Johnny struggles to learn by the slowest and most inefficient process known to man. Similarly, when he approaches the composition course, the student produces *Riding my bicycle, a dog chased me*. Then with raised pencil and rising temper, the teacher has corrected him "No, Johnny, not *Riding my bicycle, a dog chased me*, but *Riding my bicycle, I was chased by a dog*." Thus Johnny struggles to learn by the same slow, painful method. Nevertheless, largely because structures such as the preceding are rare in the only form of the language that the student controls, he cannot handle them on paper.

Writing teachers as a whole do little to remedy the occurrence of such errors because they do little to help the student control the second form of the language, formal written English. Usually, the manner in which most instructors attack the teaching of composition presupposes the student's knowledge of written English. At best, current methodology expects the student to learn the written form of the language by the process of osmosis; he reads the works of the great stylists both ancient and modern in the hope that their use of the language will seep through his brain and into his pen. From here on, he is supposed to learn by writing, making errors and correcting them according to the teacher's instructions—the trial and error method again.

There are no longer any good reasons for teaching composition this way. The establishment of both the grammatical patterns and the vocabulary of formal written English within the student's productive capabilities could be accomplished without changing the framework of current composition courses. To do this, both the teacher's approach to the subject and the use of the materials in the average course would have to change. But the framework of the course could remain the same.

Down)," *College Composition and Communication*, 7 (December, 1956), 181–87. These articles have all been reprinted in Harold B. Allen, *Readings in Applied English Linguistics* (New York, 1958).

Of these changes, the teacher's reorientation of his approach to the subject demands priority. Instead of viewing the readings and essays in the course as sources of "great ideas," the teacher will have to regard them as the source of language, formal written English. Furthermore, instead of viewing himself as ye-olde-editor raising his red pencil in the correction of heinous errors, the teacher will have to think of himself as a person who aids the student in building up a stock of responses or linguistic habits acceptable in written English.

In the first place, this requires that the student be made aware of the types of patterns in the structure and the vocabulary of the written language. To do this, the teacher will have to acquaint his pupils with a minimum of grammatical analysis. For this exercise, one of the many competing models for grammatical analysis will have to be chosen. Almost any one can be used if it provides an accurate analysis without conveying misinformation. Through the use of such a model, the student should be made to understand the structure of the sentences which are selected as examples, and which are taken from the readings in the course. But this is only the first step.

In the second place, the student must practice using these structures and this vocabulary until both the structures and the vocabulary become an easily produceable part of his linguistic repertoire. The student writer needs this type of practice because in writing as in speech the vehicle of expression, the language, should flow easily and readily so that the substance of expression, the ideas, might receive full attention. As in mastering a foreign language, the degree of fluency increases in direct proportion to the amount of effective practice expended. Under present methods of teaching composition, this type of practice scarcely exists since the student, especially the poor student, spends a great deal of his time practicing errors.

In other words, when students produce written work for current composition courses, they spend a lot of their time writing sentences like this:

> He felt standing before them despair.
> Gary's future was sublimated when he attended Columbia University.
> Toward supper-time he found his appetite to be insatiable which usually happened.

Now these sentences are considered errors not because their structure contradicts the rules of grammarians or because the use of words does not agree with the dictionary definition of some lexicographer. They are treated as errors because the type of structure exhibited by the first and third sentences does not occur in standard written English with the meaning which the student is attempting to convey. Similarly, in the second sentence *sublimate* is not distributed or used this way in the writing of English. Now the possibility of restraining the student from practicing all errors does not lie within the reach of current teaching methods. In even the best language courses students make some errors. But the minimization of the practicing of errors can be accomplished.

In an effort to do this and to remedy the faults of composition courses already noted, the following steps were taken in the University of Maryland (Far East Division) course which I am currently teaching: (1) Vocabulary practice in diagnostic frames. (2) Structural analysis of model sentences. (3) Controlled practice of sentence and paragraph structure. These three methodological devices were put to use in the following manner.

After oral introduction of vocabulary items, the writing class practiced these items orally. Oral practice was used in the belief that (1) language is primarily speech and the use of language on any level is frequently associated with some form of vocalization, (2) oral practice takes less time than written drill and hence a single item can be practiced approximately ten times orally in the same amount of time that it takes to practice it once in writing, and finally, (3) the distribution of a word, that is, its occurrence in certain types of sentences and situations, must be learned as well as its meaning. Only in oral practice can the teacher control the distribution of words well, and only in oral practice can the teacher correct a mistake soon after it occurs.

Furthermore, this type of language practice or drill is necessary because the student's productive linguistic repertoire does not include the structures or the vocabulary of the written language. Scholars and educators both have long recognized the difference between a vocabulary of recognition and a vocabulary of production. They have seldom, however, recommended ways in which the recognition can be made production. By reading and the use of a dictionary, the student can add to the structures and the vocabulary which he recognizes. But reading does not necessarily aid the student in expanding his productive capabilities in language. Only producing language structures with an ever-increasing vocabulary will do this.

Thus the use of drill to help the student master a particular type of language can be likened to the scales which the developing musician must practice endlessly before he begins producing either the music of others or his own compositions; it can be compared to the equations which the young mathematician solves on the instruction and with the examples of his peers before he tackles real problems of his own; and it can be compared to the pirouettes which the fledgling ballet dancer produces by mimicking an instructor before she can perform before an audience. Language learning is not problem solving. Stimulus-response bonds or Gestalt patterns can only be established by effective practice.

For these reasons, in the vocabulary practice the class repeated sentences like the following after the teacher:

I *relinquished* my claim to a piece of property. I gave up my claim to a piece of property.

He *relinquished* his hold on the life raft. He let go of the life raft; then, he slid under.

While the students were repeating the sentences in unison, the instructor wrote the word being treated, *relinquished,* on the blackboard to acquaint the student with its graphic form. Each of the sentences was repeated twice. After such an exercise, very few words need further definition since the sentences themselves have provided a definition and also indicated at least two of the situations in which this word could be used.

Once five or six items have been introduced this way, the instructor then gives cue sentences and an individual student selects one of the words which are being practiced. For instance, the teacher says:

He gave up his citizenship.

The student should choose the correct word and respond:

He relinquished his citizenship.

Sentences which the teacher judges correct are repeated by the whole class; if the student makes an error in the selection of a vocabulary item, the teacher gives the desired version and the whole class repeats. Finally, individual students are asked to compose sentences orally employing one of the words under consideration, and if any of these were acceptable, the class would be asked to repeat them in unison. Fifteen to twenty minutes of this type of drill prepares students to produce written sentences using an otherwise foreign vocabulary. Contrary to expectation, the students, who are mature people connected in some way with the armed services did not resist or object to the oral drilling. One student commented that the words stuck with him better after they were drilled orally.

When it came to the analysis of written sentences, the materials prescribed for the course and the primary objective of the course presented a problem for the method of teaching suggested here. According to the instructions given English teachers, "The first objective of English 1, 2, and 14 . . . is the attainment of proficiency in expository writing." But the first reading assignments deal with short stories from the Angus Burrell and Bennett Cerf anthology in the Modern Library Series.[2] Because of the aims of the course, only those short stories which have at least some passages approxi-

[2] Angus Burrell and Bennett Cerf, *An Anthology of Famous American Stories* (New York, 1953).

mating expository writing were assigned. Sometimes these were difficult to find. (This difficulty does not continue throughout the course since expository writing is assigned later on.[3]) Stories, however, such as F. Scott Fitzgerald's "The Rich Boy," have some passages which provide good models of expository writing. The first two paragraphs, for instance, are of such a nature; consequently, they were analyzed closely with attention given to the different sentence types, the varying sentence lengths and the vocabulary.

In order to provide students practice in producing the structure of sentences in written English, certain types of sentences were chosen for the students to duplicate. (Oral structural drills could also be used for relatively short sentence types: the memory span of students limits the complexity and length of sentences drilled orally.) From "The Rich Boy," students built sentences on the same pattern as the following example:

> When I hear a man proclaiming himself an "average, honest, open fellow," I feel pretty sure that he has some definite and perhaps terrible abnormality to conceal.[4]
> As the Yale tradition slipped into the past he became more and more of a popular figure among his classmates in New York, more popular than he had ever been in college.[5]

For each class period, ten sentences were assigned to be written according to the structure of the model sentences. In these sentences, students were also required to use the vocabulary practiced on the day of the assignment. In this manner, various types of sentence structures were practiced in carefully controlled drills until by mid-semester or shortly after the students duplicated the structure of whole paragraphs, and finally wrote their own paragraphs and compositions towards the end of the semester.

During the whole course, I attempted to follow certain ground rules. For instance, as few negative statements as possible were written in correcting papers during the first weeks. Many students become unteachable in the composition course because of traumatic experiences brought on by the use of a heavy red pencil on the first few themes. For the same reason, no grades were assigned to the papers in the early part of the course although a record of the students' progress was kept in detail. By and large the students appreciated this. When told that the next paper would receive a grade, the students themselves asked that they not be given grades for another week.

In every phase of teaching, a deliberate effort was made to refrain from

[3] James R. Kreuzer and Lee Cogan, *Studies in Prose Writing* (New York, 1961).
[4] Burrell and Cerf, p. 1045.
[5] *Ibid.,* p. 1053.

telling the students what *not* to do. Many composition teachers become preoccupied with telling the student what not to do, and many courses emphasize all the errors that students should not make. This not only gives any course a negative outlook, but it also leaves unexplored the infinitely great variety of things that can and should be done. Besides this, making the students dwell on errors draws their attention to them and may cause them to repeat these mistakes unconsciously.

In this manner, the entire course concentrates on teaching the student what he should do and drilling him on these things. Whether or not a course built on these principles succeeds in producing better writers than the customary composition course remains to be demonstrated by a carefully controlled set of experiments. Nevertheless, from my point of view, this much is certain: The course is more satisfying to teach.

STYLE

MONROE C. BEARDSLEY / *Style and Good Style*

Recently I had occasion to look over a couple of manuscripts that had been pretty heavily copy-edited for the press. The copy-editors had very different suggestions for ideas about the ideal direction in which to mould the hapless works that had come their way, but one thing they did thoroughly agree upon: namely, that the authors did not know how to write, and would be helpless without an editor. The main trouble was apparently not grammar, or punctuation, or consistency of capitalization, but style.

Reading these manuscripts, comparing the harshly-cancelled original sentences with the neatly-written substitutes between the lines, led me to reflect again on the puzzling nature of style—a quality so evident to the sensitive reader, and yet so difficult to lay hold of and to talk sensibly about. It brought home to me the paradox of the situation in which one person undertakes to improve the style of something written by another. *A* writes his piece of discursive prose, say, and shows it to *B*. *B*, the style-improver, may be a copy-editor or a teacher correcting a composition by a student, or may even be *A* himself at some later time. How is it possible for *B* to improve *A's* work? It can't be that *A* has failed to say what he wanted to say, because if he hasn't said it, how does *B* know what it is? And if *A has* said what he wanted to say, what can be wrong with the style?

Whether or not this is a real paradox, and, if so, how deep it goes, is one of the questions that I shall be trying to answer. Evidently it calls for a

From *Reflections on High School English*, edited by Gary Tate. Tulsa: University of Tulsa, 1966, pp. 91–105. Reprinted by permission of the University of Tulsa and Monroe C. Beardsley.

289

careful consideration of the nature of style: what style is precisely, and what it means to change the style of a sentence.

It's just as well for us to recognize at the start that there are several very different concepts of style, or uses of the term. I will distinguish the three main ones briefly, so as to get my bearings.

First, there is the concept of *a* style (that is, the distinctive style of an author or a particular work). When we think of *a* style, in this sense, we have in mind, no doubt, certain recurrent features of the writing. *A* style is a set of stylistic features. To escape a futile circularity in this definition, we must go on to say what a stylistic feature is—that is, what features of a discourse count as elements of style, and which do not.

Second, there is the concept a *good style*. The style-improver claims to make the style better, and presumably is guided by some criteria of evaluation. He must be able to say what is a fault of style, and why it is a fault, and how that fault can be eliminated—without creating some other fault.

Third, there is the concept of style itself—a part or aspect of the discourse, somehow distinguishable from what is called the substance or content.

The first concept will not concern us here; it is of aesthetic interest and importance, but we can set it aside. My chief attention will be on the second concept. My aim is to look at certain problems about style from the point of view of the style-improver—especially of the teacher who hopes not only to improve particular pieces of work by his students, but also to give them some guiding principles, or at least teach them a knack, so that they may become, as far as may be, their own style-critics.

Because of the special point of view I am adopting, I feel free to use the term "good style" in a modest way. When I speak of good style in this context I do not mean excellence or distinction—style that can claim special aesthetic merit. I mean only *not-bad style,* that is, style that is free of faults. It may seem over-generous to award this commendation to what may, at its best, pass unnoticed; but I think experienced teachers will agree with me that to achieve good style, even in the modest sense, is no mean feat. And it is no small ambition for a teacher or copy-editor to set himself the task of eliminating stylistic faults and helping others eliminate the faults in their own writing.

But in order to inquire what good style, or better style, is, I must lay the groundwork by giving, in summary, my answer to the third, and most fundamental question: what is style itself? [1] There are, then, three parts to

[1] The view sketched here has been formulated more precisely and fully in my *Aesthetics: Problems in the Philosophy of Criticism* (New York: Harcourt, Brace and World, 1958), pp. 221–27. How much I have learned from, and relied upon, William K. Wimsatt, Jr., will be evident to anyone who has read his essay on "Style as Meaning" in *The Prose Style of Samuel Johnson* (New Haven: Yale University, 1941; paperbound 1963).

my discourse: I shall consider what style is, and what good (or better) style is, and I shall discuss some of the practical consequences.

I

Many charming, clever, and memorable things have been said about style—most of which turn out to be highly misleading when subjected to analysis. One of the best things was said by Pascal, in his twenty-third *Pensée*, and I would like to take it as my text: "Words differently arranged have a different meaning, and meanings differently arranged have different effects."[2] When this double-barrelled aphorism is properly understood (that is, when I have gotten through telling you how *I* want to construe it), it sums up concisely the two theses I shall defend here, and it contains the two truths (the *only* two really general and fundamental truths) about style. Anyone who grasps their implications, and follows them out consistently in practice, will find that the consequences are far-reaching.

The clearest way to say what style is, I think, is to say what a *difference* in style is. Take two sentences or parts of sentences, S_1 and S_2. We say that they differ in style when two things are true about them. First, they differ to some extent in *meaning*. And second, the difference is not on the plane of overt or explicit meaning, but on the plane of covert or implicit meaning. The distinction between explicit and implicit meaning is one that requires a certain amount of analysis to elucidate, but let me say in a general way what sorts of things I have in mind, and leave it to the examples to clarify the distinction. Implicit meaning includes what we would ascribe to the connotations rather than to the plain dictionary sense of a word, and it includes what we would consider to be merely suggested, or hinted, or intimated by a sentence rather than to what the sentence plainly states.

It is relatively easy to see what we are talking about when we compare two similar English expressions with respect to their style. If they don't differ at all in meaning, there is no difference in style (but this, as Pascal says, is almost impossible, for if there are different words, or the same words in a different order, there is almost certain to be some difference in meaning, however small and subtle). If the meanings differ in some explicit way, there is no difference in style. It follows from this analysis that the concept of style is inherently comparative, and therefore variable with the context of concern. To isolate a particular stylistic feature in any discourse is always to think of a particular element of implicit meaning in terms of which that discourse might differ from some other one. This is the first of my two theses, then: that style is detail of implicit meaning.

[2] Trans. W. F. Trotter (New York: Modern Library, 1941), p. 11.

To clarify and support this thesis I require a few examples. And I will take them from a book on style that is regarded by many people with great affection and respect—the E. B. White revision of William Strunk, Jr.'s *The Elements of Style*.[3] I'm not choosing this as a bad example; when I speak critically of it, I do so more in sorrow than in anger. I can only say: what a pity that even so sound and sensible a book is so confused! In the final chapter, contributed by White, the view of style I have been sketching above is clearly stated and subscribed to: "Style has no such separate entity; it is non-detachable, unfilterable" (p. 55)—in other words, it is inseparable from meaning. But unfortunately the logical implications of this thesis are seldom kept in view.

Consider first the advice to use the active voice rather than the passive voice or constructions based on the verb "to be." "Many a tame sentence of description or exposition," say Strunk and White (p. 14), "can be made lively and emphatic by substituting a transitive in the active voice for some such perfunctory expression as *there is,* or *could be heard."* Here is a clear-cut example of stylistic advice: how to make your sentence more lively and emphatic. Now take a look at some of their examples. The first one is this: Don't say "There were a great number of dead leaves lying on the ground;" but say "Dead leaves covered the ground." Granted there is a significant difference in style here. But isn't that a difference of meaning? For one thing, there are more leaves in the second sentence. The second one says that the ground was covered; the first one only speaks of a "great number." Stylistic advice is a rather odd sort of thing if it consists in telling students to pile up the leaves in their descriptions. Suppose the student brings the corrected paper back to his instructor and says, "Pardon me. You told me to say the leaves covered the ground, but actually they didn't; there was quite a bit of ground showing through. Still, there *were* a great many. Do I get a lower grade just for telling the truth?" What answer can the conscientious style-expert give to that?

Now, you may say, well it's not as if the student had used an exact number. Suppose he wrote, "There were 261 leaves on the ground," and his instructor commented in the margin: "Don't say there were 261; say there were 893—that will be more effective." This would of course be telling the student to lie. Since this difference in meaning would be explicit, the change from 261 to 893 would not be a change in style. But isn't the change from "a great many leaves" to "covered the ground" a kind of lie, too—or at least a considerable exaggeration? Naturally it is more lively and emphatic, but is it honest? True, the deception will be partially concealed, because it is conveyed implicitly rather than explicitly, but that does not make it less reprehensible.

[3] New York: Macmillan, 1959.

Take another example that Strunk and White use to illustrate the same rule about liveliness and emphasis. Don't say "The reason he left college was that his health became impaired; say "Failing health compelled him to leave college." What's the difference here? Again, it is a difference in meaning—in the picture of the situation that is conjured up by the different words and different grammar. In the one case, the health grew worse, and finally after some indecision, he left college—though health was not necessarily the sole consideration. The second sentence implies worse health: it left the student no choice. Naturally it is a more dramatic story. But is this what stylistic advice is all about? Are Strunk and White saying, "Never mind about the exact truth; always try to make things as dramatic as possible, provided you don't get caught in any explicit and easily detectable misstatements"?

The same sort of question can be raised about a great many of the Strunk-White examples. "Put statements in a positive form," they urge—"Make definite assertions" (p. 14). For instance, don't say "He was not very often on time," but rather "He usually came late." Now it seems to me that if I were asked about so-and-so's punctuality I might very well reply, "He was not very often on time," if I wanted to be careful not to overstate the matter, or to suggest that so-and-so came *very* late, or that he was deliberate and inconsiderate in coming late, etc. I am saying precisely what I want to mean, and ought to mean. What right has anyone to tell me *not* to mean this?

One more example: "Use definite, specific, concrete language," say Strunk and White (p. 15). If you take this seriously, it means, "Don't write philosophy, because that will require abstract language." But here is one of their examples: don't say "A period of unfavorable weather set in;" say "It rained every day for a week." But this is like the leaves example; the second sentence gives us a higher rainfall.

My immediate purpose is not to question the advice given, though I suppose some of my skepticism has already emerged. I am coming to the question of good style shortly. My argument is that a difference of style is always a difference in meaning—though implicit—and an important and notable difference of style is always a sizeable difference in meaning. Some of the Strunk-White examples involve so considerable and obvious a change that it is questionable whether they are really stylistic changes. For example: don't say "He did not think that studying Latin was much use;" say "He thought the study of Latin useless" (p. 14). Now being useless (i.e., having no use at all), and not being of much use, are clearly different things. If anybody advised me to say the second after I had said the first, I would be rather annoyed—I would tell him not to go putting words in my mouth. I don't think that studying Latin is much use; but I would certainly not want to say that it is useless. I'm afraid our style-advisers got carried away on this one.

I can't resist one more example—this one not from Strunk and White but from a religious publication via the filler-spaces in *The New Yorker*.

> Words that sound happy put your reader in the right frame of mind to say "yes" to your request. Remember that a negative word or an unfriendly expression should never be used if there is a positive way to express the same thought. You might say: "We regret that we are unable to supply you with the item ordered. Is there another item which we may send you on the same subject?"
>
> But your reader-reaction will be 100 per cent improved if you rephrase that sentence to read: "Fortunately for you, although the specific item you ordered is out of print, we have another which might serve your purpose."

Nothing could be plainer than that this change of style is a radical change in meaning. None of us would countenance such a bland invitation to write "words that sound happy" in order to con the subnormal reader into the appropriate "reader-reaction"—so that he gets the impression that you are practically doing him a favor by not sending him the item he ordered. But we encourage this sort of confusion when we speak of style as though it *were* detachable and manipulable independent of meaning—when we define style as the "how" of writing vs. the "what"—when, in short, we lose sight of the fact that style is nothing but meaning. That is what encourages people to entertain the absurd idea that, as this writer says, there is both a "positive" and a "negative . . . way to express the same thought."

II

Now, if we are agreed about what style is, we can go on to the second question: what is *good* (i.e., not-bad) style? I assume that there are such things as *faults* of style—or at least there are pieces of discourse that are faulty *in* style—and so the basic question is what such a fault may be. Then the absence of such faults will be goodness of style.

There is one sort of problem about good style that I want to make sure we set aside here. A person who accepted a dinner invitation at the White House in a long Faulknerian sentence, or who wrote a letter of condolence in early Hemingwayese, has no doubt committed some sort of error involving style. The error is not an error *of* style, I think, but an error in the choice of style; the result is not bad style, necessarily, but *inappropriate* style. It is a lack of decorum. In fact, it is just the sort of error that one might commit if he took some of the Strunk and White advice too earnestly. "The latter sentence [the one not recommended] is less direct, less bold, and less concise," they say at one point (p. 13). But what kind of reason is this? In effect, they are saying, "Always write so as to *appear* like a bold, decisive, forthright sort of person. Never mind how you actually feel, or what the occasion is; just act bold."

What I am concerned with, then, is stylistic fault, and again I take my cue from Pascal. "Meanings differently arranged have different effects"—or, as I should put it, when meanings are combined, some combinations are better than others. But there are different ways of being better. When explicit meanings are wrongly combined, you get a logical fault (this is over-simplifying somewhat, but take it as a first approximation). The trouble with a sentence like "He married his widow's younger sister" is that it describes a logical impossibility. There's nothing wrong with the style. Free-dom from logical error is good logic—though of course it may not be great cogency. But suppose the fault lies in the way explicit meanings are combined with *implicit* meanings. Then we have a fault of style. My second thesis is that such a fault is also a logical fault, though its locus is different from ordinary explicit logical error. In short, good style is logical congruity of explicit and implicit meaning. When what a sentence suggests or hints, and what its words connote, bear out the implications of the explicit meaning of the sentence, we have no fault of style; but when there is a clash, something must be remedied. And since we take the explicit meaning as primary, we think of the implicit meaning as what requires to be altered, so we say that the style is bad—just as we say that the hat is too small for the head, rather than that the head is too large for the hat.

As Wimsatt puts it (paperbound ed., p. 10), "Bad style is not a deviation of words from meaning, but a deviation of meaning from meaning."

To prove this thesis would be more of a task than I could undertake here—it is, in fact more of a task than anyone has ever undertaken. But a few examples will show how it can be supported, and you can test it further on your own favorite examples of horrible style.

My examples will come, again, from Strunk and White—and it is a tribute to their slim volume that it yields so many provocative examples. "Place the emphatic words of a sentence at the end," they advise at one point, in boldface italics (p. 26). "The proper place in the sentence for the word or group of words that the writer desires to make most prominent is usually the end." This puts the cart before the horse. It is not correct to say that the emphatic words of a sentence should be placed at the end; it is cor-rect to say that whatever words *are* placed at the end of an English sen-tence will thereby be given emphasis. In all practical discussions of style, it is essential to distinguish two kinds of thing that can be said. They are related as the factual and the evaluative, the *is* and the *ought*.

The first kind of statement it what might be called a *stylistic fact,* or a rhetorical fact. For example, "Whatever you place at the end of a sentence will tend to be emphasized." Or, "In general, the active voice carries with it a tone of greater assurance and decisiveness than the passive voice." Many inexperienced writers make mistakes because they do not grasp these facts about the very nature of English constructions. And the teacher can help a great deal merely by pointing these things out. "Look, by placing this at the end, you implicitly claim that it is more important than what you put earlier. Is this what you want to claim?" Or, "Look; here you use the passive voice; the active voice would make the sentence more direct and forthright. Which do you prefer?" In this way, a teacher sensitizes his students to stylistic facts so that they become more and more aware of exactly what they *are* saying, implicitly. But there is no call for the Strunk-White imperative here. The instruction is in the conditional form, like instruction in checkers, gardening, golf, or winemaking: "If you do such-and-such, then such-and-such a meaning will result." Strunk and White's second sentence can be taken in this conditional form.

So there are stylistic facts; are there also *stylistic rules,* or recommendations? There may be, as I said, rules of appropriateness: such-and-such is the accepted style for a thank-you note. But what more can we say? What reason can we give for condemning style, quite apart from what the writer wished to do? Some of the Strunk-White examples of poor style break down at once if we suppose a different context. Take the first example under the sentences just quoted. They reject this sentence: "Humanity has hardly advanced in fortitude since that time, though it has advanced in many other ways." They substitute: "Humanity, since that time, has advanced in many other ways, but it has hardly advanced in fortitude." Suppose you wrote the first sentence, and your copy-editor substituted the second one. Couldn't you simply reply that the first one says exactly what you want to say? From this reply there is no appeal. The second sentence, but not the first one, suggests that what is important is the lack of advance in fortitude. As far as style is concerned, one sentence is no better than the other; they simply say (implicitly) different things, and the question is (or ought to be) which is true.

But when Strunk and White condemn one sentence and praise the other, it is clear that they are making a hidden assumption. They are thinking of the sentence in the context of a sort of Baconian essay on the subject of fortitude. It's not easy to illustrate this assumption very briefly. But imagine something like this foreshortened context:

Man is a miracle, or many miracles; but the most miraculous fact about him is his fortitude, his capacity to endure and to survive incredible hardships. Think of the conditions under which neolithic man kept going—the winters, the wild animals, the long distances of his migrations. Humanity has hardly advanced in fortitude since that time, though it has advanced in many other ways.

Here if we feel a slackness at the end, and a sort of betrayal of expectations, we can affirm a fault of style. For the end of the last sentence implicitly denies what the first sentence quite explicitly states: namely, that fortitude is the important topic under discussion. So there is a logical conflict after all, and this is the stylistic fault. Note that it is quite independent of the writer's intention and the reader's antecedent desires: it is internal to the discourse itself.

Compare another example that illustrates the same principle, though Strunk and White place it under the heading of active vs. passive voice. They cite: "I shall always remember my first visit to Boston," and continue "This is much better than 'My first visit to Boston will always be remembered by me'" (p. 13). But what's wrong with the latter sentence? If we look for the relevant stylistic fact, we find that it is the same one just considered. Putting the personal pronoun at the end rather than at the beginning of the sentence gives it an emphatic position, and the emphasis is increased by the unusual syntax. Compare these two analogous sentences:

(1) The police department will always remember my first visit to Boston.

(2) My first visit to Boston will always be remembered by the police department.

It would be silly to say that in this case the passive voice makes the second sentence "less direct, less bold, and less concise." I suppose it is less direct, but it is more dramatic and striking, because of its ominous overtones.

So it is not the active-passive difference that is important here. The difference is that the second sentence given by Strunk and White ("My first visit to Boston will always be remembered by me") implicitly claims that there is something noteworthy about *my* remembering it, as opposed to somebody else's remembering it. It says, in effect, "Others may forget it, but *I* certainly won't." Now this suggestion in itself can't make the sentence stylistically bad. One could invent a context in which it would be better than the sentence Strunk and White recommend. But they are tacitly thinking of it as in a context where the main topic under discussion has been, or is to be, the trip itself, its causes and consequences. And in *this* context, the implicit suggestion that there is something significant about *my* remembering it rather than somebody else introduces an irrelevant point. In effect, the sentence says, "It is important that *I* remember it," but the context shows that it is *not* important, because it has no logical bearing upon the other matters at hand.

At one point in their book, Strunk and White come close to making this point explicitly. They begin unpromisingly by giving advice that verges upon complete nullity. First they state their rule: "Use the active voice" (p. 13)—just like that, in so many words. But a little later they say, "This rule does not, of course, mean that the writer should entirely discard the passive voice, which is frequently convenient and sometimes necessary." All we need now is some explanation of how to tell when it is convenient and when necessary—but the much-praised conciseness of *The Elements of Style* naturally prevents them from pausing to give any such explanation. However, their example and comment are important. Compare "The dramatists of the Restoration are little esteemed today" with "Modern readers have little esteem for the dramatists of the Restoration." The authors add, "The first would be the preferred form in a paragraph on the dramatists of the Restoration; the second, in a paragraph on the tastes of modern readers." Excellent; right to the point. The difference in style is a difference in what is suggested about the focus of attention in the whole discourse. And the rightness or wrongness of the style depends on how that suggestion actually comports with the remainder of the discourse.

Some people may be puzzled by this sort of talk about style. In order to show what style is, and what good style is, you have to work out the implicit meanings and state them baldly for examination. Then they are no longer implicit, of course, and the explication of them may seem forced and artificial. But implicit meanings can be understood and can be stated explicitly; and that is the only way to exhibit their connections or divergences. This is what I call style-analysis. And it is essential if our discussions of style are not to degenerate into murky rhapsody or painfully misleading aphorism.

Perhaps I am stacking the cards too much for my second thesis by choosing examples that have already been selected, or constructed, to illustrate particular stylistic faults. So let me venture out of the laboratory for a brief field trip in the outside world of prose. My first specimen is one that came to hand not long ago in a book review by Elizabeth Janeway. She referred to the author of this book [4] as "a mistress of nearly impenetrable prose," and offered the following sample:

> The tyranny of happiness forms the nucleus of the defense apparatus employed by the woman who does not quite dare to break out, though restless, but who must continually seek a validation for her way of life.

Now granted this would be much clearer if we had a context in which "the tyranny of happiness" was defined. But even with that explanation on hand,

[4] Edith de Rham, *The Love Fraud* (New York: Clarkson N. Potter, 1965); see *The New York Times*, March 28, 1965.

there would still be stylistic trouble. And that comes largely because the connotations of the words are constantly working against the basic logical pattern proposed by the very same words. They are also working against each other.

We are told that the woman does not "dare to break out" of something (I suppose, the frustrations of her second-class status as married woman); she is compelled to "seek a validation" for her way of life. So far, so good, though we could follow the logical order of relationships better if the sequence of phrases in the sentence reflected that order. The next step—which would be clearer if it followed rather than preceded the end of the sentence—is to note that in order to find that validation, the woman requires a "defense apparatus." But "defense" is hardly the *mot juste* here, since it suggests some sort of enemy or attack, and leads us to look around in the context for hints as to what it is—only to return empty-handed. Then the "defense apparatus" is said to have a "nucleus," and again we try to fit the connotations into the picture—if there is a nucleus it holds things together, or is the center, or is surrounded by other material, etc. No apparatus that is readily conceivable has, in the strict sense, a nucleus—though it may have a most important part. Finally (but this is put first), the nucleus is said to be formed by the tyranny of happiness. Is it the tyranny itself, or the acceptance of such tyranny, or some theory about such tyranny, or something else, that the woman relies on for her validation? The syntax, apparently elliptical, claims a causal connection that is unwarranted by the rest of the context, as far as we have it here. And that is the secret of its failure—as style.

It is always interesting, and often instructive, to see what reviewers pick out as objectionable in the style of the books they review. Recently Joseph Epstein, reviewing a book [5] in the *New Republic* (June 5, 1965), wrote:

> Although every so often Coser will get off a cleanly barbaric sentence like "Geographical dispersion shades into or overlaps with functional differentiation," he occasionally achieves a graceful prose style and almost always commands a forceful one.

This example suggests many reflections—more than I will try to tease out now. It is just the sort of sentence of which Strunk and White would be likely to say: "Avoid abstract nouns. Be concrete. Be definite. Be forceful." But the trouble does not lie in the abstract nouns, I think, and they would not even obtrude on our attention if it weren't for the *active* and *concrete* verbs between them—namely "shades into" and "overlaps with." It is the connotations of these words that throw us off and leave us baffled when we

[5] Lewis Coser, *Men of Ideas* (New York: Free Press, 1965).

try to figure out what is the exact relationship between geographical dispersion and functional differentiation that is being asserted.

Last week, in a hotel in Denver, I found a booklet containing information about restaurants and other tourist attractions.[6] One of the items read as follows:

> LE PROFIL—1560 Sherman St. (222-0758).
>   Richly adorned and unique of its kind, here dinner is an experience. French and Continental cuisine with an air of Paris sophistication is skillfully prepared and served with care. This is truly a swish dining emporium. The atmosphere is relaxed but polished.

I'm sure any composition teacher would itch to get at this piece of prose; it exhibits such a fascinating range of defects. But I pass by the dubiously attached modifier and the curious redundancy in the first sentence, and what philosophers would call a "category mistake" in the second sentence (I mean that it is not strictly the cuisine but the food that is served). These certainly introduce meanings that distract from the basic order of thought— they strew logical red herrings along the path of sense. But my favorite sentence is the third. "Truly a swish dining emporium"! It would be hard to find two words whose connotations—whose whole ambiances of meaning— are more at odds with one another.

III

I promised some concluding remarks on practical applications, but as I look back it seems to me that I have drawn the practical consequences pretty much as I went along. However, it may be well to summarize my argument concisely, and take one more look to see whether other useful points emerge.

The steps of my argument are these. (1) Different words or a different order of words make different meanings—at least, they do if they make a difference in style, because style is detail of implicit meaning. (2) Therefore, if the teacher advises a change of words, or of word order, he is recommending a different meaning. And if he says one stylistic feature is better than another, he is saying that it is better to mean one thing rather than another. (3) No meaning as such is better than any other, considered solely from the stylistic point of view. (Of course there are moral and political and religious and other criteria in terms of which it is better to mean one thing rather than another.) (4) Therefore, if a change of meaning betters the

[6] *Colorado Guestguide,* Vol. 7, 1965 summer edition, p. 8.

style, that betterment must lie in the relationships of meanings. (5) The objective relationships that meanings have to each other are logical; meanings are compatible or incompatible, they are connected by causation, implication, coordination, subordination, etc. (6) Therefore, faults of style must be faults of logic; and good style must be compatibility of implicit and explicit meaning.

The practical problem for the writer is that of managing his implicit meanings so that they do not impede or divert or conceal or obstruct his explicit meanings. It is a continuous tactical problem. The strategy of writing is large-scale organization of meanings—the main steps of the argument, explicit logical relationships. What is left is management of the small-scale, subtler, and under-the-surface meanings to make them carry the thought forward, adding details on the side (so to speak), but details that fit in and enrich the thought—and perhaps show how the writer looks upon his own argument: how confident or doubtful he is, how detached or involved, how serious or playful, and so on.

A teacher who fully realizes that to change style is always to change meaning will never take his role as style-critic lightly, I think. He will shy away from simple absolute rules. He will not speculate about intentions, but focus on the discourse itself, and the way its parts work, or do not work, together. His main effort will be to help his pupils understand what I have called stylistic facts, so that they can become sensitive and discerning readers of their own work. And above all when he is faced with a hard writing-problem, he will insist that the sovereign remedy is to think out the logical connections clearly, and then make sure that the syntax and diction mirror those connections as clearly as possible.

I think I have time to play around with one final example from Strunk and White—or rather from White's concluding chapter—and to draw another moral from it. The moral (to state it first) is that the doctrine of style as meaning and of good style as logical relevance has a liberating effect on the style-critic (the teacher or copy-editor); if he really accepts the doctrine, and all its consequences, he should become tolerant of very different styles and undictatorial about his own recommendations.

White has some fun with variations on Thomas Paine: "These are the times that try men's souls." And the last and most outrageous variation is this: "Soulwise, these are trying times." White raises the question what is wrong with this—but he wisely makes no attempt to answer this question. Less wisely, no doubt, I rush in to fill the gap. Because it may seem that here, at any rate, is a stylistically bad sentence whose stylistic badness has nothing to do with logic, and therefore a sentence that can be rejected out of hand without taking into account relationships of meaning at all. Now of course, this sentence is a comedown from the original, and we can see how it differs and why it differs. "Trying times" and "times that try men's souls" are far from synonymous—a situation can be trying, in the modern sense, without constituting a real trial of one's whole self. And the "X-wise" construction has taken on foundation-board and executive-level overtones, besides its native vagueness and indeterminateness. "Soulwise, these are trying times" is flippant in tone, not deeply concerned. It reminds me of a crazy line from an S. J. Perlman television script: "A man in my position doesn't have as much freedom, choicewise."

But now suppose young Tom Paine were to bring you the first install-ment of a political piece he is writing, called *The American Crisis.* You open it up and read the first sentence: "Soulwise, these are trying times." Somehow it won't do. But what can you tell him? First, you can help him see the relevant stylistic facts, so that he knows exactly what he has said, explicitly and implicitly. You cannot prove to him, I think, that his sentence in itself is bad style. It might make an excellent beginning of a piece by Perlman. But, second, you can ask what kind of book this sentence is to be the beginning of—you can read further into the context. If the next sentence says, explicitly, that these times are not for the summer soldier and the sunshine patriot, but call for deep commitment and solemn pur-pose, then you can tell him that, in this context, the first sentence is bad style. For it says, implicitly, that the situation is not serious and that the writer does not care deeply about what is happening.

Let us suppose that, armed with this new insight, Tom Paine goes away to meditate. If you have helped him discern the logical jarring in his dis-course, and have made him want to eliminate it, you have done your job. The rest is up to him. But of course if he returns the next day saying, "I've got it! Listen to this: 'These are the times that try men's souls,'" then you can congratulate yourself, as well as him. Unfortunately, few of our students are likely to come up to this level. So we had better be content with the more limited purpose of showing what is wrong, and why. But—and this is my parting plea—when we give reasons to argue that the style is faulty, let us make sure that we give *good* reasons. For bad reasons are worse than none at all.

WALKER GIBSON / *An Exercise in Prose Style*

We have been hearing a good deal of rhetoric lately about rhetoric, and I take it most of us feel that this is mostly a good thing. At the very least, the fashion for rhetoric has provided a slight change of scene, and like most changes of scene it is refreshing. Teachers who have been around for a while can recall other fashionable changes in the recent past; while none of them exactly solved all our problems, they were at least temporarily enlightening and they provided some refreshment of spirit. At my university our English department has just moved its offices by a couple of blocks, and quite aside from the fact that our new quarters are considerably more posh than most English teachers are accustomed to, the very move itself has been a source of new dignity and delight. So it may be with rhetoric. To put the matter in the humblest way possible: so long as we keep moving our methods and manners, we must, let us hope, be doing something right.

But we do not need to be all that humble.

Let me be concrete about such refreshment as I have myself been experiencing in recent weeks, thanks to the new, really the very old, rhetoric. Having selected one of the new rhetoric-inspired textbooks, I find myself this fall teaching Plato's *Phaedrus* to a class of average freshmen. What a pleasure it is, for teacher and student, to find Socrates saying so many things so immediately relevant. I mention one. You recall that in that

From *Rhetoric: Theories for Application,* ed. Robert M. Gorrell. Champaign, Illinois: National Council of Teachers of English, 1967, pp. 99–106. Reprinted by permission of the National Council of Teachers of English and Walker Gibson.

dialogue Socrates utters an eloquent speech defending the lover over the nonlover, and in doing so he finds it necessary to talk about the immortality of the soul. Any reference to the immortality of the soul is likely to leave an average freshman uneasy, not to say hostile, and in this prejudice I am on the side of the freshman. But see how Socrates introduces the topic:

> To tell what the soul really is would be a matter for utterly superhuman and long discourse, but it is within human power to describe it briefly in a figure; let us therefore speak in that way.

And there follows the magnificent and elaborate figure of the charioteer and the pair of winged horses. Here Socrates faces, with characteristic charm and good humor, an essential quandary about language and about metaphor. If only one could *tell* what the soul really *is!* Perhaps it is an injustice to Plato to add: if only one could tell what *anything* really is! In any case, the student who can recognize that to say what things "really are" is quite literally superhuman has already grasped a fact about language and reality that I, as a freshman myself many years ago, never dreamed of. And if the student, emulating Socrates, can thereupon be forthright and self-conscious in choosing his logic, his metaphor, his style, then surely he is on the way to wisdom. "Let us therefore speak in that way."

Socrates ends the dialogue, you may remember, by attacking the very value of writing itself. It is a sobering attack, though doubtless very wholesome for the teacher of rhetoric and his student.

> Writing, Phaedrus, [Socrates says] has this strange quality, and is very like painting; for the creatures of painting stand like living beings, but if one asks them a question, they preserve a solemn silence. And so it is with written words: you might think they spoke as if they had intelligence, but if you question them, wishing to know about their sayings, they always say only one and the same thing. And every word, when once it is written, is bandied about, alike among those who understand and those who have no interest in it, and it knows not to whom to speak or not to speak; when ill-treated or unjustly reviled it always needs its father to help it; for it has no power to protect or help itself.

Can we imagine a more alarming statement about the nature of writing than that? Here are some serious misgivings about the fixed quality of written matter as against the flexible nature of oral speech, with its tones of voice and kinesics, its ability to respond to feedback. In Marshall McLuhan's much discussed new book, *Understanding Media,* there are some similar doubts about the written word, though in his case the alternatives are more spectacular than oratory or spoken conversation: they are the telephone and radio, tape recorder and TV. As long as we are the slaves of the printing press, says McLuhan, we will see the world in nice linear blocks of justified type. But the new media define a different world, involving the listener or viewer in versions of experience that are simply foreign to the reader. The medium, he says, *is* the message.

If one wished to raise a question about the future of writing, we could cite McLuhan or we could cite Socrates, but in either case we are forced to scrutinize assumptions that few of us have often questioned. Insofar as our current interest in rhetoric leads to such scrutinies, it seems to me all to the good.

But it is not altogether seemly to insist—to this of all audiences—that the future of the written word may be dim. If indeed the teacher of composition is becoming obsolete, we are all bravely behaving as if we thought it not so. For our purposes, I assume blandly that the written word is here to stay a while longer, and I propose to offer here a modest, practical contribution to our rhetorical revival. What I am about to present is little more than a Teaching Aid, an exercise, for conveying to students something about *choice* in prose style.

There is an analogy between what rhetoricians have had to say about style and the earlier pronouncements from scholarship in linguistics. The most conspicuous practical effect of linguistics on classroom procedures and attitudes surely has been our increasing reluctance to use those dirty words, *good* and *bad,* our renewed awareness that there are various kinds of language appropriate to various human predicaments. (Obviously no novel discovery—but it has now begun to penetrate into classrooms where formerly a black-and-white schoolmarmism about language prevailed.) The analogy for rhetoricians and students of style lies in the equally commonplace truism that there is no easily defined or absolute good or bad style, but many styles appropriate to countless occasions. Such relativism makes the teacher's job not easier, of course, but harder. We hear much of the desirability of showing to students the variety of his choices. Robert Gorrell puts it well in the current issue of the *4C's Journal:*

> A theory of rhetoric attempts to describe accurately and consistently and fully what happens; practical rhetoric is concerned with choices. The teacher of writing is concerned with the effects of different grammatical alternatives, so that he can offer advice about which choices to make for different circumstances.

Now my problem, like yours I hope, is severely pragmatic. How can I, as a teacher, dramatize for my students "the effects of different grammatical alternatives"? How can I show my students that their problem as writers is not a matter of learning the right language, whatever that is, and eschewing the wrong, but instead a matter of being aware of the possible choices and choosing with wisdom and self-consciousness?

My exercise or teaching aid occurs in three stages.

I begin with the first day of class in the fall—a day when many of us like to have our students write something there and then. What shall it be? "My Summer Vacation." Not quite, but I offer a topic almost as corny and as disarming. "Write me a few sentences," I say to them, "in which you describe the circumstances of your birth and early life, as if you were beginning some sort of autobiography. Just a few sentences. Ten minutes."

Samples from these effusions, dittoed and distributed at the next class, comprise of course a display of stylistic miscellany. One can begin one's task of demonstrating the basically dramatic character of all expression by asking the students to describe or classify the various voices created by the quotations before them. There are sure to be a few jokers, some traditional literary types, some solemn tones, an illiterate or two—the usual assortment.

I illustrate from my own current batch of freshmen. Here for example is the pretentious literary manner so familiar to us all:

> September evenings are cool and breezy in Illinois, relieving the hot hours of the day. Autumn is near and the land awaits anxiously for the new season to begin.
> It was then that I came.

Here is another voice using the same word *land* but with an ironic sense of cliché:

> September 10, 1946, was a rainy, miserable, stormy day in Orange, N.J. At four minutes after the hour of noon, a new voice (lyric soprano, I believe) was heard in the land.

At a much lower level of sophistication, students give us the pieties they think we must be looking for.

> When a baby is born into a family it is a time of great happiness. It is a time when your parents can pass on to you, all the ideals and values they have learned through the years.

Some young students, in response to an assignment that seems to reach them where they live, will give us a collage of memories that is perhaps better and more moving even than it was meant to be.

Shortly after my third birthday my sister was born, I wet my bed, and the following Christmas I received a rocking horse. About that time our Irish Setter bit the milkman and had puppies. The lady next door used to give us stale ginger snaps. Then, there was the year of the guppies, a bee stung me, my tooth came out and my father died.

This is all pleasant enough, but of course it says little more than that the world is full of a number of creatures, and that we all pose ourselves before one another in different attitudes, choosing our rhetoric accordingly. My next step—stage two—will perhaps seem a little more respectable, for it is more conventionally literary. Here are two other writers who purport to say something about the circumstances of birth and early life.

Passage 1

Whether I shall turn out to be the hero of my own life, or whether that station will be held by anybody else, these pages must show. To begin my life with the beginning of my life, I record that I was born (as I have been informed and believe) on a Friday, at twelve o'clock at night. It was remarked that the clock began to strike, and I began to cry, simultaneously.

In consideration of the day and hour of my birth, it was declared by the nurse and by some sage women in the neighborhood who had taken a lively interest in me several months before there was any possibility of our becoming personally acquainted, first that I was destined to be unlucky in life; and secondly, that I was privileged to see ghosts and spirits: both these gifts inevitably attaching, as they believed, to all unlucky infants of either gender born towards the small hours on a Friday night.

Passage 2

I am an American, Chicago born—Chicago, that somber city—and go at things as I have taught myself, free-style, and will make the record in my own way: first to knock, first admitted; sometimes an innocent knock, sometimes a not so innocent. But a man's character is his fate, says Heraclitus, and in the end there isn't any way to disguise the nature of the knocks by acoustical work on the door or gloving the knuckles.

Everybody knows there is no fineness or accuracy in suppression: if you hold down one thing you hold down the adjoining.

My own parents were not much to me, though I cared for my mother. She was simple-minded, and what I learned from her was not what she taught, but on the order of object lessons. She didn't have much to teach, poor woman.

A class invited to describe the narrator in each of these passages should have little difficulty producing at least a few primitive distinctions. The first narrator sounds old-fashioned, they will say, the second more up-to-date. The first one shows considerable wit—perhaps they will mention the play of "to begin my life with the beginning of my life." The second narrator is almost dead serious. The first one is easy with the reader, at ease with himself—the word *urbane* may appear. The second narrator is tense, absorbed with himself, and doesn't seem to be giving the reader much attention at all. Other suggestions will certainly crop up among reasonably interested students—for instance, the proposition that the first narrator is British and traditionally educated, while the second, obviously American, is self-educated, independent, perhaps younger. The expressions "chip-on-the-shoulder" and "self-made man" have appeared in reference to the second narrator. It is a difference between saying "I record that I was born . . ." and "I will make the record in my own way."

Whatever descriptions of the narrators the students are able to provide, either more or less than I have suggested, the question *why* is of course crucial. What is it in the language of the passages that tells us what sort of person is talking? What is there in the way they put sentences together that tells us what we say we know about their characters and backgrounds?

Once you get past the business of plain statement—after all, one of them *says* he was born in Chicago—it is possible to focus some attention on a few rhetorical matters, asking only for what the students are able, with whatever prodding, to supply themselves. One distinction they seem to identify fairly easily is a difference in verb forms: there are some half dozen passive verbs in passage 1, none at all in passage 2. What does this imply about the kind of person talking, his relation to his subject? (Some students will have forgotten what a passive verb is, naturally, but this discussion, by providing a little practical usefulness for the term, may remind them that a nodding acquaintance with a modest grammatical vocabulary may actually be worth something in talking about writing. Note too that I am operating only within conventional terms of traditional grammar.) The uses of subordination may occur to the students, for in the first passage a good deal more than half of the text occurs inside subordinate clauses, whereas in the second it is a much smaller fraction. Does this suggest, for passage 1, a speaker who knows and is ready to assert differences between what's important and what isn't? The *position* of subordinate constructions in the sentence is significant: our first speaker consistently begins his sentences with subordinate clauses and phrases, the second begins with subjects and verbs. A reading of that balanced phrasing in the opening sentence of passage 1 ought to suggest a mind that knows just what it's going to say before it opens its mouth. A sentence from passage 2 will dramatize the difference: "My own parents were not much to me, though I cared for my mother." The clause at the end of the sentence, occurring almost as an afterthought, supports the colloquial voice almost as much as the vocabulary does, or the message.

What else might students notice here, in a rhetorical way, to help explain their understanding of who is addressing them in these two passages? They may mention that the first passage seems to "flow" (this is their word), while the second is periodically interrupted. Those dashes in the first sentence of passage 2 may be mentioned in evidence; again it is a willingness to intrude with an afterthought or qualification, as in colloquial speech. Supporting the same impression are the contractions of the second passage—"she didn't have much to teach, poor woman." This device would be unthinkable in the mouth of our first speaker, for all his ease and his good humor.

So much for stage two of this exercise—you may all be adding other distinctions of this kind, and the list may be increased as long as you and your students can stand it. We should now have illustrated for them our faith that an understanding of style has something to do with concrete matters of grammar and rhetoric. Now—stage three—how can this faith, at this crude level, be applied to the students' own composition?

The students return to their own statements about birth and early life. They are to rewrite those statements—twice. They are not to alter their vocabulary or their content any more than convenient, but they are to follow certain rules that the class discussion has listed. For example, in their first rewriting, one might ask them to put half of their verbs in the passive voice, more than half of their statement in subordinate clauses, place some subordination ahead of the subject-verb structure in their sentences, and use no contractions. Their second rewriting, of course, would proceed contrariwise: use no passive verbs, little subordination, place subordination after the subject-verb, interrupt the syntax with a dash or two, and include a few contractions. One can then ask them, in whatever way seems desirable, to observe and describe what has happened to their statement—and to themselves—as they have changed their rhetoric.

A few—probably not many—may discover, through such a mechanical game of word-play, a way of expressing themselves that seems improved over their original phrasing. But that is not the whole point. The point is to illustrate, even in this heavyhanded way, the fact of choice. Some, a surprising number actually, will discover that their own original rhetoric was much closer to that of Dickens than to that of Bellow. For such students, it is as important to see the value of another style as it is for the student who never subordinated in his life to try on the more formal dress of Victorian prose. In any case, the making of a decision about one's rhetoric has consequences—that is the lesson of the day. And some of the consequences have to do with self-discovery or self-creation. The question of whether I place my clause before or after my subject-verb, or between my subject and verb (as in this very sentence), has something to do with the kind of person I present myself as, before my reader.

What actually do students produce when put through this particular pressure cooker? I illustrate with two examples, aware how disappointing these fragments are likely to sound in the light of my pretentious ambitions in this exercise. Yet the contrasts in tone are obvious enough. The first one is by a young man already pretty literary:

> It would certainly be an interesting affair to relive one's early life with the awareness and consciousness that is gained with time and with constant receptivity to those daily experiences which become precious only in memory and nostalgia. The summer of 1947 . . .

First rewriting:

> If one were to live one's early life with the awareness and consciousness that is gained with time, the experience would certainly be an interesting one.

Second rewriting:

> Why isn't anybody aware of what's going on around him when he's young? I want to relive those early years. It would be interesting to know what I missed.

My second student offers a plainer style to begin with:

> In March, 1947, I was born as the second child in our family. My sister, three and one half years older than I, had been a war baby; and my parents felt that two children were enough for anyone, thus sealing my fate as the "baby" of the family. Our family circumstances at the time were rather modest; my father was the proprietor of a small business . . .

First rewriting:

> Since my sister, a war baby, had been born three and one half years before I was, and since it was felt by my parents that two children were enough for anyone, when I was born in March 1947 as the second child in our family my fate as the "baby" was . . .

Second rewriting:

> We weren't exactly the most opulent family at the time. My father—he was a small businessman—owned a service station, and the house we lived in wasn't exactly upper-middle class.

One or two final comments. With exercises like this, as most teachers well known, it is possible to remind our students, and ourselves, that our professional activity is not always divisible into three parts. There is much to be said for defining the study of English as the study of language, literature, and composition—but there is more to be said for defining it as all three at once. Obviously one can't operate three-dimensionally all the time, but an exercise like the one I have been describing may show our students that some rudimentary knowledge of grammar is a nice thing to have when you talk about literature, and that the grammar you use as a reader-critic of literature may be useful to you as a writer. It is one of the virtues of our new concern for rhetoric that it is not easily pigeonholed in any of our three areas of English.

I would also add a good word for playing games with style. I spoke of this exercise as a "mechanical game of word-play," and to an extent it is only that. But word-play is also a serious business of life, as students ought to know well after moving around from physics lab to history lecture to art seminar. After all, they take courses called *"The* History of Western Civilization," and they must be aware how playful language like that has to be if it is to stay sane. When we talk with one another aloud, we can build a little tone and irony into our voices and remind one another of the playfulness of it all. But writing prose comes harder. Socrates is a little severe about the shortcomings of written expression, but surely he is right when he pleads for playfulness:

> The man who thinks that in the written word there is necessarily much that is playful, and that no written discourse, whether in metre or in prose, deserves to be treated very seriously . . . —that man, Phaedrus, is likely to be such as you and I might pray we ourselves may become.

And Phaedrus, that amiable straight man, answers, "By all means that is what I wish and pray for." I hope it is not frivolous for me to conclude, as a teacher of rhetoric: that is what we all wish and pray for.

EDWARD P. J. CORBETT / *A Method of Analyzing Prose Style with a Demonstration Analysis of Swift's* A Modest Proposal

Most of us teachers have felt rather frustrated in our efforts to analyze prose style, either for ourselves or for our students in the classroom. This frustration has been brought on not only by a certain vagueness about what style is but also by the lack of a technique for analyzing prose style. As a result, we content ourselves in the classroom with enunciating such general, subjective labels for a particular author's style as "vigorous," "urbane," "ponderous," "curt," "mannered," "jaunty," "explosive," and that favorite all-purpose epithet "smooth-flowing." Some of us may have arrived at the point where we feel confident enough to designate more specific features of a prose style, such as the preponderance of Latinate diction, the mannerism of balanced sentence structure, or the high proportion of concrete images. But usually by the time we have gone that far, we have exhausted our resources for describing prose style, and we spend the rest of the class period discussing the ideas of the essay under consideration.

The New Criticism, especially as it was presented in Brooks and Warren's influential textbook *Understanding Poetry,* gave us teachers a technique for analyzing the verbal strategies of a poem. Consequently, we feel very secure when we come to analyze poetry for or with our students. What we need now is comparable training in a method of analyzing prose style.

What would lay the groundwork for the development of such a method would be a number of descriptions of prose style comparable to the descrip-

From *Reflections on High School English,* edited by Gary Tate. Tulsa, Oklahoma: The University of Tulsa, 1966, pp. 106–24. Reprinted by permission of the University of Tulsa and Edward P. J. Corbett.

tions of English grammar that we have had from modern linguists. It is surprising how few of these studies have been produced. At the end of the last century, Edwin H. Lewis's *The History of the English Paragraph* (University of Chicago Studies, 1894), L. A. Sherman's *Some Observations upon Sentence-Length in English Prose* (University of Nebraska Studies, 1892), and G. W. Gerwig's *On the Decrease of Predication and of Sentence Weight in English* (University of Nebraska Studies, 1894) presented statistical studies of several prose stylists. In this century, we have had a few stylistic studies of specific authors, such as Warner Taylor's *The Prose Style of Johnson* (Madison, 1918), Zilpha E. Chandler's *An Analysis of the Stylistic Techniques of Addison, Johnson, Hazlitt and Pater* (Iowa City, 1928), and W. K. Wimsatt's *The Prose Style of Samuel Johnson* (New Haven, 1941).[1] Very shortly, I understand, Mouton of the Hague will publish Louis Milic's study of Jonathan Swift's style.

As more of these stylistic descriptions appear, we will gain a basis for more valid generalizations about English prose style, and we may find that we have to relinquish some of our illusions about how certain writers create their stylistic effects. Such studies will also help us to develop techniques for analyzing style and to prepare textbooks for the classroom. Those of use who are interested in doing something with style in the classroom are looking forward to the publication of textbooks on style now being prepared by such teachers as Richard Ohmann, Francis Christensen, Winston Weathers and Otis Winchester, Harriet Sheridan, and Josephine Miles.

I will outline here a procedure for analyzing prose style. There will be very little in this proposed method that is original. I have merely brought together what I have learned about style from the ancient rhetoricians and from modern expositors of verbal strategies. After I have outlined the various features of style that one might look for in studying any prose piece, I will illustrate the method with a fairly detailed analysis of one of the most anthologized prose essays in English literature, Jonathan Swift's *A Modest Proposal*.

Any stylistic analysis must start out, I think, with some close observation of what actually appears on the printed page. One might, for instance, sense that a particular author uses a great many short sentences. Now, sentence-length is one of the features that can tell us something about an author's style. But it should be obvious that we cannot make a tenable generalization about an author's characteristic sentence-length until we have determined, by some rather tedious counting and tabulating, just how long or short his sentences are. Such a procedure would make counters and measurers of us

[1] We must not forget, of course, the pioneering work that Morris W. Croll did in the 1920's on sixteenth and seventeenth-century English prose style. These studies will soon be published in a single volume.

all—"a slide-rule method," to use Leslie Whipp's term,[2] that we humanistically trained teachers may find repellent—but this is a necessary step if we are to learn something about style in general and about style in particular.

If teachers and students survive the tedium of such counting and tabulating, they will then have a chance to bring to bear their aesthetic sensibilities. The next step in the procedure—and a more significant step—is to relate what the statistics reveal to the rhetoric of the piece being analyzed. Determining the length of a prose sentence is much like scanning a line of verse. Just as it is fairly easy to determine that a particular line of verse is written in iambic pentameter, so it is easy to determine that a particular sentence in prose is, say, twenty-one words long. But so what? The more important consideration is the function of that meter or that sentence-length. What contribution does this meter or this sentence-length make to the effect that the writer was seeking to produce? Here is where our judgment or our aesthetic sensibility or our rhetorical sense will have an opportunity to exercise itself. And it is here, in our relating of fact to function, that we will experience a perceptible growth in our powers of analysis and criticism.

A note of caution should be raised at this point. Inductive logic has taught us that the strength of a generalization rests partly on the number of observed facts. Just as one swallow does not make a summer, so a prevalent stylistic feature observed in a single piece of prose does not necessarily constitute a characteristic of the author's style. An author's style may change as his subject-matter or his purpose or his audience changes. Moreover, his style may have evolved over a period of time, and the stylistic feature that we have observed in this particular prose piece may be a mannerism that he eventually outgrew. True, certain characteristics of an author's style will be fairly constant, but we would be wise to withhold any generalizations about those constants until after we have studied a reasonably large body of a man's prose. All that we may be able to conclude from our inductive study of a single essay is that this particular stylistic device is a feature of this particular prose piece. But of course even that limited generalization represents some gain in our knowledge of an author's style.

Another caution is that we must be careful in our effort to relate fact to function. Dr. Johnson, you recall, said about Pope's celebrated doctrine of suiting sound to the sense, "This notion of representative metre, and the desire of discovering frequent adaptations of the sound to the sense, have produced, in my opinion, many wild conceits and imaginary beauties." We can indeed become excessively ingenious in our efforts to make a stylistic feature fit a rhetorical function. The pitfalls of such speculation, however, should not discourage us from at least making the attempt. Even a strained

[2] See Leslie T. Whipp and Margaret E. Ashida, "A Slide-Rule Composition Course," *College English*, XXV (October, 1963), 18–22.

speculation about the aptness of a particular stylistic feature is better than leaving an observed fact hanging in mid-air. We can later revise or reject our forced speculation when our knowledge or skill grows. If I may indulge in a platitude, nothing ventured, nothing gained.

With these general observations and cautions about the method in mind, we can now look at a listing of some of the objectively observable features of style. These features will be considered under the three main heads of words, sentences, and paragraphs.

What is there that we can observe about words or, to use the more common rhetorical term, diction? Well, we can seek to determine whether an author's diction is predominantly general or specific; abstract or concrete; formal or informal; polysyllabic or monosyllabic; common or special; referential or emotive. Judgments about the either-or will be more subjective in some cases than in others. We can, for instance, determine precisely the proportion between monosyllabic and polysyllabic diction; but since the difference between, say, formal and informal diction is relative, our judgments about some words on this score will necessarily be subjective. Making allowances for those subjective judgments, however, we still can determine, in cases of relative difference, the general tenor of a man's diction. After studying the diction of an A. J. Liebling piece on boxing, for instance, we would find it fairly easy to conclude that although Mr. Liebling adroitly mixes formal and informal words, his diction is predominantly informal.

The frequency of proper nouns in a piece will also tell us something about a man's style. In the readability formula that Rudolf Flesch devised several years ago, the incidence of proper nouns was one of the factors that enhanced the readability of prose. Then too there will always be some few words in an essay that will tell us a great deal about an author's period, milieu, range of interest, education, and bias. We would do well to look for such indicative words.

Studying the diction of a prose piece from these various angles will help us to determine the "weight" of a man's style and to account for the effect that a man's style creates. Sometimes, for instance, when we get the general impression that a man's style is heavy and opaque, we are surprised to learn, after a close study of the diction, that the peculiar texture of his style has *not* been produced by his choice of words. And that kind of revelation is a real gain for us, because then we know that we will have to look elsewhere for the cause of the ponderous effect.

In moving on from a study of word-choice to a study of words in collocation, we find that the most fruitful syntactical unit to study is the sentence. What can we look for when we study the sentences in a prose piece? For one thing, we can study the length of sentences (measured in number of words). Once the total number of sentences and the total number of words are known, we can, by a simple exercise in long division, figure out the average sentence-length. We can then get an idea of variations of sentence-length by tabulating the percentage of sentences which *exceed,* and the percentage which *fall short of,* the average by a specified number of words.

One can also make a study of the *kinds* of sentences in a prose piece. One can tabulate the grammatical types of sentences (simple, compound, complex, compound-complex); or the rhetorical types (loose, periodic, balanced, antithetical); or the functional types (statement, question, command, exclamation). In studying varieties of sentence patterns, one can look at such things as inversions of normal word-order, the frequency and kinds of sentence-openers (infinitive, gerund, or participial phrases; adverb clauses; absolute constructions; expletive patterns; conjunctive words and phrases); and the methods and location of expansion in the sentences.

Although tropes (words with transferred meanings) could be observed when we are studying diction, and schemes (unusual sentence patterns) could be observed when we are studying sentences, it is probably better to make a separate step of recording figures of speech. Under tropes we would be noting such things as metaphor, simile, synecdoche, metonymy, irony, litotes, oxymoron, antonomasia. Under schemes we would be noting such things as anaphora, apposition, parallelism, antithesis, chiasmus, climax, anastrophe. The study of schemes and tropes can reveal a great deal about the degree of vividness, vivacity, and ornateness in an author's style.

The rhetoric of the next largest unit, the paragraph, has been one of the most neglected aspects of stylistic study. Modern rhetoric books have paid a great deal of attention to the topic sentence, to the various methods of developing paragraphs, and to the qualities of unity, coherence, and emphasis, but a study of these aspects does not reveal very much about a man's style. Perhaps the reason why classical rhetorics did not deal at all with the paragraph is that classical rhetoric was concerned primarily with spoken discourse. Paragraphing of course is a typographical device to punctuate units of thought in written discourse only, and this kind of punctuation often reveals no more about a man's style than the punctuation used within sentences. But there must be an approach to the study of the paragraph that would reveal something about style, and perhaps Professor Francis Christensen's projected book on the rhetoric of the sentence and paragraph will provide the approach that will yield significant information about the style of the paragraph.

As a beginning, meanwhile, we can look at such things as the length of paragraphs (measured in number of words and/or number of sentences), the various levels of movement or development in the paragraph, the means of articulating sentences within the paragraph, and the transitional devices used between paragraphs. By observing the length of paragraphs and the modes of development and articulation, we will get a sense of the density, pace, and readability of an author's style.

The tabulation of objectively observable items, such as I have been out-lining, might be called the stage of "gathering the data." It is a wearisome, time-consuming inductive exercise, but it is a necessary stage if our general-izations about a man's style are to be at all tenable. Needless to say, one does not have to look at *all* of the features in every stylistic analysis, and one does not have to follow the order outlined above. Sometimes concentration on a few salient features will bring us closer to the essence of a man's style than will an exhaustive analysis. Style is a complex of many linguistic devices cooperating to produce a peculiar effect, but it may not always be necessary to expose all of the linguistic devices in order to account for the effect.

Let me recommend one fruitful practice for this gathering of the data. You might try copying out by hand long passages of the essay or even the entire essay. You will be amazed at the number of additional things you will detect about a man's style when you write out his text. From my experience with transcribing a text, I would estimate that by copying you will detect at least three times as many features as you will by merely reading and re-reading the text. In gathering the data for my analysis of Swift's *A Modest Proposal,* I detected some of the most significant features of his style only after I had laboriously copied out the entire text of the essay.

Gathering the data is a prelude for the more important, the more difficult stage—relating this data to the author's rhetorical strategies. It does not take much intelligence to gather the data; it takes only patience and accuracy. But it does take intelligence and perhaps a good measure of imagination to be able to see the rhetorical function of a particular stylistic features.

The "why" of any stylistic feature can be answered only in relation to something else—the subject-matter or the occasion or the genre or the au-thor's purpose or the nature of the audience or the ethos of the writer. To be able to relate stylistic features to their rhetorical function then, we must have a secure knowledge of the essay we are analyzing. As a minimum, we must know its purpose, its thesis, and its organization. In addition, we may need to know something about the author, something about the situation that prompted the essay, something about the audience to whom the essay was directed. We should be able to gain a good deal of this kind of knowl-edge from internal evidence alone. But we may find it helpful to resort to external sources in order to supplement what internal evidence tells us. So we may have to turn to biographical reference works, to literary histories, to critical articles. The point is that the more profound our understanding of the essay is, the easier it will be to relate a stylistic feature to its rhetorical function.

Before launching into my analysis of *A Modest Proposal,* let me suggest some follow-up exercises. Once your students have done an analysis of one or more stylistic features of an essay, they can be asked to study another essay by the same author. They may discover thereby that an author's style changes noticeably as his subject-matter or his purpose or his audience changes. The value to your students of such an observation will be the realization that an author must be in command, not of one style, but of many styles. Next, you may want to direct your students to study another author, either from the same period or from a later period, preferably an author writing on a similar subject or with a similar purpose. Such comparisons can make meaningful to the students Buffon's famous statement, "Style is the man." And such comparisons can also make the students aware that styles change not only as the subject or genre or audience or purpose changes but as the period changes. Twentieth-century style in general is distinctively different from seventeenth-century style, and it will represent a real gain in the students' education if they come to realize that the radical changes in modern man's way of life have had a marked influence on the dominant style of the age.

Eventually, students should be turned loose on an analysis of their own prose style. This exercise may well be the most fruitful one for the students. They will be fascinated not only by what they learn about their own style but also by what they learn from comparing their style with that of professional writers. Let us hope that the students will be intelligent enough to recognize that the differences between their style and other authors' styles do not mean that their style is necessarily inferior to the styles of the other authors.

The best themes I have received from students during my teaching career have been those written by freshmen who were asked to comment on what they had learned from a series of stylistic studies. One of the reasons why these themes were fascinating enough to keep me up until 2:00 in the morning reading them was, I think, that the students were writing from a body of specific knowledge that they themselves had derived inductively. In other words, the problem of invention having been solved for them, the students had something to say—and somehow, for the first time, they were finding apt words to say what they had to say. Try this with your students. You may for the first time in your teaching career become excited about a batch of themes.

I have gone on long enough now about a general procedure for analyzing prose style. The method should become more meaningful for you as I apply it to a specific piece of prose—in this case, Jonathan Swift's famous satirical essay *A Modest Proposal*.

I might begin this stylistic analysis by defining what kind of discourse *A Modest Proposal* is, since genre makes its own demands on the kind of style that an author will employ. With reference to the literary genres, *A Modest Proposal* can be classified as a satire, and with reference to the four forms of discourse, satire must be classified as argumentation. If we were using the classical rhetorician's three kinds of persuasive discourse to further specify what type of argumentation we have here, we would classify *A Modest Proposal* as an instance of "deliberative" discourse, since Jonathan Swift is bent on changing the attitude of the propertied class toward the Irish poor and ultimately on moving this class to take some action that would remedy the lot of the poor.

In 1728, a year before *A Modest Proposal* was published, there had been a devastating famine in Ireland caused by three successive failures of the harvest. This famine had aggravated the misery of a people that had already been reduced to abject poverty by years of heavy taxation, repressive laws, and absentee landlordism. As Louis A. Landa has pointed out,[3] Swift hoped to expose the contradiction between a favorite maxim of the mercantilist economic writers—namely, that people are the riches of a nation—and the practice of reducing the majority of subjects to a condition of grinding poverty. The prevalence of the poverty was plain to see, and there had been no lack of proposals, from the political economists, of ways to remedy the condition of the poor. But the ruling class and the absentee landlords were not listening; battening on the revenues from the land, they were not much concerned about the condition of the peasants who were producing their wealth. Swift was determined to get their ear. He would shock them into attention. And he would shock them into attention with a monstrous proposal presented by means of two of his favorite satiric techniques—using a mask and using irony.

To make his use of the mask or *persona* effective, Swift must create a character who is consistent, credible, and authoritative. This must be a character who, in a sense, "sneaks up" on the reader, a character who lulls the reader into expecting a sensible, practicable solution of the Irish problem and who, even after he has dropped his bombshell, maintains his pose and his poise. This character will exert a curious kind of ethical appeal—a man who at the beginning of the essay gives the impression of being serious, expert, and well-meaning but who gradually reveals himself to be shockingly inhuman and naive. The character that eventually emerges is that of a fool whose insanity becomes, as Martin Price puts it, "a metaphor for the guilt of responsible men."[4]

---

[3] See Louis A. Landa, *"A Modest Proposal* and Populousness," *Modern Philology,* XL (1942), 161–70, and "Swift's Economic Views and Mercantilism," *Journal of English Literary History,* X (1942), 310–35.

[4] Martin Price, *Swift's Rhetorical Art* (New Haven: Yale University Press, 1953), p. 88.

One of the consequences of this use of a *persona* is that the style of the essay will not be Swift's style; rather it will be a style appropriate to the character that Swift has created. True, some of the characteristics of Swift's style will be present; no author can entirely submerge his own style, except perhaps when he is engaged in writing a parody of another author's style. But if Swift does his job properly, the message of the essay will be conveyed to us in a style that differs, at least in some respects, from the style that Swift displays when he is speaking in his own voice.

One of the respects in which the style of *A Modest Proposal* differs noticeably from Swift's usual style is the sentence-length. The average sentence-length in this essay is 56.9 words per sentence. And we note some remarkable variations above and below that average. Although 46 per cent of his sentences are composed of less than 47 words, almost 30 per cent of his sentences are longer than 67 words (see Appendix for additional statistics on sentence-length). It is interesting to compare this sentence-length with that in two other works where Swift used a *persona*. In studying 200 paragraphs of *Gulliver's Travels* and 100 paragraphs of *A Tale of a Tub*, Edwin Herbert Lewis discovered the average sentence-length to be 40.7 words—almost 50 per cent shorter than the average sentence in *A Modest Proposal*.[5] What has happened to the "conciseness" that Herbert Davis says is the most distinctive quality of Swift's style?[6] What has happened of course is that in *A Modest Proposal* we are listening to a man who is so filled with his subject, so careful about qualifying his statements and computations, so infatuated with the sound of his own words, that he rambles on at inordinate length.

We note this same tendency to qualify and ramify his thoughts in other characteristics of the proposer's sentence structure. We note this, for one thing, in his frequent use of parentheses. Sometimes the parenthetical matter throws in a gratuitous aside—"(as I must confess the times require)"; or editorializes—"(although indeed very unjustly)"; or qualifies a statement—"(I mean in the country)"; or insinuates an abrupt note of ethical appeal —"(it could, I think with humble submission, be a loss to the public)." Interpolated gestures like these, especially when they are as frequent as they are in this essay, betray a man who is unusually concerned for the accuracy of his statements and for the image he is projecting to his audience.

Something of the same tendency is evident in the many absolute constructions in the essay. Most of these occur at the end of fairly long sentences —e.g. "the charge of nutriment and rags having been at least four times that

[5] Edwin H. Lewis, *History of the English Paragraph* (Chicago: University of Chicago Press, 1894), pp. 35–36.
[6] Herbert Davis, "The Conciseness of Swift," *Essays on the Eighteenth Century Presented to David Nichol Smith* (Oxford: At the Clarendon Press, 1945), pp. 15–32.

value" (para. 7); "their corn and cattle being seized and money a thing unknown" (para. 33). These trailing-off phrases create the effect of a thought suddenly remembered and desperately thrown in. What is clever, though, about Swift's use of these trailing-off phrases, placed as they are in an emphatic position, is that in many cases they carry the real sting of the sentence. Here is that topsy-turviness of values that constitutes one of the main strategies of the essay—important things couched in ironical terms or hidden away in weak structures.

This tendency to ramify, qualify, or refine statements is evident too in the proposer's habit of compounding elements. I am referring not so much to the common eighteenth-century practice of using doublets and triplets, of which there are a conspicuous number in *A Modest Proposal,* as to the proposer's habit of stringing out words and phrases beyond the common triad, so that we get the effect almost of an exhaustive cataloguing of details or qualifiers. I am referring to instances like these:

> stewed, roasted, baked, or boiled (para. 9)
> of curing the expensiveness of pride, vanity, idleness, and gaming in our women (para. 29)
> equally innocent, cheap, easy, and effectual (para. 32)
> by advancing our trade, providing for infants, relieving the poor, and giving pleasure to the rich (para. 33) [7]

What is observable about the proposer's amplifications is that his epithets are rarely just synonymous variations, such as the displays of *copia* that were common in Anglo-Saxon poetry and Euphuistic prose. In a phrase like "innocent, cheap, easy, and effectual," each adjective adds a distinct idea to the predication.

Along with this heavy compounding, Swift occasionally uses the scheme of polysyndeton—e.g. "in the arms or on the back or at the heels" (para. 2); "dying and rotting by cold and famine and filth and vermin" (para. 19). Multiplying conjunctions like this has the effect of further stringing out the list. Swift sometimes adds to the compounded elements the scheme of alliteration, as in the just-quoted "famine and filth and vermin" or in the triplet "parsimony, prudence, and temperance" (para. 29). In these examples, we get the impression of a man who is beginning to play with words. In the only other conspicuous use of alliteration, "in joints from the giblet" (para.

---

[7] There is nothing in *A Modest Proposal* that approaches the crushing catalogue of words in Book IV of *Gulliver's Travels:* "Hence it follows of necessity that the vast numbers of our people are compelled to seek their livelihood by begging, robbing, stealing, cheating, pimping, forswearing, flattering, suborning, forging, gaming, lying, fawning, hectoring, voting, scribbling, star-gazing, poisoning, whoring, canting, libelling, free-thinking, and the like occupations."

18), our impulse to laugh at this sporting with words is suddenly restrained by our realization of the horror of the image. At other times, Swift will reinforce the compounding with the scheme of climax, as in the two or three examples in the first paragraph of the essay, or with the scheme of anti-climax, as in the example quoted above from paragraph 33.

Although all of this compounding is done within the framework of parallelism, parallelism is not a characteristic of the proposer's style or of Swift's style in general. But Swift demonstrates that he knows how and when to use parallel structure. In paragraph 29, the key paragraph of the essay, he lays out his long enumeration of "other expedients" on a frame of parallel structure. The list is long, the list is important, and Swift wants to make sure that his readers do not get lost in this maze of coordinate proposals.

Another thing that the long rambling sentences and the frequent compounding might suggest is a "spoken" style. If one compares spoken style with written style, one notes that spoken style tends to be paratactic—a stitching together of coordinate units. We have just observed this kind of rhapsodic structure in the word and phrase units of *A Modest Proposal,* but when we look at the kinds of grammatical sentences (see Appendix), we observe a marked predominance of the subordinate structures that typify a sophisticated written style. Over half of the sentences are complex, and almost a third of the sentences are compound-complex. Although there are five simple sentences in the essay, there is not a single compound sentence, which is the commonest structure in extemporaneous spoken discourse. So although the essay may give the impression of a certain colloquial ease, this impression is not being produced by the syntax of the sentences.

Further evidence of a calculated literary style is found in the proposer's inclination to periodic structure. As Walter J. Ong said in a recent article on prose style, "Oral composition or grammatical structure is typically non-periodic, proceeding in the 'adding' style; literary composition tends more to the periodic." [8] We see this periodic structure exemplified in a sentence like the first one of paragraph 4: "As to my own part, having turned my thoughts, for many years, upon this important subject, and maturely weighed the several schemes of other projectors, I have always found them grossly mistaken in their computations." No one *speaks* a sentence like that; sentences like that are produced by someone who has time to plot his sentences.

This tendency to delay the main predication of the sentence is most pronounced within another structural pattern that is so common in the essay as to be a mannerism. I refer to the proposer's habit of putting the main idea

[8] Walter J. Ong, "Oral Residue in Tudor Prose Style," *PMLA,* LXXX (June, 1965), 149.

of the sentence into a noun clause following the verb of the main clause. These noun clauses follow either personal structures like "I am assured by our merchants that . . . ," "I have reckoned that . . . ," "he confessed that . . ." or impersonal structures like "it is not improbable that . . ." and "it is very well known that. . . ." There are at least nineteen instances like these, where the main idea of the sentence is contained in the noun clause. And frequently the proposer further delays the main idea by making us read almost to the end of the noun clause before he gives us the main predication. A prime example of this is the final sentence of paragraph 18:

> Neither indeed can I deny, that if the same use were made of several plump young girls in this town, who, without one single groat to their fortunes, cannot stir abroad without a chair, and appear at the playhouse and assemblies in foreign fineries, which they will never pay for, the kingdom would not be the worse.

Reading a sentence like this, we wonder whether the man will ever get to the point, and in this case, when the point is finally reached, we find that it is deflatingly anti-climactic.

This tendency toward periodic structure is evidence not only of a deliberate written style but of a habit of the *persona* that suits Swift's rhetorical purpose. I suggested earlier that part of Swift's rhetorical strategy is to create a character who will, as it were, "sneak up" on the reader. The frequent use of periodic structure is one of the ways in which the proposer "sneaks up" on the reader.

And we see this same tactic in the early paragraphs of the essay. In the first two paragraphs we see the long, leisurely, meandering sentences in which the proposer, in a matter-of-fact tone, describes the present condition of the poor. There is further dawdling in paragraph 4, where in two rambling sentences he seeks to establish his credentials with his audience. Then in paragraph 6, the second longest paragraph of the essay, we are subjected to a litany of cold, hard figures or "computations." In the short paragraph 9, we hear the disturbing sputter of a lighted fuse as the proposer retails the testimony of his American acquaintance about what a delicacy a year-old child is. Then in paragraph 10, after the expenditure of almost a thousand words on preliminaries (almost a third of the essay), the proposer drops his bombshell. Nor does his pace become any more frenetic from this point on. He continues to "leak out" information, testimony, and arguments.

The noticeable periodic structure of many of the sentences, then, is part of Swift's strategy of sneaking up on the audience, of disarming the reader in order to render him more sensitive to the blow that will be delivered to the solar plexus. The proposer tells us in paragraph 27 that he is "studious of brevity." But he is not brief at all; he takes his own good time about dealing out what he has to say to his audience. This is not the curt Senecan amble; this is the rambling Ciceronian cadence. The Ciceronian cadence does not fit Jonathan Swift, of course, but it does fit the character he has created and does contribute to the rhetorical effectiveness of the essay.

We could pursue this discussion of sentences and schemes, but let us move on to a consideration of the diction of the essay. Let us see what a study of the diction tells us about Swift's strategies and about the proposer's style.

To begin with, we might advert briefly to the words and idioms that mark the essay as a product of the eighteenth century. One of the things that has often been remarked of Swift's style is that it is strikingly modern. As one of my students said to me, "When I'm reading Swift, I have the feeling that I'm reading George Orwell all over again." One of the reasons certainly for this impression of modernity is the diction and idiom. Swift uses very few words and idioms that are outdated. But he does use just enough dated words and expressions to prevent our getting the impression that we are reading the morning newspaper. I counted about a dozen idioms which were peculiar to the eighteenth century or were still current in the eighteenth century but are no longer current—expressions like "of towardly parts" (para. 6), "no gentleman would *repine* to give ten shillings" (para. 14), "I cannot be altogether *in* his sentiments" (para. 17) (see Appendix for additional examples). If one were attempting to date this piece from internal evidence, probably the two words that would be the best index of the period in which this essay was written would be *shambles* (para. 16) and the *chair* (para. 18) in which the plump young girls ride about town. The *OED* would tell us that in the eighteenth century *shambles* meant "a place where meat is sold," "a slaughter house" and that *chair* designated a means of transportation. Expressions like these give the essay its Augustan flavor, but aside from these, the diction and idiom are remarkably modern.

The Appendix carries a note about the monosyllabism of the essay. Only about one-third of the nouns in the first ten paragraphs are monosyllabic, and I suspect that there is a much higher percentage of polysyllabic, Latinate diction in *A Modest Proposal* than we will find in most of Swift's other prose works, especially in that prose where he is speaking in his own voice. This polysyllabic diction is appropriate of course for the kind of pedantic character that Swift has created in *A Modest Proposal*. The proposer wants to pass himself off on his audience as a man who has indulged in a great deal of scientific, scholarly study of the problem, so as to enhance his authority—"having turned my thoughts, for many years, upon this important subject, and maturely weighed the several schemes of other projectors" (para. 4).

The mathematical and mercantile terminology is also contributing to the image of the dedicated investigator and the political arithmetician. Besides the many figures cited, there are repeated uses of words like "compute," "reckon," "calculate," "shillings," "pounds," "sterling," "accounts," "stock," "commodity," "*per annum.*" By putting jargon like this in the mouth of his proposer, Swift is making him talk the language of the other political economists who had turned their attention to the problem. We might say of the cold-bloodedness with which the proposer delivers himself of these terms that it represents his disinterested endeavor to propagate the worst that is known and thought about the problem in the Anglo-Irish world.

The most notable of the lexical means that Swift uses to achieve his purpose is the series of animal metaphors (see the Appendix). Charles Beaumont has pointed out that Swift is here employing the ancient rhetorical device of diminution, the opposite effect of amplification.[9] Swift first reduces his human beings to the status of animals and then to the status of food furnished to the table when these animals are slaughtered. So we pass from animal images like "dropped from its dam" and "reserved for breed" to such slaughtered-animal images as "the carcass," "the fore or hind quarters," and "the skin of which, artificially dressed." We feel the impact of these metaphors when we realize that Swift is suggesting that the Anglo-Irish landlords were treating human beings no better than they treated their domestic animals. The proposer points up this inhuman treatment when he says, in paragraph 26, that if his proposal were adopted, "men would become as fond of their wives, during the time of pregnancy, as they are now of their mares in foal, their cows in calf, or sows when they are ready to farrow."

Another trope that Swift uses to achieve diminution is litotes—the opposite trope to hyperbole. Here are four prominent examples of litotes or understatement. In paragraph 2, the proposer refers to the burden of the prodigious number of beggar children as "a very great additional grievance." In paragraph 17, he speaks of the practice of substituting the bodies of young lads and maidens for venison as "a little bordering on cruelty." At the end of the periodic sentence in paragraph 18, he says that "the kingdom would not be the worse" if the bodies of plump young girls were sold as a delicacy for the table. The most notable example of litotes in the essay—and the one that serves as the chief tip-off to the irony of the essay—is found in the first sentence of the key paragraph 29: "I can think of no one objection that will possibly be raised against this proposal, unless it should be urged that the

---

[9] See Charles Allen Beaumont, "A Modest Proposal," *Swift's Classical Rhetoric* (Athens, Ga.: University of Georgia Press, 1961), pp. 15–43. After my own gathering of data, it was reassuring to me to discover that I had noted many of the same stylistic features that Beaumont had found.

number of people will be thereby much lessened in this kingdom." The frequent use of litotes fits in well with the proposer's tendency to underplay everything.

The proposer not only underplays his proposal (note "a modest proposal") and his arguments to justify the proposal but also underplays his emotions. One has a hard time of it finding emotionally freighted words in the essay. Only in paragraphs 1 and 5 do I find conspicuous clusters of what I. A. Richards calls "emotive words":

> paragraph 1: Melancholy, all in rags, helpless infants, dear native country, crowded
> paragraph 5: abortions, horrid practice, murdering their bastard children, alas, tears and pity, poor innocent babes, savage and inhuman breast

The only other place in the essay where I sense the proposer losing a tight rein on his emotions is in his outburst in paragraph 18 against the plump young girls of the town, and in this instance, the anger simmering under these words is, I suspect, the emotional reaction of the clergyman Swift rather than of the worldly proposer. And this is the one place in the essay where I feel that Swift momentarily drops the mask and speaks in his own voice.

Swift considerably enhances the emotional impact of his message by this underplaying. And the other trope that is responsible for the emotional power of the essay is irony. As I remarked before, irony is an over-arching device for the entire essay: the proposer means what he says, but Swift does not. Irony, however, is a prevalent device within the essay too. I counted at least fifteen instances of words being used ironically. Rather than weary you with the entire catalogue, let me quote a few representative examples (the ironical words are italicized):

> will make two dishes at an *entertainment* for friends (para. 10)
> the fore and hind quarters will make a *reasonable* dish (para. 10)
> will make admirable gloves for *ladies* and summer boots for *fine gentlemen* (para. 14)
> some *scrupulous* people might be apt to censure (para. 17)

The horror of this irony hits us all the harder when we realize that the proposer, in his naivety, intends his words to be taken literally. These are the places where I can almost see Swift grinning through the lines of print.

Swift does something with words in this essay that I had not noticed him doing in any of his other prose works. He repeats key words so that they almost become motifs in the essay. The Appendix lists some of these repeated words and records the frequency of repetition. Note particularly the repetitions and variations of the words *child* and *parent*. Swift realizes that the proposal violates one of the most fundamental of human relations—the child-parent relation. When this violation of the normal child-parent relation is joined with a suggestion of cannibalism, a practice that almost universally offends the sensibilities of mankind, we get a proposal of the utmost monstrosity. And if Swift can get his audience to react violently enough to the revolting proposal, there is hope that they will resort to some of the "other expedients" for a solution to the problem of poverty. Basically that is his main rhetorical strategy in the essay.

I cannot wholly account for the rhetorical function of the repetition of the kingdom-country-nation diction. Swift may be seeking to emphasize that the poverty of the people is a problem of national scope, one in which the welfare of the entire nation is crucially involved. Hasn't this been the theme that President Johnson has been urging in his efforts to promote his Poverty Program? Another explanation may be that Swift is suggesting that just as, on the domestic level, the normal child-parent relationships have broken down, the kingdom-citizen relationships have broken down on the national level.

This kind of repetition of key words and phrases is a device that we have come to associate with Matthew Arnold's style. Anyone who has read Arnold's prose extensively knows how effective this tactic can be for purposes of exposition. Although repetition is not a mannerism of Swift's style in general, we can appreciate the emotional effect that Swift achieves in this argumentative piece with these drumbeat repetitions. These insistent repetitions keep bringing us back to the full implications of the modest proposal.

Before this exhaustive analysis becomes prostratingly exhausting, I had better bring it to a quick conclusion. Maybe a good way to conclude this study is for me to quote two estimates of Swift's style and then to ask you which of these two estimates seems to be, in the light of the foregoing analysis, the more just.

The first quotation is from Dr. Johnson's *Life of Swift:*

> For purposes merely didactic, when something is to be told that was not known before [his style] is in the highest degree proper, but against that inattention by which known truths are suffered to lie neglected, it makes no provision; it instructs but does not persuade.

There is no denying that Swift's style does achieve an "easy and safe conveyance of meaning," but do you find Dr. Johnson's denial of persuasive value in Swift's style too harsh? Perhaps you are more disposed to accept Coleridge's judgment on Swift's style: "The manner is a complete expression of the matter, the terms appropriate, and the artifice concealed."

But maybe it is unfair to ask you to choose between these two estimates, for one of my points has been that in this essay we are observing not so much Swift's style as a style that Swift has created for his modest proposer. And who, after all, remembers this essay for its style? This analysis has revealed, I hope, that there is considerable stylistic artifice in *A Modest Proposal,* but hasn't this essay become memorable mainly because of the monstrousness of the proposal and the cleverness of the ironical form? As a matter of historical fact, Swift did *not* succeed in persuading his audience to do something about a lamentable situation. But he did succeed in producing a great piece of literature.

Appendix

SOME STATISTICS ON SWIFT'S *A Modest Proposal*

3474 words
  33 paragraphs
  61 sentences   (For this study, a sentence is defined as a group of words beginning with a capital letter and ending with some mark of terminal punctuation.)

Average number of words per paragraph 105.2
Average number of sentences per paragraph 1.84
  18 one-sentence paragraphs
   7 two-sentence paragraphs
   4 three-sentence paragraphs
   3 four-sentence paragraphs
   1 five-sentence paragraph (#29)

Shortest paragraph #8 (20 words)—a transitional paragraph (other transitional paragraph, #20, is 34 words long)
Longest paragraph #29 (289 words)—"other expedients" (a key paragraph)

Average number of words per sentence 56.9
Number of sentences 10 words or more *above* average 18
Percentage of sentences above average 29.5%
Number of sentences 10 words or more *below* average 28
Percentage of sentences below average 45.9%

Longest sentence .... 179 words (para. 32)
Other long sentences: 164 words (para. 6); 141 words (para. 29); 119 words
    (para. 18); 109 words (para. 4); 102 words (para. 13)
Shortest sentence .... 11 words (last sentence of para. 27)
    (other short sentence: first sentence of transitional paragraph #20)
34 Complex sentences
18 Compound-complex sentences
 5 Simple sentences (paragraphs 4, 19, 20, 27)
 4 Elliptical or incomplete sentences (paragraphs 10, 29 (two), 31)

REPEATED WORDS

child (children) .....25 ⎤
infants 6   ⎬......33
babes ....2 ⎦

kingdom ....13 ⎤
country 9   ⎬......27
nation ....5 ⎦

mother ....6 ⎤
parents ....7 ⎬......20
breed (breeders) .....7 ⎦

the year ....6 ⎤
one year old ....1 ⎥
annually 3   ⎬......16
solar year ....2 ⎥
per annum ....4 ⎦

number ....7 ⎤
compute ....5 ⎥......15
reckon ....2 ⎥
calculate ....1 ⎦

food ....7 ⎤
flesh 4   ⎬......19
carcass ....5 ⎥
plump ....3 ⎦

propose ....5 ⎤......9
proposal ....4 ⎦

gentlemen ....5 ⎤
persons of quality ....2 ⎬......12
beggars ....5 ⎦

DICTION OR IDIOM PECULIARLY EIGHTEENTH-CENTURY

(The number in parentheses refers to the paragraph in which the expression
occurs.)
    (6) of *towardly* parts
    (10) increas*eth* to twenty-eight pounds
    (13) fish being a *prolific* diet
    (14) no gentleman would *repine* to give ten shillings
    (16) *shambles* may be appointed
    (16) dressing them hot from the knife
    (17) the *want* of venison . . . for *want* of work and service
    (17) I cannot be altogether *in* his sentiments

(18) who came from *thence, above* twenty years ago

(18) without a *chair*

(19) and I have been desired to employ my thoughts what course may be taken

(19) But I am not *in the least pain upon* that matter

(19) and thus the country and themselves are *in a fair way* of being delivered from the evils to come

(25) bring great *custom* to taverns where the *vintners* will certainly be so prudent

(26) emulation among the married women, *which* of them could bring

(32) to reject any offer, proposed by wise men, *who* [which?] shall be found equally innocent, cheap, easy, and effectual

ANIMAL IMAGERY

(3) at the *heels* of their mother

(4) a child just *dropped* from its *dam*

(10) reserved for breed

(10) more than we allow to sheep, black-cattle, or swine

(10) therefore one *male* will be sufficient *to serve* four *females*

(10) to let them *suck* plentifully . . . to render them plump and fat for a good table

(10) the fore or hind quarter

(14) for the *carcass* of a good fat child

(15) flay the *carcass* . . . the skin of which, artificially *dressed*

(16) as we do roasting pigs

(26) men would become as fond of their wives, during the time of their pregnancy, as they are now of their mares in foal, their cows in calf, or sows when they are ready to farrow

(27) propagation of swine's flesh

(27) the great destruction of pigs

(27) fat *yearling* child

MONOSYLLABISM

In the first ten paragraphs of the essay, there are 1127 words; of these, (60%) 685 are monosyllabic. But since a good many of these monosyllabic words are pronouns, prepositions, conjunctions, or auxiliary verbs, we get an unreliable estimate of Swift's diction. If we look at the nouns only, we get a different picture. In these same ten paragraphs, there are 204 nouns. Of these, 73 are monosyllabic (36%), 131 are polysyllabic. If we regard only the substantive words in these paragraphs, we get, for Swift, an unusually high number of polysyllabic words.

ATTITUDES

JAMES L. FENNER / *Can "Average" Students Be Taught To Write?*

As the class enters the room and takes seats, the students begin to realize with dismay and mounting horror that the teacher is writing composition titles on the board. The feeling that they have been betrayed yields to a sticky self-pity in which the weaker souls among them may wallow for as much as seven or eight minutes. After they have devoted all they can to this fruitless enterprise, a panic seizes them as they realize that the braver and more ambitious members of the class have already begun to write. But the panic is self-limiting, because each student knows that the period will end, that the papers will be collected, that the teacher will mark them, and that he must in fact pull himself together at least enough to write *something* before the bell rings.

Fortunately, almost every student has mastered the techniques of writing without having anything to say, and since the panic-stricken ones are ill-equipped to think of anything, they begin to practice this precious skill. An opening sentence calls attention to the importance of the topic. A second discusses how deeply it is cherished by persons of all ages and sexes. A third goes on in similarly empty style with other totally meaningless phrases that serve merely to protect the student from the knowledge that no matter how many words may appear on his paper, he has written nothing.

Soon his repertoire of meaningless openers becomes exhausted, and he begins to try to think of something to write. Prayerfully, he bites his pencil and glances hopefully about the room. An idea seems to flash through his

From *English Journal*, LVI (May, 1967), 725–35, 738. Reprinted by permission of the National Council of Teachers of English and James L. Fenner.

mind, and, hastily, before it flashes back out again into the darkness, he tries to write it down. A fourth sentence has taken shape upon his paper. The panic and pencil-biting return, until mercifully another shadowy and shapeless half-thought skirts the edges of his consciousness. This too he writes down as best he can before it vanishes altogether. A fifth sentence has been produced.

This process continues for ten or 15 minutes until at the end of 15 or 20 sentences a student has produced the required number of words and is at last able to gasp a breath of air. Of course, he has not produced a composition; he has created a rambling improvisation padded as necessary to achieve the required length. And now, because he knows that the teacher will penalize him for mistakes and because he has been exhorted since childhood to reread his written papers, he sits back in his seat and begins to read.

A flush of pleasure and a swell of pride surge through him as he begins to appreciate that he has really written quite a bit and not bad at that. He hadn't realized that he could write as well as that, and it is apparent that his pitiful self-admiration has utterly clouded whatever potential faculties he may have had for self-criticism and revision. And, finally, when the bell rings, in a rosy fog compounded of anxiety and a touching but ludicrous pride, he hands in his paper and prepares to wait the six weeks it may take before he gets it back.

And that six-week figure is not intended to sound sarcastic. The correction of five sets of compositions, 180 papers in all, is a job of staggering proportions. The proofreading required to note and correct the rich flow of illiteracies in a single paper can of itself take five to ten minutes, at the end of which time the paper has been transformed by the teacher's red pencil into what might almost be considered a double essay, the one written by the student for the teacher and the other by the teacher for the student. It is a swamp of correction symbols and marginalia upon which the teacher may actually have spent more effort and thought than the student. In addition, the conscientious teacher will try to write a personal comment on the ideas a youngster has expressed, indicating her understanding and appreciation of or perhaps her disagreement with, what he has said. In the case of some few papers so highly fluent and literate as to require little proofreading, the teacher may even go on to write brief phrases commenting on the development and structure of the paper's substance. It may take a whole week of evenings for her to finish a single set of 35 papers, and five weeks for five sets is not unthinkable, even if no large chores intervene. At the end of this time, if the teacher returns the paper for filing, the student is likely to glance at his grade and file it in the waste-basket. If it is returned for correction, the teacher is saddling herself with an additional problem. Is she going to have individual errors corrected separately or have the entire paper rewritten? Is she going to grade the written work again or trust the student to correct his mistakes without making new ones? Very few teachers have found satisfactory solutions to these thorny problems.

While composition is much *given,* and while teachers spend endless hours correcting and grading written work, the actual *teaching* of composition is in reality undertaken either very seldom or very poorly. A teacher doesn't have to read very many empty papers to realize that one of the chief reasons why her students are in no position to write acceptable compositions is that they can't find anything to say. Therefore, she will often "prime the pump" before assigning the writing of a paper and conduct a preliminary discussion the day before in which the general topic—say, conformity vs. nonconformity—is explored in the classroom, in which the students' thoughts on the subject are elicited in advance, in which they are led to see beneath the surface a bit, and in which she hopes they will find some substance for the following day's composition.

If her next experience with writing is somewhat better, it is because the students do not react with dismay and panic; they are able to write for most of the period and their papers do convey the impression of greater substance. If she is very conscientious, she will try to teach her pupils to begin preliminary plans by emptying their minds of whatever miscellaneous ideas they may have on the topic. This "jotting stage" is to be followed by the crossing out of items which, on reflection, appear unsuitable or unrelated to the general drift of the others. The students are encouraged to group the ideas that have not been crossed out, so that those that belong together will be placed together. As a final step before the actual writing, they are taught to make an outline, which, lest the word *outline* sound unduly restricting and give offense, is called a "working plan."

Now again, the teacher will "give" the class a composition, and what with the pump primed by a motivating discussion and the ideas organized by the working-plan lesson, many of the students' compositions will be considerably better than previous ones. They will have greater substance than the earliest vapid ramblings had, and this time a new sense of direction and organization may appear in at least a few of the papers.

However, when the teacher sits down to read papers written under examination conditions, in high hopes that they will show genuine improvement in correctness, organization, and substance, she is likely to discover, this time to her own dismay and mounting horror, that almost every student has reverted to empty improvisation, substanceless and disorganized, for the simple reason that there has been no preliminary discussion of the various topics presented in the exam and consequently the working-plan method of organization was not sufficient to help the student. After all, how can he be expected to empty his mind of ideas on a subject about which he feels he has nothing to say? The student might have thoughts on the subject if he knew where to find them and how to frame them, but he thinks that he has none. And since he *believes* his mind is a blank, he cannot possibly go through even the teacher's initial jotting stage. If he has nothing to jot down, he has nothing to eliminate, nothing to group, nothing to outline, and nothing to write.

Why *should* students know how to write? Certainly, if we are talking about "average" students, neither severely retarded nor really college bound, their personal need for writing skill will be relatively slight. As adults, they will seldom write letters to family and friends, most of whom will live nearby. On such occasions of joy or sorrow as demand written communications, a stop at the Hallmark shop for an appropriate greeting card will often suffice. Some may write diaries and social bread-and-butter notes, but most won't. On the job, although they may have to fill out application blanks, this group will seldom have executive reports or business letters of consequence to compose for themselves.

Perhaps their greatest practical need for composition instruction stems directly from the relatively more artificial requirements of school. It is certainly true that if they are going to earn commercial or marginal academic diplomas, they are going to have to write satisfactory compositions in English, literature essays, book reports, and perhaps even term papers; and in other subjects they will have to know how to write notes, take short-answer tests, compose essay answers, and prepare documented reports such as the social studies teacher may require. And perhaps those few who may be marginally college-bound may be called upon to write brief autobiographical sketches designed to show their good judgment and powers of expression on short essays like "Why I Chose the Ivy-clad Halls of Rockbottom College."

These are far from being the deepest reasons why an average student should write. As Bacon reminds us, "writing maketh an exact man," and exactitude is a quality very much to be desired. And Hughes Mearns reminds us that in every soul there resides a spark of creativity that should be cherished and nurtured as earnestly and intensively as possible. Writing out our feelings commemorates and celebrates them; it dignifies them with the aura of importance that they truly deserve. Writing down our thoughts clarifies and sharpens them and encourages in us the development of that sense of responsibility without which "thought" verges on worthlessness. The creation of beauty for which writing can provide the occasion is something that all individuals can aspire to and even in some ways achieve. All of these reasons are in the profoundest sense far more important than the practical outcomes of practical instruction in practical composition, but I believe it is necessary to establish and insist upon distinctions between reasons for writing and reasons for *teaching* writing, between cherishing self-expression and teaching composition.

It may not be merely desirable but actually possible to teach students how to choose intelligently among the topics presented, how to see the depth, scope, and ramifications of the topic of his choice; how to narrow the possibilities down in accordance with the required essay length; how to see the questions it implies and frame them in appropriate language; how to summon, recognize, and express the answers to those questions in the form of fact or argument; how to subdivide a topic into manageable related sections; how to plan the paragraphing of a composition, for example using the first paragraph to preview it, the second to discuss the first subdivision, the third to discuss a second subdivision and the fourth to review and conclude it; how to vary sentence structure and sentence openings; and how to achieve a coherent smoothness of expression. Each of these "how to" items might well provide the basis of several periods of classroom instruction, with homework exercises, class development and discussion, and student practice and teacher guidance, so that specific separate skills could be imparted, one by one, to students in such fashion that these skills cumulatively would enable students to write intelligently, even under examination conditions. These may be uninspiring skills, but anyone who has examined even a single set of compositions knows very well that very few students possess them. It is my contention that they are practical and teachable skills and that students will see value in them, employ them, and profit from their acquisition.

Perhaps several illustrative lessons will suggest how some of these skills might be acquired. The first is a lesson to help students to form interrogative sentences accurately and thus to formulate questions whose answers would provide a suitable discussion. The teacher could have students copy down the following five-sentence paragraph, listing and numbering the sentences separately:

1. The walled medieval town was as characteristic of its period as the cut of a robber baron's beard.

2. It sprang out of the exigencies of war, and it was not without its architectural charm, whatever its hygenic deficiencies may have been.

3. Behind its high thick walls, not only the normal inhabitants, but the whole countryside, fought and cowered in an hour of need.

4. The capitals of Europe now forsake the city, when the sirens scream and death from the sky seems imminent.

5. Will the fear of bombs accelerate the slow decentralization which began with the automobile and the wide distribution of electrical energy and thus reverse the medieval flow to the city?

The teacher might ask students to prepare for homework a series of five sequentially-related questions such as those a courtroom attorney might prepare in getting ready to cross-examine an opposing witness. Each question would require for its exact answer a different one of the sentences. When the class came in the next day and the homework was placed on the board, discussion might explore how carefully the pupils had formulated and phrased their questions so that the given sentences were exact and responsive answers and so that the series of questions had its own clear, logical structure. After eliciting a question from a student, the teacher might repeat it and ask the student to read the sentence that is supposed to answer it. Pretending that this was actual dialog, he might ask members of the class to point out in which particulars the sentence was a perfect answer to the student's question and in which ones it was not. In this way a student might be led to rephrase and rework his question until he arrived at the point where the question and answer matched perfectly. After all the questions had been done, the teacher might ask a student to read his whole set and consider with the class how closely all five seemed related to each other. After doing a few such homework and classroom exercises, a class might reach the level of ability represented by the following set of questions:

1. How characteristic of its period was the walled medieval town?
2. What were its origins, charms, and drawbacks?
3. What practical purpose did it serve in wartime emergencies?
4. What is the response of cities today to such emergencies?
5. What question about population movements does the difference imply?

It seems reasonable to assume that a student who can formulate questions in this fashion can compose satisfactory expository essays. Certainly it would not be difficult for the teacher to indicate to the students the direct connection between the ability to juggle questions and the ability to put ideas in writing.

Another lesson aimed at alleviating the difficulties so many students have citing specific details in support of a generalization is the following lesson on "paragraph sandwiches." After an introduction in which the teacher asks something like, "If the opening and concluding sentences of a paragraph are like the bread of a sandwich, how are the other sentences like the meat?" and after eliciting suitable answers goes on to ask, "And how are the opening and closing sentences like the bread?" the teacher might supply the class with a pair of "bread" sentences for which the students would be asked to supply the meat. If the class is a young and unsophisticated group, perhaps an opening sentence, "My friend is a pest," and a concluding sentence, "Because he does these things, even his friends get annoyed with him," could be dictated to the class with instructions that they are to leave room between them for three additional sentences. The students then might invent suitable details showing the friend's peskiness, simultaneously amplifying the opening sentence, and leading to the conclusion expressed in the opening sentence. It may be fairly easy to elicit three such questions from a whole class of 35 students, but each one working separately may find it not at all a simple matter to think of three sentences by himself.

There is room for considerable teaching in imparting this skill. Especially where the subject matter is more elaborate or touches on a realm of discourse more complex than peskiness, it is often difficult indeed for a student to see and make the necessary connections between the generalities and concrete details that together comprise the essential ingredients of exposition. Here again, it should be a relatively easy matter for the teacher to show the class a direct connection between the exercise being performed and the ultimate objective of fluent and intelligent writing. A follow-up exercise might give the students only an opening sentence and ask them to supply both details and conclusion for themselves. Another exercise might provide the student with details only and ask him to supply an opening and a concluding sentence for the paragraph. A culminating exercise would require him to produce an entire paragraph of his own.

A friend of mine who is now a noted journalist had such a checkered intellectual career before reaching his present position, having been pianist, musicologist, philosophy major, and high school teacher during his college and later years, that I was moved to ask him one night how he learned to write. Of course, any intelligent college graduate knows how to write English, and some write it very well indeed, but he knew I did not mean that mere veneer of fluency. My real intention was to discover how he had learned to write for professional publication, how he had learned to hone his skill to the point where it was dependable, and how he had learned to exercise his fluency so that producing a prizewinning news story was as easy for him as turning on the faucet is for me. He didn't have to think long before answering me: "It was imitating models." When he began working as a cub reporter in a small town, the merits and defects of his work were as plain as day the very next morning. Reading his articles in print, alongside the work of other professionals, made him acutely conscious of where they had and where they had not done what was required of them. As his job changed and greater and more complicated demands were made, the available models were more and more professionally competent and the lapses of which he said he was occasionally guilty seemed more and more painfully obvious in print. It was a matter of writing by conscious imitation, of writing, so to speak, by formula, until the time arrived when the formula dispensed with itself. He calls it a self-limiting crutch and believes that anyone who uses it wisely and well will eventually discover that he need not use it any longer.

This idea of imitating models is commonly employed in college freshman composition courses but almost never in high school; nevertheless, a number of teachers do employ a near approximation of it when they try to train Regents candidates to write the Regents literature essays successfully. Since the student is often marked very largely on how directly and accurately he answers the question, it is easy to persuade him that in this one case at least there is a premium on exposition rather than improvisation. So the teacher tries to get him to master a formula for answering the question directly, accurately, and fully. The following typical Regents question, for example, requires a 20-point or 30-minute essay:

> In books, as in life, we meet people who face problems. From the novels and full-length plays you have read, choose a total of two books. For one book, show by definite references that a problem of a person in the book was chiefly the result of his own actions or attitude. For the second book, show by definite references that a problem of a person in that book was chiefly the result of the actions of others. Give titles and authors.

Even without going at all into the problems of answering the question, just deciphering it presents any number of serious problems to the average student: Where does the preliminary statement end and the question begin? What literary genres must I choose from? What do I have to show? Where do you draw the line between self-induced and externally caused problems? Must I show the same or different causes for each book? Must I use books studied in school? Must I write about the heroes, or may I use lesser characters, in each book? How many references does the plural noun "references" require? How definite is "definite"? How much do I have to tell about the story of the book to introduce my references properly? Will the teacher agree with my point of view? How much am I supposed to write? How much credit do I lose if I don't remember the wife's uncle's name?

Many teachers have attempted to help students solve some of these problems by suggesting a method of "boxing" the question. The sample illustration given shows the plan for a single novel; for the question above, a student would have to set up two such sets of boxes and use a different set for each book.

The way in which these boxes are employed to answer the question is illustrated in the rectangle below. A student who has filled in each square with what is called for here will have his entire essay plotted out for him even before he starts writing it out.

The normal student will experience much difficulty with even this apparently oversimplified method of setting forth the minimum information required for the answer. For one thing, it is difficult for him to see that the opening statement about the book must be a generalization formulated in direct response to the question asked. For another, it is hard for him to recall two definite references that are in fact germane to the question. It is even difficult for most students to distinguish between a definite reference and a loose generalization. It is often obvious to the student that his reference supports the generalization even if it is not clear specifically why or how, but it is far from easy for him to discipline himself to make that connection explicit for the reader. The final difficulty these boxes pose is that of making an appropriate summary and conclusion. The tight-wire between mere repetitiousness on the one hand and an irresponsible veering off into new subject matter on the other is a difficult one for him to negotiate.

Once these difficulties are at least partially removed by appropriate direct instruction, however, the student's writing task is enormously simplified if he can plan his answer intelligently in advance. The following sample Regents essay answer was written from the boxes below. The opening paragraph is a simple paraphrase of the question itself. Teachers sometimes teach students to paraphrase the question in this fashion without teaching them to construct their answer methodically and intelligently. The sample answer printed here could not fail to receive a better-than-passing grade from anyone who rated it:

In books as in life, we meet people who face problems. From the novels and full-length plays I have read, I will choose two books. For one book, I will show by definite references that a problem of a person in the book was chiefly the result of his own actions or attitudes. For the second book, I will show by definite references that a problem of a person in that book was chiefly the result of the actions of others.

In the full-length play, *Macbeth,* by William Shakespeare, the problem that the character Macbeth has (his suffering) is caused chiefly by his own actions. He murdered King Duncan, who was his benefactor, his king, and his guest, even though he should have showed him loyalty, hospitality, and protection. The feeling of guilt that Macbeth suffered as a result of this action robbed him of his sleep and haunted his mind forever afterwards. Later, Macbeth's tyrannical actions in paying cutthroats to kill Banquo and in having a band of his men massacre the innocent and helpless family of Macduff led to more difficulties. These actions made his people despise him thoroughly and made them willing to revolt, when Macduff finally returned from England with military forces to overthrow Macbeth. Thus we see that Macbeth's misfortunes, his feelings of guilt as well as his final overthrow, were brought about chiefly by his own actions in murdering Duncan, Banquo, and Macduff's family. He was truly the cause of his own downfall.

In the novel, *Giants in the Earth,* by Rolvaag, Per Hansa's problem of making wise decisions was chiefly the result of the actions of others. When Per found stakes bearing Irish names on property Hans Olsa had claimed as his own, Per had to struggle with his conscience and decide whether to reveal the stakes or destroy them. The conflict between the legal actions of the Irish and Hans Olsa's not-so-legal claim-jumping forced this problem upon Per. In the final tragic chapters, Per was again forced to make a decision, this time between common sense and safety on the one hand and his duty to his dying friend Hans Olsa on the other. Only the hounding and nagging of his wife Beret made Per go out to fight the storm in which he was killed. It is true that Per Hansa was his own master in many ways, but most of his problems came from the actions of others. The conflicting claims, first of Olsa and the Irish, and later of Olsa and Beret caused him anguish in the one case and death in the other.

It is possible to train students to plan a Regents essay *without* using boxes too. A colleague of mine uses a six-sentence catechism in which he supplies the students with the bare bones of an answer and with blanks into which, a student must insert the flesh. Students who write answers from this recipe do so in accordance with the identical principles that lie behind the box method except that instead of filling in rectangles, they fill in blanks. The chief disadvantage here is repetitiousness.

SAMPLE BOX

Type	Title	Author	What do I have to prove something about?
What do I have to "show by definite references" about it?			
definite reference #1		definite reference #2	
One incident or fact from the book that shows what is required	explanation: how does this definite ref. actually prove what you claim it does?	second fact	second explanation
Summary & conclusion: Summarize the first paragraph in one sentence so its argument and point are crystal clear. Add a concluding sentence if you wish.			

FIRST BOOK

full-length play	*Macbeth*	Shakespeare	the problem that the character Macbeth has (suffering)
was chiefly the result of his own actions.			
definite reference #1		definite reference #2	
Macbeth killed Duncan even though Duncan was his benefactor, his king, and his guest.	Therefore, a feeling of guilt haunted Macbeth, robbing him of sleep & peace of mind.	Macbeth's tyrannical behavior in killing Banquo & in having Macduff's family murdered made trouble for him.	These acts made the people despise him & made them more willing to revolt when Macduff raised army to overthrow Macbeth.
We see that Macbeth's misfortunes, his feelings of guilt as well as his final overthrow, were chiefly caused by his own actions in murdering Duncan, Banquo, and Macduff's family.			

SECOND BOOK

novel	*Giants in the Earth*	Rolvaag	Per Hansa's problem (of making decisions wisely)
was chiefly the result of the actions of others.			
definite reference #1		definite reference #2	
Per finds Irish stakes on Olsa property & has to decide whether to reveal them or destroy them.	The legal action of the Irish & Hans Olsa's illegal claim-jumping made this decision necessary.	In the final tragic chapters, Per has to decide between safety & his "duty" to his dying friend, Hans Olsa.	Beret's insistence makes Per brave the storm in which he is killed.
Although Per Hansa was very much the captain of his fate in many ways, most of his problems came from the actions of others. The conflicting claims of Olsa & the Irish, & Olsa & Beret, caused him anguish on the one hand & death on the other.			

1. In the (*type*) (*underlined title*) by (*author's name*), the problem, (*mention the problem*), faced by the character (*character's name*), was chiefly caused by his own actions.

2. One indication that this is the case is that (*here put first fact, incident, or reference, to conclude this sentence*).

3. This reference shows that his problem was of his own making because (*put first explanation here*).

4. Another thing that shows how he created his own troubles is (*2nd reference*).

5. I say this because (*2nd reference*).

6. Thus it seems that (*character's*) problem is caused by himself because (*here mention 1st reference briefly*) and (*2nd reference*).

These Regents essay formulas are obviously intended for marginal students incapable of fluent writing in response to a direct and restricting question and incapable as well of summoning easily or organizing coherently the material that such an answer must consist of. Neither of these formulas is appropriate for the ordinary college-bound student. He should and would quite properly regard it with a certain grand contempt. It is for the non-college-bound or marginally college-bound that the methods suggested above are intended to be helpful. One more composition formula device should be described before leaving this mechanical world of models and imitations. It has been suggested that any student who can frame two related questions about a topic can write a four-paragraph composition on it, if for each question he can merely supply two or three answers of his own. The recipe goes like this: Divide the topic into two related questions. In your first paragraph, tell first why the topic is interesting or important; second, write down the two related questions in succession; and third, write a concluding statement about them.

Example   (topic—"The Lure of Luxury"):

> Everybody is attracted by luxuries. What are some of the luxuries that are most in demand? Why do we want them so badly? The answers to these two questions may help us to understand ourselves better.

For paragraph two, first change question one into statement form. Then supply one argument or substantiation with an explanation if necessary. Third, supply another argument or substantiation as above and another explanation if desired. Do the same for other supporting statements as required. Example:

> The most popular luxuries are desired by almost everyone. Some of these are the kind that provide physical comfort and pleasure. Fur

coats, cars, and cigarettes are examples of this kind of luxury. Others, like TV, books, and concerts, provide mental stimulation and entertainment. Still others are for showing off with. Cadillacs, landscaped gardens, and uniformed butlers seem to belong in this last group.

For the third paragraph, do the same thing. First, change question two into statement form. Second, offer an item of argument or factual substantiation with optional explanation if needed. Third, another item of concrete detail with optional explanation, and continue with further details and explanations as required. Example:

It is not hard to imagine some of the reasons why people want such things as these as much as they do. One reason may be that we don't always have them. Many of the luxuries we want always seem to be just out of reach. And then there are always some people who do have the things we don't have. This creates a desire in us because we never want the next fellow to be better off than we are. A third reason is that advertisements make them sound more important than they really are sometimes. Often a luxury is given such a buildup that it almost seems like a necessity.

In the final paragraph, first summarize paragraph two, then summarize paragraph three, and third, answer the question, "So what?" in a concluding sentence. Example:

Luxuries give us many things, like comfort, entertainment, and status. They satisfy deep desires within our hearts. It is hardly any wonder that they lure us strongly and have the power to make us miserable when we lack them and happy when they are ours.

For the intelligent adult, for the college-bound teen-ager, and for the teacher of English, such a formula will appear unduly restricting if not downright insulting. For the teacher with some respect for creative work, the whole idea of producing compositions by formula may be anathema. Nevertheless, for the non-college-bound student, for the future white-collar or blue-collar worker, some such crutch may be necessary if he is to succeed on school examinations and in preparing the papers and term reports that his teachers will from time to time require. The skills involved in producing a composition according to these models are far from simple. Indeed it is extremely difficult for the average student to formulate two related questions about a topic at all, doubly difficult to formulate two that he can answer at any length; and the difficulty is compounded further by the requirements of substantiation and explanation and by the summaries called for at the end. They are skills that most of our average students must be taught because they need them and do not have them. They are skills in which a student can take both interest and pride, and they are amenable to successful direct instruction. It may be impossible to give a lesson on how to write a composition, but it is quite feasible to teach students to summarize a paragraph or subdivide a topic, to substantiate a generalization, or to justify and explain the substantiation.

This business of imitative writing must not be permitted to come under attack from those who have a due and proper respect for creative enterprises. I hold with those who believe that creative work, whether in writing or elsewhere, is the one supremely noble activity and achievement of mankind. And I hold with those who insist that students in high school can, should, and must be given opportunities to exercise the creative energies they may possess. But my reverence for this important work does not prevent me from finding merit in the teaching of imitation. Man is in fact an imitative species. Writing skills can indeed be fostered through the practice of imitation, which as a pedagogical device has had a long and honorable history in all the arts. Composers of music are taught to write in the styles of past masters. A visit to any art museum on a weekday when it is not crowded will reveal students industriously imitating with charcoal or paintbox the great works hanging on the walls. Ballet dancers imitate set movements at the cost of great physical and mental concentration, to the end that they may one day be free from the necessity of slavish imitation. Piano students are taught, hopefully, to imitate as best they can the intentions of the composer as indicated by the printed notes on the music page. As a matter of fact, most music instruction is imitation teaching wherein the teacher supplies the model, shows the pupil the required movements, and gives him a method of practicing them. At the end of his week of solitary labor, the student shows the teacher the quality of his imitation so that he can hear it criticized and learn what and how to imitate next.

Imitation is in many respects self-rewarding. It is instantly obvious when an attempt at imitation is successful, and even the "average" pupil can derive real enjoyment from the study of composition if he is encouraged to take pride in the quality of his imitations. If composing expository pieces involves many and difficult skills, they are nevertheless all knacks that the student can learn and in whose acquisition he can take genuine and spontaneous pleasure.

How can we evaluate our work and that of our students? Certainly not by mere proofreading. But if the teacher will show his pupils what to write and how to write it, where to find ideas and how to look for them, how to summon, recognize, and sort them, how to frame questions, supply answers, and provide explanatory connections, and how to coordinate and summarize his ideas, then he can give composition assignments that are in reality good tests of the degree to which the student has acquired the skills the teacher has in fact imparted. A teacher who does this will be able to concentrate in the reading of even the most illiterate paper on what the student has written, on how he has ordered and connected it, and on showing the student through brief comments how he could have made it better.

The New York City Board of Examiners has in recent years been evaluating certain essays for "written English" only. In practice this means that the candidate must write on a given topic for 500 words or so, but need not necessarily say anything sensible, intelligent, or even correct. All he need do is avoid errors in English, and if he manages this little, he must pass. Teachers have long been rightly and righteously indignant at this. I can think of few greater indignities to a thinking human being than asking him to write 500 words of written English; yet in many cases this is what teachers are asking of their own pupils on composition day. The alternatives are clear and attractive. We must teach our pupils how to find ideas and what to do with them. We must write brief but instructive remarks on the student's paper to show him what he should have done. Instead of writing "Vague," we must write, "Tell what you mean;" instead of writing "Too general," we must write, "Give examples," or "Show how," or "Say why," or "Tell more." We must note and comment upon the sequence of topics paragraph by paragraph, and only then proofread the paper for mistakes. We must get students to revise—not merely recopy—their work. We must teach, not "give," composition.

A teacher who will attempt such a regimen as this cannot fail to produce better results than the one with whose misadventures this essay began.

ROBERT L. ALLEN / *Written English Is a "Second Language"*

Structural linguists were among the first to show convincingly that a person's first language interferes with his learning of a second language. They have also been in the forefront of those who have called attention to the existence of different varieties or "dialects" within any one language. Much of what we know today about the specific differences between different varieties or dialects of English we know as the result of studies made by these linguists. And yet most structural linguists seem to have overlooked the possibility that *written English* may be a dialect of English quite distinct from spoken English. Perhaps because of their original preoccupation with spoken languages which had no written form—or even because of their great success in improving the teaching of foreign languages through their emphasis on the oral-aural approach—structural linguists seem to have accepted, almost without question, the dogmatic assertions in Bloch and Trager's *Outline of Linguistic Analysis* (Linguistic Society of America, 1952) that "A LANGUAGE is a system of arbitrary *vocal* symbols by means of which a social group cooperates" and that "WRITING is a secondary visual representation of speech."

On the contrary, written English is one of the systems of English—a separate dialect, if you will—with its own rules, its own conventions, its own signals. There is nothing in spoken English, for example, to correspond to the indentation for a new paragraph that one finds in writing. As a matter of fact, there is nothing in spoken English that corresponds in all instances to the spaces that one finds between written words. Again, there is nothing

From *English Journal*, LV (April, 1966), 739–46. Reprinted by permission of the National Council of Teachers of English and Robert L. Allen.

in spoken English—as there is in written English—which would make it possible to distinguish between the expression *the little girl's dolls,* referring to the dolls belonging to one girl, and the expression *the little girls' dolls,* referring to the dolls belonging to more than one girl. Still another convention of written English, that of spelling, precludes any ambiguity in a question like the following:

What do you think of Lydia's new beau?

If this question were asked orally, the hearer might take the last word as referring to something that Lydia is wearing. Spoken English does not distinguish between these two words, but written English does. In fact, if the hearer should misinterpret the question, the speaker might well resolve the ambiguity *by means of the conventions of written English rather than by any use of spoken English:*

"What do you think of Lydia's new beau?"
"Lydia's new bow? Where? I don't see any bow?"
"I mean her *b-e-a-u,* not her *b-o-w.*"

Such conventions as paragraphing, punctuation, and spelling are just as truly conventions of the English language as are different degrees of stress or different levels of pitch. Indeed, as English teachers, we have to be more concerned with the former than with the latter: even though our children may have mastered the structure of spoken English by the time they first enter school, most children learn the signals of written English *in school, from their teachers—as a second language.* When Henry Lee Smith, Jr., says, in *Linguistic Science and the Teaching of English* (Harvard University Press, 1956), that "the complex systems through which human communication goes on . . . are thoroughly learned and internalized by all physiologically normal human beings in all cultures at about five and a half years of age," he is ignoring the fact that one of the most important forms of communication in our modern world is the kind of communication that goes on between a writer and his readers. It is only through the systems of written language that writers of a hundred or more years ago continue to communicate with us today. Much of our education and much of our culture is communicated to us by means of the system of written English. It is for this reason that a person is not considered to be truly educated until he can read and write.

But obviously the systems of spoken English and of written English, though separate and distinct, do overlap at many points. It is not surprising, therefore, that students tend to carry over patterns of the spoken system which they already know to the written system which they are trying to learn, just as someone studying a foreign language is likely to impose the word order of his own language on the words of the new language. For example, when students who are learning the system of written English are already speakers of some form of non-standard English, it is very probable that they will transfer conventions of their non-standard English to the English that they write. But it is not so much the conventions of non-standard English that plague our students' writing as it is the conventions—or at least, the accepted patterns—of spoken English. Many high school handbooks devote much space to exercises designed to teach students to avoid such "errors" as sentence fragments, comma splices, run-on sentences, and faulty agreement. But these are all transgressions against the conventions of *written* English—and of *formal* written English, at that—rather than transgressions against the conventions of spoken English. Elliptical sentences, for example, are normal in spoken English: a speaker who used only full or "complete" sentences in his conversations would sound stilted and pedantic. As a recorded transcription of almost any free oral discussion will show, we tolerate false starts, repetitions, pauses, extraneous "words," sentence fragments, and even lack of agreement between subject and verb or between pronoun and antecedent *in each other's speech,* although the conventions of formal written English do not allow such phenomena.

But that our students already know the structure of spoken English when they come to us gives us as English teachers a great advantage that teachers of foreign languages lack. We do not have to start our teaching of the structure of written English from scratch. We can start with those features of English which are identical in both the written system and the spoken system and can build our teaching around them. We can make use of the fact that our students already know—even if not consciously—those grammatical devices of English which are the same in both written English and spoken English.

Yet it is essential, before we teach written English, that we know which features of English are the same in both the written system and the spoken system and which are different. Unfortunately, the two systems have been so constantly confused that labels which are used for features of one system are also used for features of the other system, even when the features themselves are not identical. A "syllable" in written English, for example, is not the same as a "syllable" in spoken English. A convention of written English requires that when we divide a word containing a double consonant into "syllables," we separate the two consonants, so that the two "syllables" of the written word *minnow* are *min-* and *-now*. But in the spoken form of *minnow* there is only one /n/ sound; in spoken English, therefore, the two "syllables" of this word are /min/ and /ō/. Again, in written English the third person singular morpheme has, not three variant forms, but only two—namely, -s and -es. This is as much a fact of the structure of English as is the fact that in spoken English the third person singular morpheme has three forms—namely, /-z/, /-s/, and /-ɨz/. (Indeed, we English teachers are necessarily more concerned with the two written forms than with the three spoken forms.) Even *words,* as we commonly use this term, are primarily units of written English: it is probably only when we first see an expression like *have to* or *used to* or *a lot* or *all right* written down, with a space in the middle, that most of us realize that the expression is made up of two "words." And is the name for the kind of "tree" on which a person hangs his hat made up of one "word" or of two "words"? Does the name for the time of day when one eats supper consist of one "word" or of two "words"? Pronunciation does not help us to answer such questions; most of us would probably not be sure we knew the right answer until we had consulted the dictionary.

Recently several linguists have become interested in—and have initiated studies in—so-called "grapheme-phoneme correspondences," that is to say, in the correlations between spelling patterns and sound patterns. I suggest that such studies represent exactly the kind of contrastive linguistic analyses that many linguists consider so important for foreign language teaching. From the very first step we take in teaching first-grade children or even kindergarten children to read, we are teaching them a *second* language: we are teaching them to respond to an entirely different set of signals from those to which they have responded in speaking and hearing English. But this is true not only of beginning reading. At even more advanced stages in their reading, our students must learn to respond to written signals which, even though they may have counterparts in spoken English, do not themselves form any part of the system of spoken English. I have already mentioned several such signals, but I would like to underscore again the crucial importance of such written signals as periods and question marks, especially in more advanced stages of reading.

One of the most important grammatical relationships in English is the relationship holding between the subject of a sentence and its predicate. To be able to comprehend a complicated sentence and to read it intelligently, a student must be able to recognize the boundary line between its subject and its predicate. Unfortunately, however, the definitions that one finds in most traditional handbooks—and even the definitions that one finds in some linguistically oriented grammars—are of little help in the identification of complicated subjects.

The feeling that all native speakers of English—including even small children—have for the difference between subjects and predicates is probably related, as Smith suggests, to the difference between the nominal (and adjectival) kind of material that usually turns up in subjects and the verbal kind of material that usually introduces predicates.[1] As long as sentences are of the type *That funny old man likes cats* or even *That funny old man in the house across the street likes cats,* a child may have little difficulty in "accumulating" the whole subject in his memory storage until he comes upon verbal material (that is, the word *likes*). But when the subject itself includes verbal material, most children probably find it much more difficult to grasp the structure of the sentence without special assistance or training. For example, a child who has "stored up" the words *That funny old man* to be related as subject to verbal material that will turn up later, may "release" this stored up subject at the first occurrence of any verbal material and thus assume (unconsciously) that *That funny old man* is the subject of *lives in the house across the street* in a sentence like the following:

That funny old man who *lives in the house across the street* likes cats.

When the child finally reaches the words *likes cats* in his reading of the sentence, he finds that he has words "left over." A good reader, of course, would go back and re-analyze the sentence; many poor readers, however, would probably not know how to re-analyze the sentence, even if they realized that something was wrong.

Another kind of subject that is likely to cause many children difficulty in their reading is a subject containing participles—and yet the use of so-called participial phrases is one of the distinctive features of formal written English as opposed to informal English (which makes more use of clauses strung along one after the other in linear sequence). Even a poor reader would probably have little difficulty in reading and understanding a sentence like the following:

Is that girl writing a letter?

The sentence clearly asks a question about what "that girl" is doing. But many poor readers would have much more difficulty in reading the following sentence:

Is that girl writing a letter your sister?

[1] See Henry Lee Smith, Jr., "Superfixes and Syntactic Markers," *Monograph Series on Languages and Linguistics,* No. 9 (Washington, D. C.: Georgetown University Press, 1957), pp. 7–23.

A poor reader might well assume that the subject in this sentence consists of the words *that girl,* the predicate of the words *writing a letter,* and that this sentence, like the preceding one, asks a question about what the girl is doing. Such an analysis, of course, would take no account of the "left over" words *your sister;* but I suspect that many poor readers, if not most, read not by sentence units but by minimal word-groups, plunging forward desperately from one such word-group to the next in the hope that they may be able to get at least some meaning out of what they read. Such readers have probably long since come to accept the existence of "left over" words that don't quite fit in anywhere as a fact of written English.

Even a good reader, of course, might have started out reading that last example sentence as if its subject consisted of only the words *that girl* rather than of the words *that girl writing a letter.* But a good reader, on coming upon the words *your sister* before the terminal question mark, would go back and re-analyze the sentence in such a way that all the words would fit into the possible positions for an English sentence. *His re-analysis of the sentence, however, would in no way depend upon any spoken or phonological clues.* The crucial signals in the recognition of the structure of this question are not terminal contours but rather the absence of a question mark after the word *letter,* the lack of a capital letter in the word *your,* and the presence of a question mark after the word *sister*—that is, the signals which show that the words *your sister* form an integral part of this sentence.

I know of no linguists who would advise the teacher of a foreign language to devote much class time (if any) to a discussion of his students' native language. And yet some linguists seem to suggest that we should tell our students all about stresses and pitches and junctures, even when we are trying to teach them to read and write—and this in spite of the fact that our students are supposed to have mastered the structure of spoken English by the time they enter first grade. I doubt if detailed descriptions of the suprasegmentals are of really much value in helping students to read more effectively. Instead of teaching our students to analyze written sentences orally, we need to teach them to analyze written sentences visually. The way in which a person reads a given sentence aloud does not *lead* to his analysis of its structure, but rather *reflects the syntactic analysis of the sentence he has already made mentally, through his eyes.*

Again, a mastery of the system of spoken English will be of little help to a student when he wants to know how to divide a word at the end of a line, or whether to write a compound as one solid word or as a hyphenated word or as two words. For this kind of help, he will have to turn to his dictionary. Nor will his knowledge of spoken English enable the student to determine whether a group of words that he has written with a capital letter at one end and a period at the other, really constitutes a "complete sentence." But here his dictionary cannot guide him. Even a traditional handbook will probably be of little assistance to him: the "completeness" of a thought does not necessarily guarantee the "completeness" of a sentence. Even an added statement to the effect that a sentence must also contain a subject and a predicate is not enough: so-called "subordinate clauses" contain subjects and predicates, but by themselves they do not constitute acceptable sentences in formal written English. And our students *must* learn to write acceptable sentences—*acceptable, that is, by the conventions of formal written English.*

I do not mean to intimate that phonological signals are unimportant. They are of primary importance—*in speech.* Our ability to understand spoken sentences depends upon our ability to recognize phonological signals. But I do not believe that the ability to understand written sentences depends upon a mastery of the spoken sentences of the language in which they are written. There are scholars who can translate hieroglyphics into English even though they do not know how to pronounce the Egyptian language which the hieroglyphics represented. Written English is "secondary" to spoken English only in the sense that we learn to read English after we learn to speak it. Both written English and spoken English are of prime importance in our country today; no one can say that one is "secondary" to the other except in specific contexts. As L. M. Myers pointed out in the October 1961 issue of *College English,* "written English, especially since the invention of the printing press, has been exerting an absolutely inescapable influence on the spoken form. Writing . . . is not merely a passive reflection of speech, and it can not be effectively treated as if it were." In any event, our students have already mastered the fundamentals of spoken English by the time they reach us; it is our job to teach them the fundamentals of *written* English. For this we need an accurate description of the structure of written English.

After long and intensive study of structural grammar and structural grammars, I have come to the conclusion that other, less well-known linguistic techniques than those of the early structural linguists hold greater promise as ways of providing the kind of analysis of English structure that can help our students to read and write more effectively.

One such technique derives from Zellig Harris' and Noam Chomsky's concept of "transformations," that is, of rules that show how certain kinds of sentences in English can be analyzed most precisely as transforms of other sentences—and perhaps in no other way. A passive sentence, for example, is obviously related in some manner to the corresponding active sentence; I know of no better way to describe this relationship than as a transformation. Again, it seems to me that a sentence like *I heard John calling* must be derived from such sentences as

> John was calling.
>
> I heard (   ).

But I do not think that transformational grammar is especially helpful in teaching students to recognize the difference between the two questions *Is that girl writing a letter?* and *Is that girl writing a letter your sister?* Admittedly, these two questions can be shown to be derived from different source sentences, but a student who comes across such sentences in his reading does not have the time to trace back their derivational histories as a means to identifying their subjects before reading the sentences aloud. An approach to linguistic analysis which is much more helpful in cases like these—indeed, an approach to linguistic analysis which seems to me to be perhaps the most promising of all—derives from Kenneth L. Pike's concept of "tagmemes," that is, of the correlations between grammatical positions and the kinds of units that can fill those positions. Recognition of the nominal *your sister* as the filler in the complement position in the question *Is that girl writing a letter your sister?* leads to the realization of the fact that the words *writing a letter* cannot fill the verb and object positions and must therefore fill a post-nucleus position within the subject. This kind of embedding, or nesting, of one construction within another is an important feature of English; it is in its recognition of constructions as higher-layered units in the grammatical hierarchy of the language that Pike's tagmemic theory is particularly useful.

But perhaps the one technique of linguistic analysis that has proved most useful in helping high school students and even elementary school students to identify sentence-units is the technique of testing by "shifting." The application of this technique can best be demonstrated by means of examples. Both of the following sentences, for instance, begin with the words *last winter*:

> *Last winter* Joe's parents went to Florida.
>
> *Last winter* was unusually cold.

To the unsophisticated, the word-group *last winter* in both sentences may seem to answer the question "When?"—but only one of the two is adverbial. The adverbial word-group is the one that must be *shifted to the end of its sentence* when we change both statements to "Yes-No" questions, that is, to questions that can be answered by either "Yes" or "No":

> Did Joe's parents go to Florida *last winter?* (Yes.)
>
> Was *last winter* unusually cold? (Yes.)

The potentiality for shifting from one end of the sentence to the other marks the included clause *as I was going to St. Ives* in the following sentence as also being adverbial:

> *As I was going to St. Ives,* I met a man with seven wives.
>
> I met a man with seven wives *as I was going to St. Ives.*

The shifting test also provides us with an easy way of identifying subjects: if we compare the statements *Last winter was unusually cold* with its corresponding Yes-No question *Was last winter unusually cold?*, we find that the subject is marked off by the two positions of the word *was*. In other words, the subject is that construction around which the word *was* shifts (or "orbits") when the statement is changed into a Yes-No question:

> *Last winter* was unusually cold.
>
> Was *last winter*   unusually cold?

The words that "orbit" around subjects include both auxiliaries and the finite forms of the verb *to be*. For lack of a better term, I call them "X words," and the two positions in every sentence which can be occupied by such words I call "the X positions." By shifting an X word from one of its two positions to the other, we can easily identify the subjects in the example sentences which I have already discussed:

X   X
Is *that girl*   writing a letter?
 That girl is writing a letter.

X   X
Is *that girl writing a letter*   your sister?
 That girl writing a letter is your sister.

X   X
 That funny old man who lives in the house across the street   likes cats.
Does *that funny old man who lives in the house across the street*   like cats?
 That funny old man who lives in the house across the street does like cats.

Indeed, it appears that the only feature shared in common by the subjects in most if not all major English statements—including the subjects in such statements as *It is raining*—is just this potentiality for serving as the hub around which some X word must shift to change the statement to a Yes-No question.

In 1940, in his *American English Grammar* (Appleton, 1940), Charles C. Fries wrote as follows concerning traditional grammar:

> It is the point of view of this report that *a study of the real grammar of present-day English has never been used in the schools* and that the conclusions concerning its effectiveness relate only to the type of "grammar" that has been tried.

The conclusions voiced by several writers concerning the ineffectiveness of linguistically oriented materials in helping students to improve their writing may also "relate only to the type of 'grammar' that has been tried." Grammarians, like L. M. Myers and Ralph B. Long, have called attention to the short-comings of the structural grammars now available, but unfortunately their criticisms have not been taken seriously by most linguists. In a way this is ironic, since of all people the linguists themselves should have been the first to recognize the reasons for the inappropriateness of such grammars for the teaching of reading and writing.

We need new grammars, then—grammars which will incorporate such linguistic concepts as the concepts of transformations, of tagmemes, and of shifting, but above all grammars which will describe written English in terms of its own signals and conventions rather than in terms of the signals and conventions of spoken English. I believe that it is not too much to hope that, when we do get such grammars, we will be able to teach a much larger number of our students while they are still in the elementary grades to recognize the structure of the sentences they meet in their reading, and to produce similar sentences in their own writing, especially the kind of "complete sentences" that are appropriate to formal written English. And then perhaps, in our high school classes, we will not have to devote so much time to the purely linguistic aspects of reading and writing, but will be able to concentrate on such matters as organization, logic, rhetoric, and creative expression.

VIRGINIA F. ALLEN / *Teaching Standard English as a*
Second Dialect

Few people today need to be told that standard English is virtually a
"second language" for millions. Almost every teacher knows students who
cannot speak, read or write the sort of English that educated persons consider standard, even though some variety of English may be the student's
mother tongue. Not only is the problem prevalent, of course, it is also old.
It dates back past the days of Huck Finn and Topsy to the eighteenth
century, and beyond.

Yet two facts do appear to come as news—good news.[1] One is that some
teachers are developing a fresh and clearer view of what is involved in
learning a standard dialect of English in school when some other dialect is
spoken in the home. A second newsworthy fact, and an even more cheering
one, is that these fresh insights have suggested some practical classroom
procedures which are being tried with encouraging results. Some of those
promising procedures will be described in this paper.

Standard English

First, however, it would be wise to show what the term "standard English"
will mean in the context of this discussion. For our present purposes,

[1] For front page news in the literal sense, see for example *The Wall Street Journal*,
January 19, 1966, which featured an account of several current programs and approaches in standard English as a second dialect.

From *Teachers College Record*, LXVIII (February, 1967), 355–70. Reprinted by permission of Teachers College, Columbia University and Virginia F. Allen.

standard American English is the kind of English *habitually* used by most of the *educated* English-speaking persons in the United States.

Thus "He doesn't want any" would qualify as a sample of standard English—not because some "authority" has certified it as being "correct," but because evidence suggests that educated speakers habitually *say* "He doesn't want any" in situations where less educated speakers might say "He don't want none."

It is important to note the emphasis on *habitually* and *educated* in this definition of standard English. A teacher who undertakes to familiarize her students with the standard dialect of English as here defined is careful to focus attention upon grammatical forms which educated speakers are in the *habit* of using. For instance, even though some grammar books decree that the "comparative" form *more* "should" be used in place of the "superlative" form *most* when only two are being compared, an enlightened teacher today would be undismayed if a student said, "Both Pete and Bill get good grades in school, but I think Pete really has the most sense." Habitual usage among educated speakers is what counts—whether or not that usage obeys some grammarian's rule.

On the other hand, the stress on the word *educated* in this definition is significant, too. What is being advocated here is emphatically *not* an "anything goes" approach to English usage. Standard English, as defined here, is the variety of English generally used by the *educated* members of the American speech community. Statistically speaking, one has reason to suspect that the number of Americans who say "you was" exceeds the number who say "you were." This fact does not establish "you was" as standard usage, however. Standard English is what the majority of *educated* speakers habitually use.

Teachers who start with this definition then go on to link it up with their student's experience and observation. They point out that the kind of English they have in mind is the sort used on radio and television by announcers, sportscasters, civil rights leaders, and news commentators, as well as by practically all TV heroes, including Batman, Superman and Flash Gordon. It is the English heard in the public statements of astronauts, bankers, congressmen, and movie stars. It has been called "the language of educated ease," because it is used by people who *know* they sound "educated" and so do not have to think about their use of language.

When the target language is defined in these terms, even young children know what the teacher means by "standard English." Martin Joos, who has made a special study of people's attitudes toward language, says:

> Long before any teacher began to correct his English, the child has learned all he needs to know, at his age, about people and their

places; he has developed considerable skill in judging adults by their speech . . .[2]

Morality and Comprehensibility

Class time invested in discussing standard English along such lines is time well spent. For one thing, such discussions remind both teachers and students that the presence or absence of standard forms in a person's speech is not a moral or ethical issue; among announcers, congressmen and movie stars there are some who are moral, honest and upright and some who are not; yet both kinds are speakers of standard English.

Then, too, such discussions give the teacher an opportunity to grant that people who speak standard English do not always and invariably communicate any more clearly or forcefully than speakers of non-standard dialects do. Since the students themselves will doubtless have observed this fact, they will appreciate the candor of teachers who acknowledge that a person's grammatical usage has little effect—for better or for worse—upon the clarity and vigor of his message. Too often, teachers try to convey the opposite impression by feigning incomprehension when a student says something like "I don't have no pencil"—a statement whose import is perfectly clear, as the student well knows. The reason for learning to say "I don't have any pencil" has little to do with comprehensibility; when teachers imply that the standard English way is better because it is clearer, students can hardly be blamed for regarding English teachers as "phoneys" or, more charitably, as living in an unreal world.

There is a further advantage to be gained from discussing standard English in terms of professional groups who characteristically use it. Such discussions help to dispel the impression that what the class is being urged to learn is a language spoken chiefly by teachers, by *English* teachers, at that. As a motivating force, such an impression has very low potential.

A Scale of Importance

Moreover, a definition which identifies the target of instruction as "the kind of English habitually used by educated speakers" gives teachers a useful scale for weighing the relative importance of various items found on English tests and in English textbooks. Textbook "rules" which would teach the class usages no longer habitual among most educated Americans can be

[2] Joos, Martin. "Language and the School Child," *Word Study,* Vol. XI, No. 2, December, 1964.

passed over lightly or omitted altogether, and time thus saved can be more profitably spent in a study of usages that actually do distinguish the standard dialect from other varieties.

Thus far we have been concerned with identifying the kind of English that teachers should be helping their students learn to use. We have stressed the need for frankness and realism. It is good strategy to acknowledge that this standard dialect, this variety of language habitually spoken by educated Americans, has no inherent virtue of its own, unpossessed by other dialects. It as not divinely bequeathed to some Moses on tablets of stone. Furthermore, language problems are very different from arithmetic problems, though for centuries this difference has traditionally been ignored. Standard English is not a set of "right" answers, like the answers found at the back of an arithmetic textbook. (The right answer to "two plus two" is "four"; any other is, has always been, and doubtless always will be, wrong. Yet one cannot in the same sense assert that it would be "wrong" for a slum child in a rat-ridden flat to say to his mother, "That landlord, he *mean*. Ain't nobody no meaner'n him.") Hence, in good programs for students of standard English as a second dialect, the terms "right" and "wrong" are not often used. When they are, "right" means "appropriate to the situation," and "wrong" means "likely to put the speaker at a disadvantage," much as one might say it is "wrong" to chew gum while being interviewed for a job.

Standard vs. Non-Standard

There is another truth that teachers in modern programs publicly acknowledge. Students whose families speak some variety of English other than the standard dialect appreciate being told that several features of their home language were once characteristic of standard speech. In seventeenth century England there would have been nothing non-standard about a sentence like "My brother and his family, they live in Atlanta." After all, the authors of the King James version of the Bible wrote: "Thy rod and Thy staff, they comfort me." Double negatives, too, were features of standard English for hundreds of years: Chaucer and Shakespeare often used them. For that matter, double negatives are regularly used in Spanish even to this day.

Teachers who share this sort of information with their students earn a reputation for honesty and reasonableness that stands them in good stead when the hard work of learning the standard dialect begins. For of course the standard dialect must be taught, and it should be learned. Even though there is nothing inherently "wrong" or "bad" about using a non-standard dialect, there are times when it can harm the person who uses it. No matter how tastefully he may dress, no matter how impeccable his grooming may be, the applicant for white collar employment does not enhance his chances by saying, "I come because I seen your ad."

"Front Door English"

Undemocratic and unfair as it may seem, the fact is that standard English is "front door" English. And American schools are committed to the task of making it possible for every citizen to enter by the front door if he wishes to do so.

Just as candor and a clear view of the facts are essential in defining what standard English is, so also one needs to be factual and frank in saying why the standard dialect ought to be learned. The student needs to understand that a command of standard English is vital to any American (particularly any "minority-group" American) who aims to associate with speakers of the standard dialect on anything like an equal footing.

Note the phrase: "A *command* of standard English." To command something is not merely to have a vague notion of it, but rather to be able to *summon it up at will*. The student must be given the ability to summon up the standard dialect whenever he himself wants to use it, in any situation where fluency in that dialect would be to his advantage.[3]

Often, in the development of such fluency, the school can count on little help from the environment outside. In urban "gray areas," for example, and in the rural South, a non-standard dialect is generally the medium of communication for most members of the student's immediate community, standard English being used only by members of the school staff. It is then entirely up to the school to teach young people how to use the standard dialect with ease and self-confidence when occasions demand.

Teachers are well aware of this responsibility, and they have worked at the task, year in and year out, but often with little success. Why? Partly because many a teacher antagonizes the very people she is trying to help. She makes her students feel that their natural way of talking is a shameful thing, marred by "errors" that need to be rooted out. She seems determined to wrest the students' familiar dialect from them, leaving in its place a language that may well estrange them from homefolks and lifelong friends. Small wonder that many students resist!

[3] Of course there are other reasons for teaching standard English—reasons more palatable to those who dislike treating language as a status symbol (which, in America, it is). Quite apart from the fact that nonstandard English makes a poor impression, there is the obvious fact that the standard dialect is the medium for imparting information and ideas in print and on the air.

Towards Linguistic Versatility

Nowadays, luckily, there *are* teachers who recognize that other varieties of English have validity for many communication situations profoundly important to their students. Such teachers offer standard English as a second—or additional—dialect without demanding that it *supplant* the students' home language.

In Europe, such a view of the standard dialect would be taken as a matter of course. In France, for example, it is taken for granted that a citizen will learn to use a standard dialect of the national language for communication in relatively formal situations involving educated speakers, and in conversations with persons from regions other than his own. It is not expected, however, that the standard dialect will replace for all time and for all occasions the dialect the individual learned at home. He retains his local dialect and uses it when he goes back to his home community, switching from one language-track to the other as he moves from scene to scene. This two-track versatility in language usage seems to be characteristic of most societies, especially the older ones. It is unfortunate that the possibility of achieving such versatility has been given so little systematic attention in the United States. To the traditional teacher in America, any and all nonstandard utterances have seemed like evil tendencies, to be stamped out with Calvinistic zeal.

In earlier times, this may have been because so many teachers in American public schools were themselves members of immigrant families, to whom the learning of English had meant an unremitting struggle. Frequently, by dint of prodigious effort and some pain, these teachers had cut their ties with families whose "broken English" posed a threat to the teachers' own hard-won status as new members of an American middle class. One can understand how the experience could have accounted for a teacher's inability to tolerate the thought that a non-standard dialect might have a right to live on in some of the relationships her students held dear.

One of the new things to be said about the teaching of standard English is that some teachers now feel secure enough in their own middle class status to view the school's language-teaching responsibility in a somewhat different light. Such teachers try not to treat non-standard forms with abhorrence and disdain. At the same time, they press vigorously toward the goal of developing in every student the *ability* to use the standard dialect in any situation that *requires* its use. When this is the teacher's policy, many students eventually do stop using non-standard varieties of English altogether. They find themselves moving over to the standard dialect in a widening range of situations as they develop fluency and confidence in handling the standard modes. In time, many are willing to risk speaking standard English with family and friends. But even if a student continues to use the home dialect with his family and peer-group associates, the teacher need not feel that the language program has failed. The test of success is the student's readiness to "turn on" the standard dialect in situations where his standing as a person will be judged in part by his speech.

Instructional Strategy

Sometimes, however, even when the teacher has managed to avoid arousing hostility through her attitude toward the home dialect, results have fallen short of success. A realistic, understanding attitude is not enough: one must also take stock of tactics and techniques.

Just what must be done by anyone who tries to become fluent in standard English when his home dialect is something else? His problem is much like that of someone learning a foreign language in school. Of course there are differences, too. On the debit side, the learning of a second dialect is harder to motivate than the learning of a language entirely foreign and new. And on the other hand, the non-standard dialect speaker has at least the advantage of knowing far more of the *meanings* of the target language than the foreign learner knows.

Still, despite these differences, the needs of second-dialect students and second-language students are alike in one important respect: in both cases the learner needs to develop a new set of language *habits*. He needs new habits that will enable him to utter appropriate responses instantaneously, whenever the need arises, without having to stop and think.

A student who has to stop and think whether to say "I done it" or "I did it" in a standard English speech situation has not *mastered* the target dialect. A person who has mastered a language or a dialect is no more conscious of making such decisions than he is conscious of deciding how to tie his shoes. The problem for teachers, then, is how to lead students to develop a repertoire of routine habits in connection with the forms and arrangements that make up the grammar of the standard dialect.

Clues from Foreign Language Teaching

Teachers of foreign languages give much thought to this matter of "automatic control over the patterns of the language" as it is often called. Hence some of the foreign language teacher's procedures will suggest useful strategy to teachers of standard English as a second dialect.

The first element in the foreign language teacher's strategy is *selection*. Even the most skillful teacher cannot give a student a thorough mastery of every individual linguistic feature. The teacher (or the textbook writer) tries to select the smallest possible number of really essential items to be learned. The students concentrate on these, item by item, until they are able to "produce" each essential type of utterance without hesitation. After that, if time remains, attention is turned to finer points, minor patterns, alternate forms of expression. And once the student has been given a substantial start through the development of control over the major patterns of the language, he is able to fill in the remaining gaps on his own, through observation and analogy.

What does this mean for teaching English as a second dialect? It suggests that teachers and students need to concentrate their energies on features that truly do distinguish standard English from non-standard usage. These need to be taught before items that do not conspicuously characterize one dialect or the other—items which are prescribed or proscribed by some grammar books, but which are used in much the same way by speakers of both standard and non-standard dialects.

Some concrete illustrations may be needed in order to clarify this point. In the list below, certain sentences contain obvious examples of non-standard usage. Any novelist who put those sentences into the mouths of his bankers, stock brokers, optometrists, head nurses or airline hostesses would be accused of having a poor ear for talk. Other sentences in the list would seem quite at home in the discourse of educated Americans. Let us sort out the fifteen sentences, noting which ones would sound out of place in the "language of educated ease"—and which ones would not.

1. Cartwright don't want nobody to help him.
2. They give the burglar five dollar, which was all they had.
3. The man die after he had drank the poison.
4. This author explain why everything cost more now.
5. They always trying to find a way to get rich, no matter how it hurt other people.
6. Their children has went to Washington to spend six week with Mrs. Green sister.
7. I hope William and his family, they going to be more happier now.
8. In my opinion, neither Adams nor Reeves are really qualified for the job.
9. In each of these novels, the hero has to choose between riches, fame and happiness.
10. Somehow this hotel looks different than it did the last time we stayed here.
11. Both Detroit and Denver have possibilities, but I believe Denver would be the best for our conference.

12. But who could Patty stay with if we went abroad without her?
13. Even though I try not to be over-protective, I can't help but worry every time the children are away from home.
14. Carson is efficient, but Peters is certainly easier to work with.
15. Don't look so startled, Janice; it's only me!

Every one of the fifteen sentences contains something that violates some "rule" in grammar books still extant in American schools, but that fact is beside the point here. What has significance to the teacher of standard English as a second dialect is that only seven of the fifteen sentences would sound out of place in conversations among educated Americans. Those are sentences one through seven. The patterns represented by those sentences are the ones that need to be given intensive study by students who are trying to master the standard dialect. If the class has not yet learned to use these high-priority features of standard English, it will be pointless to spend valuable time on grammar-book rules which are "violated" by sentences like the last eight above—rules which condemn usages like "different than" and "neither are." It will be futile and foolish to dwell upon rules governing *between* and *among* and *who* and *whom*. It is sad to think how much precious energy is being squandered on such esoteric distinctions in courses for students who need all the help they can get in mastering the basic hallmarks of standard speech.

In essence, then, the strategy of teaching a second dialect (as in teaching a foreign language) amounts to teaching the smallest possible number of vitally significant items—and *teaching each of them hard*.

Teaching vs. Scolding

What does a teacher do about a language pattern when she really wants students to learn it? Above all, she gets the students to *use* the pattern, to say sentences illustrating the pattern, again and again, until that mode of speech begins to sound natural to the students themselves. The skillful teacher of a second dialect does not simply remark in class, "Stanley should have said 'I saw it,' not 'I seen it.' You remember that, Stanley, don't you? All right then, let's go on."

Yet this is the sort of "teaching" that often takes place, and it has not been of much help to children from non-standard dialect homes. Year after year they have brushed briefly up against the same features of standard English; they have been "corrected" for the same "mistakes" from grade to grade in the same reproachful but off-hand way.

Now to get back to Stanley, a hypothetical child in perhaps the third or fourth grade. Supposing he has just said, "I seen it on my way to school this morning." Supposing the teacher has murmured, "You *saw* it, Stanley. You know that, don't you?" and Stanley has mumbled, "Yeah."

As a matter of fact, Stanley probably does "know it"—in a way. That is, he has heard something about *I seen* as opposed to *I saw* a number of times before. The trouble is, no one has ever made him settle down on this bit of the standard dialect long enough to learn to use it. He has never been given a chance to *command* the form "I saw." Naturally, then, even in situations where he would be willing to use standard English—if only to mollify the teacher—the standard form is just not *in* him to be summoned up. If the teacher wants Stanley to *focus* on this bit of language, the very least she can do is ask him to repeat the sentence after her: "I saw it on my way to school this morning." (And she waits while Stanley repeats the sentence.) If several of the students share Stanley's problem, and she wants the class to master this use of *saw*, something like the following has to take place:

TEACHER: Let's practice using *saw* in some standard English sentences. Let's start by saying Stanley's sentence: I saw it on my way to school this morning. Class!

CLASS: (in unison): I saw it on my way to school this morning.

TEACHER (to Thomas): Thomas, *when* did Stanley see it? Use *saw* in your answer.

THOMAS: He saw it on his way to school this morning.

TEACHER: Right! Gloria, *who* saw it on his way to school? Use *saw* in your answer.

GLORIA: *Stanley* saw it.

TEACHER: Yes! Now let's all mention things we saw on our way to school this morning. *I* saw a fire engine. What about you, Paul?

PAUL: I saw a garbage truck on my way to school.

TEACHER: Good! Laura, tell us what Paul saw, and then tell us something *you* saw.

LAURA: Paul saw a garbage truck on his way to school. I saw a . . . a . . . I saw a black kitten in front of the supermarket.

TEACHER: Fine! Anthony, what did Laura see?

ANTHONY: She seen . . .

TEACHER: She *saw*. Please say, "She saw . . ."

ANTHONY: She saw a kitten.

TEACHER: Yes. And what did *you* see?

ANTHONY: I seen . . . I saw a . . . a motorcycle.

TEACHER: Good. Class, what did Anthony say he saw? Use *saw* in your answer.

CLASS: He saw a motorcycle.

TEACHER: Right! Now, then, let's play the game in a different way. Did anyone see a taxi or a jeep on the way to school today? Gregory, did you see a taxi or a jeep?

GREGORY: I didn't see a jeep, but I saw a taxi.

TEACHER: Good. Daphne, did you see any dogs or horses on your way to school?

DAPHNE: I seen—saw some dogs, but I didn't see no horse.

TEACHER: I didn't see *any* horses. That's the standard English way to say it. Say: "I didn't see any horses."

DAPHNE: I didn't see any horses.

TEACHER: Fine! George, what did Daphne see, and what didn't she see?

GEORGE: She . . . she . . . (silence)

TEACHER: Daphne, tell George what you saw and what you didn't see.

DAPHNE: I saw some dogs, but I didn't see no . . . I didn't see *any* horses.

TEACHER: Good for you Daphne! You did it the standard English way without any help. Say it again.

DAPHNE: I saw some dogs, but I didn't see any horses.

TEACHER: Fine! George, what did she tell us?

GEORGE: She saw some dogs, but she didn't see any horses.

(And so on, with contributions from all who need to gain command over this feature of the standard dialect. The last to speak is Stanley, who is asked to say what various classmates saw on their way to school.)

This is the kind of drill—disguised as a conversation—that has become important in foreign language teaching. Its aim is to make a language pattern begin to sound natural, feel right, through repeated uses in sentences that have some interest and meaning for the speaker and his listeners. It belongs, in fact, to the species of drill that is often called "pattern practice" or "substitution practice." For several years it has been widely used in courses for students of English as a Foreign Language (or Second Language); and it is used when people teach foreign language along "audio lingual" lines today.

True, it takes time to teach patterns of speech in this way. The easier way is merely to mention the student's "error"—or to give him a workbook exercise that he can do at home—though he probably won't. But to deal thus with a language habit is not to deal with it at all. Next year Stanley and the rest will still be using the same non-standard forms on occasions that call for the standard dialect, and next year's teacher will still deplore and nag, rather than teach. True, too, the list of items to be learned is long (particularly if the student's home dialect differs greatly from the standard) but the number of really crucial items is finite: these *could* be mastered during the many years English teachers are given for the task. In no other subject do teachers in all grades try to work on everything at once. Why can't English teachers divide up the list of linguistic habits to be learned? If the fourth grade teacher could make her students fluent with regard to a specified few of the items on the list, the fifth grade teacher could go on from there, and so on up through the grades.[4]

Some Sources of Help

As yet little has been written about the possibilities of this kind of "fluency practice" for students of standard English as a second dialect, but three helpful studies will be mentioned here. One is Marjorie Barrows' *Good English Through Practice*,[5] which shows how to use a set of cleverly devised games for getting junior high school students to use many troublesome standard English forms over and over again while taking part in entertaining, creative language activities.

A second helpful text is Ruth Golden's *Improving Patterns of Language Usage*,[6] in which the problems and attitudes of students learning the standard dialect are analyzed, and many language-learning activities are suggested, including games, stories and role-playing skits.

There is irony in the fact that both *Good English Through Practice* and *Improving Patterns of Language Usage* perpetuate in their titles the older, unhelpful policy of condemning non-standard dialects as intrinsically "worse" than the standard dialect and needing to be "improved." Fortunately, however, the attitudes reflected in the texts themselves are more harmonious with the spirit of modern courses in this field.

A third, and particularly fruitful, source of help for teachers is San-su C. Lin's report on a three-year research project financed by the U. S. Office

[4] Below grade four, the teacher's most essential task is to help children learn how to read and write the English they already know. They need to learn how letters and combinations of letters are used for representing sounds and combinations of sounds that are already familiar. They need to hear stories of the sort the children of educated Americans hear their parents read aloud. They need games that call their attention to rhymes, games that make them notice words. Above all they need to be listened to, and they need help in learning to use their minds. Activities directed toward these ends should be central to the language curriculum for grades one through three.

[5] Barrows, Marjorie Wescott. *Good English Through Practice*. New York: Henry Holt, 1956.

[6] Golden, Ruth I., *Improving Patterns of Language Usage*. Detroit: Wayne University Press, 1960. See also her report on *Effectiveness of Instructional Tapes for Changing Regional Speech Patterns*, Detroit Public Schools, 1962.

of Education, in which Dr. Lin and her associates experimented with pattern-practice techniques as a means of helping students in South Carolina master standard English.[7]

The setting for the Lin program was Claflin College, a small, church-supported school serving mainly Southern Negroes from rural communities. The speech of many freshmen at Claflin included patterns like these: *three apple; nine childrens; I arrive here last week; Claflin have a new dormitory; They looks after theirselves; He don't want nothing; She's more prettier; She sang beautiful; I had wrote it; My uncle, he work in Richmond*. It was evident that the efforts of students and staff would need to be concentrated upon the mastery of basic grammar patterns distinguishing the standard dialect (in writing and in speech) from non-standard varieties. Consequently, problems of pronunciation were not permitted to occupy the center of attention in the Claflin project. However a few pronunciation problems (such as difficulties in adding the -s and -ed endings) did come within the scope of the project because these interfered with the mastery of grammatical forms.

Early in 1961, when the Claflin Project was conceived, there were few guidelines for teachers of a second dialect. Dr. Lin's 1965 report tells an absorbing story of trials, false starts, frustrations, accomplishments, and—above all—cumulative learnings on the part of both students and staff. The report tells of questions to which answers were found. First there was the need to understand why the problem existed:

> What makes a college freshman from a culturally deprived Negro community persist in the use of a nonstandard dialect in spite of many years of English instruction through high school and elementary school? The dialect, no matter how other people may judge it, has evidently proved socially and psychologically satisfactory to the individual who uses it. It is the language of his family—a symbol of security and love. It is the language of his initiation into life—from the dawn of awareness through successive steps in which he learned to adjust to different groups and to establish rapport with the world around him.[8]

Next came the questions of approach, growing out of the staff's analysis of the human aspects of the problem. Certain fundamentals had to be established:

> First of all, the teacher must become aware, and help the student become aware, of the infinite variations that exist in the many dialects of

[7] Lin, San-su C., *Pattern Practice in the Teaching of Standard English to Students with a Non-Standard Dialect*. New York: Teachers College Press, 1965.
[8] Lin, San-su C. *Ibid*.

American English, both regional and social. Both teacher and student must also understand the social implications of these variations. If any change is desirable, the decision to change must come from the individual himself. The teacher, with sympathetic understanding, can help speed the process of change by supplying the necessary methods and materials.[9]

In their search for procedures that could help these students achieve proficiency in the use of standard English, the Claflin staff turned to the field of foreign language teaching, particularly to the teaching of English as a foreign language, in which Dr. Lin had had training and experience. As the report points out:

> . . . there has been little recognition among English teachers of the need for a program basically different from the English program catering to those who speak standard English at home. Not only are these linguistically different young people more sensitive to intolerance and tactless criticism, they also differ from standard speakers in being faced with the task of establishing a new set of language habits. In other words, if they are learning a second language to be added to their indigenous dialect, they must be taught with methods and procedures that are used in learning a second language.[10]

However, after a few weeks' experience with the "repeat-after-me" type of practice material found in most language-learning laboratories, the Claflin staff realized that major adaptations had to be made, since English was, after all, not a foreign language to these American students. Quite apart from the psychological resistance to having one's national language treated like a foreign tongue, there were difficulties arising from the fact that standard English and a non-standard dialect of English are so closely related that, as San-su Lin puts it, "the socially significant differences may be over-shadowed by the similarities and fail to present a real challenge to the students." Moreover, much as the students themselves wished to acquire skill in using standard English, they naturally resented having their entire Freshman English course devoted to drill on grammar patterns: they wanted to learn about literature, composition, stylistics, and other matters that they considered appropriate to a college course.

Thus the Claflin staff was faced with the task of devising procedures and materials that would give the students the kind and amount of drill they needed for mastery of the standard patterns, while at the same time satisfying the students' natural desire for "college level" instruction. Since much

[9] Lin, *Ibid*.
[10] Lin, *Ibid*.

this same task is faced everywhere by teachers whose students are already fluent in some variety of English, Dr. Lin's report on solutions to the problem offers much practical advice. The Claflin staff learned to avoid the use of example sentences and drill sentences that merely illustrated a grammar pattern without offering information or ideas. They learned to construct practice exercises that gave these students information about science, etiquette and job-hunting techniques. They learned to design drills that increased a student's vocabulary, or improved his spelling and punctuation, while simultaneously strengthening his control over standard grammar forms.

For example, noting that the students needed to acquire the habit of using the -s ending for the third person singular form of verbs, the staff prepared an exercise which required each student to use third-person singular forms again and again while discussing "college level" vocabulary words that he knew he needed to learn to pronounce and spell.

The exercise was conducted about as follows: The teacher mentioned a polysyllabic word, such as *curriculum*. A student was then directed to analyze the word, using this sequence of sentences:

> The word *curriculum* begins with the letter *c*.
> It ends with the letter *m*.
> It contains two *r*'s.
> It has four syllables.
> The accent falls on the second syllable.

A second student would then analyze another word (e.g. *accommodation*), using the same set of sentences:

> The word *accommodation* begins with the letter *a*.
> It ends with the letter *n*.
> It contains two *c*'s and two *m*'s.
> It has five syllables.
> The accent falls on the fourth syllable.

The exercise would continue in the same way, until most members of the class had had an opportunity to construct sentences in this mold, each sentence containing at least one word with an -s ending. If any student said, "It *end* with . . . ," or "The accent *fall* . . ." he was asked to repeat the sentence, using the -s ending appropriately. In this way, for the first time, the -s ending began to "sound natural" and "feel right" to these students, because they had said and heard it over and over again. Moreover, they had accepted the drill as being appropriate to their level of educational maturity because it sounded like "college English."

Conducting Meaningful Drills

Exercises of this sort are not nearly as easy to construct as they may seem. First the teacher must know precisely what grammatical point it is that the students need to have illustrated and repeated again and again; and then the teacher must elicit many repetitions of the pattern from the students in the course of a discussion that is more than a mere mechanical drill.

In the Claflin project, the staff realized that just one drill on the -s ending would not be enough to ensure the ready use of this feature of standard English when next the student found himself in a situation calling for fluent, effortless use of the standard dialect. There were many other exercises leading to the same goal by different routes. For example, on one occasion the class discussed reading techniques, within the framework of "Five Things a Good Reader Does." Each student offered his own five sentences, based on a discussion of reading in the essay anthology. Sentences constructed by the class included the following:

> A good reader keeps his mind on his work.
> A good reader looks for answers to certain questions in his mind.
> A good reader distinguishes between main ideas and details.
> A good reader summarizes the writer's ideas from time to time.

(Note that this exercise would have lost its effectiveness so far as practice on the third-person -s ending was concerned if the students had been permitted to alternate between "a good reader" and "good readers." What they needed was to say and to hear a singular subject plus the -s form of the verb again and again, in order to forge a link between the form of the subject and the form of the verb.)

In similar fashion, the Claflin project students practiced the -ed ending for verbs within the context of a discussion of a chapel program, in which, they said, "The president introduced the guest speaker. The speaker talked for twenty minutes. He described . . . and explained that . . . , etc." Once again the strategy called for an oral account, with contributions from all members of the class, carefully elicited by the teacher so as to ensure many repetitions of the standard English form (in this case, the -ed ending) over which the students needed to develop control.

Role Playing

In addition to these "structured discussions" or "fluency drills," the Claflin staff experimented with skits and other role-playing activities. The most successful skits were those that simulated life situations in which standard English would obviously be the appropriate dialect to use. Some dialogs illustrated forms of etiquette relevant to job interviews, employer-secretary conferences, and the like. After the students had taken part in skits written by the project staff, the students themselves—working in small groups— wrote a number of role-playing exercises. Each student practiced his part with the aid of a taped standard English recording of it in the language laboratory. The best skit in each class was chosen for performance in a chapel program. The students found the experience interesting and helpful: among a few students, the speech patterns changed dramatically as a result.

Although the Claflin project extended from 1961 to 1964, a different Freshman class participated during each of the three years. Thus no student was enrolled in the program for more than one academic year. As the final report pointed out, it would be wrong to claim (in San-su Lin's words) that "any method can, in nine months, give the student a full command of the standard dialect when it is psychologically and socially difficult for him to use anything but the non-standard dialect in his daily life, even on a college campus."

Even so, some very encouraging results emerged. From the taped interviews which formed part of the evaluation data, it was evident that the students had become more self-confident and more determined to develop dialectal versatility. Their enunciation had become clearer, they found it easier to communicate, and they appeared more ready to correct themselves after using non-standard forms. On the locally prepared grammar test, the project students proved to be more successful than the control group in identifying non-standard patterns and "translating" them into standard modes. In addition to items that were indisputably non-standard, the test also included items like "Everyone was supposed to bring their lunch," and "This color is different than that"—usages decried by grammar books but often heard in the speech of educated persons. Since such items had been given little attention in the experimental program, most of them were "missed" by project students on the final test. However, in terms of the conspicuous hallmarks of standard English (as contrasted with the non-standard dialect) the experimental students demonstrated significant improvement.

Reading and Writing

Nor were the gains at Claflin limited to matters of speech and social dialect. Somewhat to the surprise of the staff, scores on the Cooperative English Test revealed that the experimental group made greater gains in *read-*

ing after a year of grammar pattern practice than did the members of the control group (which had engaged in free conversation in place of the structured grammar drills). What made this result the more striking was that the control group (the group not employing the experimental techniques) had given more attention to reading, as such, and to discussions of the material read. The Lin report points out that apparently "the use of pattern practice techniques can sharpen students' awareness of structural matters in such a way as to improve their comprehension of material that they read. After a year of working systematically and intensively with various patterns of English, the experimental students were apparently better equipped to read passages which required an alert attention to structural signals."

Another skill which benefited from the application of second-language teaching techniques in the Claflin project was *writing*. At the end of the second year of the program, the director reported [11] that the compositions written by students in the project were "not only more free of errors, but more purposeful and more interesting" than any she had previously read during seven years' experience at the same institution.

Above all, what has been proved by the Claflin project (and by similar programs) is that speakers of non-standard dialects can make significant progress toward the mastery of standard English, even in a program of very short duration. (It should be remembered that no Claflin student was involved in the project for more than nine months.) How much could be accomplished if teachers at all levels of the instructional ladder were to apply the lessons learned from such experiments!

Target Language

Fortunately, more and more teachers are coming to realize that attitudes, approaches and procedures germane to the teaching of foreign languages have relevance to the teaching of standard English as a second dialect. More and more teachers are defining the target language as "the kind of English habitually spoken by most of the educated members of the American speech community." Guided by this definition, classes for non-standard speakers are concentrating upon language usages which indisputably characterize "the language of educated ease." Teachers are thus freeing class time for practice upon these crucial features of the target dialect by passing lightly over esoteric distinctions that carry little or no weight outside some grammar textbooks.

[11] Lin, San-su C. "An Experiment in Changing Dialect Patterns: The Claflin Project," *College English*, May, 1963, pp. 644–47.

In their classrooms, these teachers guard against treating the students' home dialect as something faulty, flawed and inferior. They are willing to grant that the home dialect may even be the "right" one for a student to use in some interpersonal relationships deeply important to him. At the same time, they help their students achieve fluency in standard English by patiently guiding the class through practice exercises based on second-language teaching techniques, but adapted to second-dialect purposes with artistry and tact.

In programs conducted along these lines, there is much hope for students striving to command the dialect that is required for advancement in our national life—for entering fully into American affairs, through the front door.

BIBLIOGRAPHIES

A Minimal Professional Reference Library for Teachers of Secondary School English—1968

Prepared by the NCTE Secondary Section Committee (John C. Maxwell, Upper Midwest Regional Educational Laboratory, chairman, assisted by William J. Scannell, NCTE Curriculum Materials Associate).

Suggested as a basic list of essential publications to which schools may add titles as funds become available.

PROFESSIONAL JOURNALS

Elementary English. National Council of Teachers of English.*
English Journal. National Council of Teachers of English.*
College English. National Council of Teachers of English.*
College Composition and Communication. National Council of Teachers of English.*
Journal of Reading. International Reading Association, Box 119, Newark, Delaware 19711.
Media and Methods. Media & Methods, 134 Thirteenth Street, Philadelphia, Pa.
The Speech Teacher. Speech Association of America, Statler Hilton Hotel, New York, New York 10001.

THE CURRICULUM SERIES OF THE NATIONAL COUNCIL OF TEACHERS OF ENGLISH

The English Language Arts. New York: Appleton-Century-Crofts, 1952.*
The English Language Arts in the Secondary School. New York: Appleton-Century-Crofts, 1956.*

* Available from the National Council of Teachers of English, 508 South Sixth Street, Champaign, Illinois 61820.

From *English Journal,* LVII (January, 1968), 116–19. Reprinted by permission of the National Council of Teachers of English.

GENERAL BOOKS ON CURRICULUM AND METHODOLOGY IN
SECONDARY ENGLISH

Burton, Dwight L., and John S. Simmons (eds.). *Teaching English in Today's High Schools.* New York: Holt, Rinehart and Winston, Inc., 1965.

Dixon, John. *Growth Through English* (Report on the Anglo-American Dartmouth Seminar for the profession: National Council of Teachers of English, National Association for the Teaching of English, Modern Language Association). Reading, England: National Association for the Teaching of English, 1967.*

Evans, William H., and Jerry L. Walker. *New Trends in the Teaching of English in Secondary Schools.* Chicago: Rand McNally & Company, 1967.

Gordon, Edward J., and Edward S. Noyes (eds.). *Essays on the Teaching of English.* New York: Appleton-Century-Crofts, 1960.*

Guth, Hans P. *English Today and Tomorrow: A Guide for Teachers of English.* Englewood Cliffs, N.J.: Prentice-Hall, Inc., 1964.

Holbrook, David. *English for the Rejected: Training Literacy in Lower Streams of the Secondary School.* New York: Cambridge University Press, 1964.

Hook, J. N. *The Teaching of High School English,* Third Edition. New York: Ronald Press Company, 1965.

Lacampagne, Robert J., Roger K. Applebee, and James R. Squire (eds.), *High School Departments of English: Their Organization, Administration, and Supervision.* Champaign, Ill.: National Council of Teachers of English, 1965.*

Loban, Walter, Margaret Ryan, and James R. Squire. *Teaching Language and Literature.* New York: Harcourt, Brace & World, Inc., 1961. (Revised edition now in preparation.)

Muller, Herbert J. *The Uses of English* (Report of the Anglo-American Dartmouth Seminar for the public: National Council of Teachers of English, National Association for the Teaching of English, Modern Language Association). New York: Holt, Rinehart and Winston, Inc., 1967.*

Reeves, Ruth (ed.). *Ideas for Teaching English: Grades 7-8-9.* Champaign, Ill.: National Council of Teachers of English, 1966.*

Sauer, Edwin H. *English in the Secondary School.* New York: Holt, Rinehart and Winston, Inc., 1961.

SPECIALIZED BOOKS AND REFERENCES

Composition and Rhetoric

Braddock, Richard, Richard Lloyd-Jones, and Lowell Schoer. *Research in Written Composition.* Champaign, Ill.: National Council of Teachers of English, 1963.*

College Composition and Communication and *College English* (collection of reprints). *The Sentence and the Paragraph.* Champaign, Ill.: National Council of Teachers of English, 1966.*

Corbin, Richard. *The Teaching of Writing in Our Schools.* New York: The Macmillan Company, 1966.*

Gibson, Walker. *Tough, Sweet and Stuffy.* Bloomington, Ind.: Indiana University Press, 1966.

Gorrell, Robert M. (ed.). *Rhetoric: Theories for Application.* Champaign, Ill.: National Council of Teachers of English, 1967.*

Hook, J. N. *Guide to Good Writing: Grammar, Style, Usage.* New York: Ronald Press Company, 1962.

Judine, Sister M., I.H.M. *A Guide for Evaluating Student Composition.* Champaign, Ill.: National Council of Teachers of English, 1965.*

Mearns, Hughes. *Creative Power,* Second Revised Edition. New York: Dover Publications, Inc., 1959.

Perrin, Porter G. *The Writer's Guide and Index to English,* Revised Edition by Karl W. Dykema and Wilma R. Ebbitt. Glenview, Ill.: Scott, Foresman and Company, 1965.

English Language

Allen, Harold B. (ed.). *Readings in Applied English Linguistics,* Second Edition. New York: Appleton-Century-Crofts, 1964.

Anderson, Wallace L., and Norman C. Stageberg (eds.). *Introductory Readings on Language,* Revised Edition. New York: Holt, Rinehart and Winston, Inc., 1966.

Baugh, Albert C. *History of the English Language,* Second Edition. New York: Appleton-Century-Crofts, 1957.

Bryant, Margaret M. *Current American Usage.* New York: Funk & Wagnalls Co., 1962.

Evans, Bergen and Cornelia. *Dictionary of Contemporary American Usage.* New York: Random House, Inc., 1957.

Fowler, H. W. *A Dictionary of Modern English Usage,* Second Edition, revised and edited by Sir Ernest Gowers. London and New York: Oxford University Press, 1965.

Francis, W. Nelson. *The English Language.* New York: W. W. Norton & Company, Inc., 1965.

Gleason, Henry A., Jr. *Linguistics and English Grammar.* New York: Holt, Rinehart and Winston, Inc., 1965.

Goldstein, Miriam B. *The Teaching of Language in Our Schools.* New York: The Macmillan Company, 1966.*

Hayakawa, S. I. *Language in Thought and Action,* Second Edition. New York: Harcourt, Brace & World, Inc., 1964.

Hogan, Robert F. (ed.). *The English Language in the School Program.* Champaign, Ill.: National Council of Teachers of English, 1966.*

Marckwardt, Albert H. *Linguistics and the Teaching of English.* Bloomington, Ind.: Indiana University Press, 1966.

Sapir, Edward. *Language: An Introduction to the Study of Speech.* Harcourt, Brace & World, Inc., Harvest Books, HB 7.

382   BIBLIOGRAPHIES

Shane, Harold G. *Linguistics and the Classroom Teacher.* Washington, D.C.:
Association for Supervision and Curriculum Development, NEA, 1967.*
Shipley, Joseph T. *Dictionary of Word Origins.* Paterson, N.J.: Littlefield,
Adams & Co., 1964.
Shuy, Roger W. *Discovering American Dialects.* Champaign, Ill.: National
Council of Teachers of English, 1967.*
Shuy, Roger W. (ed.). *Social Dialects and Language Learning.* Champaign, Ill.:
National Council of Teachers of English, 1965.*
Thomas, Owen P. *Transformational Grammar and the Teacher of English.*
New York: Holt, Rinehart and Winston, Inc., 1965.
Wilson, Graham (ed.). *A Linguistics Reader.* New York: Harper & Row, Pub-
lishers, 1967.

Literature

Booth, Wayne C. *The Rhetoric of Fiction.* Chicago: University of Chicago Press,
1961.
Brooks, Cleanth, and Robert Penn Warren. *Understanding Fiction,* 2nd ed. New
York: Appleton-Century-Crofts, 1959.
Brooks, Cleanth, and Robert Penn Warren. *Understanding Poetry,* 3rd ed. New
York: Holt, Rinehart and Winston, Inc., 1960.
Burton, Dwight L. *Literature Study in the High School,* Rev. ed. New York:
Holt, Rinehart and Winston, Inc., 1964.
Ciardi, John. *How Does a Poem Mean?* Boston: Houghton Mifflin Company,
1960.
Forster, E. M. *Aspects of the Novel.* New York: Harcourt, Brace & World,
Inc., 1947; also Harcourt, Brace & World, Inc., Harvest Books, HB 19.
Frye, Northrop. *The Educated Imagination.* Bloomington, Ind.: Indiana Uni-
versity Press, 1964.
Frye, Northrop. *The Well-Tempered Critic.* Bloomington, Ind.: Indiana Uni-
versity Press, 1963.
Gordon, Edward J. (ed.). *Writing and Literature in the Secondary School.* New
York: Holt, Rinehart and Winston, Inc., 1965.*
Hamilton, Edith. *Mythology.* Boston: Little, Brown and Company, 1942; also
Grosset & Dunlap, Inc., Universal Library; and New American Library, Men-
tor Books, MP 665.
Moffett, James. *Drama: What Is Happening—The Use of Dramatic Activities
in the Teaching of English.* Champaign, Ill.: National Council of Teachers of
English, 1967.*
Richards, I. A. *Practical Criticism.* New York: Harcourt, Brace & World, Inc.,
1929. Harvest Books, HB 16.
Rosenblatt, Louise M. *Literature as Exploration,* Revised Edition. New York:
Noble & Noble, 1967.
Rosenheim, Edward W. *What Happens in Literature: A Student's Guide to
Poetry, Drama, and Fiction.* Chicago: University of Chicago Press, 1960; also
University of Chicago Press, Phoenix Books, P 77.

Stafford, William (and the NCTE Commission on Literature). *Friends to This Ground: A Statement for Readers, Teachers, and Writers of Literature.* Champaign, Ill.: National Council of Teachers of English, 1967.*

Thrall, William Flint, Addison Hibbard, and C. Hugh Holman. *A Handbook to Literature, Revised and Enlarged Edition.* New York: The Odyssey Press, 1960.

Mass Media

Boutwell, William D. (ed.). *Using Mass Media in the Schools.* New York: Appleton-Century-Crofts, 1962.*

Hazard, Patrick D. (ed.). *TV as Art: Some Essays in Criticism.* Champaign, Ill.: National Council of Teachers of English, 1966.*

McLuhan, H. Marshall. *Understanding Media.* New York: McGraw-Hill Book Company, 1964.

Postman, Neil, *et al. Television and the Teaching of English.* New York: Appleton-Century-Crofts, 1961.*

Sheridan, Marion C., *et al. The Motion Picture and the Teaching of English.* New York: Appleton-Century-Crofts, 1965.*

Reading

Bamman, H. A., *et al. Reading Instruction in the Secondary School.* New York: David McKay Co., Inc., 1961.

Karlin, Robert. *Teaching Reading in the High School.* Indianapolis, Ind.: Bobbs-Merrill Co., Inc., 1964.

Massey, William T., and Virginia D. Moore. *Helping High School Students To Read Better.* New York: Holt, Rinehart and Winston, Inc., 1965.

Strang, Ruth, Constance M. McCullough, and Arthur E. Traxler. *Improvement of Reading,* Third Edition. New York: McGraw-Hill Book Company, 1961.

Aids for Selecting Books for Adolescents

Alm, Richard S. (ed. for the National Council of Teachers of English). *Books for You.* New York: Washington Square Press, 1964.*

A Basic Book Collection for High Schools. Chicago: American Library Association, regularly revised.

A Basic Book Collection for Junior High Schools. Chicago: American Library Association, regularly revised.

Carlsen, G. Robert. *Books and the Teen-age Reader.* New York: Harper & Row, Publishers, 1967; also Bantam Books, Inc., 1967.*

Emery, Raymond C., and Margaret B. Houshower (eds.). *High Interest—Easy Reading for Junior and Senior High School Reluctant Readers.* Champaign, Ill.: National Council of Teachers of English, 1965.*

Perkins, Ralph M. (ed.). *Book Selection Media.* Champaign, Ill.: National Council of Teachers of English, 1967.

Willard, Charles B. (ed. for the National Council of Teachers of English). *Your Reading: A Book List for Junior High Schools*. New York: New American Library, Inc., Signet Books, 1966.*

Miscellaneous Professional References

Bennett, Robert A. (ed.). *Speech in the English Classroom*. Champaign, Ill.: National Council of Teachers of English, 1961.*

Bruner, Jerome S. *The Process of Education*. Cambridge: Harvard University Press, 1960.

Bruner, Jerome S. *Toward a Theory of Instruction*. Cambridge: Harvard University Press, 1966.

Carruthers, Robert B. *Building Better English Tests*. Champaign, Ill.: National Council of Teachers of English, 1963.*

Committee on National Interest. *The National Interest and the Teaching of English*. Champaign, Ill.: National Council of Teachers of English, 1961.*

Committee on the Right To Read (Edward R. Gordon, chairman). *The Students' Right To Read*. Champaign, Ill.: National Council of Teachers of English, 1962.*

Corbin, Richard, and Muriel Crosby (eds.). *Language Programs for the Disadvantaged*. Champaign, Ill.: National Council of Teachers of English, 1965.*

DeCecco, John P. (ed.). *Educational Technology: Readings in Programmed Instruction*. New York: Holt, Rinehart and Winston, Inc., 1964.

Directory of Assistantships and Fellowships for Graduate Study in English and the Teaching of English, a yearly special issue of *College Composition and Communication*. Champaign, Ill.: National Council of Teachers of English.*

Frederick, Anthony, S.M. (ed.). *Annotated Index to the English Journal 1944-63*. Champaign, Ill.: National Council of Teachers of English, 1964.*

Frye, Northrop (ed.). *Design for Learning*. Toronto: University of Toronto Press, 1962.

Schreiber, Morris (ed.). *An Annotated List of Recordings in the Language Arts*. Champaign, Ill.: National Council of Teachers of English, 1964.*

Taba, Hilda, and Deborah Elkins. *Teaching Strategies for the Culturally Disadvantaged*. Chicago: Rand McNally & Company, 1966.

Wilhelms, Fred T. (ed.). *Evaluation as Feedback and Guide*. Washington: Association for Supervision and Curriculum Development, NEA, 1967.

JAMES R. BENNETT / *An Annotated Bibliography of Selected Writings on English Prose Style*

GENERAL [1]

Aurner, R. R. "The History of Certain Aspects of the Structure of the English Sentence," *PQ,* II (1923), 187–208.
  Assessed by Williamson in *The Senecan Amble,* p. 39.
Brownell, W. C. *The Genius of Style.* New York: 1924.
  Chapter IV, "English Prose Tradition," depores the loss of "aesthetic" style and the ascendancy of the scientific "plain" style; surveys "aesthetic" stylists during the last three centuries.
Earle, John. *English Prose: Its Elements, History and Usage.* New York: 1891.
  A highly provocative study of English prose style which argues the thesis that there have been three epochs in the history of English prose at which the language has culminated into a standard: the tenth century, the fifteenth, and the nineteenth. Saintsbury has written: "If anybody should say, 'Why do you quote Earle? He is quite obsolete as a scholar,' my answer is ready: 'Please show me any scholar of the present day who has shown himself to be equally conversant, *from the literary point of view,* with Old, Middle, and Modern English.' I know one, perhaps two; but neither has written *in extenso* on the matter."
Gerwig, G. W. *On the Decrease of Predication and of Sentence Weight in English Prose.* Nebraska University Studies, Vol. II, No. 1, 1894.
  Discussed by Lewis in *English Paragraph,* p. 58.
Lewis, Edwin H. *The History of the English Paragraph.* Chicago: 1894.
  Argues that the English paragraph has increased in the number of sentences and in the quality of its structure.

[1] I am indebted to the assistance of Professor Marjorie Ryan in the collection of titles for this bibliography.

From *College Composition and Communication,* XVI (December, 1965), 248–55. Reprinted by permission of the National Council of Teachers of English and James R. Bennett.

Potter, Simeon. "The Sentence," *Our Language*. London: 1950.
    Describes the historical continuity of the English sentence, and distinguishes
    the loose, balanced, and periodic sentences.
Read, Herbert. "Unity," *English Prose Style* (1928). Boston: 1952.
    An effort to define the essential English prose tradition. Considers Dryden
    the "starting point of the main traditional style in English"; argues in op-
    position to the majority of scholars that before Dryden there was "no
    corporate literary sense."
Saintsbury, George. "English Prose Style," *Specimens of English Prose Style from
    Malory to Macaulay*. London: 1886.
    A not always safe historical sketch of English prose from the beginning of
    printing to the end of the nineteenth century. He discerns three general de-
    velopments: experiment and individualism in the sixteenth and seventeenth
    century, establishment of regularity and order in the Restoration and
    eighteenth century, and a return to ornate individualism in the nineteenth
    century.
————. *A History of English Prose Rhythm*. London: 1912.
    The most famous and comprehensive of studies of prose rhythm.
Scott, John H. *Rhythmic Prose*. University of Iowa Humanistic Studies, Vol. III,
    No. 1, 1925.
    Although not historically oriented the book is packed with detailed analyses
    of individual writers covering several centuries.
Scott, John H., and Z. E. Chandler. *Phrasal Patterns in English Prose*. New
    York: 1932.
Sherman, L. A. *Analytics of Literature: A Manual for the Objective Study of
    English Prose and Poetry*. Boston: 1893.
    Lewis praises this book for its historical understanding of the English
    sentence. Sherman discusses the stages through which English prose has
    passed: coordinative, subordinative, "suppressive," and steady decrease in
    predication.
Thompson, J. A. K. *Classical Influences on English Prose*. London: 1956.
    Historically oriented discussions of a wide variety of stylistic problems; for
    example, chapters nine and ten treat the plain and ornate styles, chapter
    sixteen the classical rhetorical background.

FROM ALFRED TO MORE

Atkins, J. W. H. *English Literary Criticism: The Medieval Phase*. London:
    1952.
Aurner, R. R. "Caxton and the English Sentence," *Wisconsin Studies in Lan-
    guage and Literature*, No. 18 (1923).
    Discussed by Williamson, p. 39.
Baugh, Albert C. Various chapters in Book I, Part II of *A Literary History of
    England*. New York: 1948.
Bennett, H. S. "Fifteenth Century Secular Prose," *RES*, XXI (1945), 257–63.
    Qualifies Chambers' stress upon religious and homiletic prose as the chief
    instruments of continuity. Denying Chambers' argument that secular prose
    in the fifteenth century was not in the true English tradition, since it was

spoiled by clumsiness and pedantry, Bennett claims for secular prose an important place in the development of the main English tradition of the clear and easy plain style.

Chambers, R. W. *On the Continuity of English Prose from Alfred to More and His School.* London: 1932.

> Chambers agrees with Krapp concerning the nature of the essential English prose tradition (clarity and intelligibility, simplicity and directness), but he traces this tradition back to Alfred, and then forward through Aelfric and Wyclif to More and modern prose. The prose of the eleventh century derived directly from the tenth, and the fifteenth century prose directly from the eleventh. The sudden output of English prose in the late fourteenth century that Krapp emphasizes as the proper starting point is a survival of the old prose of Alfred and Aelfric. The full revival of English prose in the fifteenth century, therefore, is the consequence of the steady development of English prose since Alfred, which was a tradition of plain and open style, typified by the *Ancren Riwle,* and the writings of Rolle and Hilton, all of which were forecasts of the prose of More, and therefore of Bunyan, Defoe, Dryden and modern prose.

Craik, Sir Henry. *English Prose; Selections with Critical Introductions to Each Period.* Vol. I. New York: 1893.

Graves, Robert, and Alan Hodge. "The Beginnings of English Prose," *The Reader Over Your Shoulder.* New York: 1944.

Greenwood, Alice D. Chapters III, XII, and XIV in *The Cambridge History of English Literature,* ed. A. W. Ward and A. R. Waller, New York: 1908.

Krapp, George Philip. *The Rise of English Literary Prose.* New York: 1915.

> Discovers the same "spirit" in More, Tindale, Hooker, Milton, Burke, and Carlyle, indeed in "all the great masters of expositional and oratory prose in the English language." But he believes that the true English prose tradition did not commence until the late fourteenth century with Wyclif, the "father" of English prose, "the first intelligent writer of English prose."

Malone, Kemp. Book I, Part I, Chapter X, "Literary Prose," *A Literary History of England,* ed. A. C. Baugh. New York: 1948.

Wilson, R. M. "On the Continuity of English Prose," *Mélanges Fernand Mossé.* 1962, pp. 468–94.

FROM TYNDALE TO BROWNE AND TAYLOR

Allen, Don Cameron. "Style and Certitude," *ELH,* XV (1948), 167–75.

> Describes the transition from early to late Renaissance, suggests causes "for the discarding of the Ciceronian prose method."

Barish, Jonas, A. *Ben Jonson and the Language of Prose Comedy.* Harvard: 1960.

> A thorough study of Jonson's prose style and of his place in the history of English prose style.

———. "The Prose Style of John Lyly," *ELH,* XXIII (1956), 14–35.

Beum, Robert. "The Scientific Affinities of English Baroque Prose," *EM,* XIII (1962), 59–80.

Chittick, Roger Dale. "The Augustinian Tradition in Seventeenth Century English Prose," *DA,* XVII (1957), 2606 (Stanford).

Christensen, Francis. "John Wilkins and the Royal Society's Reform of Prose Style," *MLQ*, VII (1946), 279–90.

Cook, Albert S. (ed.). *The Bible and English Prose Style*. Heath: 1892.

Crane, William G. *Wit and Rhetoric in the Renaissance: The Formal Basis of Elizabethan Prose Style*. New York: 1938.

Croll, Morris. "Introduction: The Sources of the Euphuistic Rhetoric," *Euphues: The Anatomy of Wit*. Ed. Harry Clemons. New York: 1916.

————. "'Attic' Prose in the Seventeenth Century," *SP*, XVIII (1921), 79–129.

————. "Attic Prose: Lipsius, Montaigne, and Bacon," *Schelling Anniversary Papers*. New York: 1923.

————. "Muret and the History of 'Attic' Prose," *PMLA*, XXXIX (1924), 254ff.
> "In an article, "'Attic' Prose in the Seventeenth Century" *Studies in Philology* (April 1921), I discussed the theory of this Anti-Ciceronian movement of 1575–1600, and especially its relations to its classical models and authorities. An object of the present study is to show its relations with the movement of ideas in its age. An article, "Lipsius, Montaigne, and Bacon," in *Schelling Anniversary Papers* (1923), carries the history into the generation following Muret. Another study, "Juste Lipse et le Mouvement Anti-Ciceronien" (*Revue du Seizième Siècle,* July 1914), now calls for revision at several points."

————. "The Baroque Style in Prose," *Studies in English Philology: A Miscellany in Honour of Frederick Klaeber*. Minneapolis: 1929.
> Whereas in his other essays on the anti-Ciceronian movement Croll had concentrated chiefly upon the *theory* of the style, in this essay he attempts to describe the *form* of anti-Ciceronian, or, as he calls it here, "baroque" prose.

Daniells, Roy. "Baroque Form in English Literature," *UTQ*, XIV (1945), 393–408.

Fisch, Harold. "The Puritans and the Reform of Prose-Style," *ELH*, XIX (1952), 220–48.

Hamilton, K. G. *The Two Harmonies: Poetry and Prose in the Seventeenth Century*. Oxford: 1963.

Harkness, S. "The Prose Style of Sir Philip Sidney." *University of Wisconsin Studies,* II (1918), 57–76.

Hendrickson, G. L. "The Origin and Meaning of the Ancient Characters of Style," *AJP*, XXVI, 249–90.

————. "The Peripatetic Mean of Style and the Three Stylistic Characters," *AJP*, XXV, 125–46.

Howell, Wilbur S. *Logic and Rhetoric in England, 1500–1700*. Princeton: 1956.
> Traces theories through two centuries. Chapter 4 on Ramus.

Jones, Richard F. "The Attack on Pulpit Eloquence," *JEGP*, XXX (1931), 188–217.

Knights, L. C. "Elizabethan Prose," *Scrutiny*, II (1934), 427–38.

Lowes, John Livingston. "The Noblest Monument of English Prose," *Essays in Appreciation*. Boston: 1936.
> Describes how, when the translators of the Bible came to do their task, they found a medium ready to their hand: the simple, direct vigor of native English combined with the majesty and stateliness of the Latin of the Church.

Macdonald, Hugh. "Another Aspect of Seventeenth Century Prose," *RES*, XIX (1943), 33ff.
> Controverts Joan Bennett.

Mitchell, W. Fraser. *English Pulpit Oratory from Andrewes to Tillotson*. New York: 1932.

Oliver, H. J. "Izaak Walton's Prose Style," *RES*, XXI (1945), 280–88.

Randolph, Gerald Richard. "An Analysis of Form and Style in the Prose Works of Thomas Nashe," *DA*, XXIII (1963), 3890–91 (Fla. State).

Staton, Walter F., Jr. "The Characters of Style in Elizabethan Prose," *JEGP*, LVII (1958), 197–207.
> Analyzes the three "characters" of style in Elizabethan prose: low, middle, and lofty; argues that "low" or "plain" style always existed (one of the three kinds of style commonly recognized by Elizabethan critics), and that, therefore, seventeenth-century plain prose was not so much a reaction as is sometimes thought.

Tempest, Norton R. "Rhythm in the Prose of Sir Thomas Browne," *RES*, III (1927), 308–18.

Thompson, Elbert N. S. "Milton's Prose Style," *PQ*, XIV (1935), 1–15.

———. "The Seventeenth-Century English Essay," Ch. X of *Style of the English Essay*, University of Iowa Humanities Studies, Vol. III, No. 3, 1925.
> A summary of the varieties of prose styles in the seventeenth century, dealing especially with the rise of the simple-direct style, thereby indicating the developments that prepared for the eighteenth century.

Umbach, Herbert H. "The Merit of Metaphysical Style in Donne's Easter Sermons," *ELH*, XII (1945), 108–25.

———. "The Rhetoric of Donne's Sermons," *PMLA*, LII (1937), 354–58.

Uve, Peter. "Introduction," *Seventeenth-Century Prose, 1620–1700*. London: 1956.

Webber, Joan. *Contrary Music: The Prose Style of John Donne*. Madison: 1962.
> "What I have done here, then, is to read Donne's prose in the light of the traditions he knew, and to show how and why he made of them what he did." A model of prose analysis.

Williamson, George. *The Senecan Amble: A Study in Prose from Bacon to Collier*. Chicago: 1951.
> An outstanding work of scholarship. Chapter I, for example, analyzes the Ciceronian-Isocratian styles and the reactions against them; Chapter III is a technical analysis of Euphuistic and Senecan styles and the varieties of anti-Ciceronian styles in the seventeenth century.

Wilson, Frank Percy. *Seventeenth Century Prose: Five Lectures*. Berkeley: 1960.
> Primarily a survey of the types of prose.

FROM SPRAT TO JOHNSON

Bennett, Joan. "An Aspect of the Evolution of Seventeenth-Century Prose," *RES*, XVII (1941), 281–97.
> Focuses on the separation of prose from poetry during the last half of the seventeenth century. "The prose writer's new purpose was to deal with matters of fact, that could be verified."

Bredvold, Louis I., Robert K. Root, and George Sherburn. "Introduction," *Eighteenth Century Prose*. New York: 1932.

Chandler, Zilpha Emma. *An Analysis of the Stylistic Technique of Addison, Johnson, Hazlitt, and Pater*. University of Iowa Humanistic Studies, Vol. IV, No. 3.

Emden, Cecil S. "Rhythmical Features in Dr. Johnson's Prose," *RES*, XXV (1949), 38–54.

Hnatko, Eugene. "Studies in the Prose Style of Laurence Sterne," *DA*, XXIII (1963), 4685 (Syracuse).

Jefferson, D. W. "Introduction," *Eighteenth-Century Prose, 1700–1780*. London: 1956.

Jones, Howard Mumford. "American Prose Style: 1700–1770," *Huntington Library Bulletin*, VI (1934), 115–51.

Jones, Richard F. "Science and English Prose Style in the Third Quarter of the Seventeenth Century," *PMLA*, XLV (1930), 977–1009.
> An excellent examination of the influence of science on English prose style.

Lannering, Jan. *Studies in the Prose Style of Joseph Addison*. Cambridge, Mass.: 1951.

Lawton, George. *John Wesley's English: A Study of His Literary Style*. London: 1962.

Sutherland, James. *On English Prose*. Toronto: 1957.
> General chapters on the development of English prose. Chapter III, "Age of Prose," deals with the rise of modern prose in the seventeenth and eighteenth centuries.

Sutherland, James, and Ian Watt. *Restoration and Augustan Prose*. Los Angeles: 1956.

Williamson, George. *The Senecan Amble*. Chicago: 1951.
> Chapter 9, "Reform and the Royal Society," argues (in opposition to Jones) that the reforms of the Royal Society were part of the long anti-Ciceronian efforts. Chapter 11, "Pert Style in Neo-Classic Times," summarizes the stylistic developments in the seventeenth century and traces the development of the Senecan style in the eighteenth and, briefly, in the nineteenth centuries.

Wimsatt, William. *The Prose Style of Samuel Johnson*. New Haven: 1941.
> Chapters I–IV discuss the elements of his style; Chapters VIII–IX place him historically according to antecedents and effects.

——. *Philosophical Words: A Study of Style and Meaning in the "Rambler" and "Dictionary" of Samuel Johnson*. New Haven: 1948.
> This book is "a development of several pages of my earlier study *The Prose Style of Samuel Johnson* and diverges from the whole of that study in placing a greater emphasis upon origins."

FROM WORDSWORTH TO PATER AND HUXLEY

Allott, Kenneth, and Miriam Allott, eds. "Introduction," *Victorian Prose 1830–1880*. The Pelican Book of English Prose, Vol. V. London: 1956.

Brewster, W. T. *Studies in Structure and Style*. New York: 1902.
> Contains extended analyses of about six essays by nineteenth-century writers.

Buckler, William E., ed. "Introduction," *Prose of the Victorian Period*. Boston: 1958.

> Evaluates Allott, Elton, Culler, Svaglic. Of Allott and Elton, Buckler writes: "In these two critics at least we have apparent agreement on Victorian prose: (1) it was a positive literary achievement; (2) its chief characteristic was energy; (3) it had more formal excellence than Elizabethan prose and more range than Augustan prose; and (4) a change in prose style came about toward the end of the Victorian period. . . ." Emphasizes Pater's "Style" as containing a set of critical principles for the judgment of Victorian prose. Brief sections on Mill and Huxley, Macaulay, Arnold, Carlyle, Ruskin, and Newman.

Craik, Sir Henry. *English Prose: Selections with Critical Introductions to Each Period*. Vol. V. New York: 1893.

Culler, A. Dwight. "Method in the Study of Victorian Prose," *VN*, No. 9 (1957), 1–4.

Earle, John. *English Prose*. New York: 1891.

> Contains a long, general section on the nineteenth century; urges the thesis that "The Nineteenth Century is characterized by two conspicuous movements, namely, the higher organization of the paragraph, and the progress in restitution of vernacular English" (especially shorter sentences).

Elton, Oliver. *A Survey of English Literature, 1830–1880*. 2 vols. London: 1920.

Gibson, Walker. "Behind the Veil: A Distinction Between Poetic and Scientific Language in Tennyson, Lyell, and Darwin," *VS*, II (1958), 60–68.

Graves, Robert, and Alan Hodge. *The Reader Over Your Shoulder*. New York: 1944.

Harrison, Frederic. *Tennyson, Ruskin, Mill, and Other Literary Estimates*. New York: 1900.

> Chapter 2 evaluates Ruskin as the master of nineteenth-century prose.

Holloway, John. *The Victorian Sage: Studies in Argument*. London: 1953.

> "Examines the rhetorical methods of Carlyle, Newman, Disraeli, Arnold, Eliot, and Hardy, emphasizing the emotional and imaginative qualities of their work."

Houghton, Walter. *The Art of Newman's "Apologia."* New Haven: 1945.

> An outstandingly perceptive and suggestive analysis of style.

———. "The Rhetoric of T. H. Huxley," *UTQ*, XVIII (1949), 159–75.

Hyman, Stanley Edgar. *The Tangled Bank: Darwin, Marx, Frazer and Freud as Imaginative Writers*. New York: 1962.

Levine, Richard A. "Carlyle as Poet: The Phoenix Image in 'Organic Filaments,'" *VN*, No. 25 (1964), 18–20.

Minto, William. *A Manual of English Prose Literature*. Boston: 1901.

> Detailed analyses of De Quincey, Macaulay, and Carlyle, with comparisons relating them to the history of English prose style.

Ohmann, R. H. *Shaw: The Style and the Man*. Middletown: 1962.

> A linguistic exploration of the style underlying Shaw's thought; although unhistorical, this book is an important contribution to the study of non-fiction prose that provides new tools and opens new doors.

Roellinger, Francis X., Jr. "The Early Development of Carlyle's Style," *PMLA*, LXXII (1957), 936–51.

Schweik, R. C. "Method in the Study of Victorian Prose: A Criticism," *VN*, No. 10 (1957), 15–16.

Sherman, L. A. *Analytics of Literature*. Boston: 1893.
> Has some useful analysis of the nineteenth-century sentence.

Sutherland, James. *On English Prose*, Toronto: 1957.
> Chapter IV, "The 19th Century and After."

Svaglic, Martin J. "Method in the Study of Victorian Prose: Another View," *VN*, No. 11 (1957), 1–5.

Townsend, F. G. "Newman and the Problem of Critical Prose," *VN*, No. 11 (1957), 22–25.

Woodring, Carl. "Introduction," *Prose of the Romantic Period*. Boston: 1961.

THE TWENTIETH CENTURY

Beach, Joseph W. *The Outlook for American Prose*. Chicago: 1926.
> Unhistorical discussion of the faults and virtues of writers of the twenties. Modern prose generally criticized for sloppiness.

Beck, Warren. "William Faulkner's Style," *William Faulkner: Two Decades of Criticism*, ed. Frederick J. Hoffman and Olga W. Vickery. East Lansing: 1951.

Connolly, Cyril. *Enemies of Promise & Other Essays*. Garden City: 1960.
> Discusses the "vernacular" and "Mandarin" styles. Pp. 70–80 are a shrewd analysis of Hemingway and the revolt against "fine" style in the twentieth century.

Corin, Fernand. "Steinbeck and Hemingway—A Study in Literary Economy," *Révue des Langues Vivantes*, XXIV (1958), 60–75.

Dobrée, Bonamy. *Modern Prose Style*. Oxford: 1934.
> Part IV, "Modern Prose Style," compares Browne and William James, then examines briefly the styles of Pepys, Sidney, Shakespeare, Gosse, Stein, Woolf, Bagehot, Henry James, and D. H. Lawrence. General comments about changes of style from the seventeenth to the twentieth century.

Douglas, Wallace W. "Drug Store Gothic: The Style of Robert Penn Warren," *CE*, XV (1954), 265–72.

Forster, E. M. "English Prose Between 1918 and 1939," in *Language, Style, Ideas*, ed. Sumner Ives and S. O. Mitchell. New York: 1964.

Graves, Robert, and Alan Hodge. "Recent Prose," *The Reader Over Your Shoulder*. New York: 1944.

Higashida, Chiaki. "On the Prose Style of D. H. Lawrence," *Studies in English Literature* (Tokyo University), XIX (1939), 545–56.

Hopkins, Viola. "The Ordering Style of *The Age of Innocence*," *American Literature*, XXX (1958), 345–57.

Levin, Harry. "Expressive Voices: The Emergence of a National Style," *Times Literary Supplement*, Sept. 17, 1954, pp. xii–xiv.

Moore, Geoffrey. "American Prose Today," originally in the *8th Mentor Selection, New World Writing*. Reprinted in *Modern Prose: Form and Style*, ed. William Van O'Connor. New York: 1959.

Munson, G. B. *Style and Form in American Prose*. Garden City: 1929.
> Chapter XV, "Quest of the Perfect Style," complains against the decline of American prose.

Oldham, J. N. "Matter of Idiom; the Effect of Science on Contemporary Fiction and Poetry," *Sewanee Review,* XLII (1934), 436–44.

Short, R. W. "The Sentence Structure of Henry James," *American Literature,* XVIII (1946), 71–88.

Slatoff, Walter J. "The Edge of Order: The Pattern of Faulkner's Rhetoric," *Twentieth-Century Literature,* III (1957), 107–27.

Smith, Logan Pearsall. "Fine Writing," *Reperusals.* London: 1936.
>   A very general discussion of plain-ornate prose and a plea for ornate ("fine") writing in modern prose. In the opinion of Connolly, "The most convincing attack on the realism of the thirties."

Troy, William. "Virginia Woolf: The Poetic Style," *Symposium,* III (1932), 153–56.

Tuell, Anne K. "Creed of the Concrete," *Sewanee Review,* XXXVIII (1930), 210–16.

ADDITIONAL READINGS

The bibliographical items are arranged alphabetically under the same headings as used in the body of the book. In some instances, we found that an article would fit under more than one of our categories. We decided, however, to list each item only once.

Teachers are urged to consult *Resources for the Teaching of English,* a pamphlet distributed annually by the National Council of Teachers of English to all its members, for a listing of books, pamphlets, and articles that can be ordered at discount rates or for a nominal charge from NCTE.

Abbreviations used in this listing:

CCC *College Composition and Communication* (an NCTE publication devoted to Freshman English on the college level)

CE *College English* (an NCTE publication concerned with various aspects of English on the college level)

EJ *English Journal* (an NCTE publication concerned with various aspects of English on the secondary level)

GENERAL

Applebee, Roger K. "National Study of High School English Programs: A Record of English Teaching Today," *EJ,* LV (March, 1966), 273–81.

Bernstein, Abraham. *Teaching English in High School* (New York, 1961).

Braddock, Richard, Richard Lloyd-Jones, and Lowell Schoer. "The State of Knowledge about Composition," *Research in Written Composition* (Champaign, Ill., 1963), pp. 29–53.

Bronson, David B. "Reading, Writing, and McLuhan," *EJ,* LVII (November, 1968), 1151–55, 1162.

Clegg, A. B., ed. *The Excitement of Writing* (London, 1965).

Dixon, John. *Growth Through English* (New York, 1967). A report of the Dartmouth Conference.

Draper, Arthur G. "Teach the Process of Writing," *EJ*, LVIII (February, 1969), 245–48.

Dunning, Stephen. "Some Pragmatics of Composition," *Reflections on High School English: NDEA Institute Lectures 1965*, ed. Gary Tate (Tulsa, Oklahoma, 1966), pp. 49–65.

Fowler, Mary Elizabeth. *Teaching Language, Composition, and Literature* (New York, 1965), pp. 129–62.

Freedom and Discipline in English: Report of the Commission on English (New York, 1965).

Gordon, Edward J., ed. *Writing and Literature in the Secondary School* (New York, 1965).

"Guidelines for the Preparation of Teachers of English," *EJ*, LVII (April, 1968). Three-fourths of this issue is devoted to this subject.

Guth, Hans. *English Today and Tomorrow: A Guide for Teachers of English* (Englewood Cliffs, 1964).

Hagstrum, Jean H. "Research in Written Composition," *CE*, XXVI (October, 1964), 53–56.

Hook, J. N. *The Teaching of High School English* (New York, 1958).

Loban, Walter, Margaret Ryan, and James R. Squire. *Teaching Language and Literature* (New York, 1961), pp. 485–541.

Lowe, Lee Frank. "Writers on Learning to Write," *EJ*, LIII (October, 1964), 488–95.

Lueders, Edward. "Teaching Writing Today—Composition or Decomposition?" *EJ*, LVI (January, 1967), 103–8.

Mersand, Joseph. "What Has Happened to Written Composition?" *EJ*, L (April, 1961), 231–37.

Moffett, James. *Teaching the Universe of Discourse* (Boston, 1968).

———. *A Student-Centered Language Arts Curriculum, Grades K-13: Handbook for Teachers* (Boston, 1968).

Muller, Herbert J. *The Uses of English: Guidelines for the Teaching of English from the Anglo-American Conference at Dartmouth College* (New York, 1967).

Murray, Donald M. *A Writer Teaches Writing: A Practical Method of Teaching High School Composition* (Boston, 1968).

———. "Finding Your Own Voice: Teaching Composition in an Age of Dissent," *CCC*, xx (May, 1969), 118–23.

Olson, Helen F. "What Is Good Teaching of Written Composition?" *EJ*, L (April, 1961), 238–45.

Pooley, Robert C., ed. *Perspectives on English: Essays to Honor W. Wilbur Hatfield* (New York, 1960).

Royster, Salibelle. "A Backward Glance at High School Composition," *EJ*, LVI (November, 1967), 1187–88.

Sauer, Edwin H. *English in the Secondary Schools* (New York, 1961), 81–117.
Schwartz, Joseph. "One Method of Training the Composition Teacher," *CCC,* VI (December, 1955), 200–4.
Shugrue, Michael F. *English in a Decade of Change* (New York, 1968).
Simonson, Solomon S. "The Teaching of Composition," *EJ,* LV (April, 1966), 472–75, 495.
———. "Is Composition Obsolete?" *EJ,* LVI (January, 1967), 100–2, 108.
Smith, Eugene H. *Teacher Preparation in Composition* (Champaign, Ill., 1969).
Squire, James R. *High School Departments of English: Their Organization, Administration, and Supervision* (Champaign, Ill., 1964).
———. "National Study of High School English Programs: A School for All Seasons," *EJ,* LV (March, 1966), 282–90.
Squire, James R., and Roger K. Applebee. *High School English Instruction Today* (Champaign, Ill., 1968).
Tate, Gary, ed. *Reflections on High School English: NDEA Institute Lectures 1965* (Tulsa, Oklahoma, 1966).
Tate, Gary, and Edward P. J. Corbett, ed. *Teaching Freshman Composition* (New York, 1967).
Thorp, Willard. "The Well of English, Now Defiled, or Why Johnny Can't Write," *Princeton Alumni Weekly,* LIX (September 26, 1958), 6–9.
Tovatt, Anthony, and Ebert L. Miller. "The Sound of Writing," *Research in the Teaching of English,* I (Fall, 1967), 176–89.
Weiss, M. Jerry, ed. *An English Teacher's Reader* (New York, 1962), pp. 91–146.
West, William W. "Written Composition," *Review of Educational Research,* XXXVII (April, 1967), 159–67.
Whitehead, Frank. *The Disappearing Dais* (London, 1966), pp. 152–218.
Wilkinson, Andrew. "English and the Training of Teachers," *A Common Purpose* (Champaign, Ill., 1966), pp. 180–82.
Woodward, John C., and Arthur G. Phillips. "Profile of the Poor Writer," *Research in the Teaching of English,* I (Spring, 1967), 41–53.

CURRICULUM

Anderson, Lorena A. "Ways and Means in the Teaching of Writing," *EJ,* LI (December, 1962), 621–24.
Andrews, Katherine A. "New Concepts in Composition," *EJ,* LVIII (January, 1969), 96–101.
Arnold, Carroll C. "Some Preliminaries to English Speech Collaboration in the Study of Rhetoric," *Rhetoric: Theories for Application,* ed. Robert M. Gorrell (Champaign, Ill., 1967), pp. 30–36.
"But What Are We Articulating *With?* Freshman English in Ninety-five Colleges and Universities," Prepared by the NCTE Committee on High School-College Articulation. *EJ,* LI (March, 1962), 167–79.
Barry, James D., ed. *The Future of the English Curriculum* (New York, 1967).

Blau, Harold. "Written Composition and Oral Discourse," *EJ*, LVII (March, 1968), 369–71.

Carlsen, G. Robert, and James Crow. "Project English Curriculum Centers," *EJ*, LVI (October, 1967), 986–93.

Dell, William C. "Creative Writing in the English Classroom," *EJ*, LIII (October, 1964), 500–3.

Dilley, David R. "A Business Manager Looks at Business Writing," *EJ*, L (April, 1961), 265–70.

Dusel, William J. "Planning the Program in Writing," *EJ*, XLV (September, 1956), 320–7.

Dykstra, Gerald, and Christina Bratt Paulston. "Guided Composition," *English Language Teaching*, XXI (January, 1967), 136–41.

Elbow, Peter. "A Method of Teaching Writing," *CE*, XXX (November, 1968), 115–25.

Erwin, Gloria. "The Overhead Projector—Aid to the Composition Program," *EJ*, LIII (January, 1964), 48–50.

Estrin, Herman A. "Articulation of High School and College English: A Program in Action," *EJ*, LV (February, 1966), 211–3.

Fotos, Joseph P. "Teaching the Paragraph in the Junior High School," *EJ*, LV (November, 1966), 1071–72, 1104.

Frazier, Alexander. "The Teaching of Writing as Writing," *EJ*, LIII (September, 1964), 435–38.

Furness, Edna L., and Gertrude A. Boyd. "231 Real Spelling Demons for High School Students," *EJ*, XLVII (May, 1958), 267–70.

Gregory, Emily Betts. "Managing Student Writing," *EJ*, XLIV (January, 1955), 18–25.

Grommon, Alfred H. "Coordinating Composition in High School and College," *EJ*, XLVIII (March, 1959), 123–31.

Grose, Lois M. "Teaching Writing in the Junior High School," *EJ*, XLIX (February, 1960), 89–94.

Hach, Clarence W. "Needed: A Sequential Program in Composition," *EJ*, XLIX (November, 1960), 536–47.

———. "Needed: Sequences in Composition," *EJ*, LVII (January, 1968), 69–78.

Henry, George H. "The Unit Method: The 'New' Logic Meets the 'Old,'" *EJ*, LVI (March, 1967), 401–6.

Heys, Frank, Jr. "The Theme-a-Week Assumption: A Report of an Experiment," *EJ*, LI (May, 1962), 320–22.

Higbee, R. W. "A Speaking Approach to Composition," *EJ*, LIII (January, 1964), 50–1.

Hook, J. N. "Logic, Grammar, Rhetoric: A Presumptuous Essay on Their Relationships," *EJ*, LV (April, 1966), 417–24.

Horton, Stephen H. "The Place of Devices in Composition," *EJ*, XXXIX (May, 1950), 271–72.

Johnson, Eric W. "Stimulating and Improving Writing in the Junior High School," *EJ*, XLVII (February, 1958), 68–76, 91.

Joseph, Lois. "A Disciplined Approach to Creative Writing," *EJ*, LI (October, 1962), 468–73.

Keables, Harold. "Creative Writing in the Secondary School," *EJ*, LVII (March, 1968), 356–9, 430.

Klein, Anna Lou. "Expository Writing for Amateurs," *EJ*, LIII (January, 1964), 16–22.

Lin, San-su C. *Pattern Practice in the Teaching of Standard English to Students with a Non-Standard Dialect* (New York, 1965).

Littwin, Maxwell F. "Three Methods of Developing Imagination in Pupil Writing," *EJ*, XXIV (October, 1935), 654–61.

McCafferty, John. "Beginning Composition in the Senior High School," *EJ*, XLIX (December, 1960), 636–38.

McElheny, Kenneth. "Cows and Colors: Imaginative Writing in High School," *EJ*, LV (January, 1966), 53–56, 61.

Madden, Edgar. "Evolution of a Writing Program," *EJ*, LIII (January, 1964), 34–39.

Maloney, Henry B. "Stepsisters of Print: The Public Arts in the High School English Class," *EJ*, XLIX (November, 1960), 570–79.

Mayo, T. F. "Integration of the Teaching of English in High Schools and Colleges in Texas," *CCC*, VII (February, 1955), 18–19.

Mills, Barriss. "Writing as Process," *CE*, XV (October, 1953), 19–26.

Moffett, James. "Rationale for a New Curriculum in English," *Rhetoric: Theories for Application*, ed. Robert M. Gorrell (Champaign, Ill., 1967), pp. 114–21.

Norton, James H. "Teaching Expository Writing Using Skill Levels," *EJ*, LVI (October, 1967), 1015–1024.

Olsen, James. "Some Suggested Guidelines for Writing and Adapting Materials for the Disadvantaged," *EJ*, LV (December, 1966), 1207–9.

Parkins, William L., Jr. "Motion Pictures and Written Composition," *EJ*, LII (January, 1963), 31–36.

Peterson, R. Stanley. "Once More to the Well: Another Look at Creative Writing," *EJ*, L (December, 1961), 612–19, 637.

Pollock, Thomas Clark. "Spelling Report," *CE*, XVI (November, 1954), 102–9.

Redford, Grant H. "Of Teachers, Students, and Creative Writing," *EJ*, XLII (December, 1953), 490–96, 509.

Renwick, Ralph, Jr. "Writing 'Construction': An Aid in Teaching Composition," *EJ*, XLVI (November, 1957), 491–94.

Rogers, Robert W. "Articulating High School and College Teaching of English," *EJ*, LIV (May, 1965), 370–74, 381.

Ross, Frank E. "For the Disadvantaged Student—A Program That Swings," *EJ*, LIV (April, 1965), 280–83.

Schiff, Lillian. "*Showing* the Average Student How to Write—Again," *EJ*, LVI (January, 1967), 118–20.

Shanker, Sidney. "Is Your Vocabulary Teaching Obsolete?" *EJ*, LIII (September, 1964), 422–27.

Sheeley, Stuart L. "Tape Recorders and Writing: Innovation in Indianapolis," *EJ*, LVII (May, 1968), 637–40.

Shugrue, Michael F., Carl A. Barth, and Leo Ruth. *An Evaluation of the Use of English Institute Materials Center Curriculum Materials in NDEA Summer Institutes in English* (New York, 1966).

Simon, Charles. "A Trial in Programmed Composition Teaching," *CCC*, XIII (December, 1962), 16–19.

Smiley, Marjorie. "Gateway English: Teaching English to Disadvantaged Students," *EJ*, LIV (April, 1965), 265–74.

Smith, Eugene H. "English Composition in the Advanced Placement Program," *EJ*, LIV (September, 1965), 495–501.

Spogue, William T. "Teaching Written and Oral English in Nonselective Secondary Schools," *A Common Purpose* (Champaign, Ill., 1966), pp. 90–91.

Steinberg, Erwin R., Robert C. Slack, Beekman W. Cottrell, Lois S. Josephs, "The Inductive Teaching of English," *EJ*, LV (February, 1966), 139–57.

Stephenson, Claude E. "A Sequential Approach to Advanced Composition," *EJ*, LI (February, 1962), 114–16.

Stern, Adele H. "Using Films in Teaching English Composition," *EJ*, LVII (May, 1968), 646–49.

Trainor, Francis X., and Brian McLaughlin. "An Inductive Method of Teaching Composition," *EJ*, LII (September, 1963), 420–25, 467.

Turner, G. R. "But My Spelling Is Terrible," *EJ*, LV (November, 1966), 1091–93.

Veidemanis, Gladys. "The Teaching of Speaking and Writing: An Articulated Approach," *EJ*, LII (March, 1963), 172–77.

Wallace, Karl R. "Towards a Rationale for Teachers of Writing and Speaking," *EJ*, L (September, 1961), 384–91.

———. "The Primacy of Substance and Ideas in the Teaching of Practical Discourse," *EJ*, LIII (January, 1964), 1–9.

Ward, W. S. "High School-College Cooperation in English," *CCC*, VII (May, 1955), 93–96.

Warner, John L., Jr. "Anthologies in the High School Classroom?—Never!" *EJ*, XLVIII (October, 1959), 382–87.

Watson, Bruce. "The Master-Apprentice Approach to Teaching Writing," *EJ*, LIII (January, 1964), 41–44.

"Writing's the Theme: Research Findings and Best Judgments Concerning the Teaching of Composition," *Curriculum Report* (Washington, D.C.: Curriculum Service Center, National Association of Secondary School Principals, December, 1964).

Wykoff, George S. "Practical Helps in Teaching Written Composition," *EJ*, XLI (June, 1952), 310–12.

Zoellner, Robert. "Talk-Write: A Behavioral Pedagogy for Composition," *CE*, XXX (January, 1969), 267–320.

RHETORIC AND COMPOSITION

Becker, A. L. "A Tagmemic Approach to Paragraph Analysis," *CCC*, XVI (December, 1965), 237–42.

Bilsky, Manuel, McCrea Hazlett, Robert E. Streeter, and Richard M. Weaver. "Looking for an Argument," *CE*, xiv (January, 1953), 210–16.

Bloom, Lynn V., and Martin Bloom. "The Teaching and Learning of Argumentative Writing," *CE*, xxix (November, 1967), 128–35.

Booth, Wayne C. " 'Now Don't Try to Reason with Me': Rhetoric Today, Left, Right, and Center," *The University of Chicago Magazine*, lx (November, 1967), 12–15; Part ii, ibid, December, 1967, 17–21.

Braddock, Richard. "Teaching Rhetorical Analysis," *Rhetoric: Theories for Application*, ed. Robert M. Gorrell (Champaign, Ill., 1967), pp. 107–13.

Bryant, Donald C. "Rhetoric: Its Functions and Its Scope," *Quarterly Journal of Speech*, xxxix (December, 1953), 401–24.

Burke, Virginia. "The Composition-Rhetoric Pyramid," *CCC*, xvi (February, 1965), 3–6.

———. "The Paragraph: Dancer in Chains," *Rhetoric: Theories for Application*, ed. Robert M. Gorrell (Champaign, Ill., 1967), pp. 37–44.

Christensen, Francis. *Notes Toward a New Rhetoric: Six Essays for Teachers* (New York, 1967).

———. "A Generative Rhetoric of the Paragraph," *CCC*, xvi (October, 1965), 144–56. Reproduced in Christensen's *Notes Toward a New Rhetoric*.

Corbett, Edward P. J. "The Usefulness of Classical Rhetoric," *CCC*, xiv (October, 1963), 162–64.

———. "A New Look at Old Rhetoric," *Rhetoric: Theories for Application*, ed. Robert M. Gorrell (Champaign, Ill., 1967), pp. 16–22.

———. "The Relevance of Rhetoric to Composition," *Kentucky English Bulletin*, xvii (Winter, 1967–68), 3–12.

Duhamel, P. Albert. "Traditional Misconceptions of Traditional Rhetoric," *Rhetoric: Theories for Application*, ed. Robert M. Gorrell (Champaign, Ill., 1967), pp. 23–29.

Elledge, Scott B. "Invention and Topics: or, Where to Look for Something to Say," Text of a kinescope produced by the Commission on English, College Entrance Examination Board, 1965.

Fichtenau, Robert L. "Some Rhetorical Considerations for Teaching Young Writers," *EJ*, liv (November, 1965), 720–23.

Gibson, Walker. "The Voice of the Writer," *CCC*, xiii (October, 1962), 10–13.

Gorrell, Robert M., ed. *Rhetoric: Theories for Application* (Champaign, Ill., 1967). Several articles from this NCTE publication are listed in this section.

Guth, Hans P. "Rhetoric and the Quest for Certainty," *CE*, xxiv (November, 1962), 131–36.

Hughes, Richard E. "The Contemporaneity of Classical Rhetoric," *CCC*, xvi (October, 1965), 157–59.

Jennings, E. M. "A Paradigm for Discovery," *CCC*, xix (October, 1968), 192–200.

Kane, Thomas S. "Rhetoric and the 'Problem' of Composition," *CE*, xxii (April, 1961), 503–6.

Karrfalt, David. "The Generation of Paragraphs and Larger Units," *CCC*, xix (October, 1968), 211–17.

Larson, Richard L. "Discovery through Questioning: A Plan for Teaching Rhetorical Invention," *CE*, xxx (November, 1968), 126–34.

Lecky, Eleazer. "Rhetoric, Semantics, and Composition," *Rhetoric: Theories for Application*, ed. Robert M. Gorrell (Champaign, Ill., 1967), pp. 5–15.

Lockerbie, D. Bruce. "The Speaking Voice Approach Joins the Rhetoric Parade," *EJ*, lvi (March, 1967), 411–16.

McCrimmon, James M. "Will the New Rhetorics Produce New Emphases in the Composition Class?" *CCC*, xx (May, 1969), 124–30.

Miles, Josephine. "What We Compose," *CCC*, xiv (October, 1963), 146–54.

Moffett, James. "I, You, and It," *CCC*, xvi (December, 1965), 243–48.

Perrin, Porter G. "Freshman Composition and the Tradition of Rhetoric," *Perspectives on English: Essays to Honor W. Wilbur Hatfield*, ed. Robert C. Pooley (New York, 1960), pp. 119–32.

Pitkin, Willis L., Jr. "Discourse Blocs," *CCC*, xx (May, 1969), 138–47.

Rockas, Leo. "Further Comments on the Paragraph," *CCC*, xvii (October, 1966), 148–51.

Rodgers, Paul C., Jr. "A Discourse-centered Rhetoric of the Paragraph," *CCC*, xvii (February, 1966), 2–11.

Rogers, Joseph A. "Analog Rhetoric," *EJ*, lv (April, 1966), 453–56, 460.

Rohman, D. Gordon. "Pre-Writing: The Stage of Discovery in the Writing Process," *CCC*, xvi (May, 1965), 106–12.

Saalbach, Robert P. "Teaching Students to Organize," *EJ*, xlvii (November, 1958), 505–7.

Smith, Charles Kay. "Toward a 'Participatory Rhetoric': Teaching Swift's *Modest Proposal*," *CE*, xxx (November, 1968), 135–49.

Steinmann, Martin, Jr., ed. *New Rhetorics* (New York, 1967).

Stoehr, Taylor. "Details and Generalizations," *CE*, xxx (November, 1968), 162–71.

"Symposium on the Paragraph," *CCC*, xvii (May, 1966): Francis Christensen, 60–66; A. L. Becker, 67–72; Paul C. Rodgers, Jr., 72–80; Josephine Miles, 80–82; David H. Karrfalt, 82–87.

Ulanov, Barry. "The Relevance of Rhetoric," *EJ*, lv (April, 1966), 403–8.

Weathers, Winston. "The Rhetoric of Certitude," *Southern Humanities Review*, ii (Spring, 1968), 213–22.

Weaver, Richard M. "To Write the Truth," *CE*, x (October, 1948), 25–30.

Williams, George. "Organization—Rhetorical and Artistic," Text of a kinescope produced by the Commission on English, College Entrance Examination Board, 1965.

LINGUISTICS AND COMPOSITION

Allen, Harold B. "From Prairies to Mountains: Linguistics and Composition," *CE*, xxvi (January, 1965), 260–66.

Bateman, Donald R. "More Mature Writing through a Better Understanding of Language Structure," *EJ*, l (October, 1961), 457–60, 468.

Bateman, Donald, and Frank Zidonis. *The Effect of a Study of Transformational Grammar on the Writing of Ninth and Tenth Graders* (Champaign, Ill., 1966).

Black, Karen L. "The Application of Linguistic Principles to the Teaching of Freshman English," *CCC*, xvi (December, 1965), 270–73.

Carroll, John B. "Psycholinguistics and the Teaching of English Composition," *CCC*, vii (December, 1956), 188–93.

Cook, Philip H. "Putting Grammar to Work: The Generative Grammar in the Generative Rhetoric," *EJ*, lvii (November, 1968), 1168–75.

English, Hubert M. "Linguistic Theory as an Aid to Invention," *CCC*, xv (October, 1964), 136–40.

Francis, W. Nelson. "Modern Rhetorical Doctrine and Recent Developments in Linguistics," *CCC*, v (December, 1954), 155–61.

Gorrell, Robert M. "Grammar in the Composition Course," *CE*, xvi (January, 1955), 233–38.

Hall, Robert A., Jr. "To Hyphenate or Not to Hyphenate," *EJ*, liii (December, 1964), 662–65.

Hartung, Charles V. "Doctrines of English Usage," *EJ*, xlv (December, 1956), 517–25.

Higgins, V. Louise. "Approaching Usage in the Classroom," *EJ*, xlix (March, 1960), 181–86.

Hunt, Kellogg W. *Grammatical Structures Written at Three Grade Levels* (Champaign, Ill., 1965).

———. "Improving Sentence Structure," *EJ*, xlvii (April, 1958), 206–11.

———. "A Synopsis of Clause-to-Sentence Length Factors," *EJ*, liv (April, 1965), 300, 305–9.

Ives, Sumner. "Grammar and Style," *EJ*, lii (May, 1963), 364–70.

———. "The Relevance of Language Study," *CCC*, xx (May, 1969), 131–37.

Kraus, Silvy. "A Comparison of Three Methods of Teaching Sentence Structure," *EJ*, xlvi (May, 1957), 275–81.

McGuire, Eileen J. "Sentence Building and Transformational Grammar," *EJ*, lvi (May, 1967), 747–50.

Malmstrom, Jean. "Linguistic Atlas Findings versus Textbook Pronouncements on Current Usage," *EJ*, xlviii (April, 1959), 191–98.

Myers, L. M. "Linguistics and the Teaching of Rhetoric," *CCC*, v (December, 1954), 166–71.

Newsome, Verna L. "Expansions and Transformations to Improve Sentences," *EJ*, liii (May, 1964), 327–35.

Pike, Kenneth L. "A Linguistic Contribution to Composition," *CCC*, xv (May, 1964), 82–88.

Pooley, Robert C. "Dare Schools Set a Standard in English Usage?" *EJ*, xlix (March, 1960), 176–81.

Postman, Neil, and Charles Weingartner. *Linguistics: A Revolution in Teaching* (New York, 1966).

Roberts, Paul. "Linguistics and the Teaching of Composition," *EJ*, lii (May, 1963), 331–35.

Sledd, James. "Grammar or Gramarye?" *EJ*, XLIX (May, 1960), 293–303.

Smith, Dora V. "Teaching Language as Communication," *EJ*, XLIX (March, 1960), 167–72.

Stageberg, Norman C. "Some Structural Ambiguities," *EJ*, XLVII (November, 1958), 479–86.

———. "Structural Ambiguity: Some Sources," *EJ*, LV (May, 1966), 558–63.

Struck, Herman R. "The Myth about Initial Conjunctions," *EJ*, LIV (January, 1965), 42–44.

Suggs, Lena Reddick. "Structural Grammar versus Traditional Grammar in Influencing Writing," *EJ*, L (March, 1961), 174–78.

Thomas, Owen. "Generative Grammar: Toward Unification and Simplication," *EJ*, LI (February, 1962), 94–99, 113.

Tibbetts, A. M. "The Case Against Structural Linguistics in Composition," *CE*, XXI (February, 1960), 280–85.

———. "The Real Issues in the Great Language Controversy," *EJ*, LV (January, 1966, 28–38.

Warfel, Harry R. "Structural Linguistics and Composition," *CE*, XX (February, 1959), 205–13.

Womack, Thurston. "Teachers' Attitudes toward Current Usage," *EJ*, XLVIII (April, 1959), 186–90.

Young, Richard E., and Alton L. Becker. "Toward a Modern Theory of Rhetoric: A Tagmemic Contribution," *Harvard Educational Review*, XXXV (Fall, 1965), 450–68.

Zais, Robert S. "The Linguistic Characteristics of Punctuation Symbols and the Teaching of Punctuation Skills," *EJ*, LII (December, 1963), 677–81.

LITERATURE AND COMPOSITION

Ashmead, John. "Good Writing from Great Books," *CCC*, XV (February, 1964), 29–33.

Bell, Marvin. "Poetry and Freshman Composition," *CCC*, XV (February, 1964), 1–5.

Calderwood, Natalie. "Composition and Literature," *CCC*, VIII (December, 1957), 201–4.

Cohen, B. Bernard. "Writing Assignments in a Course with Readings in Imaginative Literature," *CCC*, XIX (October, 1968), 225–29.

Eschbacher, Robert L. *"Lord Jim,* Classical Rhetoric, and the Freshman Dilemma," *CE*, XXV (October, 1963), 22–25.

Fillion, Bryant. "The Case for Freedom in Composition and Literature," *EJ*, LVII (January, 1968), 52–58.

Friedrich, Gerhard. "The English Teacher and the Process of Communication," *EJ*, LV (January, 1966), 19–27. The use of précis-writing and literature.

Gladding, Walter M., Jr. "The Short Story in Composition," *CCC*, XV (February, 1964), 16–20.

Greenhut, Morris. "Great Books and English Composition," *CE*, XXIV (November, 1962), 136–40.

Irmscher, William F. "An Apology for Literature," *EJ*, LII (April, 1963), 252–56, 294.

Judy, Stephen, "Style and the Teaching of Literature and Composition," *EJ*, LVI (February, 1967), 281–85.

Lockerbie, D. Bruce. "Solomon Was Wrong," *EJ*, LII (November, 1963), 596–600. The "speaking voice" approach to teaching literature and composition.

Murphy, Charles P. "The Teaching of Fiction as Composition," *EJ*, LV (March, 1966), 331–34.

Murphy, Richard. "Teaching Rhetorical Appreciation of Literature," *EJ*, LV (May, 1966), 578–82.

O'Malley, William J., S.J. "Literary Craftsmanship: The Integration of Literature and Composition," *EJ*, LII (April, 1963), 247–51, 268.

Purves, Alan C., and Victoria Rippere. *Elements of Writing about a Literary Work: A Study of Response to Literature* (Champaign, Ill., 1968).

Roberts, Edgar V. *Writing Themes about Literature* (Englewood Cliffs, N.J., 1964).

Rogal, Samuel. "Composition and Literature: Suggestions for a More Sensible Balance," *Peabody Journal of Education*, XLIV (September, 1966), 91–94.

Rubinstein, S. Leonard. "Composition: A Collision with Literature," *CE*, XXVII (January, 1966), 273–77.

Stone, William B. "Teaching 'The Dead': Literature in the Composition Class," *CCC*, XIX (October, 1968), 229–31.

Wilcox, Thomas W. "Composition Where None Is Apparent: Contemporary Literature and the Course in Writing," *CCC*, XVI (May, 1965), 70–75.

ASSIGNMENTS

Adler, John C. "The Metatextbook Factor in Writing," *EJ*, XLVIII (December, 1959), 511–17. A plea for unstructured writing assignments in the early stages.

Allen, Andrew E. "An Individual Vocabulary-Building Device," *EJ*, LI (March, 1962), 205–7.

Arnold, Lois V. "Writer's Cramp and Eyestrain—Are They Paying Off?" *EJ*, LIII (January, 1964), 10–15.

Bergman, Floyd L. "Individualization: Key to More Writing," *EJ*, LI (March, 1962), 192–96.

Bouise, Oscar A. "Generating a Composition," *EJ*, LVI (October, 1967), 1011–14.

Brogan, H. O. "The Freshman Research Paper," *CCC*, XI (December, 1960), 224–26.

Buchan, Vivian. "Priming the Pump and Controlling the Flow," *EJ*, LVI (January, 1967), 109–13.

Chalpin, Lila. "On Ending with a Bang Not a Whimper," *EJ*, LIII (January, 1964), 46–48. Models for effective conclusions.

Cook, Luella B. "Writing as Self-Revelation," *EJ*, XLVIII (May, 1959), 247–53.

Cummins, Paul F. "Composition as the Expression of Personality," *EJ*, LVIII (January, 1969), 92–95.

Daniels, Edgar F. "The Dishonest Term Paper," *CE*, xxi (April, 1960), 403–5.

Deighton, Lee C. "Developing Vocabulary: Another Look at the Problem," *EJ*, xlix (February, 1960), 82–88.

Dressel, Paul, John Schmid, Jr., and Gerald Kincaid. "The Effect of Writing Frequency upon Essay-Type Writing Proficiency at the College Level," *Journal of Educational Research*, xlvi (December, 1952), 285–93.

Farrell, Edmund J. "The Beginning Begets: Making Composition Assignments," *EJ*, lviii (March, 1969), 428–31.

Geller, Robert. "What to Write About: A Return to Humanity," *EJ*, lv (April, 1966), 457–60.

Houghton, Donald E. "Paperback Research: Some Shortcomings," *CCC*, xi (December, 1960), 203–6.

Hunting, Robert. "Recent Studies of Writing Frequency," *Research in the Teaching of English*, i (Spring, 1967), 29–40.

Jordan, John E. "Theme Assignments: Servants or Masters?" *CCC*, xiv (February, 1963), 51–53.

Judy, Stephen. "On Clock Watching and Composing," *EJ*, lvii (March, 1968), 360–66.

Keavy, Hubbard. "The Simpler Sentence: Key to Better News Writing," *EJ*, xlviii (November, 1959), 462–65.

Kerner, David. "A New Way to Teach Composition: Controlled Material," *CE*, xxi (April, 1960), 384–88.

Keskinen, Kenneth. " 'Shooting an Elephant'—An Essay to Teach," *EJ*, lv (September, 1966), 669–75.

Kilburn, Patrick E. "Every Man His Own Pedagogue: A Project in the Teaching of Freshman Composition," *The Journal of Higher Education*, xxxiii (February, 1962), 89–95.

Kogan, Bernard. "Three and a Half Ways of Looking at Control: or, The Controlled Paper Controlled," *CCC*, xi (May, 1960), 77–81.

LaBrant, Lou. "Inducing Students to Write," *EJ*, xliv (February, 1955), 70–74, 116.

Lokke, Virginia, and George Wykoff. "Doubling Writing in Freshman Composition," *School and Society*, lxviii (November, 1948), 437–39.

Love, Glen A., and Michael Payne. "The Research Paper: Does It Belong in High School?" *EJ*, lvi (May, 1967), 739–41.

McCampbell, James F. "Using Models for Improving Composition," *EJ*, lv (September, 1966), 772–76.

Minton, Arthur. "Thinking-Composition," *EJ*, xl (January, 1951), 7–11.

Nelson, Lawrence E. "In the Beginning," *EJ*, lv (March, 1966), 342–45. Specific models for introductions to themes.

O'Connor, Marie E. "The Research Paper and the Tape Recorder," *EJ*, lvii (May, 1968), 652–53, 660.

Perry, William G., Jr. "The 600-Word Theme and Human Dignity," *CE*, xiv (May, 1953), 454–60.

Pitt, Jack. "A Caveat for Deductive Reasoning," *EJ*, lvi (March, 1967), 407–10.

Plotka, Marie, and Arnold Lazarus. "Teaching Interpretive Expository Writing," *EJ*, LVII (January, 1968), 59–64. A lesson plan for writing on Anne Frank's *Diary of a Young Girl*.

Reeves, Bruce. "The Object Lesson," *EJ*, LV (March, 1966), 328–30, 334. Descriptive-writing exercises.

Rideout, Ray. "Building a Background for High School Composition," *EJ*, LVIII (February, 1969), 242–44.

Rockas, Leo. "The Freshman Journal," *CE*, XX (October, 1958), 18–20.

Rodabaugh, Delmer. "Assigning and Commenting on Themes," *CE*, XVI (October, 1954), 33–7, 48.

Rogers, C. D. "The Sedulous But Successful Ape," *EJ*, LVI (December, 1967), 1309–11.

Roth, George L. "The Controlled Materials Method of Teaching the Research Paper," *The CEA Critic*, XX (December, 1958), 2, 7–8.

Rounds, Robert W. "Using the *New Yorker* as a Composition Text," *CCC*, XIX (October, 1968), 223–25.

Rozsnafszky, Jane. "Teaching Unity in Composition: Another Approach to the Book Report," *EJ*, LV (November, 1966), 1073–75.

Salmon, Webb. "Selecting Topics for Composition from a Study of Literature," *Reflections on High School English: NDEA Institute Lectures 1965*, ed. Gary Tate (Tulsa, Oklahoma, 1966), pp. 125–36.

Schroeder, Fred E. H. "How to Teach a Research Theme in Four Not-So-Easy Lessons," *EJ*, LV (October, 1966), 898–902.

———. "How Not to Assign 'What-Did-You-Do-Last-Summer': A Cumulative Course in Writing Personal Narratives," *EJ*, LVII (January, 1968), 79–84.

Shaffer, Virginia, Simeon Round, Anna Bloom, Ellis Newton, and Dorothy Kell. "A Realistic Pattern for Writing Assignments," *EJ*, XLVI (February, 1957), 89–99.

Spencer, D. H. "Two Types of Guided Composition Exercise," *English Language Teaching*, XIX (July, 1965), 156–58.

Summerfield, Geoffrey. *Topics in English* (Champaign, Ill., 1968).

Van Dyk, Howard A. "Teach Revision—It Works!" *EJ*, LVI (May, 1967), 736–38.

Wagner, Linda Welshimer. "Practice Without Pain: The In-Class Journal," *EJ*, LVII (February, 1968), 221–22.

Wallace, Robert. "A Writing Exercise That Works," *EJ*, XLIX (October, 1960), 489–90. Exercise in imitation.

Weeks, Robert P. "The Case for the Controlled Materials Method," *CCC*, X (February, 1959), 33–35.

Wilson, Grace E., ed. *Composition Situations* (Champaign, Ill., 1966).

Wolfe, Don M. "How to Begin? The First Writing Assignment," *EJ*, XLIII (May, 1954), 244–48.

———. "Fruitful Long Paper: The Autobiography," *EJ*, XLV (January, 1956), 7–12, 38.

Yaggy, Elinor. "The Shorter Research Paper," *CE*, XVIII (April, 1957), 369–70.

EVALUATION

Andrews, Joe W. "Redpencilitis: Cause and Cure," *EJ*, XLII (January, 1953), 20–24.

Baker, William D. "An Investigation of Characteristics of Poor Writers," *CCC*, V (February, 1954), 23–27.

Bernadette, Sister Miriam. "Evaluation of Writing: A Three-Part Program," *EJ*, LIV (January, 1965), 23–27.

Blackman, Ralph. "Accentuate the Positive and Save the Red Pencil," *EJ*, LIII (January, 1964), 31–33.

Burke, Virginia M. "A Candid Opinion on Lay Readers," *EJ*, L (April, 1961), 258–64.

Canfield, Sally Martin, and Harriette B. Kolker. "Correcting the Impossible Theme," *EJ*, LII (November, 1963), 619–21.

Coward, Ann F. "A Comparison of Two Methods of Grading English Compositions," *Journal of Educational Research*, XLVI (October, 1952), 81–93.

Daigon, Arthur. "Computer Grading of English Composition," *EJ*, LV (January, 1966), 46–52.

Derrick, Clarence. "Tests of Writing," *EJ*, LIII (October, 1964), 496–9.

Diederich, Paul B., John W. French, and Sydell T. Carlton. "The Measurement of Skill in Writing," *School Review*, LIV (December, 1946), 584–92.

Diederich, Paul B. "How to Measure Growth in Writing Ability," *EJ*, LV (April, 1966), 435–49.

Dusel, William J. "Some Semantic Implications of Theme Correction," *EJ*, XLIV (October, 1955), 390–97.

———. "How Should Student Writing Be Judged?" *EJ*, XLVI (May, 1957), 263–68, 299.

Estrin, Herman A. "How Do You Grade a Composition?" *CCC*, XII (December, 1961), 234–35.

Fleece, Jeffrey. "Teacher as Audience," *CE*, XIII (February, 1952), 272–75.

Fletcher, Paul F. "What Doesn't Happen in Writing—and Why It Doesn't," *EJ*, LIII (January, 1964), 27–30.

Ford, Paul M. "Lay Readers in the High School Composition Program: Some Statistics," *EJ*, L (November, 1961), 522–28.

Gerber, John C. "Testing and Evaluation in the Skills of Communication," *CE*, IX (April, 1948), 375–84.

Girr, Francis X., Jr. "Group Paragraph Revision," *EJ*, XLIX (December, 1960), 630–32.

Halverson, Nelius O. "Two Methods of Indicating Errors in Themes," *CE*, II (December, 1940), 277–79.

Harris, David P. "The Testing of Student Writing Ability," *Reflections on High School English: NDEA Institute Lectures 1965*, ed. Gary Tate (Tulsa, Oklahoma, 1966), pp. 137–45.

Hovelsrud, Joyce. "No Wonder Students Can't Write," *EJ*, LVIII (February, 1969), 249–51.

Keene, Katherine. "Students Like Corrections," *EJ*, xlv (April, 1956), 212–215.

Krueger, Paul H. "Some Questions on the Lay Reader Program," *EJ*, l (November, 1961), 529–33.

Larson, Richard L. "Teaching the Analysis of Expository Prose," *EJ*, lvii (November, 1968), 1156–62.

———. "Training New Teachers of Composition in the Writing of Comments on Themes," *CCC*, xvii (October, 1966), 152–55.

Leahy, Jack Thomas. "Objective Correlation and the Grading of English Composition," *CE*, xxv (October, 1963), 35–38.

Lowe, Lee Frank. "Theme Correcting via Tape Recorder," *EJ*, lii (March, 1963), 212–4.

Mahnke, Marcia. "Aide-to-Order for the Composition Teacher," *EJ*, liii (January, 1964), 40–1.

Masters, George D. "A Rosetta Stone for Composition," *EJ*, lvii (October, 1968), 1015–16.

Palmer, Orville. "Sense or Nonsense? The Objective Testing of English Composition," *EJ*, l (May, 1961), 314–20.

———. "Seven Classic Ways of Grading Dishonestly," *EJ*, li (October, 1962), 464–67.

Perrin, Porter G. "Maximum Essentials in Composition," *CE*, viii (April, 1947), 352–60.

Pudlowski, Victor. "Compositions—Write 'em Right!" *EJ*, xlviii (December, 1959), 535–37.

Schumann, Paul F. "What Criteria Do *You* Use in Grading Compositions?" *EJ*, lvii (November, 1968), 1163–65.

Schwartz, Marjorie Xenia. "Non-academic Writing: Requirements and Evaluation," *EJ*, lv (April, 1966), 468–71.

Singleton, Clifford G. "Honors Students as Lay Readers," *EJ*, liii (January, 1964), 44–46.

Smith, Eugene H. "Composition Evaluation: A Problem of Voice," *EJ*, lvi (November, 1967), 1189–94.

Stern, Arthur A. "How to Write Less Efficiently," *EJ*, lvi (January, 1967), 114–17.

Thomas, William Miles. "Technical Errors in the Compositions of the Average High-School Senior," *The School Review*, lxxi (Summer, 1963), 188–207.

Van Schaick, Sally. "The Composition-Reading Machine," *EJ*, xlix (April, 1960), 237–41. Using lay readers.

Wagner, Linda Welshimer. "The Student-Graded Theme Series," *EJ*, liii (December, 1964), 689–90.

STYLE

Ash, Irwin O. "An Experimental Evaluation of the Stylistic Approach in Teaching Written Composition," *Journal of Experimental Education*, iv (September, 1935), 54–62.

Ashida, Margaret E., and Leslie T. Whipp. "A Slide-Rule Composition Course," *CE*, xxv (October, 1963), 18–22.

Christensen, Francis. "The Problem of Defining a Mature Style," *EJ*, lvii (May, 1968), 572–79.

Davidson, Donald. "Grammar and Rhetoric: The Teacher's Problem," *Quarterly Journal of Speech*, xxxix (December, 1953), 425–36.

Frank, Yakira H. "Stylistics in the Classroom," *EJ*, lv (November, 1966), 1051–55, 1075.

Gibson, Walker. *Persona: A Style Study for Readers and Writers* (New York, 1969).

Greiner, Charles F. "Stafford's 'Traveling Through the Dark': A Discussion of Style," *EJ*, lv (November, 1966), 1015–18, 1048.

Hayes, Curtis W. "Edward Gibbon: Linguistics, Syntax, and Style," *CCC*, xix (October, 1968), 204–10.

Kaplan, Milton A. "Style *Is* Content," *EJ*, lvii (December, 1968), 1330–34.

Love, Glen A., and Michael Payne, ed. *Contemporary Essays on Style* (Chicago, 1969).

Lynskey, Winifred. "Macaulay as Teacher," *CE*, xvi (November, 1954), 127–29.

———. "Imitative Writing and a Student's Style," *CE*, xviii (May, 1957), 396–400.

Milic, Louis T. "Theories of Style and Their Implications for the Teaching of Composition," *CCC*, xvi (May, 1965), 66–69, 126.

———. "Metaphysics in the Criticism of Style," *CCC*, xvii (October, 1966), 124–29.

———. "Unconscious Ordering in the Prose of Swift," *The Computer and Literary Style*, ed. Jacob Leed (Kent, Ohio, 1966), pp. 79–106.

———. "The Computer Approach to Style," *The Art of Victorian Prose*, ed. George Levine and William Madden (New York, 1968), pp. 338–61.

Nist, John, ed. *Style in English* (Indianapolis, 1969).

Ohmann, Richard. "Generative Grammars and the Concept of Literary Style," *Word*, xx (December, 1964), 423–39.

———. "Literature as Sentences," *CE*, xxvii (January, 1966), 261–67.

Riffaterre, Michael. "Criteria for Style Analysis," *Word*, xv (April, 1959), 154–74.

Stoehr, Taylor. "Tone and Voice," *CE*, xxx (November, 1968), 150–61.

Weathers, Winston, and Otis Winchester. *Copy and Compose: A Guide to Prose Style* (Englewood Cliffs, N.J., 1969).

Weathers, Winston. "The Rhetoric of the Series," *CCC*, xvii (December, 1966), 217–22.

ATTITUDES

Almer, Alvin T. "Teaching Composition: A Few Hints," *EJ*, lvii (February, 1968), 213–14, 257.

Bishop, Jonathan. "Criteria for an Adequate Composition Course," *CCC*, x (December, 1959), 243–48.

Carlsen, G. Robert. "Conflicting Assumptions in the Teaching of English," *EJ*, xlix (September, 1960), 377–86, 424.

Cromwell, Otelin. "Preparation for Freshman Composition," *EJ*, xxv (September, 1936), 551–56.

Dean, Dennis R. "Slang Is Language Too!" *EJ*, li (May, 1962), 323–26.

Douglas, Wallace W. "Composition and the Editorial Process," *Reflections on High School English: NDEA Institute Lectures 1965,* ed. Gary Tate (Tulsa, Oklahoma, 1966), pp. 76–90.

Estrin, Herman A. "Teachers of English Can Create Prize-Winning Authors," *CCC*, xix (October, 1968), 218–22.

Grose, Lois. "Essential Conditions for Teaching Written Composition," *EJ*, l (April, 1961), 246–51.

Hilkert, Robert N. "Language Competencies Required by Occupational Choice," *EJ*, xxxix (March, 1950), 137–44.

Johnson, Eric W. "Avoiding Martyrdom in Teaching Writing: Some Shortcuts," *EJ*, li (September, 1962), 399–402.

Kitzhaber, Albert R. "New Perspectives on Teaching Composition," *CE*, xxiii (March, 1962), 440–44.

LaBrant, Lou. "The Individual and His Writing," *EJ*, xxxix (April, 1950), 185–89.

———. "Writing Is More Than Structure," *EJ*, xlvi (May, 1957), 252–56.

———. "Writing, Most Difficult of the Language Arts," *NEA Journal*, xlvii (March, 1958), 189–90.

Macrorie, Ken. "Words in the Way," *EJ*, xl (September, 1951), 382–85.

O'Dea, Paul. "Five Myths in the Teaching of Composition," *EJ*, liv (April, 1965), 328–30.

Russell, Robert. "The Question of Composition—A Record of a Struggle," *CE*, xxx (November, 1968), 171–77.

Sheridan, Marion C. "Can We Teach Our Students to Write?" *EJ*, xl (June, 1951), 320–24.

Spiegler, Charles G. " 'If Only Dickens Had Written about Hot Rods,' " *EJ*, liv (April, 1965), 275–79. How to reach the disadvantaged student.

Steinberg, Erwin R. "Some Basic Assumptions for Courses in English Composition," *CCC*, ii (October, 1951), 11–16.

Stewart, Stanley. "Composition: Teaching as Obstacle," *EJ*, lvii (January, 1968), 85–86, 95.

Sweet, John. "Some Notes for Student Writers," *EJ*, lvi (February, 1967), 257–61.

Walker, Clifford J. "The Opposite of a Tree: Motivation for Composition," *EJ*, lv (April, 1966), 450–52.

Wonnberger, Carl G. "They All Can Learn to Write," *EJ*, xlv (November, 1956), 455–61.

———. "Writing—A Way of Life," *EJ*, xlviii (February, 1959), 66–73.

BIBLIOGRAPHY

Blount, Nathan S. "Summary of Investigations Relating to the English Language Arts in Secondary Education," *EJ*, lv (May, 1966), 591–608; ibid, lvi (May, 1967), 681–96; ibid, lvii (May, 1968), 710–24.

Braddock, Richard, Richard Lloyd-Jones, and Lowell Schoer, "References for Further Research," *Research in Written Composition* (Champaign, Ill., 1963), pp. 117–42.

Doherty, Paul C. "Stylistics—A Bibliographical Survey," *The CEA Critic,* xxviii (May, 1966), 1, 3, and 4.

Lynch, James J., and Bertrand Evans. *High School English Textbooks: A Critical Examination* (Boston, Mass., 1963).

Milic, Louis T. *Style and Stylistics: An Analytical Bibliography* (New York, 1967).

Strom, Ingrid M. "Summary Investigations Relating to the English Language Arts in Secondary Education," *EJ,* xlix (February, 1960), 119–30; ibid, l (February, 1961), 111–25; ibid, li (February, 1962), 123–40; ibid, lii (February, 1963), 118–36; ibid, liii (February, 1964), 110–35; liv (March, 1965), 238–55.